Imperialism and Postcolonialism

History: Concepts, Theories and Practice

Series editor: Alun Munslow, University of Staffordshire

The New History
Alun Munslow

History on Film/Film on History
Robert A. Rosenstone

Imperialism and Postcolonialism
Barbara Bush

Imperialism and Postcolonialism

BARBARA BUSH

PEARSON

Longman

Harlow, England • London • New York • Boston • San Francisco • Toronto
Sydney • Tokyo • Singapore • Hong Kong • Seoul • Taipei • New Delhi
Cape Town • Madrid • Mexico City • Amsterdam • Munich • Paris • Milan

Pearson Education Limited

Edinburgh Gate
Harlow CM20 2JE
United Kingdom
Tel: +44 (0)1279 623623
Fax: +44 (0)1279 431059
Website: www.pearsoned.co.uk

First edition published in Great Britain in 2006

© Pearson Education Limited 2006

ISBN-13: 978-0-582-50583-4
ISBN-10: 0-582-50583-6

British Library Cataloguing in Publication Data
A CIP catalogue record for this book can be obtained from the British Library

Library of Congress Cataloging in Publication Data
Bush, Barbara, 1946–
   Imperialism and postcolonialism / Barbara Bush. — 1st ed.
      p. cm. — (History: concepts, theories and practice)
   Includes bibliographical references and index.
   ISBN-13: 978-0-582-50583-4 (alk. paper)
   ISBN-10: 0-582-50583-6
   1. Imperialism.   2. Imperialism—Case studies.   3. Postcolonialism.   I. Title.   II. Series.
JC359.B89 2006
325′.32—dc22

2005058622

10 9 8 7 6 5 4 3 2 1
10   09   08   07   06

Set by 35 in 11/13pt Bulmer MT
Printed and bound in Malaysia

The Publisher's policy is to use paper manufactured from sustainable forests.

Contents

Foreword

It gives me great pleasure to write the foreword to this book written by my colleague, Barbara Bush. To produce something as comprehensive as she has done here – a work that examines empires from ancient times through to the current American embroilment in Iraq and which investigates them from a wide range of economic, political, social, and cultural perspectives – requires special resources not only of intelligence but of optimism and energy also. Such works are always open to attack from the specialists who claim that their own field has been misrepresented or misunderstood. They can also easily be criticised because of what, despite the impressive 800 or so sources listed in the bibliography, they – inevitably – leave out. But so much research and writing on so many different aspects of empire, imperialism and post-colonialism has appeared in recent decades that books such as Barbara's are essential from time to time to give a sense of the state of play in the subject, to remind us to take account of each other's labours and, most of all, to give students an overview of the landscape before they go off to tend their corner of the terrain. It is impossible now, without a deliberate and time-consuming effort of the kind made here, for anyone to 'know the field' as one might have been able to do 50 years ago when the number of interested historians was much smaller and when perspectives on the subject were, anyway, much narrower than they are today. Even those scholars who are sniffy about general works such as this will no doubt sometimes be caught consulting it in search of a quick introduction to that 'background' without which their own endeavours would be rather less meaningful.

The rush of publication and the widening of the debate on empire to include all those aspects which are conveniently rendered under the title 'postcolonialism' inevitably raises the perennial problem as to how to define words like 'imperialism' and 'colonialism'. Barbara acknowledges the huge range of possible definitions and wisely avoids plumping for any one of them. It is only necessary to read a few pages of her book to see why this is so: if, as the dictionary says, a definition is 'a precise statement of the essential nature of a thing' then a word like 'imperialism' is similar to others like 'liberty' or 'freedom' which resist that precision. Imperialism is what the philosopher William Gallie many years ago called an 'essentially contested concept'; and the variety of ways of describing and dissecting it register not so much confusion or even the enormous complexity of the subject matter as the fact that historians' visions of empires, whether formal or informal, ancient or modern, are based fundamentally on moral assumptions that are sometimes so deep that the protagonists are only dimly aware of the inflection that they give to their work. And, as our moral perceptions change so do our histories: at this moment, American activities in Iraq are not only stimulating new debates on what imperialism is but are also beginning to shape our reflections on what it was in the past. Historians are condemned by the nature of their task to make interim statements only: Barbara's book is valuable because it gives us a much better overview of the bulletins the profession is issuing at the beginning of the 21st century.

Barbara gives more space to postcolonial writings influenced by the 'cultural turn', and especially by Said, than she does to the more conventional, often economics-inspired, Eurocentric literature that had its origins in the heyday of European imperialism. That is as it should be because the former has attracted most of the attention in recent years and because it was essential to make the shift to a more de-centred perspective in order to be faithful to the rich legacy left by the great European empires of modern times and to reflect changes in awareness and interest both in the West and in the formerly colonised nations. What is perhaps needed now, as Barbara indicates, is more fertile interaction between the old and the new. In Chapter 3 she shows that the debate as to whether imperialism is a distressing atavism or a bringer of modernity can bring together thinkers as diverse and time-distanced as Schumpeter, who wrote his famous essay in 1919, and postmodernists like Dipesh Chakrabarty. Moreover, the ongoing discussion about modern globalisation and its relationship with imperialism, which Barbara skilfully dissects in Chapter 6, is inevitably bringing economics and geo-politics back nearer to the centre of discussions of the subject again.

For myself, the most valuable sections of Barbara's book are the short but concentrated case studies – of tropical Africa, China, Japan and Ireland – which show not only an impressive range of reference but which, in their different ways, demonstrate as clearly as possible that no satisfying imperial histories can be written without some blending of the older and the newer ways of writing them. This melding of different approaches could be taken much further: it has often seemed to me, for example, that the distance between Ronald Robinson's idea of collaboration and Homi Bhabha's notion of hybridity is rather less than champions of either approach have been prepared to consider. In that context, the last case study on how the empire has been represented in Britain, where Barbara faithfully records the debates and the contests, seems to be an area wherein a rather large gap has opened up between cultural historians and those who write in a more traditional vein; a gap that the next generation of imperial historians will, hopefully, begin to fill.

Peter Cain
Research Professor in History
Sheffield Hallam University

Preface to the series

History: Concepts, Theories and Practice is a series that offers a coherent and detailed examination of the nature and effects of recent theoretical, methodological and historiographical developments within key fields of contemporary historical practice. Each volume is open to the idea of history as a historicist cultural discourse constituted by historians as much as it is reconstructed from the sources available about the past. The series examines the discipline of history as it is conceived today in an intellectual climate that has increasingly questioned the status of historical knowledge.

As is well known, questioning of the status of history, indeed of its very existence as an academic subject, has been seen in several recent scholarly developments that have directly influenced our study of the past. These include the emergence of new conceptualizations of 'pastness', the emergence of fresh forms of social theorizing, the rise of concerns with narrative, representation and the linguistic turn, and a self-conscious engagement with the issues of relativism, objectivity and truth. All these are reflected in the appearance of new historical themes and frameworks of historical activity.

In acknowledging that history is not necessarily nor automatically authorized by one foundational epistemology or methodology and that history cannot stand outside its own genre or form, all volumes in the series reflect a multiplicity of metanarrative positions. Nevertheless, each volume (regardless of its own perspective and position on the nature of history) explains the most up-to-date interpretational and historiographic developments that fall within its own historical field. However, this review of the 'latest interpretation and methodology' does not diminish the broad awareness of the 'challenge to history as a discipline' reflected in the tensions between referentiality, representation, structure and agency.

Each volume offers a detailed understanding of the content of the past, explaining by example the kinds of evidence found within their own field as well as a broad knowledge of the explanatory and hermeneutic demands historians make upon their sources, the current debates on the uses to which evidence is put, and how evidence is connected by historians within their field to their overall vision of What is history?

Alun Munslow

Author's acknowledgements

For help and encouragement in the preparation of this book I would like to thank my colleagues in the History department at Sheffield Hallam University, in particular Peter Cain; Josephine Maltby (University of Sheffield) for her reading of the final draft and helpful suggestions and, finally, my students for ideas and gifts of old books and ephemera of empire that they knew I liked to collect. Thanks also go to the general editor of this series, Alun Munslow, the editorial staff at Pearson Education for helping me see this book through to completion and, of course, my family for their consistent support. There are many others – too numerous to mention – whose published research, ideas and arguments I have found helpful in defining my own approaches to imperialism and postcolonialism. They have all broadly contributed to this book and are credited in the Bibliography.

Publisher's acknowledgements

We are grateful to the following for their permission to reproduce copyright material:

Map 4 reproduced with permission, British Library Maps.183.q.1.(13); Figure 1.1 reproduced with permission, British Library 9604.bbb.29; Figure 1.3 reproduced with permission, British Library YA.1998.a.4414; Figure 3.1 reproduced with permission, British Library 4766.dd.25; Figure 3.2 reproduced with permission, British Library 09055.b.10; Figure 4.1 reproduced with permission, British Library PA.1998.a.4414

In some instances we have been unable to trace the owners of copyright material, and we would appreciate any information that would enable us to do so.

List of maps

List of illustrations

Map 1   'The Roman Empire under Diocletian and Constantine' showing the extent of the Western and Eastern empires *circa* AD 284–305 from George Willis Botsford, *A History of Rome* (New York, London, The Macmillan Company, 1909)

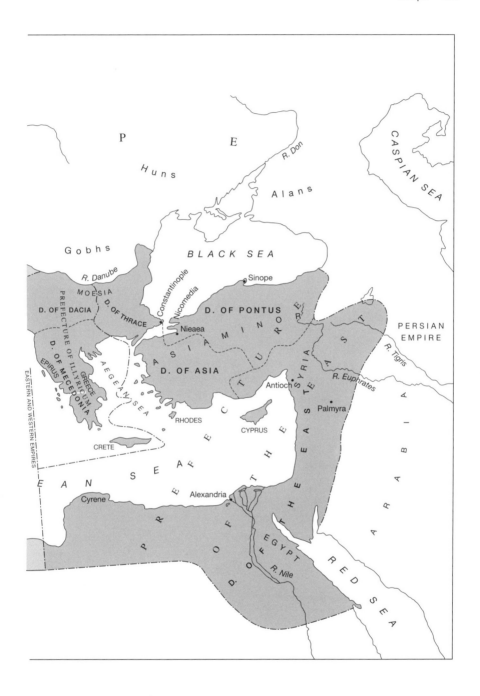

Map 2 'Persian Empire at its greatest extent, 525 BC' from Sir Percy Molesworth Sykes, *A History of Persia* (London, Macmillan & Co., 1921, 2nd edn; first published, 1915), 2 vols, vol. 1

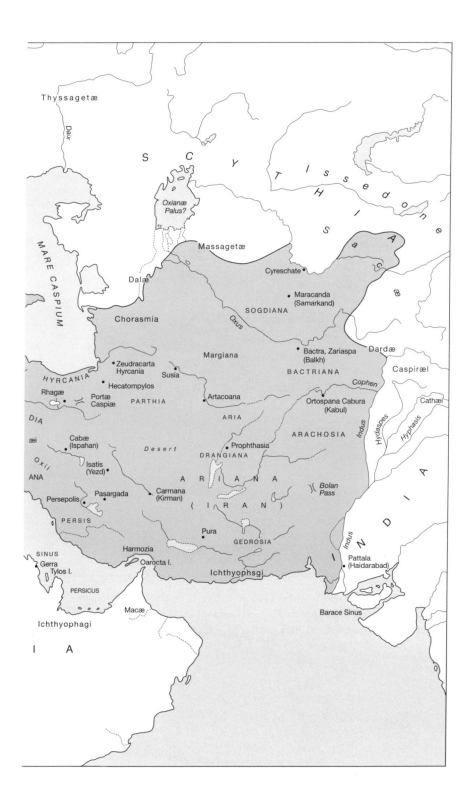

Thyssagetæ

Daïx

S   C   Y

T I s s e d o n e

SCYTHIS

Oxianæ
Palus?

MARE CASPIUM

Massagetæ

Cyreschate

Dalæ

Chorasmia

SOGDIANA

Maracanda
(Samarkand)

Oxus

Margiana

Bactra, Zariaspa
(Balkh)

Dardæ

Zeudracarta
Hyrcania

Susia

BACTRIANA

Caspiræl

HYRCANIA

Cophen

Hecatompylos

Ortospana Cabura
(Kabul)

Cathæi

Rhagæ

Portæ
Caspiæ

PARTHIA

Artacoana

Indus

Hydaspes

Hyphasis

DIA

ARIA

æi

ARACHOSIA

Cabæ
(Ispahan)

Desert

Prophthasia

Oxii

Isatis
(Yezd)

DRANGIANA

ANA

A   R   I   A   N   A

Bolan
Pass

I   N   D   I   A

Persepolis

Pasargada

Carmana
(Kirman)

(I R A N)

PERSIS

Pura

Indus

Harmozia

GEDROSIA

Pattala
(Haidarabad)

SINUS

Oarocta I.

Gerra
Tylos I.

Ichthyophsgi

PERSICUS

Macæ

Barace Sinus

Ichthyophagi

I   A

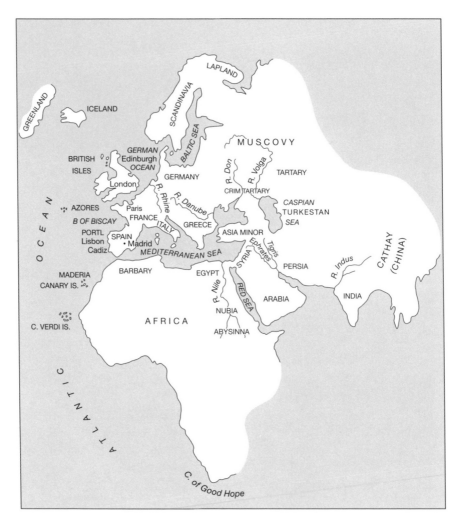

Map 3 'The known world in 1475' from Rev. C. S. Dawe, *King Edward's Realm: The Story of the Making of the Empire* (London, The Educational Supply Association Limited, c. 1902), p. 19

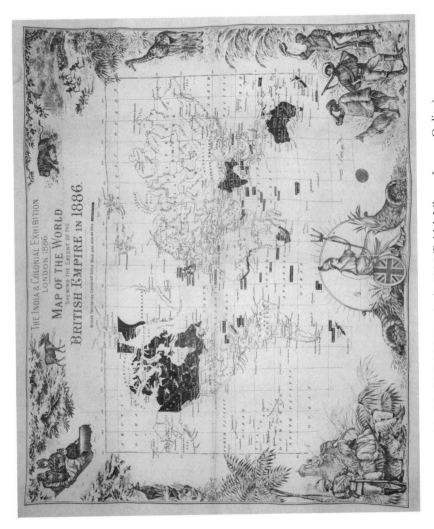

Map 4   Map of the World: British Empire in 1886 (British Library Images Online)

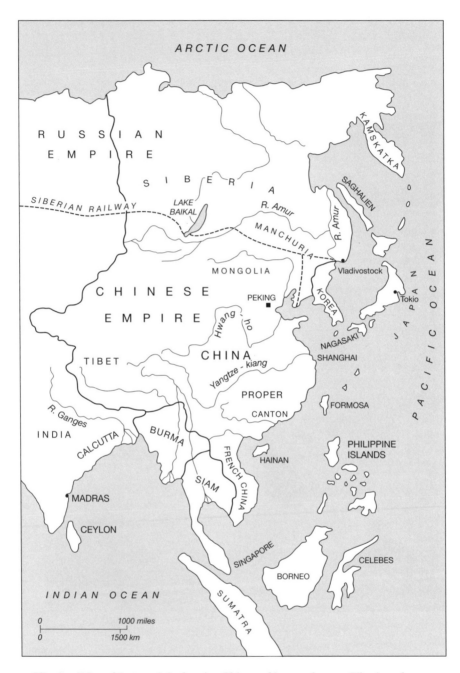

Map 5   'Map of Eastern Asia showing China and its vassal states, Siberia and Japan, pre 1885' from Michael J. F. McCarthy, *The Coming Power: A Contemporary History of the Far East, 1898–1905* (London, Hodder and Stoughton, 1905)

Introduction

In the popular Western imagination empires are either a thing of the past or the empires of cinema fantasy, as in the *Empire Strikes Back*. In the political rhetoric of 1980s Reaganite America, the last stronghold of 'real' as opposed to fantasy imperialism was the 'Evil Empire', the USSR, that threatened the free world. With the collapse of communism this threat was superseded by the 'axis of evil' states (Iraq, Iran, North Korea) and globalized terrorism counterpoised against the 'good empire' of the USA. Empires and imperialism, however, remain as relevant today as in the past, reflected in the growing popularity of imperial history. As Michael Hardt and Antonio Negri pointed out in *Empire* (2001), imperialism as we knew it may have passed but empire is alive and resurgent, carving a new economic, cultural and political globalized order. Critical interrogation of the meaning of empire and imperialism, the link between imperialism, modernity and capitalism and the impact of imperialism on global structures and national cultures, past and present, is the central focus of this book. But is it imperialism or imperialisms that we need to consider? Is imperialism inevitable and will it always exist? What is the difference between imperialism and expansionism? What constitutes an empire?

In the 1940s, Sir Keith Hancock commented on the different meanings given to the word 'imperialism', including political, military, racial and economic aspects of the concept (Hancock, 1943, p. 9). 'Empire' and 'imperialism' are blanket terms and demand careful consideration (Doyle, 1986). Blurring, contradiction and confusion over the nature of imperialism are reflected in the different terminology used in published works within different disciplines and written from different ideological perspectives. Different meanings are ascribed to empire over time. Empire, *imperium, reich*, commonwealth, all imply expansion of states outside their territory, a widening of geographical space, either by land or sea, extending boundaries of power and influence. 'Empire', a bounded geographical entity, is a less loaded term than 'imperialism', which inscribes social, cultural and political relations of power between the empire and its subordinated periphery. 'Imperialism', then, is a subjective term that is ideologically loaded and conveys a range of conflicting meanings. The term was first used in Britain in the early nineteenth century in relation to hostile French ambitions and gained greater currency after 1850, but it was the emergence of anti-imperialism at the end of the nineteenth century that strengthened the negative connotations of the term. If we are to develop a less Eurocentric perspective, a study of imperialism must interrogate empires *and* imperialism.

In explaining the rise and fall of empires, some political historians have favoured the term 'Great Powers' (Kennedy, 1988), prioritizing the powerful modern nation-state. Is this applicable to 'powers' which created empires before the modern age? Lieven defines an empire as

> . . . a great power that has left its mark on the international relations of the era . . . a polity that rules over wide territories and many peoples . . . by definition not a democracy . . . [where] the management of space and multi-ethnicity is a perennial dilemma . . .
>
> (Lieven, 2002, p. xiv)

Yet this focus on 'Great Powers', whether acknowledging empire or not, obscures the importance of transnational structures of global power established through capitalism (Wallerstein, 1996) and the fact that colonies have always been pawns in global power games (Osterhammel, 1997, p. 3). Empires and imperial discourse may differ considerably within and between different eras, but oppression of colonized groups is a unifying characteristic. How is capitalism linked to imperialism? Can imperialism exist outside the formal boundaries of empires? These thorny and unresolved questions have evoked fierce debates about informal imperialism and neo-imperialism which have raged since the 1960s but are crucial to understanding the nature of imperialism, past and present, including the contemporary global power of the USA.

Can 'good' empires exist without the more negative and exploitative characteristics of imperialism? The concept of commonwealth is relevant here. Commonwealth may be defined as 'a group of politically discrete but related polities collectively distinguishable from other polities or commonwealths by a shared culture and history' (Fowden, 1993, pp. 6, 169). Arguably, there can be no commonwealth without a preceding empire. From this perspective, a commonwealth is a reformed empire premised on an 'association of equals' and 'partnership' between centre and periphery, as reflected in the rhetoric of the British Commonwealth (Wilkinson, 1944, p. 193). Thus, unlike empire, commonwealth has positive connotations. The concept has a long history stretching back to late antiquity when the Islamic empire developed into a more loosely structured 'commonwealth', centred on trade and Islamic religion and culture (Lieven, 2000, pp. 11–12, 16). The word *reich*, as applied to the Germanic Holy Roman Empire (962–c. 1806) from the fourteenth century, is also an early conception of 'commonwealth'; the empire was, in effect, a loose association of states ruled through a legislative body, the *Reichstag*, and the powers of the emperor/Kaiser were limited. Yet there is a dangerous slippage between 'empire' and 'commonwealth'. The first use of the term 'commonwealth' in relation to England and its colonies was during the sixteenth and seventeenth centuries, but wealth and prosperity accrued largely to England. It was, indeed, Britain's 'First Empire' (Armitage, 2001). The move from Empire to Commonwealth from the late 1930s onwards can be interpreted as a strategy of the British establishment to hold on to power in the face of mounting colonial resistance (Bush, 1999).

In this book I want to explore recent intellectual, theoretical and conceptual developments in imperial history, including interdisciplinary and postcolonial perspectives. I am not entering into theoretical debates about the causes of imperialism, which have been meticulously and extensively developed since the 1960s and revived by the postcolonial challenge (Cain and Harrison (eds), 2001). Like Wolfe (1997), I use the term 'imperialism' in a generalized way to embrace a range of perspectives on the nature of Western hegemony. I will undoubtedly be accused of adopting too wide a definition and overemphasizing the impact of imperialism at global, national and local levels. Yet, for too long, imperial history has been delinked from other aspects of the 'national story' of the imperial power, whereas empire and domestic history are arguably intimately intertwined. Can the Industrial Revolution in Britain really be fully understood without reference to its colonies (Pomeranz, 2000)? When students flock to courses on the Third Reich, do they realize that they are studying an aberrant descendant of the first Reich, the Holy Roman Empire? European history has been divorced for too long from its vital imperial context.

Additionally, academic research and teaching still favour the narrow local, rather than the broader global, focus. Concepts and definitions relating to empire and imperialism in a broader context have been marginalized in favour of micro studies of aspects of imperial cultures (predominantly relating to the British Empire) and/or detailed empirical analysis. As David Cannadine observes, in a world of historians populated by macro/overview 'parachutists' and micro/detail 'truffle hunters' and frequently marred by polarized rancour and dispute, there is a need for both approaches and more productive interconnections between the general and particular (Cannadine, 2002). Christopher Bayly has argued for a return to world history and study of global interconnections after the postmodernist 'abrasure' of the link between human experience and political economy (Bayly, 2004, p. 38). Globalization in the context of world history has attracted far more interest since the 1990s (Hopkins (ed.), 2002). My focus here is on interconnections and comparisons between empires and imperial power within wider developments in world history, from the Roman to the present-day American Empire. As empires and imperialism are of interest to historians, social scientists, and literary and cultural theorists, the scope is interdisciplinary.

I am also concerned with continuities between the colonial and 'postcolonial'. The word 'empire' stretches back 2,000 years to the Latin *imperium*. Empires have waxed and waned, merged and dissolved for thousands of years and, without such empires, there would be no 'modern world'. In the words of Dominic Lieven (2000), 'to write the history of empire would be to write the history of the world' and understanding imperialism is essential to understanding the contemporary world (p. xvi). How else can we explain continued racial tensions in the ex-imperial powers of western Europe; the problematic nature of 'Britishness'; the contradictions within the French concept of citizenship, which prioritizes a common unifying culture over racial difference, yet fails to address racial exclusions or to accept cultural diversity? How can contemporary identities of minorities (including African-Americans) be fully interrogated without reference to the migrations, forced and voluntary, that sustained the changing labour needs of empires and created global diasporas? As Patrick Wolfe writes:

> Questions of balance aside, the fact remains that Europe and its others were co-produced in and through their unequal interactions . . . To begin to evoke the multifaceted fullness of imperialism . . . we not only have to bring it home, wherever that might be. We also have to trace its complex interrelations.
>
> (Wolfe, 1997, pp. 406, 409)

The dialogue between postcolonial and orthodox approaches to imperial history has opened up fertile new research into these aspects of imperial history that were previously marginalized in the historiography. Studies influenced by postcolonial theory have challenged West-centred paradigms of the imperial past and present. There has been more emphasis on how colonialism was shaped in struggle and the ways in which colonial discourse and imperial policies were deeply affected by the actions of the colonized (Stoler and Cooper (eds), 1997, p. ix). Finally, new perspectives on race, class, gender, sexuality, the psychology of violence, the interplay of economics and culture and the dialectics of the colonial encounter, areas formerly neglected or marginalized in imperial histories, have provided a more nuanced understanding of empires and their aftermath.

With the postcolonial 'turn' imperial history became 'sexy' (literally, in terms of preoccupations with sexuality and the body, and figuratively, in increased popularity). Other disciplines, in particular geography and cultural and literary studies, have muscled in on an area formally dominated by historians and political scientists. Almost every facet has now been covered: gender, sexuality, homosexuality, law, sport, the ecological impact, medicine and imperialism and the 'empire at home'. As a researcher and teacher of imperial history, however, I have become keenly aware of the need for a text of this nature. Most of the works addressing theoretical and conceptual issues date from the 1960s to the mid-1980s and are located in the debates of the era, which were framed by the impact of decolonization and the Cold War (Owen and Sutcliffe (eds), 1972; Etherington, 1984; Mommsen, 1980). Pieterse's *Empire and Emancipation* (1990) is a valuable newer contribution to understanding the relationship between imperial power and resistance, but does not address some of the key debates opened up by the postcolonial challenge. Howe (2002) does examine what the idea of empire has meant throughout history but it is, as the title implies, a very short history. Sauer and Rajan (2004) provide a critical study of historical, literary and postcolonial scholarship on imperialism from 1500 to 1900, but omit important developments in the twentieth century. Most overview works remain focused on the British Empire from *circa* the eighteenth century (Johnson, 2003; Smith, 1998; Porter, 2004) and deal mainly with conventional debates, although Cain and Hopkins (2001) provide a stimulating study of the changing nature of British imperialism over time and address the concept of globalization.

More historical studies are now moving beyond the conventional debates and there has been interesting work on non-Western and ancient empires (Alcock *et al.*, 2002), but imperialism is still conceptualized predominantly within a modern West-centred context. As Michael Adas (1998) points out, much can be learned from applying concepts of colonialism and imperialism, reserved for the study of European or American domination to, for instance, the Chinese Qing Empire, which was engaged in colonial ventures akin to those of expanding European states, using similar techniques, and demonstrating a similar mix of colonial systems within a diverse empire. Yet the omissions in the authoritative *Oxford History of the British Empire (5 vols, 1998–2000)* revealed the durability of conventional and/or Eurocentric tendencies in imperial history. There is still far less published on anti-imperialism than on imperialism and West-centred, particularly British-centred, studies still predominate. Conventional imperial history (like conventional history in general) established narrow boundaries delineating what constituted 'valid' historical research and evidence that impeded fruitful interdisciplinary approaches. My position is that new approaches to imperial history need to build upon existing conventional studies within a critical framework that incorporates fresh insights informed by postcolonial theory. Additionally, we need to go beyond the preoccupation with British or European empires from the late eighteenth to the mid-twentieth century. As Anthony Hopkins stresses, what is needed is a fundamental reappraisal of world history to establish

> . . . a link between the history of empires, which embraces the world and the universality of problems that are the residue of their demise . . . This would capture the differences between empires and their dynamism and leave few parts of the globe untouched.
>
> (Hopkins, 1999, pp. 199, 203–4, 241)

It is with this challenge in mind that this book has been conceived. I develop a comparative framework which locates the later era of imperialism from the eighteenth century onwards in the *longue durée*. Historiographical developments catalysed by the renaissance in studies of imperialism stimulated by postcolonial theory provide the conceptual framework. Chapters 1 and 2 are foundational chapters. Chapter 1 explores the nature of empires from ancient to modern and queries the unique nature of European imperialism. Chapter 2 interrogates continuity and change in the historiography of imperialism and theoretical and conceptual developments stimulated by postcolonial theory. The following chapters develop themes and issues introduced in these foundational chapters, including imperialism and modernity; culture and imperialism; representations of empire, and, finally, the nature of the 'post-imperial' era. Each chapter will provide an overview of the range of relevant research and key controversies and debates. Case studies of Ireland, China and Japan, Africa and imperialism and national identity in Britain demonstrate how theories and concepts help to illuminate different facets of imperialism in practice.

The focus embraces resistance and imperial power as these two facets of imperial history are implicitly linked (Bush, 1999). For the same reasons, gender perspectives have been integrated where relevant, rather than dealt with separately. I have not provided a detailed analysis of decolonization as the literature on this specialized topic is now vast: with postcolonial critiques it became one of the fastest-growing areas of new research (Le Sueur, 1997). Nor have I been able to include detailed debates over the economics and costs and benefits of empire. I have, however, tried to contextualize my analysis of the cultures of empire, a dominant focus in the historiography since the 1980s, within broader political and economic developments outlined in Chapter 1. Economic history has been marginalized in the cultural 'turn', yet there are many fine studies that need to be more fully integrated into cultural analyses and are essential to a more holistic understanding of the nature of imperialism.

My fundamental premise is that imperialism is one of the most influential forces which has shaped, and is still shaping, the world. There was no sharp hiatus as the colonized moved to independence with decolonization, and the colonial and postcolonial must be conceptualized as seamless. How else can we explain what is happening in the Middle East, except in reference to the ebb and flow of differing imperial interests? We need to be constantly alert to ahistorical analyses of contemporary developments that assume history does not matter (Snooks, 1993). This works in the interests of the powerful in perpetuating their privilege and wealth as, without historical understanding, challenges to power become diffused, fragmented and undermined.

Finally, I must stress that when writing about imperialism it is difficult to be value-free; interpretations of imperialism and contemporary structures of global power depend on where individuals were/are positioned within empires, or the aftermath of empires, and in relation to vested political and economic interests and personal family histories. African migrants facing racial exclusion in London or Paris have a different, and more painful, relationship to the imperial past than white Europeans. Non-Western intellectuals are more likely to see empire in a negative perspective than a British imperial historian whose past family prosperity derived from the Empire. A Marxist historian like Eric Hobsbawm will adopt a different conceptual framework in writing about imperialism from a liberal, free-market enthusiast such as Niall Ferguson. Political ideologies – left, liberal, reformist or right – have generated different interpretations of the relationship between capitalism and imperialism, the nature of globalization and world systems and the impact of Western culture on the rest of the world. Thus, in writing about empire or imperialism as a concept there is always the danger of accusations of bias, but also the rewards of engaging in challenging, stimulating and continuously contentious debates.

Untangling imperialism: comparisons over time and space

The quintessential explorer [Christopher Columbus] personified the whole ambitious, outward thrust of early modern Europe and its . . . determination to break out of the confines of the familiar, to make known the unknown, to defy the constraints of nature and conquer all that was conquerable.

(Sale, 1990, p. 201)

Thus began the mythologizing of European history around the Columbus legend and the Eurocentric prioritization of imperialism from the seminal date, 1492, the 'discovery' of the Americas. At this time Europeans had no special advantage, so why was the conquest so successful? How unique is Europe? In different manifestations the Chinese Empire lasted from 221 BC to 1911, compared with a brief 400 years of European empires. Should we be referring to imperialisms rather than imperialism? How do we interpret changes over time and differences between empires? What can we learn from comparisons between ancient and modern empires? Firstly, this foundational chapter charts the ebb and flow of empires over time, in the *longue durée*. These include land-based (continental) and maritime, formal and informal empires and those which combine some or all these features, synchronically (Rome) or at different periods in the lifespan of the empire (England/Britain). The second section compares empires, past and present, in defining the nature of empires and understanding the West's ascendancy over the 'Rest'. I argue that empires had negative consequences for the majority of colonized subjects and mainly benefited a minority in the imperial centre and colonial periphery. This given, imperialism also generated dynamic cultural change and resistance that challenged the inequalities inherent in imperialist relations.

Early and later empires were similar in that they were premised on military power and conquest of peoples to accrue wealth through a combination of trade, colonization, mining, taxation and tribute. The conventional starting point for modern imperialism and the restructuring of the world through capitalist expansion and globalization is the Spanish and Portuguese conquest of the Americas in the sixteenth century. Yet complex relations already existed between Europe and the Ottoman, Chinese and extensive Islamic trading empires, including the Mughal Empire of Northern India. In central and South America the Spanish conquistadores encountered the extensive Inca and Aztec empires. Eventually, with varying degrees of damage and over different time-spans, all these empires declined and succumbed to European power. Why did 'we', the Europeans, colonize 'them', the Asian, African and American 'others', and not the other way round (Brown, 1963)? Is it this 'uniqueness' which helps to explain how Europe and then the West came to dominate the rest of the world?

Three broad arguments can be forwarded in support of the 'uniqueness' of Europe: the rise of capitalism, European modernity (Chapter 3) and fortuitous ecological and physical factors or, in the words of Jared Diamond, 'we are all equal but the playing fields are not' (Diamond, 1997). All three have some validity. Assumptions of the 'exceptionalism' or uniqueness of Europe and the West are reflected in the historiography. From the 1960s to the 1980s, change and continuity in imperialism were at the heart of debates centred on the New Imperialism, *circa* 1870–1914. Historians who stressed continuity did not go back much further than the emergence of the Second British Empire in the late eighteenth century, a Eurocentric position that excluded important developments in earlier periods, even prior to 1492 (Armitage, 2001). Such Eurocentricism has been criticized as an ethnocentric 'colonizer's view' of the world (Blaut, 1993). This has ignored the ways in which empires have been shaped in relation to each other since early antiquity and has prioritized the influence of the West, neglecting the Eastern contribution to Western development (Chaudhuri, 1990; Hobson, 2004). It has also precluded fruitful comparative analyses.

World systems analysis, pioneered by Braudel (1984) and Immanuel Wallerstein (1974, 1980, 1989), has also been criticized for prioritizing the rise of European capitalism since the fifteenth century. Archaeologists have extended Wallerstein's analysis to ancient societies and empires, establishing that significant commercial exchanges and divisions of labour across borders created early economic world systems (Chase Dunn and Hall, 1997). Frank and Gills (1993), Arrighi (1994) and W. R. Thompson (2000) have argued that long-term economic growth, based on cycles of innovation, peace and stability maintained through a strong hegemony, has had a continuous history since the tenth century. In the eleventh and twelfth centuries, the Sung Chinese Empire developed powerful political and military systems combined with maritime and economic innovation. Hegemonic instability, however, resulted in a reordering and stabilizing of the international system and China was challenged by the aggressive Mediterranean trading states that were, in turn, displaced by Western Europe. A cycle of the rise of empires through concentration, decline through deconcentration, and reconcentration in new imperial centres thus began (W. R. Thompson, 2000, pp. 13–14).

Such studies raise important questions about continuities, differences and similarities between empires across the epochs. Change was generated by competing power interests but also resistance to hegemonic imperial agencies by the oppressed. Empires, ancient and modern, have all waxed and waned but, as Alcock (2002) points out, old empires never entirely die but have an afterlife through 'emulation and . . . rejection . . . of the mores of one empire by another' (p. 370). Thus 'empires of nostalgia' claim the imperial tradition and outward trappings of the extinct empire. Byzantium and the Carolingian Empire of Charlemagne in the eight and ninth centuries mapped on to large parts of the former Western and Eastern Roman Empire (see Map 1, p. xvi). Russia inherited the Byzantine Christian legacy and Spain claimed legitimate decent from the Carolingian and Roman empires (Barfield, 2002). Later British and American empires also harked back to Rome, the archetypal, *Ur* empire past and present.

Time and change: the ebb and flow of empires

Before modern Europe

Empires emerged with the great civilizations of antiquity such as Old Babylonia (1800 BC), which bequeathed mathematics, science and the written word to future Middle Eastern and European cultures. The Greek Empire (c. 750–550 BC) created colonies around the Eastern Mediterranean and Black Sea and established some of the essential characteristics of later European empires, including an early form of orientalist discourse. The Achaemenid Persian Empire (c. 550–330 BC) was one of the earliest 'world empires', stretching from the Egyptian frontier to Uzbekistan (Kuhrt, 2002).

(See Map 2, p. xviii) Led by Xerxes, the Persians invaded Greece in 480 BC and destroyed Athens. In the writings of the Greek historian, Herodotus (c. 450 BC), superior democratic, rational and progressive Greek identities were contrasted with inferior barbaric 'others' of the autocratic Persian Empire. Partly motivated by revenge, between 336 and his death in 323 BC, Alexander the Great defeated the Persians and incorporated their empire into his own, which extended as far as the Hindu Kush. Colonies were established and over 30 settlements named 'Alexandra' from Egypt to Alexandra Eschate, or Farthermost, in what is now Tajikistan. Alexandrian myths and claims of direct descent from the Greeks still persist in many parts of Asia (Wood, 2004).

Ancient empires were often transient and fragile (Howe, 2002, p. 37) but during late Antiquity, 'world empires' were created, of an area large enough to pass for 'the world', that could maintain control without serious competition (Fowden, 1993, p. 6). Late Antiquity covers the period from the second century, the peak of Rome's prosperity, to the ninth century and the onset of the decline of the Islamic empire. This *orbis terrarum* (the whole world) stretched from the Eastern Mediterranean to the Iranian plateau but excluded China. Christian missions, however, had reached as far as India and the Chinese court by the third century, initiating the first travel writings (ibid.).

The Roman Empire (c. 55 BC to AD 410) established important principles of imperial rule that echoed down to the later nineteenth-century European empires. The Roman *imperium* was not simply a territory but encapsulated the Roman notion of commands given by a general or governor, the *imperator*. The Roman dream was that, through conquest, a vast area of peace, prosperity and unity of ideas could be created. At its zenith, 27 BC to AD 235, the Roman Empire incorporated vast tracts of Europe, the Near East, Egypt and North Africa. *Pax Romana* lasted for centuries, although there was rarely 'peace' throughout the empire and on the Rhine frontier the Germanic tribes were never pacified. The Romans envisaged empire as a single civic community, 'a fortress on a macrocosmic scale' which kept at bay those incompatible with community (Lintott, 1993, p. 186). Like the present-day American Empire, the Romans were engaged in an endless struggle against disorder and barbarianism and empire ended with the sack of Rome by the allegedly barbarian Visigoths in AD 410.

Antiquity's contribution to the technique of empire, suggests Fowden, was the discovery of a 'non-military . . . partially political basis for self perpetuation'. This was facilitated by the emergence of monotheism. Formerly pagan empires were now defined by cultural and political universalism, rooted in the unifying religions of Christianity and Islam that justified the exercise of imperial power and made it more effective. In its latter years, the Roman Empire was reconceptualized as a Christian world empire with a destiny to prepare the way for the kingdom of God, a universal society rather than an *imperium* created by conquest, although, stresses Lintott, this remained an aspiration rather than a reality (Lintott, 1993, p. 193). Nevertheless, the Emperor Constantine's Byzantine Empire (AD 324–37), a direct descendant of polytheist Rome, had some success in unifying the fragmenting Roman Empire through Christianization (Fowden, 1993, pp. 3, 127, 170).

The apogée of late Antiquity was the Islamic empire founded by the Umayyed dynasty, the direct descendants of the prophet Mohammed. In 750 AD the Umayyeds were overthrown by the Abbasids and moved to Spain, France and North Africa. The Abbasids replaced Damascus with a new capital, Baghdad (founded 762 AD), the 'City of Peace', located near the Babylon of ancient Mesopotamia. At the 'crossroads of the universe' and of 'fabulous wealth', Baghdad stood for the 'universalism, self sufficiency and completeness of the Islamic empire'. A prophesy attributed to Mohammed, however, warned of the 'catastrophic downfall' of Baghdad as a city where the 'kings and tyrants of the world will assemble' (Fowden, 1993, pp. 50–1). This has a peculiar resonance, given the US/British invasion of Iraq in 2003. The Islamic empire was characterized by religious and cultural tolerance, in stark contrast to contemporary media perceptions of Islam as fanatical, violent and at war with Christianity. During this era there was fruitful contact between Muslims and Christians in the Mediterranean through trade and interchange of technology. Even during the protracted twelfth-century Crusades, which brought the Christian 'West' into conflict with the Muslim 'East', some Christians accepted that they had much to learn from Islam; Muslims were less interested in the West, creating a cultural divide which is still unresolved (Fletcher, 2003).

The 'Dark Ages' is a purely Eurocentric concept, given the developments outside Europe in this period. As Fowden points out, 'not all roads out of antiquity lead to the European Renaissance' and 'non-Latin' perspectives on the past are now given more attention (Fowden, 1993, p. 9). When Genghis Khan died in 1227 he ruled over an empire that extended from the Caspian to the Pacific and was twice the size of the Roman Empire (Man, 2004). The Mughal Empire of North India (1529–1757) was founded by descendants of Genghis Khan, who had assimilated the Islamic culture and religion of the Middle East but retained military skills and other cultural facets that reflected their Far Eastern origins. A strong Chinese Empire and a reinvigorated Islam in Al Andalus (Islamized Spain and Morocco) shaped global developments from 900 to 1492. The period from 600 to 1600 also witnessed the rise of the

Turks, nomadic warrior Turkoman or Turkik peoples who spread from Central Asia into what is now modern-day Turkey.

In the sixteenth century the vast Islamic and Chinese empires were, in terms of economic development, cultural sophistication and technological innovation, equal, if not superior to Europe. In Iran, the Safavid dynasty (1501–1736) was characterized by military might, artistic brilliance, economic prosperity, dynamic developments in science, philosophy, religion (the establishment of Shiism) and architecture (Newman, 2005). The Safavids engaged in war and treaties with the Ottoman Turks, who defeated Byzantium at the Siege of Constantinople, 1453, reassembled most of the fragmenting Islamic empire and expanded into the Balkans (Halden, 2000). Constantinople, the capital of the earlier Byzantine Empire (c. 330–1453), became the centre of this new Ottoman Empire that lasted until 1924. The Turks were converts to Islam but their culture remained open, tolerant, pluralistic and assimilationist, building flexibility and dynamism into the Ottoman Empire (Inalcik and Quateart, 1994). Before the defeat of the Ottoman navy by the Holy League (Spanish, Venetian and Papal ships) at the Battle of Lepanto (Greece) in 1571, the Ottoman Empire became the most formidable state in Europe, disciplined and highly motivated. Ottoman military and technological leadership was second to none and the Sultan's territories and revenues greater than those of any Christian rivals (Lieven, 2000, p. 139). By 1800 the picture had completely changed.

The rise of modern European empires

Tectonic shifts in the fates of empires refigured global relations during the fifteenth century. For centuries Western Europe had been on the wild fringes of Europe, firstly incorporated into the Roman Empire, and then overshadowed by the medieval Mediterranean maritime city states of Genoa, Venice, Amalfi and Pisa, whose power marked the beginning of the ascendancy of Europe. These maritime states, like the earlier Phoenician city state, created trade networks but attempted to extract wealth without occupation of a large territory and lacked the autonomy that defined them as empires (Barfield, 2002, p. 38). Additionally, Western Europe was initially not strong enough to take on the powerful Chinese, Mughal and Ottoman empires. But the Renaissance instilled new vigour into Western European society and economy. The *reconquista*, the expulsion of Islamic influence from the Iberian Peninsula, combined with improvements in navigation, facilitated the Spanish and Portuguese seaborne empires (Boxer, 1969; Scammel, 1989) and the European remapping of the world. Spain dominated in Latin and Central America and the Caribbean but also colonized the Philippines and ruled the Spanish Netherlands. The Portuguese trading networks in Asia were initially similar to those of the maritime city states and could not be classed as an empire. Indeed, the Portuguese faced increasing competition from the Dutch, who expelled them from Japan in the 1630s (Subrahmanyam, 1993). Eventually empire in Asia, Africa and Brazil (after negotiations with the Spanish) was secured (Boxer, 1969; Russell-Wood, 1992; Newitt, 2001; Lockart and Schwartz, 1983).

The epochal moment was the conquest of the Americas. The mood of the times in Europe was pessimistic after a century of famine, disease and violence. Repressive and corrupt regimes also stimulated the beginning of humanism and rationalism associated with the Renaissance. Exploration held the promise of contrasting utopias; Cristóbal Colón (Christopher Columbus) was driven by a religious vision and the desire to discover a 'terrestrial paradise' (Sale, 1990, pp. 30–1). Dreams of power and fantastic visions of Eldorado thus fired the imaginations of the first conquistadores, setting the precedent for future empires. The new navigators were initially searching for a western passage through to China and the riches of the Orient. Instead Columbus 'discovered' the 'West Indies'; America was named after the explorer, Amerigo Vespucci (see Figure 1.1) and Columbus's voyages inspired further explorations, including Sir Walter Raleigh's ventures into Virginia in 1586 that resulted in the formation of the Virginia Company in 1606 and colonization (Thomas, 2004).

The 'known' world in 1492 was centred primarily on Europe and Asia (see Map 3, p. xxii). From a Eurocentric perspective this was the heart of civilization and the world unknown to Europeans was there to be conquered. The concept of 'discovery' of the Americas assumed a 'new world' of 'virgin' territory for Europeans to freely colonize. This has now been challenged. Archaeological evidence from Michigan, New England, Newfoundland and other sites suggests that North America was discovered and temporarily settled by Norse explorers as early as 1000 AD (Sale, 1990, pp. 69–71). Kamen (2002) also disputes the Spanish national myth of the 'New World' as an epic tale of organized empire building carried out by heroic Spanish conquistadors for the greater glory of King and God. The conquest that resulted in the cruel destruction of the Aztecs and Incas was, in effect, an international venture of ruthless self-interested European soldiers, adventurers, entrepreneurs and opportunists (Columbus was from the Italian city state of Genoa). The real conquistadors were European diseases such as influenza, typhus, measles, diphtheria, smallpox and gonorrhoea, against which the indigenous population had no immunity (Crosby, 1986; Cook, 1998; Kamen, 2000;

Figure 1.1   'Amerigo Vespucci and the conquest of the Americas', redrawn from
Vita e lettere di Amerigo Vespucci

Restall, 2003). Spain created an 'empire by chance' and the 'conquest' succeeded through a combination of cunning, force, depopulation through disease, luck and 'very good timing' (Thompson, 2000, p. 88). Similar ecological and biological changes destroyed other indigenous communities in the Caribbean and North America, helping to consolidate white settlement. It was these factors that facilitated exploitation, not imperial policies or colonialist machinations (Klor de Alva, 1995).

When the Spanish and Portuguese arrived in the Americas, a range of diverse societies and cultures peopled the continent and populous towns existed in the Aztec and Inca empires and along the banks of the Amazon (Wood, 2003). With drastic population decline, local cultures, religion and political organization were undermined and societies transformed through Christian missions and Spanish administration (Bethell (ed.), 1987). Gold and silver now filled the coffers of the Spanish royal family, hence the 'Tower of Gold' in Seville, where plunder from the 'Indies' was landed. Plunder was soon replaced by more systematic exploitation of conquered peoples and lands, a process refined by later European empires. The Spanish colonial system was constructed in Mexico from 1520 to 1570 and between 1550 and 1800, Mexico and South America produced 80 per cent of the world's silver and 70 per cent of its gold (Kamen, 2002, p. 75). Silver from Latin America not only enriched the Spanish monarchy but stimulated early globalization; processed New World silver was exchanged for slaves, paid for Indian cotton and was traded with the Chinese for exotic luxury goods in high demand in Europe (Pomeranz, 2000, pp. 152–61).

The Dutch, French, English and Swedes soon challenged Spain, entered into competition with each other for lucrative colonies in the Americas and vied for maritime supremacy in the Caribbean (Parry, 1961; Boxer, 1965; Modelski and Thompson, 1988). By the seventeenth century Europeans had opened up 'virgin' land and established plantations producing primary commodities, stimulating the development of commerce and trade. Pamphlets encouraged men to make their fortunes as settlers and planters (*The Present Prospect of the Famous and Fertile Island of Tobago* by Captain John Poyntz, 1685). Daniel Defoe's *Robinson Crusoe* evokes the mood of these times and Moll, in his *Moll Flanders*, meticulously details her own trading ventures with Virginia, where she ends up as a convict. An ornate system of global trade developed through state-protected companies (mercantilism) and colonization, the creation of European societies in the 'new' world. There was a growing demand in Europe for new commodities, tobacco, sugar, coffee, the 'fruits of Empire' (Walvin, 1997).

Before 1750, however, European supremacy was not clear-cut. The Ottoman Empire remained powerful and Europe was under attack by the Barbary corsairs who took thousands of German, British and Dutch slaves, some of whom converted to Islam and stayed on even when freed. (Robinson Crusoe was one such slave who escaped and went to seek his fortune in the New World, becoming a slave owner himself.) Between 1677 and 1680 the Barbary 'pirates' plundered British shipping at will. British coastal dwellers were in terror of being kidnapped and up to 8,000 British men and women were enslaved (Davis, 2003). Linda Colley (2002b) also evokes the messiness of imperial relations in the early British Empire through the stories of those taken captive by 'natives'. White settlers in North America encountered resistance but were also dependent on local indigenous peoples for their survival. In Tobago from c. 1630–80 the Couronians (Kurlanders) from present-day Latvia had a vision of a free community that does not fit in with the definition of settlers as agents of the imperial power, but consistent attacks by Caribs and European invaders, fighting for valuable Caribbean possessions, forced them to abandon their settlement. The Couronian settlement is now a historic site (see Figure 1.2), upon which a modern monument has been erected by the Latvian people. Other heroic failures include the Scottish project to settle Darien (Panama) between 1698 and 1678. Support for the scheme took almost 50 per cent of Scottish wealth and promise of reimbursement of investors was a strong incentive to unification with England in 1702. The settlers survived only through developing friendly relations with the indigenous peoples, with whom they forged an alliance against the Spanish (Ibeji, 2003), but eventually abandoned the settlement. Such early settlement schemes reflected utopian dreams and the contemporary obsession with mercantile wealth rather than imperial ambitions. The industrialization of England, however, irrevocably changed the nature of imperialism.

British imperial supremacy, c. 1760–1880

The first English empire began in the thirteenth and fourteenth centuries in the reign of Edward I (1272–1307) and its dependencies were the Celtic fringes: Ireland, Scotland and Wales. Future external imperial expansion was arguably the offspring of this 'internal colonialism' (Hechter, 1975). By the reign of Elizabeth I, the empire of Great Britain, with England as the hegemon, had already developed its character as 'protestant, Anglo-British, benign and extra-European' (Armitage, 2001, p. 198) and expanded into the 'old colonial system' of the British Atlantic World. Britain's second empire, associated with

Figure 1.2 Information board marking the historic site of the Couronian Colony in Tobago, West Indies (author's own photograph)

industrial, commercial and naval dominance, began in the 1740s. Britain's natural resources, combined with social fluidity, stimulated industrialization that heralded the 'second age of discovery' of Australia and New Zealand and expansion in India (Osterhammel, 1997, p. 30). Britain defeated France and Spain in the Seven Years' War (1756–63), the first global war extending to European colonies in the New World and India. The French Empire was further undermined by the French Revolution and subsequent problems of state integration (Aldrich, 1996).

The period 1760–1830, argues Christopher Bayly (1998), was the first age of global imperialism, dominated by Britain and characterized by unpreced-ented global power shifts and developments in the international economy. It was the age of Britain's 'slave empire' (Walvin, 2000) but also a transitional period between the older colonial system based on trade in commodities, including slaves, and modern imperialism. The British Empire now became central to economic prosperity and the development of British culture and politics, nationalism and patriotism. A strong sense of national identity emerged but premised on an 'empire of liberty and freedom' defined against autocratic Spanish papist oppression. Imperial dominance and concepts of British liberty were bound together and English radicalism and anti-slavery were shaped by arguments against imperial tyranny (Colley, 1992b; Wilson, 1998). Was this the emergence of the first modern empire? Arguably, yes, given the rise of capitalism, the move from slave production to 'free labour' and from protected to free trade.

Imperial and economic strength without competition led to the expansion of 'informal' imperialism from 1840 to 1870 (Robinson and Gallagher, 1961) erroneously dubbed 'reluctant' or even 'absent-minded imperialism' (surely a contradiction in terms); imperialism now expanded into new arenas, such as Latin America, without the burdensome cost of formal colonies. As with the future US Empire, however, economic power was sustained through military might and the British were prepared to resort to war if interests were threat-ened. The Crimean War, 1854–6, fought by the British and French against Russia, supposedly over rights to guard the holy places in Jerusalem (echoes of the Crusades), was, in effect, precipitated by the expanding Russian Empire's predatory designs on the ailing Ottoman Empire and competition between Russia and Britain in the 'Great Game' in Asia (Meyer and Brysac, 2001). Britain was undoubtedly the imperial superpower of the nineteenth century, a position retained up to the outbreak of the Second World War (see Map 4, p. xxi). The war, however, heralded a revival of pro-imperialist sentiment but also increasingly fierce competition as Britain slowly lost her edge over other Western European states.

The New Imperialism: from European to Western imperialism

A new wave of colony acquisition opened up with the 'scramble' for Africa and the Far East after 1870. Colonial rule without colonization resulted in 'exploitation colonies', with separate metropolitan authorities supervising administration on the periphery (Osterhammel, 1997, p. 9). This New Imperialism resulted from a combination of factors, including the link between imperialism, nationalism and racism and the development of more sophisticated transnational capitalism. Forged through capitalist rivalry, it was associated with the decline of older empires (China, Russia, Austro-Hungary, Turkey) that were economically backward. As Lieven (2000) observes, the British and Russian empires differed considerably, not simply in relation to liberalism versus autocracy, but also in the contrast between a state at the core of the global economy and an agrarian society at the periphery (pp. 120-1). Imperialism also took on an international dimension; the Berlin Act of 1885, that divided 'the magnificent African cake', established the principle of free trade in the Congo basin (Middle Africa) and extended Western humanitarian international agreements on anti-slavery. The emergence of the USA as an imperial power ushered in the era of Western, as opposed to European, imperialism. Imperialism was now characterized by the economic, military and perceived political and cultural superiority of Western civilization.

Untangling the relationship between economic growth, capitalism and imperialism is particularly challenging in relation to the history of the USA. When colonists launched the first anti-imperial struggle of the modern era, they forged a new republic which in turn became a colonizing state, expanding the frontier westwards, colonizing Native American Indian lands. The Republic also absorbed large tracts of the former Spanish and French North American empires: the Louisiana Purchase (1803) from France; in 1845, Texas, after a war with Mexico and, subsequently, California and New Mexico. Was this simply expansion of the frontier rather than the colonization practised by European empires? What is the difference? Is American expansionism better because it was instigated by those who had thrown off the yoke of imperial oppression? A more conventional imperialist rhetoric emerged in the 1890s as the USA joined the 'new' imperialist competition. The Civil War, 1861–65, was a traumatic hiatus but also stimulated the industrialization of the North. The building and control of the Panama Canal in the early 1900s, after French failure, secured control over the strategic Central American isthmus and the naval defence of the US west coast. Panama was acknowledged by the European powers as a US protectorate. American Empire proper begins in the 1890s (Vidal, 1987). In 1895, President Grover Cleveland reasserted the Monroe Doctrine and the Spanish–American war of 1899–1900 ended the remnants of Spanish rule in the Caribbean and Asia. The USA 'liberated' Cuban nationalists from Spanish oppression and assumed formal control of the Philippines, extending its foothold in Asia. Although nominally independent until the revolution in 1959, Cuba was effectively a US colony (Jenks, 1928). The nature of US imperialism is discussed more fully in Chapter 6.

It is not my intention to go into depth about competing theoretical explanations of the New Imperialism, as these have been thrashed out in numerous publications since the 1960s (Mommsen, 1980; Owen and Sutcliffe (eds), 1972; Brewer, 1990; Etherington, 1984). Briefly, Marxists have favoured economic explanations derived from the Lenin–Hobson theses of economic imperialism. Lenin was heavily critiqued by later non-Marxist critics for over-estimating the economic benefits of imperialism (Chapter 2). Economic determinist arguments are insufficient to explain the complex phenomenon of imperial expansion, but I have yet to find a plausible explanation of modern imperialism (1880 to c. 1960s) which convinces me that economics was not the prime motive. This given, economics does not exist in a vacuum and, as Lenin and the British liberal critic of empire, J. A. Hobson, emphasized, is intimately linked to culture and politics. The socio-psychological significance of empire to national identities and cultures should also not be underestimated, a point on which Hobson had some illuminating insights, developed further by Mackenzie (1984) in his study of the 'mass psychology' of imperialism. Whatever the most plausible explanation of the New Imperialism, the reality was that by 1914 most of the non-Western world had been drawn into the orbit of Western imperialism. British and US informal imperialism had expanded in postcolonial Latin America and the few remaining independent states of Ethiopia, Afghanistan, Siam (Thailand) and Tibet were threatened by predatory imperialism on their borders. Western capital penetrated the declining empires of Turkey, China and Russia, leading to a decline in autonomy and internal conflicts that generated further weaknesses.

In conventional historiography the New Imperialism ends with the catastrophes of the First World War that precipitated the forcible decolonization of the German, Austro-Hungarian and Ottoman empires, and the decline of the British and French empires. But there are important elements of continuity between the pre- and postwar eras and 1900–30 was the heyday of colonial export economies (Osterhammel, 1997, pp. 29–38; Cain and Hopkins, 1993). The rise and decline of the Japanese Empire was a twentieth-century phenomenon (Case study 2). Fascism, the global depression of the 1930s and the Second World War catalysed the decline of European empires, but France and Britain clung on their empires until a combination of factors, including the rise of the USA to world power status, precipitated a hasty decolonization in the 1960s. The 1960s and 1970s were the great era of the newly independent Third World and optimistic new nation building. Did the ascendancy of the New Right, neo-liberal globalization and the emergence of the 'new racism' herald the era of the 'new' New Imperialism (Furedi, 1995; Balibar, 1991)? These developments opened up new debates about the relationship between globalization and imperialism which will be examined in more depth in the final chapter.

Commonalities and divergences between empires over time

How does a broad view of different empires over time help us to define the nature of empires and the differences and similarities between them? What contitutes an empire? Barfield (2002) defines primary empires as large territories that control millions of people and have common internal characteristics. Such characteristics include management of diverse peoples to exploit resources; sophisticated communications and transport systems organized to serve the military, economic and administrative priorities of the imperial centre, or metropolis, and an imperial project that imposed unity throughout the system. One could also add that primary empires support themselves through tribute or taxation. Chance and serendipity may explain some aspects of imperial conquest, but most empires were not accidental. Empire was (and arguably still is) fundamentally about power through territorial expansion for material gains and to secure hegemony over vast, subordinated areas. Nonetheless, empires need to be legitimized in the imperial centre and the periphery through justificatory ideologies articulated through the language of power (Armitage, 2001, p. 29) and ideological transformations are central to imperial dynamics, ancient and modern (Alcock and Morrison, 2002). Ideology is a difficult concept but David Brion Davis defined it succinctly as:

> . . . an integrated system of beliefs, assumptions and values, not necessarily true or false, which reflects the needs and interests of a group or class at a particular time in history. By 'interest' I mean anything that benefits or is thought to benefit a specific collective identity. Because ideologies are modes of consciousness, containing the criteria for interpreting social reality, they help to define as well as to legitimate collective needs and interests. Hence, there is a continuous interaction between ideology and the material

forces in history . . . The salient characteristic of an ideology is that whilst it is taken for granted by the people who have internalised it, it is never the external or absolute truth it claims to be.

(David Brion Davis, 1994, p. 14)

Thus ideologies originate in the interests of the powerful but become uncritically and unconsciously accepted by the masses, legitimizing imperialism, until resistance surfaces, articulating counter ideologies of liberation. The power dynamics underpinning hegemonic ideologies were first explored by Marx, developed by Gramsci and revised by neo-Marxists from the 1960s (Laclau, 1977). More recently, discourse analysis in postcolonial theory has deepened our understanding of the relationship between power, knowledge production, ideas and discourses (Chapter 2). Stuart Hall has defined a discourse as 'a way of talking, thinking or representing a particular subject' which always operates in relation to power and is 'part of the way power circulates and is contested' (Hall, 1992, p. 295). Such discourses of power are integral to dominant ideologies. As the interests of dominant groups change, so do the ideological frameworks and discourses of power that define the nature of imperialism. Understanding these changes and the links between economic, cultural, political and ideological power demands a fuller exploration of the commonalities and divergences between empires over time.

The civilizing mission and justificatory ideologies

Economic and racial oppression represented the uglier side of imperialism, but common to imperial discourse is a 'utopian vision of a purifying administration that obliterates corruption and inefficiency' (Osterhammel, 1997, p. 108). The Roman Empire presented itself as a unitary power promoting peace and justice. Tacitus' civilizing mission in Britain was designed to suppress the pagan and barbaric and turn warriors into peaceful subjects through Romanization. Universal rule was Rome's destiny, justified on the basis that some were naturally fitted to rule, others to obey – the Aristotelian justification of slavery (Garnsey and Saller, 1987, p. 18; Lintott, 1993, p. 42). To achieve these ends, Rome and subsequent imperial powers claimed the right to conduct 'just wars' at the borders against the 'barbarians' and, internally, against rebellion. Thus the concept of empire implies the construction of a new order, presented as 'permanent, eternal, and necessary' and premised on a notion of right that 'encompasses all time within its ethical foundation (Hardt and Negri, 2000, pp. 10–11). Allusions to the 'Pax Britannica', the 'Pax Romana' in modern guise, were common in British imperial discourse, whilst the administration of George W. Bush heralded the 'Second Coming of the Roman Empire', the 'Pax Americana' (Johnson, 2003).

A divine right to rule was rooted in ethical, moral, and/or religious superiority. Whereas citizenship was the basis of the Roman Empire, the Persian Empire was justified by the fact that the king was the earthly representative of the great god Ahura Mazda, who ensured the happiness of all humanity and to whom all owed reverence, obedience and tribute (Kurht, 2002, p. 103). The Mughals in Northern India also derived their right to rule directly from God. The Qing emperors (descended from nomadic Manchu peoples) were not racially pure Han Chinese and legitimacy rested on acceptance of Confucian morality, performing the correct rituals to ensure the harmony of the cosmos in accordance with the emperor's Mandate of Heaven. Thus was 'Chineseness' forged (Yates, 2002, p. 353). The Spanish *reconquista* and subsequent conquest were 'just wars' fired by a superior *Espanidad* ('Spanishness'), defined by a high class status, Catholicism, service to God and King and purity of blood through lineage (Deagan, 2002, pp. 185–6). The Islamic empire converted the 'infidels' and America's 'manifest destiny' as an exceptional republic was to spread the superior American way of life, rooted in democratic republicanism and Protestant religious values.

Civilization/superior religion was pitted against barbarism/paganism, order against disorder that threatened the civilized world, and the spread of a superior civilization provided a common justification of empires. The 'vernacular language' of British imperial ideology, of 'empire' and 'colony', was forged in the context of Anglo–Scottish relations in the 1540s and the cultural suppression of the Gaelic Irish (Armitage, 2001, pp. 36, 54) and the civilizing mission was integral to Britain's modern empire. During the Chinese Qing (Qin) dynasty (1644–1911) non-Chinese minorities were suppressed and Inner Asia (Mongolia, Turkestan and Tibet) ruled through a 'barbarian office'. Civilized status was not governed by race but the mastery of Chinese culture (Adas, 1998, pp. 386–7). Russia's colonization of Asia was justified on the grounds that land was wasted or unexploited by 'backward' nomadic herders and Russian settlers brought 'progress and civilization' (Lieven, 2000, pp. 208, 216–17). French imperialism was 'an affirmation of universalist republicanism' and civilization, a mission to spread French language, culture, and 'genius' in order to achieve political and cultural assimilation of the colonized (Jules Ferry, cited in Doyle, 1986, p. 315). Even the greedy and ruthless King Leopold II emphasized the benefits the Belgians brought to the 'natives'.

Justificatory ideologies of later European empires were influenced by the secular discourse of rights and democracy associated with the Enlightenment

(Chapter 3). Both Britain and France claimed humanitarian reasons, the eradication of slavery and barbaric cruelties, as a rationale for the colonization of Africa. A similar humanitarianism has justified the Western 'recolonization' of sub-Saharan Africa since the 1980s. The highest moral ground was claimed by Britain, who, as the first nation to abolish slavery in 1838, was transformed into the most 'progressive' state, superior to other imperial powers and self-identified champion of the oppressed. German and Portuguese colonial administrations were criticized for cruelties to 'natives' and the use of forced labour and other atrocities in the Belgian Congo became a *cause célèbre* of British liberals (Hochschild, 1999).

Both the British and American empires, argues Linda Colley, presented (and present) themselves as unique in their benevolence in contrast to other empires, including Rome, emphasizing more similarities between the British and American empires than between Washington and Rome (Colley, 2002c, pp. 4–5). But the predominant image of a benevolent British imperialism has concealed some darker moments and human rights abuses (Curtis, 2004). This has parallels in the new 'war against terrorism' precipitated by the attack on the twin towers in New York (9/11) in 2001. The USA has contravened international laws in detaining 'unlawful combatants' in the US military base in Guantanamo Bay, Cuba, and has been accused of human rights abuses against prisoners held in Iraqi jails. Britain and the USA have stressed the moral justifications for the invasion of Iraq in 2003: the eradication of evil and the liberation of oppressed people denied democratic rights. But to what extent do moral justifications of imperial power veil economic motives and belief in racial and cultural superiority?

Economic exploitation

A common theme in imperial expansion is the economic exploitation of the colonized, whether through tribute, taxes, expropriation of land, control of trade and production or a combination of some, or all these factors. European colonization was justified by the concept of *terra nullis*, uninhabited virgin territory. In early colonial art North America is depicted as a land of infinite plenty and promise, where Europeans could develop new utopian societies. In effect, Europeans appropriated from indigenous peoples ancient lands which they held sacred and then treated them with contempt (Coates, 2004). Such oppression was not restricted to seaborne empires. Russia's treatment of indigenous peoples in Siberia was characterized by appalling brutality and trade in indigenous women was a 'runner-up to furs in terms of profitability' (Lieven, 2000, p. 223). Lack of identity and rights resulting from land dispossession and cultural oppression, past and present, are the focus of 'first nation' campaigns of indigenous peoples in the 'postcolonial era' (Chapter 6).

Empires have always been about power and greed (Gigantes, 2002) and premised on the organization and exploitation of labour. Despite the rhetoric of the Pax Romana, the Romans were renowned for their cruelties, centralized control, imposition of unified systems of beliefs and values and the enslavement and exploitation of conquered peoples. The primary goals of imperial administration were collection of taxes, recruitment of soldiers and maintenance of law and order (Garnsey and Saller, 1987, p. 32). The Mughal Empire derived its wealth from land revenues and taxation, much of which went directly to the imperial treasury. European maritime empires, however, intensified exploitation as global markets became more tightly integrated. The imperatives of imperial economies were contingent on resources available in the empire and whether the economic organization of the imperial power was pre-capitalist, proto-capitalist or capitalist. Evidence relating to the Roman Empire is sparse, but land was the basis of wealth and the landed aristocracy were the dominant class; the mass of the population were at or near subsistence level and the economy underdeveloped (Garnsey and Saller, 1987, pp. 43, 51–63). Early European colonization represented a transitory proto-capitalist stage, but Spanish colonization of the Americas established a pattern of economic incorporation that was to characterize later colonial rule in Africa: enclaves where international markets directly impacted on the people; broader areas where they were only indirectly connected with international markets (for example, as producers of food for miners), while the majority only experienced empire through payment of tribute or taxes (Klor de Alva, 1995, p. 261). In twentieth-century empires, including the US Empire, the latter two groups became increasingly integrated into the global capitalist system through primary commodity production for international markets.

All empires, then, need to mobilize the labour of the colonized to produce a profit that benefits a privileged class in the imperial centre and their collaborators in the periphery. No city was as big as Rome, with its population of around one million, until late-eighteenth-century London, and its consumers needed the resources of the whole empire. Throughout the empire, cities defined the 'civilized' against the 'uncivilized' countryside and devolved bureaucracies extracted surpluses. The Roman Empire was based on the slave estate. The slave trade was well organized and slavery brutally efficient, resulting in psychic oppression, break-up of families and sexual abuse; slaves in Roman law were defined as a 'speaking tool', subject to the will of their masters (Garnsey and Saller, 1987, pp. 71–3, 83).

Slavery and other forms of unfree labour persisted well into the late nineteenth century and modern forms still exist (Archer (ed.), 1988; Bales, 1999). The Spanish introduced slavery from the beginning of conquest and under the *ecomienda* system the Crown assigned indigenous families along with land granted to private individuals, a system of forced labour that rivalled slavery in its brutality and coercion. The Spanish subsequently introduced *repartimiento* (*mita* in Peru) where every community had to assign part of the male population to labour away from home at regular intervals. This was most oppressive in the Peruvian silver mines at Potosi, where the system continued to the end of the colonial period (Osterhammel, 1997, p. 74). Where indigenous labour, in consequence of low population, disease or white genocide, could not meet the labour needs of the colonizers, as in the Caribbean and Virginia, white indentured and convict labour was introduced. Ultimately, the growing demand for labour throughout the Americas was only met through the rapid expansion of the African slave trade and slave labour contributed significantly to the building of the Americas and created the African diaspora (Blackburn, 1997; Conniff and Davis (eds), 1994; Andrews, 2004). This expansion of colonial trade and enforced migration of Africans was dependent on a huge growth in merchant and maritime shipping and also resulted in greater exploitation of the multiracial 'motley' crews through press gangs and harsh discipline (Linebaugh and Rediker, 2000).

With the ending of slavery, labour shortages were filled by indentured and free migrations of peoples. Indentured labour from the Indian subcontinent was vital to post-slavery sugar production in the Caribbean and the development of sugar plantations in Mauritius and Natal in South Africa. In the later epoch of imperialism taxes and land dispossession forced the colonized into labour for Europeans on farms or in mines. In India, West Africa and other non-settler peasant societies, taxation was used to force production of cash crops and draw peasants into the international markets (Bush and Maltby, 2004). Efficient, modern techniques of capitalist production intensified exploitation and further stimulated labour migration. Global migrations that accompanied the expansion of imperialism created ethnic diasporas and laid the foundations for postcolonial ethnic conflicts in many parts of the non-Western world (Chua, 2003).

Cultural and racial superiority

A belief in the irreconcilable difference or 'otherness' of subordinated peoples is also a continuous feature of empires and essential to the superior identities of the powerful. Davies, Nandy and Sardar have argued that:

> The two pillars of Western civilisation: Classicism and Christianity shared
> a triumphalist image. Each invented 'Otherness' to define itself and the
> process of maintaining boundaries [racial, class], required the perennial
> reinvention of real peoples.
>
> (Davies *et al.*, 1993, p. 38)

The Roman 'others' were the 'barbarians' from outlying parts of empire.
Yet there are important differences between older and newer empires. The
Romans used slave labour from culturally inferior peoples but did not enslave
on the basis of race and colour, as did Europeans involved in the African
slave trade. Romans created a genuine sense of universal imperial citizenship, something later European empires, never achieved. Potentially divisive
ethnic, racial and regional divisions were minimized by Roman law. Slaves
could be transformed into free citizens, some of whom acquired wealth
and power, and the citizen/non-citizen, victor/conquered distinction diminished in later empire. Freedmen and slaves who served emperors became
figures of power and influence (Garnsey and Saller, 1987, pp. 115-19). Such
mobility was not possible within the strict racial hierarchies of later European
empires.

From the Spanish conquest of the Americas ideologies of cultural and racial
superiority legitimized conquest and enslavement and confirmed Europeans'
perceptions of themselves as 'Lords of All the World' (Pagden, 1995). Indigenous inhabitants were increasingly racialized as inferior 'others' in travellers'
tales and official documents (Pratt, 1992). Myths about the Carib peoples of
the Caribbean are almost entirely fabrications born in the imagination of
Columbus but the invention of cannibalism and other 'savage' traits served
the purpose of justifying the deportation and enslavement of the Caribs
(Sale, 1990, pp. 132-4). European imperialism thus created the racialized
'others' of colonial possessions in Africa, Asia, Australasia and the Americas.
Race superiority and imperial power became indivisible but how this relationship was expressed depended on the cultures of the colonizing power
and the colonized and the nature of the imperial relationship. The Catholic,
Latin cultures of Portugal and Spain had a lax attitude to race mixing, giving
rise to mestizo populations. In contrast, the Protestant Northern European
states, Britain and Holland, feared race mixing (although in practice this still
occurred), and justificatory ideologies of racial superiority based on racial
'purity' became more firmly defined as imperialism expanded, stabilizing the
racial boundaries on which white prestige and power was premised (Stoler,
1997). Thus by the nineteenth century the 'Latin' empires were regarded as
weaker and inferior in consequence of race mixing.

As with imperialism, racism is a contentious concept. Indeed, the term 'racism' only came into usage in the 1930s and may not be an appropriate concept to apply to earlier epochs. Where do racial ideologies originate? Fryer (1986) dates this from the late eighteenth century, with the emergence of capitalism and justifications of the increasingly threatened pre-capitalist slave trade. David Brion Davis (1999) takes it much further back to the Arab slave trade:

> The dishonour, contempt and dehumanisation always associated with human bondage were transferred to scores of African ethnic groups that Arabs and Europeans perceived as a single race.
>
> (Brion Davis, 1999)

Images of blackness constructed through discourse, literature and art, go back to Roman times (Snowden, 1983) and thread through medieval European history. There is a consensus, however, that the modern Western concept of race coalesced through contact with Africa and slavery between the sixteenth and nineteenth centuries and so race is a historically derived social construction (Berlin, 1998). True racism, argues George Frederickson (2002), awaited the rise of modernity and its secular, rational justifications that legitimized Western imperialism. Racism was a product of the Enlightenment, applying the principle of biological unfitness, previously applied to women and the insane, to racialized groups. This explains the paradox whereby the revolutionary French government, which briefly abolished slavery in the French Caribbean, transforming slaves into citizens, reinstated slavery in 1802.

The interconnections between imperialism and racism strengthened in the later nineteenth century, although race has been neglected, or fudged, in imperial studies (Fyfe, 1992). As Jane Sampson has stressed, explorations of the link between race and empire are marked by controversy (Sampson, 2005). In *Ornamentalism* (2001) David Cannadine disputes the primacy of race in favour of class and status. Other historians have stressed the importance of racial ideologies in the operation of European/Western imperial power (Kiernan, 1969; Huttenback, 1976; Furedi, 1998; Bush, 1999). Pieterse is unequivocal:

> Racism is the psychology of imperialism, the spirit of empire, because racism supplies the element that makes for the righteousness of empire. Hence racism is not simply a by-product of empire but . . . part of the intestines of empire.
>
> (Pieterse, 1990, p. 223)

As the Tunisian anti-colonial writer, Albert Memmi, emphasized, racism was not an 'incidental detail' of colonialism (the practical workings of imperialism) but a 'consubstantial part' – the 'highest expression of the colonial system' and the basis of the 'fundamental discrimination' between colonizer and colonized (Memmi, 1957, p. 140). Imperial race discourse informed representations of colonizer and colonized and, as postcolonial writers have stressed, this has impacted on contemporary white and black identities and has contributed to continuing inequalities stemming from superior 'whiteness' (Bonnett, 2000).

Crucial to these developments was the elaboration of racial theory in the nineteenth century, when the concept of Aryanism, which derived from Central Asian settlers in India who defined themselves as 'Arya', entered European thought via new Orientalist learning. Aryanism merged with new theories of social Darwinism, scientific racism and older racial classifications to justify white superiority (Ballantyne, 2001, pp. 3 – 6). All these elements fused in the powerful discourse of Anglo-Saxonism that emphasized the greatness of Teutonic peoples, Germans, Norsemen and Anglo-Saxons, including the English, who had colonized the world and were superior to other races, including Celts and 'inferior' Southern and Eastern European peoples (Horsman, 1981, p. 63). Americans had long believed that they were the chosen people and the 'New Teutonism' found fertile ground in the USA, where

> . . . ideas and dreams indigenous to American history melded with a variety of themes from Europe to transform revolutionary idealism for human progress into an ideology of continental, hemispheric and . . . world racial destiny for a particular chosen people.
>
> (Horsman, 1981, pp. 3 –5, 77)

Whereas tension and rivalry had formerly characterized the British–American relationship, by 1900 there was greater consensus around the 'manifest destiny' of English-speaking peoples (Britain, its white settler Dominions and the USA) to spread their culture throughout the world. Strong links now developed between American, English and German racial thought in response to mounting 'threats' to the white race. The 'Yellow Peril . . . visions of Chinamen overrunning the world' and the Japanese defeat of Russia in 1905 emphasized the need for the 'White Knight' to robustly defend the 'Aryan race' (Lauren, 1996, p. 67; Kiernan, 1969, pp. 177–9).

Race, religion and nationality, argued the anti-imperialist Leonard Woolf, were 'intimately connected with the phenomenon of imperialism' (Woolf, 1928, p. 19). The 'romantic racial nationalism' (Horsman, 1981) that emerged in the USA, Germany and Britain in the later nineteenth century strengthened imperialist ambitions. The 'thematics of blood and the science of sexuality', argued Michel Foucault, revitalized the type of political power exercised in the second half of the nineteenth century:

> Racism took shape at this point, racism in its modern 'biologising' statist form: it was then that the whole policies of settlement, family, marriage, education, social heirarchization . . . property [and] health . . . received . . . their justification from the mythical concern with protecting the purity of the blood and ensuring the triumph of the race.
>
> (Foucault, 1979, p. 149)

In *Exterminate all the Brutes* (1998), the title of which is based on a quote from Joseph Conrad's *Heart Of Darkness* (1902), Sven Lindquist explores the darker, violent side of scientific racism and eugenics, arguing that racial policies implemented in the European colonies before the First World War were a 'rehearsal' for the Holocaust. Eugenics became an essential element of modern scientific racism in Britain pre-1914 and in the USA and Germany in the 1920s and 1930s (Black, 2004; Stepan, 1982). More widely, Anglo-Saxonism and its assumptions of cultural and racial superiority shaped Western racism and became institutionalized through new international organizations such as the League of Nations, strengthening Western power (Lauren, 1996).

Strategies of imperial conquest and rule

Why did colonial conquest succeed? Military and technological superiority have been an essential ingredient of imperial power from the Roman army to the present-day American military machine. It was 'armed trading', combined with technological developments and innovative financial institutions, that gave Europe (and the West) the crucial edge in consolidating global systems of power (Pomeranz, 2000, p. 19). Western military dominance in warfare in the twentieth century, argues Lieven (2000), proved that technology and economic power always win in the end (p. 416). Military and technological superiority alone, however, is insufficient to explain why the colonized were defeated. Rome had to pacify nomadic and semi-nomadic tribes and this often entailed bitter conflict: the pacification of Spain took two centuries (Miles, 1990, p. 641). Roman success in empire building was founded on military achievements, but the empire was riven by civil wars and conflict. A strategy of co-option of elites and citizenship was first extended where political stability was most precarious – Africa, Gaul and Spain (Garnsey and Saller, 1987, p. 9). Roman rule only lasted so long because of the flexibility and effectiveness of imperial administration and law, willingness to rule through local institutions and the opening up of citizenship rights to conquered peoples that co-opted potential enemies. Unity lay in the reality of participation in power (emperors came not just from Rome but Spain, Gaul and elsewhere) and economic prosperity. For this reason, argues Lintott, the empire was 'not only tolerated but appreciated by many of its subjects' (Lintott, 1993, pp. 2, 14, 12).

In later empires, the success of conquest and the longer-term imperial project also depended on local collaborators and strategies to legitimize rule and secure the consent of subject peoples. The Spanish had superior arms in muskets and steel swords, but the key factor that enabled Hernando Cortez and Francisco Pizzarro to conquer the resistant Aztec and Inca empires in 1521 and 1531 respectively, with only a few hundred Spanish soldiers, guns and horses, was exploiting local enmities and forging collaborative alliances (Thomas, 2004; Hemming, 1970). Collaboration as well as resistance accompanied the expansion of the Russian Empire. The later British and French 'pacification' of resistance to colonial annexation in Africa also depended on local collaboration (Lieven, 2000; Robinson, 1972). After conquest, power was sustained through the co-option of client groups amongst the colonized and the myriad of minor imperial agents flowing through the networks of empires, soldiers, traders, shopkeepers, migrants and colonists. Collaboration, accommodation, and hybridization of culture were integral to colonial societies. Common cultural values and a lingua franca have all bonded empires, or at least subclasses within the empire, although this was mostly in favour of the dominant culture (Chapter 4).

Empires, argues Mann (1986) are best conceptualized as intersecting networks of power. All empires were involved in skilful management of diverse cultures and competing interests through a degree of direct and indirect rule and dependence on collaborators. As Couze Venn (1996) points out, power '. . . operates on the basis of both domination and seduction, such that sections of oppressed groups often collude in . . . its exercise' (Venn, 1996, p. 32). Thus the patronage that underpinned the Roman Empire created a series of collaborative alliances between ruler and ruled. This enhanced the wealth, status and power of a minority who embraced Romanization (Garnsey and Saller, 1987, pp. 203; Lintott, 1993, pp. 168–204). The Chinese ruled through a bureaucracy that, in theory, was open to any subject of the empire who passed the exams and, like the European empires, utilized a mix of colonial systems to maintain power (Adas, 1998). The Roman and Ottoman empires used divide and rule tactics, creating imperial subcentres that collected taxes and also co-opted local elites through education and promises of mobility through the imperial administration. The Mughal Empire, whose tightly controlled administration the British Raj mapped onto, successfully managed the different religions and cultures through ensuring religious tolerance (J. F. Richards, 1993). The British favoured divide and rule policies as a strategy of holding on to power, causing divisions between its 'mimic men', who seemingly became more English than the English and were essential to administration, and 'traditional' cultures. This created the preconditions for future ethnic, religious and class conflicts.

No successful empires could have survived after conquest without sophisticated technologies of colonial governance that facilitated smooth administration with the minimum physical force and coercion. All empires, however, resorted to the 'hard' power of military might if imperial power was threatened or obstructed (see Figure 1.3). The Roman magistrate with *imperium* was a military commander above all else and many subjects of Rome experienced empire only through taxation, military conscription and enslavement. Despite the absence of elaborate government machinery, the internal coherence of empire and influence of Roman hegemony was greater than has perhaps been assumed (Lintott, 1993, p. 12). The Romans expected commands to be obeyed despite indirect rule, a superior position that also defined the later British Empire, where indirect rule was extensively applied. Later European empires harnessed technological developments, including mass communications and media, to develop new strategies to deflect threats to social order and imperial interests in both metropole and colony. Technological developments also facilitated speedier movement of soldiers from one part of the empire to police imperial subjects in another, and air power strengthened the imperial armoury (Killingray and Omissi (eds), 1999). The USA has also co-opted sections of subordinated societies through economic and cultural power but, where threatened, has provided military backing to proxy agents in securing global economic interests. The 'open door' policy of free trade has always included the 'big stick' of military might to wield if necessary.

Power, resistance and the ending of empires

Where there is hegemonic power there is always protest and resistance against the economic and cultural oppression of dominated peoples. Huamán (Waman) Poma, who was a Peruvian chief from a noble family with a record of service in high positions under the Incas, writing between 1567 and 1615 observed that:

Figure 1.3 British imperial military power in India: 'Blowing up the Cashmere
Gate' (the siege of Lucknow, 1857)

At present our Indians are overloaded and oppressed, being obliged to pay excessive taxes . . . [the] . . . Spaniards lord it over the Indians with absolute power. They can commit crimes with impunity [and] all complaint against them is stifled.

(Poma in Dilke (ed.), 1978, p. 193)

Such cruelties were graphically illustrated in his account (see Figure 1.4). Poma was writing to attract the attention of the Spanish court to the 'merits and sufferings of the Peruvian peoples under Spanish rule' (Dilke, 1978, p.15) but this plea could have been made by any literate plaintiff articulating local grievances against imperial rule from ancient to modern empires. All imperial administrations used complex and sophisticated strategies of power to suppress and contain any opposition, but the 'many headed hydra', a symbol of disorder and resistance, has constantly regenerated (Linebaugh and Rediker, 2000). In a Hegelian perspective, the essence of imperial power depended on recognition and acceptance of colonial administrators by an inferior colonized people; resistance thus threatened the self-image and identities of the dominant elites.

How did the colonized resist? Armed 'primary' or traditional resistance has a long history from Boudicca's challenge to the Roman occupation of Britain to the Ashanti and Zulu defence against encroaching British imperialism in late nineteenth century Africa. Such resistance ultimately failed. For instance, resistance to Rome, as in England or Gaul, was based on a fragile unity and chieftains were jealous and suspicious of each other and unable to withstand Roman power (Miles, 1990, p. 645). Much later, the British prevailed through superior military technology, but also by cultivating divisions and weakening resistance. When armed resistance was 'pacified' and imperial administration extended, resistance continued through guerrilla warfare, protests against taxation and labour exploitation and cultural resistance. Resistance existed in earlier empires but intensified in the twentieth-century age of mass media and communications. In the Roman Empire communities remained relatively isolated and Roman imperialism had a less transformative impact on local cultures (Miles, 1990, pp. 645–6). In the modern era new forms of protest emerged: anti-colonial nationalism, trade union protest and urban riots informed by the discourse of democracy fundamental to defining the superior culture of Western powers.

Such resistance extended to newer empires. The Japanese faced mass protest in Korea in 1919 and widespread resistance to expansion of informal empire in China. Anti-Americanism against 'Yanquis' in Latin America led to popular uprisings and movements that the USA suppressed. The USA

Figure 1.4   'Flogging an Indian' from Letter to a King: A Picture-History of the Inca Civilisation by Huamán Poma (c. 1567–1615)

intervened in the Mexican (Zapata) Revolution 1910–17 but conflict between the USA and Mexico over land/oil rights and political autonomy persisted. US tactics included support for dictators who suppressed peasant/working-class movements. The USA occupied Nicaragua, 1926–33, and funded the Contras, who undermined the popular socialist Sandinista government in the 1970s (Keylor, 1992, pp. 206–17). The USA has intervened in politics to restore or sustain right-wing governments in Chile, Argentina, Venezuela, Honduras and Guatemala. The new 'Soviet empire' also had to crush ideo-logical opposition in Hungary, Czechoslovakia and Afghanistan and the post-Soviet Russian state became embroiled in conflict in Chechnya.

Resistance to modern imperialism has been defined as any action, indi-vidual or collective, violent or lawful, covert or overt, that is critical of, opposes, upsets or challenges the smooth running of colonial rule (Engels and Marks, 1994, p. 2). This definition embraces all forms of anti-colonial and anti-imperial resistance, but also cultural resistance and the small acts of day-to-day non-compliance which frustrated colonial administrators (Chapter 4). However, the colonial relationship should not be conceptualized solely in terms of a simple dichotomy between the oppressing colonizers and the resistant oppressed; collaboration with the imperial power and divisions among activists cultivated by imperial strategies also shaped devel-opments. Responses to imperial domination, accommodationist, survivalist or resistant, involved multiple strategies, mediated by gender, class, age, ethnicity, urban or rural residence and the nature of contact with whites. Resistance, argued Said (1987), created deep antagonisms between the colonizer and colonized, powerful and powerless, but also created '. . . an overlapping, interdependent relationship' which connected them in often unacknowledged ways (p. 17).

Pieterse (1990) suggests that there is a fundamental dialectic between imperialism and emancipation, power and liberation, operating at both a global and local level. But, he concludes, 'We appear to know more about domination than about liberation . . . and more about forces of liberation in the twentieth century than in earlier epochs' (pp. vi–xii). This reflects the fact that history is always written to reflect the interests of the powerful, whose copious sources are always available, unlike the fragmented and ephemeral records of the powerless. For Pieterse these are grounds for a new perspective on imperialism that applies the concept of the dialectic to different sections of colonial societies that are in dynamic tension. This will enable us to inter-rogate more effectively the interaction between cultures on unstable colonial frontiers and the interrelations of empire and emancipation as they have changed and developed over time.

Yet Pieterse's definition of emancipation as a 'humanising and civilising contribution' to imperialism is rather too generalized. It is important to distinguish between resistance of the colonized, and minority anti-imperialist factions in the colonizing society, both of which arguably made a 'humanising contribution' but in differing ways and for different reasons. We have little evidence of metropolitan protest from earlier empires. Hugh Thomas argues that humanitarian critiques of Spanish cruelties in the Americas and debates over the nature of the Indians, first pioneered in 1512 by Bartolomé das Casas, were 'unique in the history of empires' (Thomas, 2004). In modern empires, the humanitarian values of the Enlightenment inspired anti-slavery movements and, later, a minority anti-imperialist opposition in Britain, France, Germany and the United States directed their energies to reforming or abolishing colonial rule (Thornton, 1959; Howe, 1993; Porter, 1968; Derrick, 2002; Ben Michaels, 1993). European supporters of anti-colonial causes, liberal or left, however, were not personally in resistance to racial and colonial oppression. There were, however, important differences between the metropolitan critic of imperialism and the 'colonizer who refused', for example, the white opponent of Apartheid in South Africa, who was in a more difficult and ambivalent situation in relation to the colonized than the colonizer who adopted the conventional attitudes of superiority (Memmi, 1957, pp. 86–110).

To what extent did metropolitan opposition and anti-colonial resistance contribute to the ending of empires? Pre-European empires ended for a number of reasons: imperial overstretch, changing economic fortunes, reconquest by subordinated societies and/or the rise of other empires. Resistance arguably did not play such a large role. In the Roman Empire there were only isolated incidences of rebellion, such as Spartacus' slave revolt; there was no significant literature of protest and the ideological, technological and socio-political factors that fostered modern anti-colonialism were absent. The universalism of Rome conveyed the idea that all were equal in a common subordination to and dependency on, the empire and no distinct national identities emerged. From the perspective of modern empires, the longevity of Rome is remarkable (Miles, 1990, pp. 629–31, 637). In modern European empires new liberatory ideologies and tighter globalization stimulated more widespread, organized protest. The French revolutionary fervour of the 1790s spread to the Caribbean and stimulated major slave revolts that made a contribution to the ending of slavery equal to, if not greater than, that of European abolitionists (Blackburn, 1988). In the late modern era, mass communications, the impact of two world wars and the influence of liberal democratic and socialist ideals resulted in a mass 'revolt against the West' that determined the course of twentieth-century history (Barraclough, 1973).

Anti-Westernism is closely linked to anti-imperialism but denotes a more generalized movement against Western cultural and ideological dominance, in addition to political challenges to the structures of imperial power. The 'revolt against the West' and against formal and informal imperialism was stimulated through dialogue between anti-imperialists in the West and the non-West, informed by Marxism and liberalism, that led to a fuller understanding of the global mechanisms of power. Influenced by modern Western concepts of nationalism and the state, demands were now made for full independence. London and Paris became the 'junction boxes' of anti-imperialist activity and anti-colonial nationalism. Arab nationalists from Syria, Iraq, and Palestine and petitioners from China, Algeria, Egypt and Vietnam mingled in Paris. In London, Indian, African and Caribbean activists exchanged ideas (Bush, 1999). Cultural and political exchanges took place in the contact zone between centre and periphery, but also between peripheries, creating 'interbraiding networks of resistance' (Boehmer, 2002). These networks stimulated anti-Western ideologies, such as pan-Africanism, pan-Arabism and pan-Islamism, that challenged the cultural, as well as political, power of the West.

Stimulated by uncertain economic conditions, anti-colonial resistance gained in strength after 1918. A new sense of race-consciousness strengthened anti-imperialism. The great African-American intellectual, W.E.B. Du Bois, claimed that 'the problem of the Twentieth Century is the problem of the colour line' (Du Bois, 1973, 1902, p. 54). Experiences of soldiers fighting in Europe in 1914–18 heightened the sense of racial humiliation. After the war the 'rising tide of colour', as well as the 'red menace', deeply concerned the West, particularly after the race riots in Liverpool, Chicago and Kingston, Jamaica in 1919. Race-consciousness was also stimulated by the postwar Versailles peace treaty. Despite the inclusion of Japan as an 'honorary' Western power, there were serious wranglings over the refusal of the delegates to accept the racial equality of Asians. Lack of representation from the non-Western world stimulated anti-colonialism; despite inclusion in the conference, China was also humiliated by concessions given to Japan (Lauren, 1996, p. 110).

Faced with these challenges, the imperial powers had to adopt new tactics embracing concessions as well as force. Divisions among activists were cultivated and more of the educated colonized were co-opted into imperial administration. Britain and France both had a degree of success in steering nationalism into 'safe channels' in non-settler African colonies. The French policy of incorporating an elite colonized minority into French citizenship encouraged francophilia and support for the colonial mission, although French colonial intellectuals realized the need for cultural, if not political emancipation (Atlan and Jézéquel, 1993). However, the end of European empires also led to greater repression, including censorship and imprison-ment and/or deportation of activists and, where necessary, force and violence against armed liberation struggles in British Malaya, Cyprus and Kenya; French Algeria and Indochina and Portuguese Mozambique and Angola (Carruthers, 2004; Furedi, 1997; Anderson, 2005).

All empires have an ending: the Roman Empire was undermined by imperial overstretch and inability to pacify peripheral areas (Grant, 1990). The Ottoman Empire began to decline because of a shift in trade routes after the conquest of the Americas. The Spanish Empire was weakened by the failure of Spain to modernize and succumbed to the more aggressive capitalist powers, particularly the USA (Balfour, 1997). A similar conjunction of economic decline, overstretch and resistance contributed to the ending of European empires (Springhall, 2000; Von Albertini, 1982). Historiography on European decolonization has fallen into two camps: studies of anti-colonial nationalist movements and Eurocentric analyses of the transfer of power from the perspective of metropolitan policy. The former emphasized that independence was *taken* through the active agency of the colonized (Grimal, 1978), the latter that it was *given* as a rational response to postwar pressures on the metropolitan powers and/or American global machinations (Darwin, 1991; Chamberlain, 1987; Robinson and Louis, 1994). The merging of these two strands and the influence of postcolonial theory have stimulated research into new aspects of decolonization, emphasizing interdisciplinary perspect-ives, the interrelationship between economic, political and cultural aspects of decolonization, the importance of gender, ethnicity and race in understanding anti-colonial nationalist struggles, and the impact of decolonization on both metropolitan and colonized societies (le Sueur (ed.), 2004; Howe, 2005). Conventional Western and anti-colonial nationalist historiography alike have been critiqued for adopting a masculinist construct of nationalism and imperial power (Gandhi, 1998).

Research into decolonization is now one of the fastest-growing and most dynamic areas, with more emphasis placed on resistance and the perspective of the colonized. The ending of European empires has been reconceptualized as a 'dialogical' process where metropolitan and indigenous voices carried equal weight and decolonization has been redefined as '. . . a process during which hard won battles were waged between nationalists and metropolitan colonial powers' (le Sueur (ed.), 2004, p. 2). Yet the very word *decolonization* needs to be queried as an awkward term that raises problems of definition (Betts, 1998). It assumes that imperialism ended with the disintegration of formal empires, yet strategies employed during decolonization were designed to retain Western power and influence over the 'non-Western' world.

Postcolonial theorists have rightly queried the divide between the colonial and postcolonial and reconceptualized these epochs as a seamless development of relations between the West and the 'non-West' (Young, 2001). Thus the ending of modern empires did not take the same path as that of older, pre-capitalist empires. Indeed, the decline and/or demise of older empires – Turkey, Spain, Russia – were the consequence of growing resistance within their empires but also economic weakness in relationship to the modern capitalist Western European states. This again raises key questions about the unique nature of modern empires which are explored in more depth in Chapter 3.

***

In *Imperialism and Civilisation* (1928), the British socialist intellectual Leonard Woolf argued that modern imperialism was 'a menacing movement' which had developed a unique political psychology. He added that:

> . . . although it displays some of the characteristics of conflicts of civilisa-
> tions in ancient times [modern imperialism] has some features peculiar
> to itself which make it one of the most dangerous developments in human
> history.
>
> (p. 30)

In ancient empires different civilizations could live side by side, mutually influencing one another and absorbing conquerors into the conquered. In contrast, European economic imperialism had 'revolutionized' the lives of subject peoples and the bases of their own civilization had been destroyed. Nothing on this scale had happened before (pp. 39–40). Bill Warren (1980) also argued that the 'subjective character and objective effects' of modern colonialism were quite different from earlier forms of colonialism (p. 128).

European/Western imperialism was also 'unique' in the extent of its impact on the 'non-Western' world. Clearly, the rise of European racism, forced labour and taxation, the transformation of indigenous cultures, and global migrations to meet changing labour needs that increased the wealth of the West, had a massive and irreversible impact. The debate still rages over whether colonization was good or bad. Some commentators have that the 'non-Western' world still suffers from the 'curse of Columbus' and conclude that the impact of European imperialism was more profound than that of other empires and largely negative, associated with disease, death, genocide and an adverse ecological impact (Lindquist, 1998; Crosby, 1986). European culture, argues Kirkpatrick Sale, was more hostile and antagonistic to nature than any other civilization; Europeans were more technophile and materially acquisitive and took it as their god-given right to destroy 'new world' paradises (Sale, 1990, pp. 84–8). Conversely, revisionist interpretations have emphasized the cross-cultural context, the collaboration and co-operation that transcended perceived boundaries of religions, nationality and race, as a counterbalance to the emphasis on the exploitative and confrontational dimensions of European imperialism (Russell-Wood, 1992 Preface; Forster (ed.), 1997).

No simple binary divisions or blanket generalizations suffice to address the complexities of the colonial legacy; not all colonized peoples were victims and neither were all Europeans oppressors. The impact of Europe differed depending on the specific nature of the colonized societies with which European colonizers interacted. From its inception, however, imperialism was about enriching the 'old' European world at the expense of the 'new' world through plunder, then trade and colonization: the expansion of trade and markets increased the wealth of a minority in Europe but also brought benefits to the more privileged European working classes, widening inequalities between Europe and the rest of the world. Western hegemony over the rest of the world was facilitated initially by technological, maritime, intellectual and political developments in Western Europe but ultimately through capitalism and related dynamics of modernity. Whether this hegemony of the West is now coming to an end is the focus of my final chapter.

Untangling imperialism: theories, concepts and historiography

I am all for minute and diligent archival work that will trace a concrete historical series of events in terms of immediate complexities. But the point of either is to enable us to see better what has happened and what is happening. For that we need . . . models with which to weigh significance, we need summarising concepts with which to create the knowledge which we then seek to communicate to each other.

(Wallerstein, 1974, p. 166)

Imperialism . . . is . . . a phenomenon not yet understood, as if a theatrical performance still in motion . . . If imperialism has been extensively documented and analysed, its actual character remains opaque; a situation conditioned by . . . the ongoing realities of neo-imperialism and global hierarchy.

(Pieterse, 1990, p. 22)

How has imperialism been conceptualized by historians, social scientists and postmodernists? Understanding the complex dynamics of imperialism past and present demands a multidisciplinary approach. Untangling imperialism depends on how imperialism is defined and explained and on specific conjunctions of internal and external factors relating to different imperial powers. Periodization is contingent on how imperialism is conceptualized. Imperialism is a more comprehensive concept than colonialism, but harder to define. As Wesserling observed, empire is one but not the only form of imperialism, and a theory of imperialism should embrace formal and informal empires. Imperialism is also an analytical tool for studying international relations and power politics in general (Wesserling, 1986). Imperial power relationships involve the interaction of economic, political, social and cultural 'imperialisms'. Imperial systems also differ between epochs and within empires at any given point in time; an example here is the distinction in late European empire between white settler imperialism and governance of non-settler 'tropical' colonies.

This chapter will consider the different ways in which imperialism and colonialism have been conceptualized and written about over time, and explore the problems and possibilities of theories as analytical frameworks used by historians, social scientists and, more recently, postcolonial literary and cultural theorists. Struggles over the meaning of imperialism, as Etherington (1984) pointed out, are not simply ideological; historians have always been suspicious of, and pitted against, theorists. Theories and models employed in the social sciences can be criticized for overgeneralization and a lack of specific examples, but they do provide a preliminary framework for analysing the dynamics of imperialism, often lacking in more specialized historical studies, and facilitate comparative analysis of empires over time. Most theories are associated with Western knowledge; although they are not within the scope of this study, it should be pointed out that Japanese and Chinese theorists predated European theorists, whose writings date mainly from the late nineteenth century (Wesserling, 1986, p. 8). Additionally, theories deal mainly with European/Western imperialism, predominantly from the nineteenth century, although Michael Doyle's socio-political models and Wallerstein's world systems analysis have been influential in reconceptualizing the nature of pre-European empires (Alcock et al., 2002).

Existing studies have made a significant contribution to untangling the origins and nature of modern empires and the meaning of European imperialism and colonialism. The historiography broadly divides into the general macro histories and area studies (West Africa, Southern Africa, and South Asia). Until recently there was little dialogue between these different genres of imperial history, in the same way that imperial history and domestic history were treated as though there were no interconnections. Macro histories divide into general historical surveys of one empire (Judd, 1996; Porter, B., 2004, 1976; Aldrich, 1996); comparative studies of different empires (Fieldhouse, 1982; Von Albertini, 1982) or the global analyses favoured by economic historians and social scientists (W. R. Thompson, 2000; Wallerstein, 1996). There have been a disproportionate number of studies of British imperialism, particularly in the era of New Imperialism c. 1880–1914, with debates centred on the nature of, and motives for, imperialist expansion. I have no intention of giving a detailed analysis of these debates, which are amply covered elsewhere (Cain and Harrison, 2001), as are developments in orthodox historiography

(Winks (ed.), 1999). My aim is to provide a broad overview of the dynamics of theoretical change and address key questions of how and why conceptualizations of imperialism have changed over time. Because of their predominance in the historiography, I shall restrict myself here mainly to theories centred on nineteenth- and twentieth-century European/Western imperialism.

Defining colonialism and imperialism

Complex and multifaceted, modern imperialism has generated deep contradictions and definitions depend on differing theoretical positions and political values. Lenin defined imperialism as the 'highest stage of capitalism', the New Imperialism post-1870, linked to economic exploitation of the oppressed. Dismissive of such economic determinism and emotive language, orthodox historians have produced neutral, bland definitions: '. . . a tendency of a state or society to control another by whatever means or for whatever purpose' (Fieldhouse, 1981); '. . . a political function of the process of incorporating some countries at some times into the international economy' (Robinson, 1961, cited in Owen and Sutcliffe (eds), 1972, p. 4). Ronald Hyam attempted to analyse the dynamics of empire without using 'the contentious and emotive words: imperialism, colonialism, capitalism' in his conceptualization of empire as the 'export of surplus emotional and sexual energy, not capital', an escape from dominant 'Victorian values' (Hyam, 1991, pp. 1, 135).

Definitions differ as to whether informal imperialism is included or only formal empires. A formal imperial relationship exists when the 'imperialized' country forfeits its sovereignty and is incorporated into the state or empire of the imperialist power, as was, for instance, British India or French Algeria. Also relevant here is sub-imperialism, whereby white settler states acquired more autonomy from the 'mother country' and acted as partners in the exercise of imperial power. Such colonies articulated their own interests, which did not always synchronize with metropolitan imperial policy and developed an 'internal' colonial relationship with indigenous peoples. South Africa is the classic example here. An informal relationship exists when the 'imperialized' community retains the outward trappings of sovereignty, but its freedom of political action is constrained by the presence of military bases and expatriate personnel (soldiers, sailors, merchants, missionaries), for instance, Cuba under US dominance 1900–59, China under Western dominance, c. 1880–1914. Turkey, Latin America and Persia also had a complex and dependent relationship with European powers. Informal imperialism can exist without colonialism but colonialism cannot exist without imperialism.

The contentious nature of the concept of informal imperialism is reflected in the polarized debates in the postcolonial era over the existence of neo-colonialism and neo-imperialism. Baumgart (1982) favoured the definition restricted to political and territorial domination to the less precise term 'informal'. Orthodox historians argued that imperialism ended with decolon-ization (Fieldhouse, 1999) but, for Third World nationalists and radical Western intellectuals, 'informal' imperial power relations were perpetuated by economic exploitation and political domination (Amin, 1973; Sartre, 2001). World systems theorists see capitalism rather than imperialism as the crucial dynamic in globalization and deepening inequalities. Capitalism, argued Wallerstein, distinguished the nature of the modern global order from earlier world empires and a 'world capitalist economy does not permit the *imperium* [formal empire]', hence the collapse of European empires (Wallerstein, 1974a, p. 144). For Osterhammel, also, imperialism is associated with worldwide protection of interests and capitalist penetration. He thus queries whether the term is applicable to early modern empires that were not in a position to achieve these objectives and were thus 'colonial empires without imperial-ism'. Only Great Britain and the USA, he argues, have been imperial powers 'in the full sense of the term', although the United States has practised 'imperialism without a major colonial empire' (Osterhammel, 1997, p. 22). Debates about globalization and/or imperialism in the postcolonial era are more fully explored in the final chapter.

Colonization is also '. . . a phenomenon of colossal vagueness' (Osterhammel, 1997, p. 4). Originating from the Latin *colonia*, a farm or settlement, in the Roman Empire, a colony was defined as 'a public settlement of Roman citizens (especially veteran soldiers) in a hostile or newly conquered country'. 'Colonialism', as applied to a colonial system, was not in usage until after 1850 (Klor de Alva, 1995, pp. 264–5). A colony may then be defined as 'a particular type of socio-political organisation' and colonialism as 'a sys-tem of domination' (Osterhammel, 1997, p. 4). However, relations between colony and metropolitan centre differed between maritime empires such as the British, where distance ensured difference, and continental empires like that of Russia that absorbed conquered and dependent territories into a cent-ral homogenous state (Lieven, 2000, pp. 120–1). Moreover, the chronology of the Russian and Austro-Hungarian 'continental empires' is different from that of the maritime empires of Western Europe.

Colonization associated with imperial expansion may be divided into dif-ferent types: border colonization, pushing the frontier out into the 'wilderness'

(Russia, North America); overseas settlement colonization (the Greek colonies of Antiquity and the early English settlement of North America) that were 'settlement offshoots' with relatively little military input; white settler colonies that were associated with greater conflict (Osterhammel, 1997, pp. 4–8). Examples of the latter type include French Algeria, British Kenya, North and South Rhodesia and South Africa. In such colonies whites were in the minority and their presence was more tenuous than in the white majority settlements of the United States and Britain's 'white' dominions of Canada, Australia, Newfoundland and New Zealand, although both types of settler colony suppressed indigenous peoples and expropriated their lands. Neither colonization nor colonialism had a uniform impact as this was contingent on the historical moment in time, the geographical location and the nature of the imperial relationship. These issues are explored in more detail in Case study 2 on Ireland.

Untangling concepts and theories

Concepts are descriptive categories of analysis that help to classify, order and define complex phenomena and are developed within broader theoretical frameworks. Conceptualizations of the same phenomena – for instance, colonialism – may differ, depending on which framework is adopted: Marxist, liberal, deconstructionist (postmodernism/postcolonialism). Marxism and liberalism are metatheories associated with modernity which have been challenged by postmodernism. There are also more specific theories, such as Ronald Robinson's theory of collaboration on the periphery, although these are often located within the broader metatheories. Some theories rely too much on mono-causal explanations for European imperial conquest – for instance, technological and scientific superiority (Headrick, 1981) or the economic determinism of conventional Marxist studies. Whilst they contribute insight into aspects of imperialism, they are insufficient in themselves to explain such a complex phenomenon. Similarly, both Eurocentric and peripheral theories are too limited in themselves. Arguably, the most plausible explanations of imperialism need to account for the interaction of the economic, political, social and cultural factors operating at both the local (periphery) level and within the metropolitan centre of imperial power.

Theories differ from ideologies in that they aspire to provide a coherent, rational analytical framework, derived through critical engagement with other theories, to attempt to make sense of the world. Theories and conceptual frameworks can arguably never ever be free of implicit political values. Abstract theories and ideologies, 'modernization theory' or 'neo-liberalism', for instance, translate into practical policies that have a concrete impact on people's lives (Chapter 6). Thus, when evaluating theories and conceptual frameworks, one needs to bear in mind a number of key questions. What definition of imperialism is used? How does this influence the way imperialism was/is conceptualized? What is the purpose of the theory? Is it a conceptual tool of the historian (Robinson and Gallagher, Cain and Hopkins) or linked to political critique and/or activism (Lenin, Chomsky, Hobson)? Does the theory have general application (Wallerstein) or is it imperial power-/time-/region-specific (Robinson and Gallagher)? It is also important to consider the political and cultural context in which the theory was developed. J. A. Hobson developed his critique of imperialism in the context of the South African (Boer) War, 1899–1902. Lenin's *Imperialism* was written in 1916, and influenced by the cataclysmic First World War. The Lenin–Hobson thesis became influential amongst the European left and anti-colonial intellectuals after 1918 and remained the main analytical framework for analysing imperialism until challenged by revisionist theories in the 1960s.

The leading imperial historians of the 1960s and 1970s were influenced by the mood of the times as formal empires ended and the Cold War climate stimulated liberal and conservative critiques of the Lenin–Hobson thesis. Mainstream historians, argues Etherington, have always shown 'unremitting hostility' to economic theories. Indeed, Etherington himself criticized the theories associated with the left in the 1930s as 'ragged bits of theoretical cloth stitched together without logical coherence' (Etherington, 1984, pp. 212, 203). Lenin was criticized for seeing the New Imperialism as separate and distinct from what went before, for his economic determinism and narrow definition of imperialism that blurred capitalism and imperialism in developing a polemical analysis (Fieldhouse, 1961; Robinson and Gallagher, 1961). He was also accused of Eurocentrism, although Blaut (1997) has argued that his theory of imperialism was the first strong challenge to the Eurocentric world models that dominated European thought, Marxist and non-Marxist. Revisionist historians now argued that imperialism predated capitalism and that there was no new imperialism but a continuous process of evolution. Anti-colonial nationalism and independence shifted the emphasis away from Europe to the periphery and the interplay between resistance and collaboration in African colonization (Robinson, 1972). Empires, it was argued, were secured for prestige in an era of political rivalry, not economic gain; French historians made similar arguments (Brunschwig, 1966). Marxist economic explanations of imperialism were marginalized as failing to provide an explanation of Soviet imperialism.

The Vietnam War and other manifestations of US imperial power in the 1970s re-energized Marxist analyses of imperialism, reflected in the emergence of dependency theory and world systems analysis (Chapter 6), although these never had the same amount of influence as non-Marxist studies. Influenced by the dominance of 'free-market' ideology prevalent since the early 1980s and the 'death of socialism' with the collapse of the Berlin Wall in 1989, revisionist works further eclipsed radical/Marxist alternatives to liberal/conservative academic studies. The end of the Cold War, the collapse of old certainties and the emergence of identity politics also stimulated post-modernist/postcolonial theory and a shift of emphasis to the imperial legacy in Western Europe and the ex-colonized world.

Clearly, it is important to ask why, by whom, and for whom the theory was developed. A book written by a historian distanced from the cultural milieu shaped by the national imperial enterprise will be different from that produced by a researcher who was brought up in a particular culture of empire, even one critical of such culture. Important differences in how imperialism has been conceptualized exist between metropolitan anti-imperialists, such as J. A. Hobson, and anti-colonial activists and intellectuals like Frantz Fanon, but also between those commenting on present realities (like Hobson and Fanon) and academic historians writing retrospectively about the imperial past. Such retrospective writings also differ, depending on which side of the North/South, 'West and rest' divide you are on; this is evident in the spats between British historians of India and South Asian scholars influenced by postcolonialism (see below).

There are no completely original theories and concepts. Theories evolve and develop in dialogue with existing knowledge and theoretical frameworks. The theory of 'gentlemanly capitalism' (Cain and Hopkins, 1987) emerged out of debates about the economic motives for British imperialism but also revisited older theories of Joseph Schumpeter and J. A. Hobson. Each decade has its seminal works on imperialism which advance our understanding and whose ideas are taken up by acolytes who then argue the minutiae: the impact of Ronald Robinson's theory of collaboration on the periphery and Edward Said's critique of Orientalism (below) are good examples here. From the early twentieth century, theoretical debates were predominantly focused on socialist/Marxist theories of imperialism associated with Rosa Luxemburg, Karl Kautsky and, of course, the Leninist thesis and its critics. All were associated with anti-imperialism and threats to the liberal capitalist order of the Western world, including the links between capitalism, imperialism and war

(Etherington, 1984). Interestingly, Lenin was influenced by the earlier work of the British liberal, Hobson, who wanted to reform, not destroy, the British imperial/capitalist order.

David Cannadine concludes that as imperial historians researched, debated and disagreed from the 1950s to the 1970s, they reached only contradictory and indecisive conclusions. Imperial history began to disintegrate and global theories went out of fashion, to be replaced by area studies (Cannadine, 1995, pp. 183–4, 186). Since the 1980s, new thinking about imperialism in orthodox circles has concentrated on looking at combinations of reasons, although many mainstream historians still tend to confine their study of imperialism to the age of 'formal' empires. There has been substantially more interest in culture and imperialism and popular imperialism, pioneered by John Mackenzie. Davis and Huttenback (1986) and Cain and Hopkins (1993) have continued the debates about the economic motives for imperialism and the writings of the British radical liberal and critic of colonialism, J. A. Hobson, have had a revival (Cain, 2002). Emphasizing cultural as well as economic factors motivating imperialism, Cain and Hopkin's influential theory of 'gentlemanly capitalism' has generated a large critical literature (Dummett (ed.), 1999; Akita (ed.), 2002). Lenin has remained deeply out of fashion, although in the early 1990s there was a radical riposte to the liberal scholarly tradition that divorced capitalism from imperialism and/or sought to eradicate imperialism from our consciousness. Haynes (1993) argued that liberal historians had misconstrued the meaning of imperialism as one of the different mechanisms through which the internationalization of capital has occurred. Pieterse (1990) also retained some sympathy for Marxist theories, despite critiquing the blurring of capitalism and imperialism. But he also stressed the importance of culture and race, neglected in existing studies of all theoretical persuasions. It is these very areas that have been prioritized in postcolonial theory that has enriched controversies over imperialism since the 1980s and stimulated a renaissance in imperial history.

The postcolonial challenge and its critics

Postcolonial theory and colonial discourse analysis

Rattansi (1997) has argued that 'postcolonialism' is both a historical periodization and a particular form of theorization and analysis. McLeod distinguishes between these through hyphen use. 'Post-colonial', he argues, seems more appropriate to denote a particular historical period (after empire), whereas 'postcolonialism' refers to 'disparate forms of representations, reading practices and values that can circulate across the barrier between colonial rule and national independence'. Postcolonialism, then, 'is not contained by tidy categories of historical periods or dates', although it remains firmly bound up with historical experiences (McLeod, 2000, p. 5). There are thus debates about when the postcolonial began: this has been pushed back to the American Revolution, the decolonization of Latin America and the founding of Australia. It has been argued that postcolonialism begins with colonialism itself, perhaps as far back as 1492 with the earliest practices of resistance (Ahmad, 1995, p. 14). Klor de Alva defines postcoloniality as an 'oppositional consciousness emerging from either pre-existing colonial or ongoing subaltern relations', as affecting Latin American mestizos, US Latinos or African-Americans. Its aim is to challenge and revise forms of domination, past and present (Klor de Alva, 1995, pp. 245–6).

Colonial discourse analysis, pioneered by Edward Said, was influential in the postcolonial 'turn', although Said subsequently distanced himself from the over-theorization and ahistoricism with which it became associated. (His own writing is complex but refreshingly jargon-free.) In *Orientalism* (1978) and *Culture and Imperialism* (1994) Said was influenced by the work of Frantz Fanon, the Martiniquan psychiatrist and anti-colonial intellectual and activist, whose *Black Skin, White Masks* (1993, 1952), a study of the psychological complexities of the colonial relationship, became a seminal text in postcolonial theory. In developing his arguments about Orientalism as a system of European/Western knowledge about the Orient that facilitated domination, Said drew on the apparently conflicting theories of Antonio Gramsci and Michel Foucault. Gramsci provided a dynamic model of hegemonic power and 'subaltern' resistance, and Foucault a post-structuralist analysis of power directed to suppressing resistance.

In Foucaultian analysis culture is a mechanism of repression and violence that operates through powerful discourses and the construction of knowledge (epistemologies of power) which claim to represent 'truth':

> Each Society has its regime of truth, its 'general politics' of truth, that is the types of discourse which it accepts and makes function as true . . . Truth is to be understood as a system of ordered procedures for the regulation, distribution, circulation [of discourses] . . . truth . . . is not merely ideological but a condition of the development of capitalism (or socialism in communist states). Systems of power produce, and sustain discourses . . . the problem is not simply changing people's consciousness

– what's in their heads – but the political, institutional regime of the
production of truth.

(Foucault, 1980, pp. 131–3)

Discursive production, argued Foucault, is the production of power, 'as to
describe or represent is, at the same time, to demarcate, to include and exclude
. . . to contain'. Modern states and their imperial administrations thus had the
power to police and control every area of life, including sexuality. Historians
have employed Foucault's theory of discourse in analysing the nature of
colonial power and the ways in which representations of the colonized 'other'
also defined the superior identities of the colonizers (Chapters 4 and 5).

In dialogue with Foucault and other seminal thinkers, Edward Said provided a powerful critique of Western structures of knowledge and the way
in which colonial discourse constructed the colonial subject. He defined
Orientalism as: Western teaching, writing and research focused on the
'Orient' – that is, the academic definition; 'a style of thought based on an onto-
logical and epistemological distinction made between "the Orient" and "the
Occident"' and a 'western style of dominating, restructuring and having
authority over, the Orient – the discourse of power'. Orientalism, argued Said
(1985), was characterized by a constant interchange between academic and
'imaginative' meanings of the Orient (pp. 1–3). He conceptualized the Orient
as the place of one of the West's 'deepest and most recurring images of
the Other' (p. 1), that is, the colonized/racially inferiorized subject against
which the 'Self' is measured. This concept was developed in the phenomeno-
logical tradition and informed colonial discourse analysis. The concept of
'Orientalizing' through discourses of power was subsequently expanded to
embrace contemporary relationships between the West and the 'non-West'
and representations of the 'primitive' as opposed to 'modern', that uphold
Western male self-representations as rational and in control over weaker
and inferior 'others' (Torgovnick, 1990). The nature of Orientalism is more
fully explored in Chapter 5.

Historiographical developments in imperial history, employing postcolonial and postmodernist perspectives, however, have a wider dimension
than Said's pioneering work. There is a close link between postcolonialism
and postmodernism, which inspired much of the New Cultural History
and the genre of deconstructionist history inspired by Hayden White.
Postmodernism reflected disillusion with the modernity unleashed by the
Enlightenment and was highly influential in the development of postcolonial theory (Young, 1990). French postmodernists/post-structuralists,
such as Barthes, Baudrillard and Derrida, challenged the metatheories of the

Enlightenment and their progenitors, such as Marx and Hegel. They argued that these universalizing discourses and associated bodies of knowledge, and the patriarchal and racialized order they had produced, emphasized the need to reconstitute the colonized/subordinated subject from below rather than from above.

Psychoanalytical perspectives on identity formation have been used to elaborate on the concept of the 'other' central to Said's interrogation of the relationship between culture and imperialism. Particularly influential was the Lacanian notion of 'the imaginary' in the construction of the 'other' during the pre-verbal stage in childhood, when the child goes through the 'mirror stage'. In misrecognizing his/her reflection, the child constructs the alienated self. It is called imaginary because, for Lacan, this period of narcissistic identification is a 'mythical stage', but it becomes a metaphor for the accession of the subject to the socialized sphere of symbolic relations during which repressed desires are driven underground (cited in Lowe, 1991, pp. 144–7). Freud's dream theory has also been influential in conceptualizing the 'other' as a distorted representation of reality, reflecting the external world and emotional life of the 'dreamer' (Inden, 2001, 1986, pp. 104–5), hence the use of term 'imaginings' in analysing Western representations. Inden's 'dream-like' nature of Orientalist constructions of the 'other' is echoed in the postcolonial privileging of the 'mythic' over the real in postcolonial historiography and the questioning of the existence of truth and reality in conventional historiography (Prakash, 1990).

Such theories have been applied to understand how the 'other' is constructed through the Western 'gaze'. The language of psychoanalysis may seem obscure and inappropriate in the context of real relations of power between colonizer and colonized, but it has facilitated a more complex undertanding of the colonial relationship. Put simply, the concept of the 'other' relates to the complex construction of identities under colonialism, whereby the colonizer reinforces his/her superior identity by reflecting 'inferior' aspects of his/her own nature (sexuality, primitive emotions), suppressed in civilized societies, onto the primitive or barbaric 'other'. Thus the 'other' is a distorted representation of reality and radically different from the self. There is a tension, however, between the premise in Western social sciences of the unity of human nature and the need for the racialized 'other'. Inden explains this thus:

Once the reader comes to know the natural reason for the Other's otherness, the threat of it is neutralised. [This] restores the unity of mankind with western man as its perfect embodiment. [This is done]

> through hierarchising the Others of the world by placing them in spatial,
> biological or temporal scale of forms, one which always culminates in
> Home Euro Americanus.
>
> (Inden, 2001, 1986, p. 107)

Postcoloniality, then, is about the decolonization of representation: the
decolonization of the West's theory about the non-West, and challenging
'white mythologies' (Scott, 1999; Young, 1990). The postcolonial 'turn'
represented a growing interest in the 'symbolic empire' as well as the 'real'
(Knowles, 1996). Postcolonial theorists recentred research towards literary
and visual representations of the colonial subject and reconceptualized the
imperial project in relation to Western structures of power and knowledge.
The ways in which Western systems of knowledge have been constructed,
including Western concepts of progress, have been critically interrogated
(Chakrabarty, 2000). Imperialists, it was argued, had remapped and ordered
the world to fit in with their own consciousness, creating forms of knowledge
(epistemology) that had the power to consolidate difference and uphold the
power of the West. The crude dichotomy between 'tradition' and 'modernity'
at the heart of contemporary race discourse, truth and reality in Western historiography, and Orientalist and colonial knowledge that reproduced stable
and hierarchical East–West identities, have all been challenged. Diversity and
difference and the need to decentre and 'unsettle' essentialist identities in
Western discourse have been prioritized and a more nuanced understanding
of culture proposed (Stasiulis and Yuval-Davis, 1995). The emphasis on the
cultural and social impact of imperialism was arguably necessary to redress
the heavy emphasis on the economic and political before the 1980s.

Postcolonialism, however, is not monolithic theory and postcolonial
studies encompass a wide range of topics and disciplines (Castle (ed.), 2001).
Is it possible, asks John McLeod, to talk about 'postcolonialism' with the
entire coherency that the term implies (McLeod, 2000, p. 3)? The Orientalism
critiqued by Said related specifically to the constructions of the oriental
'other' (Middle Eastern and Asian) in European Orientalist discourse and has
generated an important subgenre of the literature (Majeed, 1992; Lowe, 1991;
Inden, 1990). Colonial discourse analysis has dominated in literary and
cultural studies and has been influential in critical rereadings of representations of the colonized in travel narratives and other European literary genres
(Mills, 1991; Boehmer, 2002; Chrisman, 2000). Another focus is on postcolonial identities in the African and Asian diasporas in Europe and the USA
(Bhabha, 1994). Additionally, some studies informed by postcolonial theory
have stressed the importance of resistance in subversions of representa-

tions of colonialism as a 'civilising mission' (Sharp, 1989) and ways in which 'anti-colonial resistances inspired one another' (Loomba, 1998, p. 185). Robert Young positions postcolonial theory as a direct development from the third world anti-colonial critiques associated with the era of decolonization. A key assumption is that many of the wrongs against humanity are a product of the economic dominance of the North over the South. In this way, he argues, the historical role of Marxism remains fundamental to postcolonial thinking. However, it is distinguished from European Marxism by combining its critique of objective material conditions with detailed analysis of their subjective (cultural) effects (Young, 2001, pp. 6–7).

The impact of postcolonial theory is reflected in a plethora of edited collections, readers and anthologies. What has been the contribution of these new approaches to the developing historiography on imperialism and post-imperial societies? Postcolonial theory has addressed issues not formerly interrogated: the links between imperialism and national cultures and identities in the imperial heartlands; the link between the imperial past and the present; how the imperial past is remembered (and forgotten); the relationship between race, gender, sexuality and imperialism. It has provided the 'postcolonial' African, African-Caribbean and Asian minorities in the Western 'heart of empire' with a new conceptual framework to interrogate their identities and challenge contemporary racism. The postmodern emphasis on cultural relativity, diversity and difference, associated with anthropologists like Clifford Geertz, has stimulated struggles for greater equality, raised the profile of minority rights (particularly in the USA and African/Asian diasporas in Europe) and facilitated 'First Nation' challenges to 'white settler' historiography.

The postcolonial 'turn' has prompted creative historical explorations and opened up new interdisciplinary perspectives that go beyond the bounds of conventional imperial histories. Significant here are South Asian subaltern studies, a project to restore histories suppressed by colonialism by reading colonial texts against the grain. Subaltern studies have queried the validity of existing historiography, Western and nationalist, and prioritized the active agency and resistance of Indian classes without a voice under colonial rule – the 'subalterns' (Guha (ed.), 1982–5). Subaltern studies were pioneered by Indian and British Marxist historians, influenced by Gramsci, who focused on problems of class in recovering the consciousness of the disempowered. Subsequently, the focus of subaltern studies shifted to a 'post-Orientalist' critique of Orientalist discourse with the aim of 'disrupting and derailing the will of the powerful'. Indian Marxist historiography was critiqued for conceptualizing India's underdevelopment as a failure to modernize, thus replicating Western constructs of India as 'Third World'. 'Post-Orientalists' thus rejected the 'essentialist categories of east and west, first and third worlds' found in Orientalist, nationalist, Marxist and other historiographies (Prakash, 1995, pp. 235–6, 242–6). Postcolonial writers such as Partha Chatterjee proposed a new paradigm of nationalism (1986). These developments were influenced by a convergence of Marxist, feminist and postmodernist theories.

The most extreme 'post-Orientalists' disputed that there was any 'truth' whatsoever in colonial texts or contemporary Western historiography (Spivak, 1985) and Gyan Prakash warned of a drift into cultural essentialism, although he stressed the ongoing need for critical enquiry into how knowledge had been 'colonized' (Prakash, 1995). Subaltern challenges to Western 'Orientalist' historiography provoked critical responses from established British historians of South Asia (Washbrook, 1999). Some have been sympathetic to the subaltern project but critical of their methodologies (O'Hanlon, 1988) but the backlash from orthodox historians against subaltern studies and, more generally the postcolonial 'turn' in imperial studies, has been clamorous and, at times, vituperative. What, then, are the main criticisms of postcolonial theory and how valid are they?

Critiquing postcolonial theory

Said's *Orientalism* was a seminal text, emphasizing the need to move towards 'antifoundational' or 'postfoundational' histories that challenged the very foundations of Western knowledge. His arguments put Western scholars of the Middle East on the defensive and provoked fierce debate (MacFie (ed.), 2002). Some criticisms were constructive but much was vituperative and dismissive, particularly where the writers opposed Said's political position (Windshuttle, 1999; Lewis, 1993). All this is valuable as it is through these conceptual and theoretical engagements that the frontier of knowledge is pushed back and new ideas emerge. Said inspired new perspectives on imperial history. As Leela Gandhi (1998) points out, he made a unique contribution to the understanding of the epistemological and cultural basis of imperialism and colonialism, but his analysis could also be critiqued as ahistorical, theoretically naïve and dependent on abstract generalizations (pp. 77–9). A key criticism was that, for Said, Orientalism preceded imperialism whereas, arguably, Orientalism developed out of imperial power. Ideas are rooted in the material world, a point made by Marx in his critique of the idealist philosopher, Hegel. As Wolfe (1999) observes, we cannot reduce history to textuality, text is also context and the historical dynamism of human activities. Said also assumed a unified imperialist/Orientalist discourse that failed to accommodate difference and presupposed a simple binary division between Orient and Occident. Melman (1995) and Lewis (1996) challenged this concept of the Orient as stable and homogeneous in emphasizing the differences between male and female representations of the East. Drawing on four examples of French and British Orientalism in the nineteenth and twentieth centuries, Lowe (1991) argued that the 'Orient' was not a discrete, monolithic, essentialized formation but reflected different socio-historical contexts that produce different formations of cultural difference (pp. 9–10).

Additional criticisms have been directed to works derivative of Said in which, it is argued, the postcolonial 'others' have become simply products of our imagination through Orientalizing. Contemporary Orientalizing of the primitive, claimed Gewertz and Errington (1993), erased the complexities of cultures and the real pressures and stresses of so-called 'primitive' life. The romanticization of the primitive reflects what we in the uncertain world of the West yearn for: simpler, more coherent lives and psychological wholeness, a point made by Torgovnick (1990) in her study of representations of the primitive in Western art, anthropology and texts. Yet, conclude Gewertz and Errington, textual representations of the primitive, 'non-Western' subject have political implications that render the essentialized, primitive 'other' 'virtually irrelevant' to us in the West. This curtails our understanding of 'those forces which articulate between and shape our lives and theirs in the world system'. Orientalism also fosters another distortion: 'Occidentalism'. In Western representations of the 'other', the West also becomes understood in reified essentialist terms. Misrepresentations of ourselves as well as the 'other', they conclude, can help to sustain, rather than subvert, existing socio-political relationships and prevent relationships and interconnections between peoples (pp. 634–8).

Postcolonial theory was a child of the 1990s, when it produced a veritable haemorrhage of studies, many of them derivative and repetitive, rendering the key concepts and theories pioneered by seminal theorists, such as Said, clichéd and predictable. Like other seminal thinkers, Said has been has been bowdlerized. Although influenced by postmodern thinkers like Foucault, he was not entirely convinced by their anti-Marxism, emphasized the importance of history and was motivated by political, not theoretical concerns. Postcolonial theory, however, has located itself 'everywhere and nowhere', eclectically borrowing from other theories and disciplines (Lacan, Derrida, Foucault), regardless of their relevance to the colonial and postcolonial context. Theoretical analyses of concepts related to colonial 'otherness', such as subalternity, hybridity and mimicry, have taken the place of real-life struggles against ongoing injustices (Goldberg and Quayson, 2002). The postcolonial 'turn' was pioneered by 'third world' intellectuals writing from a diasporic status in the West, mainly within North American universities, and preoccupation with 'identities' and dismantling of the ideological and cultural legacy of colonialism have masked the continuing dominance of global capitalism (Dirlik, 1994, pp. 328–9, 343). Postcolonial writers enthusiastically engaged with the psychoanalytic perspectives on Black identities interrogated by Frantz Fanon, without retaining his political activism and analysis of the wider structures of imperial power.

David Washbrook has argued that postcolonial theory pandered to the modern rhetoric of racial and ethnic 'victimization' and fitted in with politically correct multiculturalism (Washbrook, 1999, p. 601). Similarly, Inden concludes that the postcolonial emphasis on 'identity politics', diversity and difference has resulted in an '. . . atomistic and specious . . . doctrine of cultural relativism'. Its euphemistic language has failed to address continued relations of domination and stifled debate in international forums such as the United Nations about persistent inequalities, racial and cultural (Inden, 2001, 1986, p. 125). With its emphasis on difference and ethnic identities, multiculturalism constituted a new form of the imperialist 'divide and rule'. In Australia and the United States, multiculturalism, critics argue, masks race realities, eases the liberal conscience and undercuts a more radical anti-racism to preserve the *status quo* (Goldberg (ed.), 1994; Prashad, 2001).

A further criticism is that postcolonial studies have related primarily to the British Empire in the late nineteenth and twentieth centuries and India has received disproportionate attention. Such studies overgeneralize, fail to distinguish between different kinds of colonialism – settler and non-settler – and subscribe to an 'oddly monolithic and surprisingly unexamined notion of colonialism' (Wolfe, 1999; Mishra and Hodge, 1993). Literary and cultural theorists informed by the 'linguistic turn' use 'historicism' very loosely to indicate a broad historical dimension to postcolonial critiques of colonial literature or postcolonial writings. In his critique of Said, John Mackenzie warns against reading contemporary attitudes and preoccupations into the past. This has resulted in ahistorical moral condemnations that portray Orientalism as always negative, whereas Oriental culture and arts were not always denigrated but admired and absorbed into European culture (Mackenzie, 1995, pp. 241–51). A related, but more general, criticism from conventional historians is that colonial discourse analysis homogenizes diverse forms of relationships between colonizer and colonized and overprioritizes negative representations of the colonial subject as essential in the construction of a hegemonic 'whiteness'.

Colonial discourse analysis can degenerate into a 'discourse of discourse analyses' that, like postmodernism, deconstructs but puts nothing in its place.

As Anthony Hopkins (1999) observes, postcolonial theory replaced 'modes of production' with 'modes of discourse'. Postcolonial theorists developed complex and often obscure critiques of 'crude dichotomies', yet reproduced them in generalized discussion of the colonizer and colonized and the 'colonial subject'. Overemphasis on representations of the colonial subject, suggests Hopkins, resulted in another form of the 'totalizing' theories (liberalism, Marxism etc.) that postmodernists critiqued:

> For many young historians the only point of studying European History is to unmask the derogatory racial stereotypes encoded in the modernising myths of the Enlightenment: hence the flood of publications dealing with 'representations' of the 'Other' that have appeared in recent years. By studying images and symbols, scholars can avoid grappling with reality while being *au courant* in doubting its existence.
>
> (Hopkins, 1999, pp. 198–9)

The 'discourse of imperialism' was (and still is) expressed through tangible forms of power. Criticisms that emphasized this point surfaced from the early 1990s. Parry (1987) and Ahmed (1995) stressed that, in prioritizing culture, postcolonialism neglected the material impact of imperialism and obscured the reality of oppression. A similar point was made by Anne McClintock (1993), who argued that we may be in a postcolonial, but not a postimperial age; for people in many parts of the world, there was no postcolonial condition. An emphasis on an 'undifferentiated postcoloniality' had deflected attention away from the continued dominance of Western capitalism and negated the historical rupture implied by the term 'postcolonial' (p. 296). Global inequalities generated by capitalist expansion in the epoch of formal imperialism are still deepening, fusing the lived present with the past (Chapter 6). Benita Parry (2002) conceded that some significant initiatives emerged from the postcolonial turn but argued for a 'turn from [postcolonial] rhetoric disparaging the master narratives of revolution and liberation' (which had fudged clear thinking about the politics and economics of late imperialism) and a return to political activism (pp. 77–8).

We cannot dismiss all postcolonial studies because of the excesses of a few. Postcolonial studies cover a range of disciplines and some, such as Said's writings, have reached a much wider audience than the studies of imperial historians (Howe, 1998, 2001). Despite criticisms, postcolonial theory has evolved and continued to generate academic debate (Goldberg and Quayson, 2002). Perhaps the most positive impact of postcolonial theory was that it challenged imperial historians to reflect on their methodology, defend their approaches to imperial history and explore areas of potential commonality between postcolonialism and imperial history. Constructive dialogue with postcolonial and postmodernist theory has produced a 'new' imperial history (explored in Chapters 4 and 5) and stimulated historiographical debate.

Towards a 'new' imperial history?

One of the most fundamental criticisms of postcolonial studies is that they offer little that is new except linguistic inventiveness ('re-narrating', 'racing') and a new jargon and dense language that can obscure, rather than illuminate. Yet, under the influence of postcolonial theory, historians have felt under pressure to use politically correct terminology and frameworks of analysis. Empiricist labours in the archives have been belittled as having insufficient theoretical depth and jargon-free narratives dismissed as 'fiction'. Why is it so difficult to merge the empirical with the theoretical and conceptual and achieve critical depth without joining an elite club with its own special language that deters interlopers and thus preserves its own mystique? Why are the conventional majority so antipathetic to conceptual and theoretical innovation? Possibly because postcolonial theory has challenged orthodox imperial history, exposed the 'silences' in imperial studies and opened up new, sometimes sensitive, areas of study. It has queried 'truth' in historical documents and revealed the 'past' as more diverse, chaotic and irrational than the orderings of conventional history suggest.

For Bill Schwartz, the 'moment of post-structuralism' in historical research passed quickly, as the more useful postcolonial insights were channelled down 'empirical and historical routes' (Schwartz, 1996, pp. 9–31, 21). A new intermediate position emerged in the 1990s, a 'post-anti-colonial critique' taking into account anti-colonialist and post-structuralist sensibilities, but examining them in the light of traditional methodology (Barkan, 1994, p. 180). As Kennedy (1996) stressed, postcolonial theory reinvigorated imperial studies and took it in new directions, raising provocative questions about power, culture and resistance in understanding the nature of colonial rule. These developments provoked a sometimes rancorous debate between 'old' and 'new' imperial historians, particularly in the dominant area of British imperial history (Colley, 2002a). This was reflected in the critiques of the 'old orthodoxy' represented in *The Cambridge Illustrated History of the British Empire* (CUP, 1996), edited by P. J. Marshall, and the more thorough and extensive *Oxford History of the British Empire* (5 vols, 1998–2000). These authoritative texts provide an overview of current research across a diverse range of topics but perpetuate the historiographical divide between British and imperial history, marginalize gender and concentrate predominantly on formal imperialism. Empire is seen in retrospective and more negative elements of empire are insufficiently interrogated. Both publications reflected orthodox methodology in a commitment to 'objective' historical 'truth', were hostile to postcolonial theory and interdisciplinary perspectives and provided no systematic treatment of the link between empire and race (Howe, 2001; Kennedy, 2001).

In contrast, imperial history incorporating insights from postcolonial theory reconceptualized the metropolitan centre and 'periphery' as indivisible, challenged the compartmentalization of domestic and imperial history and reconnected race, empire and nation in the formation of British culture and national identity (Marks, 1990; Colley, 1992a; Burton, 1994b; Wilson, 1998; Hall, 2002). The 'new' imperial history also gave more priority to 'underground' colonial history that incorporated the view from the colonized margins as well as the imperial heartland (Jayawardena, 1995, p. 262). There was more openness to interdisciplinary studies employing psychoanalytical, Foucaultian, anthropological and historical perspectives to new areas of study such as gender and sexuality (McClintock, 1994; Stoler, 1996, 2002; Stoler and Cooper (eds), 1997; Burton, 1999). The contribution of these new imperial histories to reconceptualizing imperialism and colonialism will be examined in more depth in Chapters 4 and 5.

***

To conclude, the postcolonial challenge and emergence of the 'new' imperial history moved historiography on from what Muriel Chamberlain (1993) described as the 'distressingly repetitive' debates rooted in the Hobson–Lenin v. Robinson–Gallagher dichotomy. Reflecting on the state of imperial history at the close of the twentieth century, Anthony Hopkins concluded:

> When the empire broke up, so did the cohesion of the subject . . . the obstacles to preparing a fresh agenda for imperial history are . . . intimidating. The imperial experience that inspired the major debates on empire is no longer to hand. In consequence, the long-running battle between conservative and radical theories that dominated much of the historiography for so long cannot simply be re-enacted.
>
> (Hopkins, 1999, pp. 199, 241)

What was needed, he suggested, was a wider vision. This would capture the differences between empires and their dynamism and leave few parts of the globe untouched. It would help to integrate less fashionable branches of history, such as economic history, with more fashionable cultural histories informed by postcolonial theory (ibid., pp. 203–4). Imperialism remains a complex and messy concept that defies historiographical compartmentalization and will continue to generate historical debate. In the case study of Ireland that follows I will demonstrate this by analysing the complex position of Ireland within the British Empire and historiographical controversies stimulated by postcolonial Irish writings exploring the impact of colonialism on contemporary Irish identities. The following chapters and case studies also consider in more depth developments in imperial history and new conceptual frameworks discussed above.

Case study 1
Conceptualizing imperialism: the case of Ireland

The history of Ireland is intimately bound up with the long era of English/British imperial expansion. The Celtic 'fringes', including Ireland, were the first to be incorporated into the new English empire and 'civilizinge' the 'rude parts' was achieved through colonization (Ohlmeyer, 1998). Bonds between the modern 'Celtic' nations in Britain and elsewhere (Brittany, Galicia) remain strong today. In the film *Braveheart,* which roused nationalist sentiment in contemporary Scotland, the heroic alliance against the brutal, hated English king, Edward I, was forged between William Wallace ('Braveheart') and an Irish noble. Both Scotland and Ireland retain memories of English oppression and the Irish famine and the famine resulting from the enforced Highland Clearances had similar consequences for both Celtic peoples. Yet Scotland was never conquered and remained an independent kingdom until the Act of Union (1707), whereas Ireland was arguably the colonial prototype, an early model for many of the processes of colonial incorporation, cultural oppression and 'pacification' campaigns that characterized the course of British imperialism (Cook, 1993, pp. 134–5).

In this case study I will argue that Ireland can be conceptualized as colonized but with important qualifications. Irish writers influenced by postcolonial theory have emphasized the cultural and psychological impact of colonial rule, but in conventional British historiography about the colonial past, historical amnesia about Ireland persists. As Stephen Howe (2000) points out, Ireland is omitted from most studies of the British Empire or covered in a superficial, poorly informed fashion. Studies of the relationship between Ireland and Empire tend to focus on the pre-nineteenth century, emphasizing its significance to the origins of the British Empire (Canny, 2001; Canny (ed.), 1998) and Irish history has been conflated with British history (Armitage, 2000, p. 3). During the period of formal Union, 1801–1922, Ireland was subsumed into 'England's unconsciousness' (Kibberd, 1996) and debates over Home Rule in the Gladstonian era relegated Ireland to an aspect of British domestic history. Fitzpatrick argues that political union allowed for ambiguous interpretations of Ireland's history although, in effect, it was a hybrid administration with 'manifest colonial elements' (Fitzpatrick, 1999, p. 495). Was Ireland's position within the British Empire unique because of close geographical proximity and the fact that for long periods it was integrated into the British state? How does the Irish experience compare with other parts of the British Empire?

A fierce debate has emerged since the 1980s between postcolonial writers influenced by the Field Day Group, founded in Derry (or Londonderry, depending on your politics) in 1980 by Brian Friel, Stephen Rea, Declan Kibberd and others, and revisionist historians who have downplayed the colonial legacy. Inspired by Edward Said, who clearly regarded Irish history as colonial (Said, 1990), Irish writers have explored the problem of Irish identities and the buried 'colonial psyche' of the Celtic Irish (Deane, 1986, p. 58). Postcolonial critiques dispute revisionist positions on Northern Ireland, the famine and nationalist struggles against British imperialism and emphasize the interconnections between colonial and postcolonial Ireland (Lloyd, 1999; Carrol and King (eds), 2003). Conversely, Liam Kennedy claims that Ireland is too 'advantaged' to be postcolonial and considers colonial concepts to be of little use in charting Irish history from 1800. Irish history, he argues, must be reclaimed from the myths promoted by nationalist historiography (Kennedy, 1996, pp. 179, 217). Stephen Howe is also doubtful about the '. . . adequacy of colonial and postcolonial frameworks for analysing contemporary Ireland', although he concedes that some aspects of Irish history need to be analysed in an imperial framework (Howe, 2000, pp. 4–5). Most recently, these historiographical debates have been condensed in the *Oxford History of the British Empire* companion volume which spans the early modern to the postcolonial period in Irish history (Kenny (ed.), 2004).

From the republican perspective, revisionists such as James Boyce and Alan O'Day (1996) and Roy Foster (1988) have distorted Irish history by taking an 'irreconcilable Anglo-Irish position' (Carty, 1996, p. 45); Connor Cruise O'Brien has been accused of Ulster Loyalist (Unionist) sympathies (Wheatcroft, 2003). Conversely, republican nationalist historiography analysed Irish struggles for independence in the wider context of the British Empire

(Curtis, 1996). Carty (1996) proritized conquest and cultural destruction as the dominant fact in Irish history; the Ulster Protestant minority were a conqueror society which developed a settler identity, now incorporated into contemporary identities (pp. 15–16). Roy Foster has queried interpretations of the Northern Ireland situation as essentially colonial (Foster, 1993) but, asks Howe (2000), how far has Unionist consciousness seen itself as colonial and to what extent have Northern Irish Protestants identified with colonial settler populations elsewhere (pp. 199–200)?

Like India, Ireland has its own nationalist mythology forged in opposition to British imperialism and emphasizing British oppression. Central to nationalist historiography is the Great Irish Famine of 1845–7 and this has consequently become a major focus of historical controversy. The famine had a huge impact on Irish society. Over one million died of starvation or famine-related illness (see Figure 2.1) and, in the mass emigrations to North America that ensued, many more died in the 'coffin ships' and quarantine centres. Irish nationalists saw the famine as 'racial genocide' (Foley, 1992, p. 5), a result of deliberate government policies, a position disputed by revisionists. Criticisms of the marginalization of the famine in revisionist histories became more clamorous with the 150-year commemoration preparations in the early 1990s. These debates prompted 'post-revisionist' historians like Christine Kinealy (1994, 2002) to revisit the famine and its impact and legacy. Kinealy argued for a midpoint between the revisionist view and the distortions and emotive half-truths of popular mythology. Cormac Ó'Gráda (1999) transcended the revisionist/post-revisionist debate by integrating folklore, ballad and song – the 'famine memory' – with detailed econometric analysis critiquing British free market economics. Such memories persisted in the Irish diaspora (Fitzpatrick, 1994).

There is now more recognition of the imperial relationship between England and Ireland, although Ireland does not fit in with classic definitions of colonialism. As David Fitzpatrick (1999) points out, Ireland had an ambiguous status as a colonized country whose people also played a prominent role as colonizers. Ireland contributed both to the building and dismantling of the British Empire. Irish soldiers, like Indian soldiers, were vital to policing other parts of the empire (Jeffrey (ed.), 1996). The memorials in the big Anglo-Irish churches in Irish cities are testimony to the Irish contribution to empire. Anglo-Irish landowners provided imperial administrators who took an equally hard line against the struggles of the Irish for land rights as against anti-colonial resistance in their colonies (Kiernan, 1982, p. 178). The fortunes of Anglo-Irish families were linked to the empire. Life in Ireland was profitable and privileged until family misfortunes mounted in the second

Figure 2.1   Remembering empire: memorial and famine graves, Skibbereen, Cork (author's own photograph)

half of the nineteenth century as land reforms changed their relationship with the Irish tenantry. But fortunes could be made by working, for instance, in expanding trade in China and the Far East, and estates saved. The empire continued to provide jobs in the military and the administration, but steep decline set in during the turbulent times after the First World War, when tenants became armed intruders, and many Anglo-Irish families left.

The conceptualization of Ireland as a colony thus needs to be qualified by a class/culture analysis. The biggest contribution the Irish made to the empire was actually as poor migrants, particularly after the famine. It was this poor, racialized element, Catholic and Gaelic, who constituted the first large-scale 'colonial' migration into Britain. Pre-1600, there were two Irelands, the Celtic clans and the Norman settlers; both were Catholic and shaped pre-conquest Irish culture. By 1600, the situation had changed. With the new English administration, the landscape was carved into large 'plantations'. The Norman lords and Celtic clans rebelled, their lands were confiscated and this stimulated the first migrations. Two new Irelands emerged, the English ruling elite and the Celtic Ireland of the colonized Irish peasantry, confined 'beyond the pale' of civilization. This divide was deepened in the seventeenth century by the establishment of Ulster and the ascendancy of the Anglo-Irish in Celtic Ireland. The consequence of these developments, argues Lyons (1979), was 'four Irelands': the Anglo-Irish Protestant ascendancy; the bourgeois Catholics (including descendants of the old English predating the Cromwellian settlements); the working-class Northern Irish Protestants with an Ulster/Scots identity and the Gaelic Irish. The point of greatest contradiction was between the latter two groups. Debates over whether Ireland can be classed as a 'settlement colony' – that is, a 'colony without colonialism' – or an 'exploitation colony' (Osterhammel, 1997, pp. 10–12) depend partly, though not wholly, on which of these 'four Irelands' you belong to.

Was Ireland, then, a colony? I will explore this question with reference to definitions of colonialism and comparisons with India, also conceived as having a unique position within the British Empire. Osterhammel defined a colony as '. . . a new political organisation created by invasion, conquest and/or settlement colonisation' and colonialism as 'a relationship of domination [where] colonisers are convinced of their own superiority and their ordained mandate to rule'. Alien colonial rulers were dependent on a geographically remote 'mother country' or imperial centre which claimed exclusive rights of possession of the colony (Osterhammel, 1997, pp. 10, 16–17). Most orthodox histories associate colonialism exclusively with 'non-European societies' under the control of a European state or the USA, ruled from a distance and with 'no necessary identity of interest' between rulers and ruled. The 'modern tropical colony' is the classic example (Fieldhouse, 1981, pp. 1–11). These definitions would seem to exclude Ireland, given its close geographical proximity to, and different constitutional and political relationship with, England. Moreover, imperial relations with Ireland were complicated by the fact that the Irish were 'white' Europeans.

Was Ireland colonized? Comparing Ireland and India

How did Ireland's relationship with Britain compare with other colonized societies in the British Empire? In 1824, the abolitionist James Cropper toured Ireland and noted that Irish poverty and West Indian slavery were 'two dark shadows' thwarting British progress, intimately linked through monopolies on plantation produce that profited English landlords (cited in David Brion Davis, 1994, p. 212). Cropper was, of course, making his case against slavery, but also highlighted similar patterns of oppression and exploitation by English colonial masters. Important similarities also exist in the legitimization of colonial oppression through a racialized discourse. This is evident in comparisons drawn between India and Ireland. John Stuart Mill, in explaining Irish 'disaffection' other than by a 'taint of infirmity in the Irish character' wrote:

> In India, as in Ireland, there is a superabundant population depending wholly on land . . . and those Englishmen who know something of India are even now those who understand Ireland best. Persons who know both countries have remarked many points of resemblance between the Irish and Hindoo character; there are certainly many between the agricultural economy of Ireland and that of India.
>
> (Mill, 1868, cited in Lebow, 1979, p. 22)

The English, he added, denied the vast majority of the Irish religious, civil and political liberties and they were left 'to plough or dig the ground and pay rent to their task-masters'. The whole of the island had been 'confiscated' to enrich powerful Englishmen and their Irish adherents and to give away to Scottish colonists to hold as 'a garrison against the Irish'. Irish manufactures were 'deliberately crushed to make more room for those of England'. 'A nation which treats its subjects in this fashion', he warned, 'cannot well expect to be loved by them' (pp. 3–4).

Affinities between Ireland and India in the nineteenth century have been explored by Cook (1993) and by Holmes and Holmes (1997), who argued that the relationship was unusually close, despite physical and cultural differences, although paths diverged after independence. Yet the relationship was ambiguous: the Irish in India were prominent as soldiers, administrators and missionaries and developed a similar superior consciousness to that of the English. Despite experiencing British rule, they were as brutal as any other conquerors and saw Ireland as a privileged colony whose citizens could share in the benefits of empire (Holmes, 2000, p. 242). This given, there were also affinities between Ireland and India in relation to colonial oppression of the poor Catholic majority which are fruitful to explore. David Potter provides a useful model for comparative analysis. Colonialism, he proposes, was legitimized through control over the colonial economy; bureaucratic/authoritarian rule aided by collaborative elites; the use of force and colonial policing; technological advantage and a hegemonic ideology of power linked to cultural and racial oppression (Potter, 1992). I would add that these strategies were also necessary to contain resistance. On the basis of these criteria, plausible arguments can be made for the colonial status of the Celtic Irish.

Control over the colonial economy

In 1601 the Catholic barons were defeated and the era of colonization and genocide began as English adventurers engaged in the pillage of Ireland. In 1641 Protestant settlers from Scotland violently evicted Catholic inhabitants. Under the 1652 Act of Settlement, Cromwellian soldiers were given gifts of land confiscated from Irish peasants. By the end of the eighteenth century, Ireland was turned into a vast estate and only five per cent of the land was in Catholic hands (Foley, 1992, p. 5). Only the rugged and harsh areas of the West Coast were spared and, in terms of land expropriation, not 'colonized'. It is in these areas that the small *Gaeltachts* (remaining Gaelic-speaking areas) of present-day Ireland are located. But such areas were not spared the cultural oppression, nor the poverty associated with subsistence farming. Subsequently, the Irish economy was distorted to meet the needs of the British (Cleary, 2003). This is comparable to the long history of exploitation in India, an exploitation which, in the late nineteenth century, contributed to nationalist grievances over the 'drain of wealth' from India to Britain (Bose and Jalal, 1998, pp. 100–1). In both India and Ireland a dispossessed peasantry and social disruptions resulting from colonial rule turned peasants into rural and urban landless labourers (proletarianization) and resulted in migration. The Irish and Asian working-class diasporas were dynamic elements in the development of empire (Asians in East Africa, Irish in Australia) and these diasporas also nourished nationalism.

In both Ireland and India the colonial relationship with Britain contributed to poverty, hunger and famine. Although there is controversy over the nature of the Irish famine in the early 1840s, it had a huge impact on Irish perceptions of English 'tyranny'. In India there were a series of famines, including the great famine in Madras in 1876–8, where up to six million people died. Government policy towards famine in Ireland, including coerced migration, was used as the model for controlling famine in India. According to Davis (2001), famines in China, India and elsewhere in the last quarter of the nineteenth century were not the result of natural disasters, but rather the imposition of Western free-market, export-oriented, cash-crop economies on the colonial world. Thus, in Ireland and India, cash crops were still exported and relief provided by the British government was inadequate. Also implicated was the rapaciousness of middlemen and collaborative landlords. These human causes of famine are brilliantly evoked in the Indian director Satyajit Ray's *Distant Thunder* (1973), a film about the great Bengal famine in 1943–4 that killed up to 3.8 million (Bose and Jalal, 1998, pp. 157–9). This was virtually written out of British histories of the period and, where it is mentioned, it is attributed to 'abnormal war conditions' with only a 'small' death-roll in comparison with the past (Wilkinson, 1944, p. 185). In both India and Ireland the experiences and memories of famine stimulated anti-colonialism.

Authoritarian rule aided by collaborative elites

Ireland had a far longer and more consistent history of oppression by Britain than India. Conquest, 1649–52, and reconquest, 1689–91, after Irish resistance, involved ruthless repression. In 1641 the Catholic lords, Celtic and Norman, rebelled against the Protestant settlers in the North and the uprising was crushed by Cromwellian forces. Between 1649 and 1653, an estimated one-third of the Irish population died, many through famine resulting from destruction of crops. From the eighteenth century, Ireland was ruled by its own 'Raj' – the landowning Anglo-Irish ascendancy and a collaborative Irish middle class who prospered under British rule. Superficially, relations between the Anglo-Irish and the tenantry were often amicable but in essence they were paternalistic and distant and the gentry remained isolated from the life around them (Lyons, 1979). Their social lives were centred on the 'big house', socializing with other Anglo-Irish, and the Church of Ireland. Like British residents in India, they sustained a lifestyle which emphasized superiority and power. Coercive measures, including military force and imprisonment, were used to suppress any Irish dissent. Ireland, like India, had a substantial 'army of occupation' and Irish colonial policing became a model for colonial policing elsewhere (Fitzpatrick, 1999, p. 516). Ireland was ruled directly from Westminster through a Lord Lieutenant or governor, and administration of the Irish peasantry though the Resident Magistrate system was similar to administration by colonial officers in other parts of the empire (Crossman, 2000).

Racial and cultural oppression

In Ireland cultural oppression began in 1366 with Statutes of Kilkenny that legislated for the eradication of Celtic culture. The Penal Code (1695–1728), the laws that facilitated the Protestant ascendancy, deprived Catholics of rights enjoyed by Protestants and suppressed Catholicism. Catholicism had to be secretly practised at mass rocks as Catholics were unable to build churches until the nineteenth century – hence the rather anachronistic modernist churches that are a familiar feature of the contemporary Irish landscape. The Irish language was also suppressed and competition between the English and Irish languages was an integral facet of an 'enduring, violent and bitter struggle between differing forms of social organisation, cultures and economies' (Crowley, 1996, p. 100). Cultural imperialism in education was a facet of both Irish and Indian experiences of British rule. With the development of the national educational system after 1831, Irish children learned nothing of their own geography or history (Fitzpatrick, 1999, p. 503). But in Ireland cultural and linguistic imperialism was far harsher than in India, where English was also imposed as the language of governance. Orientalist learning (Chapter 5) included Indian languages in order that they could be used as 'an instrument of rule' to understand the 'peculiar manners' of the Indians and to gather information to better control the peoples of India. There was also some respect for Indians and institutions that were the carriers of traditional culture (Cohn, 1996, p. 46). With the decline of respect for elite oriental culture and the diffusion of scientific racism after the Indian Mutiny in 1857, South Asian cultures and religions were increasingly regarded as inferior, but there was no active suppression of indigenous languages.

The identities of Indian and Irish colonial subjects were both constructed through racialized discourses but conventional associations between race and colonialism were subverted by the classification of the Irish as European and the prioritization of class and religious divisions over race in explaining conflicts. Thus Stephen Howe (2000) queries whether racism is an appropriate label for English attitudes to the Irish, which raises the interesting question of whether colonialism is possible without racism. Conversely, Irish postcolonial writers have prioritized the impact of colonialism and racial stereotyping in understanding contemporary Irish identities (Kibberd, 1995; Gibbons, 2001). As with other colonial 'subjects', the Irish contributed to the shaping of English identity and sense of imperial superiority. Irish peasants were condemned as dirty, emotional, shiftless, untrustworthy, undisciplined and unstable. Supposedly childlike, wild, reckless and superstitious, they despised English enterprise and civilization, creating an ever-present 'Irish problem' (Huttenback, 1976, p. 17). Simian-like imagery in popular caricature emphasized comparisons between the Irish 'yahoo' and the gorilla and Negro (Foster, 1993, pp. 184, 192–3). The Irish were racialized as the 'blacks of Europe' or white 'niggers' (Pieterse, 1992) and this suggests the essentially colonial attitudes of the British towards the subordinated Celtic Irish.

Stereotypes of the Irish, however, differed from those applied to other colonized men and women in that there was no sexual dimension. Irish men were never a threat to 'white women' nor were Irish women the repositories of forbidden, exotic sexuality, key elements of racism directed towards Africans and Asians. Religious contamination rather than racial dilution was the key threat posed by mixed marriages. As Foster emphasizes, the British working class were also represented as 'dark and brutish' and class and religion, rather than scientific racism, shaped Irish identities (Foster, 1993, pp. 184, 192–3). Yet, as Lyons has demonstrated, the Irish in the nineteenth century were not just 'second-class Englishmen' but something quite different, 'either quaintly or horribly'; Protestantism was identified with 'civilization', Catholicism with 'barbarism' (Lyons, 1979, pp. 4, 11).

With large-scale Irish immigration to England, popular English representations of the Irish began to deteriorate. In the satirical magazine, *Punch* (founded 1841), famine distress relief was attacked as subsidizing the lazy Irish and ingratitude, rather than starvation, came to be seen as the leading characteristic of the Irish (Foster, 1993, pp. 174–8, 180). But it was Fenianism which gave 'full reign to the image of the bestial and violent Irishman' (ibid., p. 185). Ireland was increasingly distinguished from Great Britain by the fanaticism, violence and 'murderous cruelties' of the Celtic people (Wilkinson, 1944, p. 150). The Irish Republican Brotherhood, or the Fenians, organized in 1858, were committed to the violent overthrow of the English in Ireland. A product of impoverished anti-British migrants in the diaspora, the Fenians attempted an uprising on mainland Britain in February–March 1867, which resulted in British civilian deaths. Irish nationalists were always more of a 'close and present' threat to the British mainland than were Indian nationalists.

Resistance and anti-colonial nationalism

Irish nationalism originated in the bourgeois nationalisms which erupted throughout Western Europe in the nineteenth century. Wolfe Tone's Protestant

United Irishmen movement of the 1790s, inspired by the French Revolution, laid the basis for a modern Irish nation-state, a separatist movement embracing native and settler, a rebuttal of the notion of two 'irreconcilably antagonistic nations' (Foley, 1992, p. 3). Conversely, Daniel O'Connell (the 'Liberator'), in furthering Catholic bourgeois interests, reinforced the 'two nation' divide which deepened when O'Connell's more moderate nationalism was challenged in 1846 by the new Young Ireland Movement. This divide was blurred once more by the alliance between the Protestant nationalist, Charles Stewart Parnell, and the Catholic activist, Michael Davitt, in the Irish Land League's challenge to exploitative landlordism and campaign for fair rents. Reforms were introduced in 1882 but fell short of demands and Parnell, an Irish MP in the British House of Commons, turned to political agitation for Home Rule. Differences now widened between Parnellian demands for constitutional change and the more radical republican position of the Irish Republican Brotherhood and Sinn Fein. There was no voice for the Irish masses until 1913 and the formation of the Irish Volunteers founded by James Connolly, a Scottish-born Marxist leader of the Irish Labour Party, who emphasized the link between socialism, working-class struggles, nationalism and independence.

Large numbers of Irish volunteered to defend Britain in the First World War, but Irish Republicanism took advantage of British weakness in the 1916 Easter Rising and Proclamation, which declared Ireland a republic. The rising was crushed and the fifteen leaders executed, including James Connolly, but in his poem, 'Easter', Yeats wrote 'a terrible beauty is born'. For Yeats and Anglo-Irish sympathetic to nationalism, the rising put paid to their vision of the fusion of the Protestant and Catholic cultures (Lyons, 1979, pp. 76–8). Repression of the Easter Rising increased support for Sinn Fein, which swept the elections in 1918 with 73 out of 105 Parliamentary seats on a platform of abstention from Westminster and the establishment of an Irish parliament. There was an upsurge in popular resistance, including withholding taxes and rents and strikes, and during the Anglo–Irish War of 1919–21. Anglo-Irish houses were attacked and guerrilla warfare waged against British soldiers or 'Black and Tans'.

After 1880, Irish nationalism became more clearly defined against the British Empire and grievances were similar to those of Indian nationalists. Maud Gonne McBride, an Anglo-Irish woman who embraced the nationalist cause and founded the Friends of Irish Freedom in Paris in 1892, wrote that Irish prisoners in Britain before 1914 were 'suffering for Ireland and the struggle against the British Empire' (Gonne McBride, 1938, p. 129). Irish nationalists also supported the Afrikaners during the South African (Boer) War (Kiernan, 1982, p. 172). The Irish patriot, Roger Casement, worked for the British Consulate Service from 1895 to 1912 and was involved in the scramble for Africa before transforming into a critic of colonialism, campaigning against the evils of colonialism in the Belgian Congo and the use of indigenous peoples of the Upper Amazon as slave labour. Casement compared European treatment of Africans with English oppression of the Irish. Now viewed by the British government as a traitor, his reputation was undermined by revelations of homosexuality in his 'Black Diaries' leaked by the British government (Mitchell, 2003). Casement was hanged for treason in 1916 for allegedly enlisting the Germans to help with the cause of Irish freedom. Controversies over whether his diaries were forged by the government to tarnish his reputation continue, although they were declared genuine in 2002 (Tilzey, 2002).

Ireland was arguably the first colony after the USA to gain independence from Britain, albeit through violent means (with support from the American Irish), and the first 'postcolonial' state in the empire. Did Ireland produce the first successful colonial liberation movement of the twentieth century? Certainly, Irish nationalism inspired Indian nationalism, which, in turn, stimulated African nationalism. Passive resistance tactics in India were influenced by the Irish 'no rent' campaigns, obstructionism and boycotts pioneered by the Irish Land League. O'Connell inspired Gandhi, Indian nationalists visited Ireland, and Indian and Irish nationalists mingled in the salons of London and Paris after 1880 (Boehmer, 2002, p. 84). Parallels also exist between the cultural nationalism of the Gaelic League, founded in 1893 to reinvigorate Irish language and culture after failed demands for home rule, and the late-nineteenth-century Bengal Renaissance. Both romanticized the past, articulated identities separate from Britain and melded tradition with modernizing elements (Chatterjee, 1986). Irish women were also involved in nationalist struggles in India. Most prominent of these were the Irish suffragette, Margaret Cousins, and the radical activist, Annie Besant, who helped launch the home rule campaign in 1916 and became the first woman president of the Indian National Congress (Chaudhuri and Strobel (eds), 1992). In sum, the developments in mass nationalism in both Ireland and India greatly stretched the British government, particularly during and after the First World War, when unstable economic and political conditions stimulated anti-colonial protest and labour unrest in the empire and growing political discontent in Britain.

Strategies to contain nationalism and maintain hegemony

In both India and Ireland nationalist protest was suppressed by use of British force, but repression in Ireland had a longer and bloodier history. In 1798, the British killed 50,000 United Irishmen and Wolf Tone died in prison, providing

Irish nationalism with its first martyr (Foley, 1992, p. 2). After 1900, the British government responded to both nationalist movements by a divide and rule policy to counteract radical Hindu nationalism and Irish Republican nationalism. This created fissures between Protestants and Catholics and Muslims and Hindus. Proposals of Irish Home Rule in 1886 and 1912 were violently opposed by the Northern Irish Protestants who had formed the Orange Order in 1795 to defend Protestant interests. Irish nationalism was represented as a threat to the essential unity of Britain; in reality, it was military might which bound England and Ireland together. The Liberal government encouraged the formation of the Ulster Volunteer Force in 1912 and the British military elite maintained close links with the Unionists (Foley, 1992, p. 10).

The massacre by the British authorities of at least 379 protestors at Amritsar in the Punjab in 1919 and the suppression of the 1916 Easter Rising stimulated mass nationalism and more extensive resistance to the British state. Popular resistance culminated in the Anglo–Irish War of 1919–21 when the British government adopted ruthless strategies to repress the Republicans who waged guerrilla warfare against the British Black and Tans. Under the 1920 Government of Ireland Act, Ireland was partitioned into Eire and British Northern Ireland. Splits in the nationalist movement, between factions supporting Michael Collins and Eamon de Valera, resulted in a bitter civil war (1922–3). British divide and rule tactics, however, promoted intercommunal religious violence. During the violent unrest which culminated in the partition of Ireland, people were shot for their religion by Catholic and Protestant militias. This foreshadowed the violence between Hindus and Muslims during the partition of India in 1947. Both partitions unleashed recurrent violence that is still unresolved, although promising developments have taken place in Northern Ireland since the late 1990s.

Ireland and empire: some conclusions

Both Ireland and India had a long imperial relationship with Britain that went through different stages and involved a complex interplay of different cultures, religions and classes which was, at certain crucial points, manipulated by the British to contain resistance. British power in India and Ireland was justified by stereotyping and inferiorization of the colonial subject: Irish and Indian postcolonial identities were shaped by experiences of oppression in the colonial era and in relation to the resultant global Irish and Indian diasporas. Experiences of British oppression also influenced the development of nationalism and there are important parallels between Indian and Irish nationalism. But India was the 'Jewel in the Crown', central to Britain's imperial prestige and Queen Victoria was also Empress of India. Conversely, Ireland was viewed as a country beyond redemption. Persistently more insubordinate than India, Irish republicans were far less accepting of the 'higher ideals' of empire epitomized in the British monarchy. Royal visits to Ireland, where, for some, Queen Victoria was the 'Famine Queen', encountered hostility as well as displays of loyal affection (Gonne McBride, 1938, p. 294). Strategies to contain nationalism were generally successful in India and independence (as opposed to extended political representation for Indians), was not on the agenda until after 1929. This contrasted with the Irish situation, where nationalism had become a serious threat to British control by the late nineteenth century.

Additional factors differentiating Ireland from other colonies include the characterization of nationalist struggle as religious sectarianism and the intimate and long-lasting connections between the English and the Anglo-Irish and Northern Irish Protestant settlers, who were also imperialists and colonizers. Northern Ireland had a strong Scottish Protestant culture and its history was shaped by the Cromwellian 'plantation' in the seventeenth century and the victory of the Orangemen over the Catholics at the Battle of the Boyne. Belfast was industrialized and integrated into the British economy, having more in common with Liverpool or Glasgow than the Celtic Irish hinterland. It was only the Western half of Ireland which was seriously affected by famine. Yet Celtic Ireland was also consistently vulnerable to English culture and language (Lyons, 1979, pp. 8–9). In effect, both Protestants and Catholics identified themselves as Irish, but the latter were subordinated to the former – a situation of 'internal' colonialism. Parallels with South Africa, where white and African inhabited one country but through a colonial relationship, are interesting here. In the postcolonial era, suggests Rian Malan (1993, pp. 13–14), the Northern Irish Protestants see themselves in a similar position to the Afrikaners or the Israeli Jews with 'nowhere to go' and besieged by a hostile, 'alien' population.

Northern Ireland has a pivotal, if ambivalent, position in debates about Irish nationalism. It was Ulster Unionists, argues Howe, not British imperialism, that created partition and subsequent sectarian politics; British imperialism or neo-colonialism is not a significant factor in contemporary Irish life. For this reason, he queries if Ireland is best described as a colony and, hence, whether Irish nationalism was anti-imperialist. He is also ambivalent about the relationship between Irish and other anti-colonial nationalisms and critical of writers like Liz Curtis who stress Irish/Indian solidarity (Howe, 2000, pp. xv, 9, 48). Both Howe and Holmes (2000) conclude that the Irish may have influenced Indian nationalism, but not vice versa. Holmes points to the fact that the Irish in India were just as susceptible to the dominant ideology of racial superiority as the British – even those from a Catholic, nationalist background – and very few Irish were involved in the Indian nationalist struggle (Holmes, 2000, pp. 238, 243).

Liam Kennedy regards Irish independence as 'secessionist', not anti-colonial, as it bore little relationship to other independence movements in Africa or Asia. Irish nationalists wanted cultural unity, not their own nation-state (Kennedy, 1996, p. 177). Stephen Howe suggests that the model of European nationalism was more influential than anti-colonialism. Was Irish nationalism inspired by European nationalist movements of the nineteenth century and/or hatred of the imperial British oppressors? Clearly, both European nationalism and socialism influenced Irish nationalism, but the same could be argued for other anti-colonial movements which followed a similar pattern. Moreover, are European and anti-colonial nationalism so distinct? As Armitage has observed, the influence of the imperial context has been left out of histories of European nationalism (Armitage, 2000, p. 14). We also need to distinguish between the bourgeois nationalism of O'Connell and Parnell that envisaged autonomy within the British Empire and republican nationalism that targeted the British state and Empire as the main enemy of Ireland and Irish culture.

***

Irish history demonstrates that there are no static conceptions of colonialism and imperialism. The imperial relationship was contingent on the shifting priorities of the imperial power, fluid power balances between colonizer and colonized, the specific class, ethnic and cultural contours of the colonized society and the dynamics of resistance. The debate over the relationship between Ireland and empire will undoubtedly rage on, as will the debate over the influences, past and present, shaping Irish identities (O'Mahoney and Delanty, 1998). As Howe points out, now Ireland is a successful 'tiger economy' in the European Union, postcolonial problems seem irrelevant. Do 'whiteness' and the booming standard of living in the 'Celtic tiger' now make comparisons with postcolonial India futile? Indeed, the increase in Irish racism against asylum seekers and 'non-white' migrant workers in Ireland indicates full membership of the ex-colonial, rather than postcolonial world. This racism is indeed ironic, given the migrant experiences of the Irish. What implications will this have for Ireland's relationship with its imperial past and its 'postcolonial' identities?

Imperialism and modernity

> Imperialism was the means through which the techniques, culture and institutions that evolved in Europe over several centuries – the culture of the Renaissance, the Reformation, the Enlightenment, and the Industrial Revolution – sowed their revolutionary seeds in the rest of the world. This culture was in many ways unique and contributed much of value to humanity.
>
> (Warren, 1980, p. 36)

For Warren, imperialism was a dynamic force in global development as the 'pioneer of capitalism'. Writing within the context of Marxist debates in the 1970s, when capitalism was critiqued for perpetuating neo-imperial relationships and underdevelopment in the colonies, Warren returned to the classical Marxist position, arguing that capitalism had the dynamic potential to empower oppressed classes and transform societies. What is the link between imperialism, capitalism and modernity in shaping global power relations? European/Western empires emerged from unique changes in Western European society, linked to intellectual, technological and scientific innovations and the development of capitalist production. Modernity fuelled the successful expansion of Western European and US empires associated with the New Imperialism that emerged in the late nineteenth century, shaping imperial identity and rhetoric. Did the Russian, Turkish, Spanish, Austro-Hungarian and Chinese empires collapse because they were not 'modern' enough and lagged behind in capitalist development? Was the defeat of the newer empires of Germany and Japan, in the First and Second World Wars respectively, related to distortions of rapid modernization stimulated by competition and conflict with other imperial powers?

Clearly, the relationship between imperialism and modernity is significant and multifaceted. Modernity is crucial to understanding differences between 'old' and 'new' empires, but also the nature of cultural imperialism, Westernization and anti-colonial resistance. Through imperial expansion, modern Western concepts of progress and linear time, capitalist modes of production, liberal democracy, and nationalism were spread globally, demonstrating the triumph of civilization over barbarity. The impact of this modernity on the rest of the world was profound and had far-reaching transformative influences on the economies, social relations and cultures of colonized peoples. This chapter, then, deepens debates raised in Chapter 1 about the 'unique' character of European/Western imperialism. It interrogates the ambiguities and contradictions inherent in the Euro/West-centric discourse of modernity and related 'civilizing mission' to spread 'enlightenment' to colonized and postcolonial societies.

Modernity, capitalism and the rise of European empires

What constitutes the modern and when did the modern begin, in the 1490s, or with the European Enlightenment and the development of modern capitalism (Thompson, 2000, p. 40)? Did European modernity begin with the fifteenth-century Renaissance, epitomized in the science of Leonardo da Vinci (1452–1519) and associated European maritime reconnaissances of the globe? Or was it during the sixteenth and seventeenth centuries when the Protestant Reformation freed human individuality and agency from the constraints of Catholicism and medieval mysticism and promoted a 'Protestant ethic' that the German sociologist Max Weber identified as a dynamic behind the development of capitalism? Alternatively, does the modern stem from the intellectual Enlightenment and the development of industrial capitalism in the eighteenth century, or accelerations in social, political, technological and economic change associated with the era of New Imperialism? There were different phases in the formation of Western modernity and all were important in creating its defining characteristics.

Most historical periodizations place Europe at the centre and map key developments in Europe and the West. Western European maritime explorations of the fifteenth century and the defining moment of Columbus's 'discovery' of the Americas mark the emergence of the modern, suggesting a discontinuity with the past and continuity with future developments.

Europe's success has conventionally been attributed to its unique harnessing of science and technology (Landes, 1969). Snooks (1996) takes the longer view of the dynamics of human society over two million years, but favours a Euro/West-centred interpretation that stresses the importance of the Industrial Revolution in creating a 'dynamic society', the 'great chariot of economic change' driven by 'materialist man'. Western 'man' (as opposed to woman) is a decision-making individual desirous of maximizing material well-being. Dynamism comes from these key agents who struggle to survive in a Darwinian competitive environment. Before this 'economic Darwinism', society was a case of simple survival, but technological change, commerce and colonization were used to improve material standards of living. 'Cultural feedback' does occur but the dynamic process is essentially determined by more basic forces (pp. 6, 11–12). Snooks charts why human societies grow, stagnate and sometimes collapse over the *longue durée*. He has rightly challenged the ahistoricism of contemporary economic theory that replicates a Eurocentric model of global economic development (Snooks, 1993), but his arguments are framed in the language and epistemology of Western modernity and the technological/economic triumph of the West. What would the world be like now, he asks, without the Industrial Revolution?

This raises central questions as to whether capitalism was associated uniquely with Europe, giving it an edge over older, non-European empires. Immanuel Wallerstein dates the development of a 'unique' modern world capitalist system from the sixteenth century, when the core of global power shifted to Spain and North West Europe and the Northern Italian states declined to semi-peripheral status, as, ultimately, did Spain in the nineteenth century. Three structural positions in the world economy – core, periphery and semi-periphery, linked through the operation of 'unequal exchanges' – had stabilized by 1640 (Wallerstein, 1974a). Imperial and capitalist expansion were thus interlinked from this point onward in the creation of modern world systems. Wallerstein has been criticized for his Eurocentric position (as well as for blurring capitalist expansion with imperialism). Frank and Gills (1993), Modelski and Thompson (1988), Pomeranz (2000) and W. Thompson (2000) have taken a longer and less Eurocentric view of the development of the global economy. Challenging conventional wisdom about the European 'miracle', they have argued that an Afro-Asian market and capitalistic practices pre-existed developments in Europe; India, China and Japan were all as advanced as Europe before the eighteenth century, with the potential for dynamism and modernity.

None of the developments associated with modernity, observes Crone (1989), were unique to Western Europe:

> ... there is something puzzling about the excitement with which European historians hail the arrival of cities, trade, regular taxation, standing armies, legal codes, bureaucracies ... and other common appurtenances of civilized societies as if they were unique and self-evident stepping stones to modernity: to the non-European they simply indicated that Europe had finally joined the club.
>
> (p. 148)

Many cities in Asia (and one or two in pre-colonial America) were larger than any European city in the eighteenth century, several were larger than London and an estimated 22 per cent of Japan's eighteenth-century population lived in cities versus 18 per cent for Western Europe (Pomeranz, 2000, p. 35).

There is some consensus, however, that with the reversal of Europe's long-term peripheral and dependent position within the Afro-Eurasian economy in the sixteenth century, a global political economy emerged. The development of long-distance trading networks in the late fifteenth century, together with overseas colonization, now gave Europe the advantage. Europe prevailed, not because it was superior, but because of 'clusters of fortuitous processes', a timely coalescence of political, economic, environmental, cultural and population changes that enabled the dynamic of capitalism and modernity to take off and facilitated (and still facilitates) dominance of the global political economy (Pomeranz, 2000, pp. 17–19; W. Thompson, 2000, pp. 34, 71–2). By 1750 a wealthier and more advanced Europe had overtaken India, China and Japan.

From this point onwards European empires, modernity and capitalism were implicitly linked. Indeed, the most advanced European empires (France, Holland, Britain) were those either most economically advanced and/or most influenced by the modernity stimulated by Enlightenment thought. In contrast, Spain, which, despite the riches of empire, had stagnated in semi-feudalism, failed to develop economically and its empire declined. Russia also declined to the level of Europe's 'second world periphery', precipitating a crisis of empire after 1870. In the eighteenth century Russia had embraced modernity and, argues Lieven (2000), openness to European innovations and foreign expertise contributed to Russia's success over the Ottoman Empire. The system of serfdom, however, was also at its highest extent and this acted as blockage to further modernization. The Russian empire continued to expand in the nineteenth century but remained a hybrid, combining aspects of a modern European empire and the tradition of autocratic land empire which stretches back to Antiquity. Russia remained economically backward, with agricultural techniques and productivity that lagged behind those of China as late as 1900 (pp. 284–6, 256–8, 419).

In interrogating the link between imperialism and modernity we must also consider the emergence of the modern nation-state and shift from autocracy to democracy. During the sixteenth century, early state building on the Western fringes of Europe (previously 'backward areas' of the Roman Empire) stimulated imperial ambitions, the formation of European overseas empires and new national identities (Armitage, 2001, p. 23). European maritime expansion now synchronized with struggles to attain hegemony in Europe as powerful states, France, England and Spain, emerged out of the warring kingdoms of the medieval period. Empires were essential to this modern state formation. As Kamen (2002) puts it, the empire created Spain rather than the other way round. In contrast, conquered areas of the world were either collapsing, loosely defined, pre-modern empires such as the Incas and the Aztecs, or *terra nullis*, empty 'virgin' territory which, in effect, was peopled by indigenous groups who had no state boundaries.

From the end of the eighteenth century, European imperialism was distinguished by a unique melding of capitalism, nationalism and democracy. States which embraced the new modernity stimulated by the European Enlightenment became stronger. A combination of a strong modern state and the most advanced capitalist economy had transformed Britain into the global hegemon by the nineteenth century. In France, the revolution forged new national identities and imperial ambitions; progress was disrupted by the Napoleonic Wars but strongly revived in the post-revolutionary era (Aldrich, 1996, p. 35). In contrast, the Spanish state, effectively an association of states under the leadership of the most powerful, Castile, was weakened in the nineteenth century by internal tensions, including civil war, and this contributed to Spain's imperial decline. Whilst modern unificatory nationalisms strengthened France, Britain and Germany, ethnic nationalisms weakened the Russian Empire and contributed to the break-up of the older Hapsburg and Ottoman empires (Lieven, 2000, p. 414).

In contrast to the pre-modern empires of China, Egypt and Rome, argues Wallerstein, the 'so-called nineteenth century empires' were, in effect, 'nation-states with colonial appendages', operating within the framework of the world economy (Wallerstein, 1974a, p. 163). Politics and economic power fused and there was more state intervention and control over imperialist policies (Hobsbawm, 1989). Imperialism was also vital to nation building and the creation of modern, unified states in the USA, Japan, Germany, Italy and Belgium. In Belgium imperialist projects diverted attention from ethnic conflicts within the artificially created state. Imperial ambitions were integral to building a strong American national identity that would heal the scars of the Civil War and transcend the ethnic identities of the large, diverse, immigrant population resulting from territorial expansion and economic development (Kaplan, 1993). In Japan, modernization of the state, precipitated by predatory European imperialism, created the conditions for Japanese imperialism (Case study 2).

So far we have established a broad link between modernity, capitalism and modern European empires. But neither imperialism nor capitalism is static and homogeneous. Capitalism was stimulated by early imperial expansion but did not emerge in its modern form until the late-eighteenth-century industrialization of Britain. Prior to that time it was merchant capital and trade that dominated, although these were informed by modern practices that differentiated them from early systems of international trade. The industrial capital generated through manufacturing and modern scientific and technological developments also differed from the finance capitalism that became increasingly important in the latter half of the nineteenth century. For Lenin, the imperialism that emerged c. 1900 was uniquely modern and distinct from early periods of colonization and colonial rule. In *Imperialism: the Highest Stage of Capitalism*, building on J. A. Hobson's critique of the imperialist impulses in modern finance capitalism, Lenin argued that:

> Capitalism has grown into a world system of colonial oppression and financial strangulation of the overwhelming majority of the people of the world by a handful of advanced countries . . . of particularly rich and powerful states which plunder the whole world . . . and out of their enormous super profits . . . bribe the leaders and an upper stratum of the labour aristocracy.
> (Lenin, 1916)

The nature of the epoch was characterized by the ascendancy of the bourgeoisie and the 'highest' stage of capitalism. This New Imperialism was different from what had gone before and was marked by a concentration of production and capital, developed so highly that it created monopolies; the fusion of banking capital with industrial capital and the creation of a financial oligarchy (ruling power elite); the export of capital, as distinguished from the export of commodities; the formation of international capitalist monopolies and the 'territorial division of the whole earth by the capitalist powers' (ibid.).

From the end of the nineteenth century until the collapse of socialism fierce theoretical debates raged between different anti-imperialist socialist and liberal intellectuals and political activists about the nature of the New Imperialism. For the Austrian socialist Karl Kautsky, this phase of 'ultra' or 'inter' imperialism was unique and characterized by peaceful co-operation rather than militaristic competition between expanding capitalist states. However, the outbreak of the First World War appeared to contradict his theories. Lenin agreed that capitalism was carving up the world but argued that war was inherent in this modern imperialism. There is some credibility in both these early-twentieth-century 'anti-imperialist' positions. After the Second World War Western imperialist states co-operated under US leadership but war remained significant in securing and defending imperialist interests.

Whether the New Imperialism represented a 'new' phase in capitalism or an acceleration of the world capitalist system that emerged in the sixteenth century is debatable. What is certain is that the era witnessed significant changes in the nature of global capitalism, the emergence of a powerful Western transnational capitalist class and a speeding up of progress. Lenin's New Imperialism also reflected the broader dominant discourse of the age: the 'new woman', the 'new journalism', the 'new' mass advertising, that reflected the acceleration of modernity through scientific, technological and social change. It arguably defined the specific characteristics of a modern imperialism which may or may not have ended with decolonization of formal empires (Chapter 6). It was also during this period that the civilizing mission intensified and a self-image of the West as 'lords of humankind' was consolidated.

Imperialism and the culture of modernity: the civilizing mission

The Enlightenment had a central role in articulating the superior, civilized nature of modern empires and is the major focus of critiques of Western modernity in postcolonial theory (Chapter 2). The 'reformulation' of empire with the Enlightenment and modernity signified an important, if imperfect, change in Western European political and cultural thought (Pagden, 1995). Commerce was now preferred to conquest in expanding European powers and humanism reshaped relations between the colonizer and the colonized. The development of the British Empire after 1750 provides an excellent example of the link between modernity, imperialism and capitalism. Cultural, political and economic changes already underway since the acquisition of an empire accelerated with industrialization and Britain reinvented itself as the most progressive and modern state. The abolition of slavery in the British Empire in 1838 removed the atavistic blockage of slave labour, and replaced it with more flexible 'free' labour. Britain's status was transformed from premier slaving nation to humanitarian 'champion of the oppressed', a democratic, liberal imperialist power with a mission to spread the 'light of civilization' into the dark and savage parts of the world (Hall, 2002). The twin elements of British modernity: secular, rational utilitarianism and evangelicalism that articulated a Christian morality for the modern world had a profound influence on British domestic culture, the nature of its imperial mission and colonial cultures (Van de Veer, 2004).

Britain was not alone in this modern rationalization of empire; Enlightenment ideals also informed French, Dutch, Belgian and German imperial discourse. All Western European powers transported the civilization of modernity to their empires, with ambivalent consequences for the colonized. Modern technology, railways, the telegraph and weapons were used to control and order colonial societies. Imperial expansion stimulated science and new botanical finds and facilitated the exploitation of 'exotic' environments, legitimizing colonial conquest. The Royal Botanical Gardens at Kew and similar gardens in other European capitals became central to the imperial 'improving' mission in the colonies (Drayton, 2000; McCracken, 1997). Imperialism thus had an important function in taming and ordering the 'wild' through the introduction of Western science: civilization was the commoditization of nature and universal technological strategies were used, regardless of the diversity of ecosystems (Adas, 1989). In India sacred land was 'wasted land' and Western technological superiority was demonstrated by 'making rivers behave' (Hill, 1995). Settlers moving into 'empty' lands had a destructive impact on indigenous ecosystems, applying science and technology to expand modern agriculture. Alfred Crosby (1986) argued that this prolific spread of Europeans, their plants, animals and diseases into 'neo Europes' over the globe, an 'empire of the dandelion', constituted ecological imperialism. Nor was a scientific interest in conservation or environmentalism – what Richard Grove (1995) calls 'green imperialism' – always beneficial, given Eurocentric perceptions of tropical nature. The tropical rainforest was 'invented' by Europeans as central to exoticization of the 'other', the myth of the 'last Eden', but also a realm of scientific study (Stott, 2001, p. 40). Conservation of the wild, linked to the European hunting and shooting craze that peaked in the 'high noon' of late imperialism, often crowded out and undermined indigenous hunting practices and thus adversely affected diets, and indigenous economic and social structures (Mackenzie, 1997, pp. 7, 81). 'Power hunting' supplanted 'subsistence hunting', the modern gun replaced the spear and hunters tamed the wild frontier. Hunting also became linked to natural history collecting and thus Western classification of colonial species (Mackenzie, 1997, pp. 36–41, 49).

The culture of modernity was spread by the white diasporas: the administrative elites in the non-settler colonies and the settlers who established mini Europes throughout the globe. When new continents were 'discovered' their indigenous names were erased – America was named after the conquistador, Amerigo Vespucci; Aotearoa became New Zealand. White settler societies transported Western progress to the 'darker', less 'enlightened', parts of the world and white settler rule was premised on spatial and cultural segregation from the indigenous peoples. Settlers' civilized status granted them full political rights and a degree of autonomy from the metropolitan imperial government, in contrast to the disenfranchised, dependent subject status of non-white colonized peoples (Evans and Grimshaw *et al.* (eds), 2003). Settlers remapped land taken from indigenous peoples and created new white spaces whose names evoked home – Victoria in Australia, New Hampshire and New York in the USA, Victoria Falls and Salisbury in Rhodesia, Windsor in Canada – or commemorated illustrious European founders, as in Melbourne and Sydney in Australia. Where indigenous names were retained (Toronto, Canada, for instance) any link with the past culture was erased. European cities, towns, churches and architecture transformed the landscape. As Aldrich writes of French Algeria:

> By the late nineteenth century, with farms and vineyards, French-style cities and European settlers, Algeria was well on the way to becoming Algérie française. The indigenous Berbers had been relegated to the background, a picturesque population living on the fringes of their own country.
>
> (Aldrich, 1996, p. 28)

This is an apt description of white settlement in general, although indigenous peoples were portrayed as more threatening presences in, for instance, British Southern Africa.

Gender was central to these Western definitions of modernity. Control of nature through science and technology was an enterprise associated with superior white masculinity. Imperial masculinity was also defined by rationality and enterprise and bourgeois values of financial prudence, the work ethic and duty (Bush, 2004). The superiority of 'civilized' white domesticity, sexuality and gender roles was central to defining a modern bourgeois colonial culture (Burton (ed.), 1999). The emancipation of white women and their relative freedom in a civilized, modern society was favourably contrasted with the drudgery, subservience, and patriarchal oppression of colonized women as typified by Oriental women, who continued to evoke seclusion behind the veil and imprisonment in the harem. In Egypt, Lord Cromer, Agent General from 1883 to 1907, was particularly antipathetic to how Islam treated women and saw it as a major obstacle to the modernization of Egypt. Feminism, argued Ahmed, served as a 'handmaid to colonialism', whether in the hands of patriarchal men like Cromer or Western feminists, and reinforced Western superiority (Ahmed, 1992). Imperial feminism in Britain and Germany articulated the importance of women to empire building and their 'maternalist role' in civilizing colonized women (Burton, 1994a; J. Bush, 1998; Wildenthal, 2001). Superior French femininity was represented through the imagery of the republican Marianne that transported to the colonies the ideal that 'the modern nation had a female incarnation' (Edwards, 2002). In the twentieth century, enfranchised Western women shared a vision of a modern empire on equal terms (Bush, 2004). Political emancipation further confirmed white women's superiority and enhanced their perceived fitness to rule over defenceless, colonized women and 'unmanly' men (Procida, 2002, pp. 141, 153). All white women have been (and continue to be) privileged by the superior white identities (Frankenberg, 1993). The emancipated status of Western women still affirms cultural superiority and the liberation of oppressed women has contributed to justifications for US intervention in Afghanistan and Iraq.

By the late nineteenth century, the USA had claimed Britain's position as the 'Empire of modernity' with a 'civilizing mission' to spread progress throughout the world. This 'historical convergence' of the USA and Europe represented a 'new world in the making', epitomized by the dominance of Western modernity (Ninkovich, 2001, p. 47). US imperialism was premised on advances in science and technology celebrated in the St Louis World Fair of 1904, themed around the centenary of the Louisiana Purchase from France and the San Francisco Panama–Pacific Exposition in 1915 that marked the completion of the Panama Canal. The opening of the canal demonstrated US superior skills in capital investment, labour management and technological expertise in contrast to the failed French initiative. While colossal women (Liberty, Columbia and the Republic) symbolized the democratic modernity of American nation, the male colossus, Hercules, evoked the mechanical triumph of the canal, as reflected in the poster advertising the 1915 exposition. In the guidebooks, the USA was represented as the inheritor of modernity and progress that could be traced back to Athens (Brown, 1993, pp. 140–6, 149).

As the most modern, humanitarian empires, the United States and Britain shared a mission to spread their superior Anglo-Saxon culture globally. US colonization of the Philippines after the Spanish American War (1898–1899) was driven by what President William McKinley called 'benevolent assimilation' which would win the 'confidence, respect and affection of the colonized' (cited in Rafael, 1993, p. 185). Vincent L Rafael observes that:

> . . . because colonization is about civilizing love and the love of civilization, it cannot but be absolutely distinct from the disruptive criminality of conquest. The allegory of benevolent assimilation effaces the violence by construing colonial rule as the most precious gift that 'the most civilized people' can render to those still caught in a state of barbarous disorder.
>
> (Rafael, 1993, p. 185)

But white love for 'little brown brothers', as Taft described Filipinos, was 'predicated on white supremacy enforced through practices of discipline and maintained by a network of surveillance'. American modernity also brought new forms of constructing the governable person. Thus, the colonial census was used to differentiate between 'wildness' and 'civility' (ibid., pp. 195, 198). This triumphalism of the West thus demands scrutiny; deep contradictions existed within the discourse of modernity as it was spread through imperialism to other parts of the globe, often with adverse consequences for colonized societies.

The contradictions of imperialism and modernity 1: race, culture and progress

Postcolonial critics and theorists have claimed that colonialism was universalizing in its assumptions about culture and modernity and this was the prime source of oppression of non-white peoples. Yet, as Colm Hogan (2000) has observed, racism and colonial ethnocentricism was, in effect, anti-universalist and assumed profound differences between cultures and peoples. The spread of modernity was double-edged and opened up fierce debates over the relationship between race, culture and progress. Anthropologists and many colonial administrators assumed a simple dichotomy between tradition and modernity and feared the negative and disintegrative impact of Western culture. Debates between assimilationists and segregationists were most intense in relation to 'primitive' peoples. In Australia and Canada assimilation into white culture until they disappeared was seen as the modern solution to the 'problem' of indigenous peoples, as they had 'weak' cultures and were unable to resist the influence of a more vigorous, superior culture. Children were taken from their families and placed in white homes and the claims of the 'stolen generation' are currently a central issue in the recognition of

Aboriginal rights in Australia (Armitage, 1995). Conversely, segregation of 'civilized' and 'savage' was advocated in other white settler societies, most viciously in South Africa, where it laid the foundation for Apartheid (Dubow, 1995). Here, as in the USA, segregation was premised on scientific racism (a term infused with the contradictions of modernity) as a defence of modernity against atavistic and decadent influences.

Throughout British Africa, segregation and separate development were defended on paternalist grounds as the best means of preserving traditional African culture from the corrupting influences of modernity. 'Alien' development on European lines was deemed harmful and the aim of British rule should be to 'create a good African and not a bad European' (Huxley, 1941, pp. 56–8). Whereas the British glorified the primitive and administered 'indirect' rule through traditional authorities, the French favoured the civilized *assimilé*, or Western-educated colonial subject who, in theory at least, could achieve equality through French citizenship. As Doyle (1986) observes, 'only in assimilation could the [modern] ideology of universal republicanism find imperialism acceptable' (p. 319). This assumed the desirability of adoption of a superior French culture and abandonment of one's own culture and has created deep problems in postcolonial France. The British adversely compared the centralized, bureaucratic French system with their system of decentralized, pragmatic, indirect rule. 'The Frenchman', wrote Margery Perham in 1933, 'does not preserve native culture because he does not share our respect for it . . . to him it is barbarism in spite of an aesthetic appreciation of its externals' (Perham, 1967). Ultimately, the British approach prevailed, gaining international endorsement at the 1919 Treaty of Versailles that established the League of Nations (Dimier, 2002, pp. 168–9).

In effect, there was little to choose between French *assimilation* and British 'indirect' rule. The Harvard professor, Robert Leslie Buell, painted a rosy picture of interracial harmony in the French African colonies (Buell, 1928, vol. 2, pp. 77–85), but other contemporary observers noted that the colour bar against *assimilés* was 'extraordinarily strong' (Gorer, 1935, pp. 77–8). The British rhetoric of 'protecting' Africans, that shaped international paternalistic humanitarianism after 1919 was premised on the 'divine right' of superior 'Anglo-Saxons' to rule the less civilized through separate development to ensure race purity. Colonial authorities also cultivated 'tradition' as a way of maintaining order lost when Africans embraced the 'less desirable' features of European culture – particularly modern forms of protest against colonial rule.

Policies of preserving 'tradition' and the scientific racism upon which they were implicitly based conflicted with the priorities of modern European colonialism, exposing contradictions in the discourse and practice of imperialism. Colonies had to be economically viable and the colonized transformed into modern governable subjects as peasant producers or urban and rural labourers. Taxation (whereby the colonized paid for the benefits of white rule) was used to coerce colonized subjects into the modern sector of the colonial economy linked into international capitalist markets (Bush and Maltby, 2004). Colonial administration thus exposed the tensions between the altruistic 'higher ideals' of modern empires and the pragmatics of colonial economics, between assimilation through progress and protection of native cultures. Frederick Lugard, Governor of Nigeria, 1912–18 and architect of British indirect rule administration, wanted to bring the 'benefits of civilization' with as little interference as possible with African laws and customs (Lugard, 1922, pp. 9, 30). Yet he ordered officials to make Africans pay in money and promoted enterprise, order, bureaucratic efficiency and economic development. Taxation, he emphasized, was a 'common burden [and universal necessity] of civilization' which African communities who aspired to be regarded as 'civilized' had to share (ibid., pp. 166–7, 208, 319).

Imperialism in Africa thus had a dual aspect as a modernizing force but also an agent of conservative reaction. In India, too, British officials and, later, nationalists were equally torn between steering India to a modern Western future or preserving an unchanging 'Oriental' culture (Washbrook, 1999, p. 420). Such dilemmas were compounded by the fact that incorporation of the colonized into the modern colonial economy introduced the less desirable and disruptive forces of modernity which threatened the colonial order. Liberal imperialists criticized those who wanted to hold back 'progress', yet they also feared the potential for chaos unleashed when dreams of preserving 'traditional culture' in aspic became futile. Postmodern theorists have been much engaged with these ambiguities of modernity but, as Marshall Berman (1983) points out, these were identified earlier by Karl Marx. Capitalist penetration through colonialism, argued Marx, compelled 'all nations' to adopt the 'bourgeois' mode of production and 'what it calls civilization', thus creating 'a world after its own image'. Yet such expansion also destroyed 'archaic and feudal orders' when:

All fixed, fast frozen relations, with their train of ancient and removable prejudices and opinions, are swept away . . . All that is solid melts into air, all that is holy is profaned, and men at last are forced to face with sober senses the real conditions of their lives and their relation with fellow men.

(Marx and Engels, 1852, pp. 39 ff.)

For Berman, Marx provided some of the most powerful insights into the nature of modernity and the links between modernist culture, economy and society. The experience of modernity was, and still is, characterized by a maelstrom of perpetual disintegration and renewal, of struggle and contradiction, possibilities and unity and disunity. Modernity, concludes Berman, alters cultures irrevocably but also offers liberation of the spirit from the constraints of 'tradition'. Imperialism involved the imposition of bourgeois order and forms of production and exchange but, in unleashing modernity, the imperialist (the agent of bourgeois values) became like Marx's sorcerer, 'who can no longer control the powers of the underworld he has summoned up' (Marx, cited in Berman, 1983, p. 101). This is clearly manifest in the dilemmas of administration created when the 'rational' order which colonial administrators tried to impose on African societies was thrown into chaos by the conjunction of modernity with the 'irrational' and 'primitive'. In this maelstrom of change, modernity thus also carried the seeds of opposition to empire and stimulated new forms of resistance.

Racism also exposed contradictions in European liberalism. As the dominant Western political discourse, liberalism had enormous power in the twentieth century, claiming to represent universal values and rights, including race and gender equality. In effect, liberalism was gendered (male) and culturally exclusive. This resulted in the exclusion or marginalization of those who failed to meet the standards set for inclusion in the democratic processes, economic benefits and intellectual and cultural projects that define Western modernity. The world's 'first' and most 'advanced' democracy, the USA, excluded its African American population until the Civil Rights struggles of the 1960s (Goldberg, 1993). In Britain modern men of supposed sensibility, committed to progress and Enlightenment humanism, still profited from the slave trade. Later modern European empires allowed only for the advancement and inclusion of Europeanized male colonized subjects. This echoed the 'protective' and paternalistic liberalism of the early nineteenth-century British utilitarians, such as James Mill, who argued that only those who were educated and thus 'civilized' were 'fit for citizenship'; the role of government was to protect the interests of those who did not fulfil these criteria (Held, 1987, pp. 66–71).

In the twentieth century these contradictions stimulated anti-imperialism and anti-Westernism. Colonial intellectuals were quick to point out the anti-democratic nature of colonial rule and during the Second World War anti-colonial nationalists demanded a more inclusive conceptualization of rights and citizenship. This incorporation of liberal democratic discourse into anti-colonial nationalism demonstrates that liberalism, like other 'isms', is not a monolithic discourse and can be interpreted both as a discourse of power and a liberatory ideology. Fundamental to philosophical liberalism is a commitment to the universal principles of reason and moral values which presuppose human rights. As David Theo Goldberg points out, such principles are not exclusively those of the dominant class, and may be contested and revised through political action (Goldberg, 1994, pp. 17–18). This progressive vision of universal liberal values helps us to understand the ways in which Black oppositional discourses reworked Western liberalism in articulating their grievances against racism and imperialism. Liberal values, as an expression of progressive modernity, were incorporated into more radical anti-imperialism or anti-racism in the colonies and imperial centres. Negotiating the complex impact of modernity constituted an important consciousness-raising process for the colonized, which progressed the forces of resistance (Gilroy, 1993). Modernity also inspired new dreams of freedom, articulated through the oppositional discourses of, for instance, pan-Africanism and pan-Arabism. But the penetration of modernity could also result in fragmented forms of consciousness which impeded and problematized Black emancipatory struggles (Bush, 1999).

The contradictions of imperialism and modernity 2: anti-democratic and atavistic forces in imperial culture

Imperial governance was undemocratic, excluding the colonized from citizenship, extending taxation without representation and implementing segregationist racial policies. Modern ideas, particularly nationalism and/or trade unionism, stimulated anti-colonialism and were thus viewed as major threats to imperial rule. European men and women had more personal power than would ever have been possible 'back home' and more remote rural areas became the personal feudal fiefdoms of administrators and settlers. Expatriates, argued the anti-imperial critic J. A. Hobson, constituted 'a superior caste living an artificial life removed from all the healthy restraints of ordinary European society' who had a 'baleful influence' in both colony and metropole, where they undermined progressive British culture (Hobson, 1988, 1902, pp. 150–1). Hobson also argued that imperialism worked against democracy in the imperial centre (Hobson, 1988, 1902). The discourse of imperialism post-1880 was framed in the language of modernity, science and progress, but there were also countervailing, anti-democratic tendencies reflected in the centralization of power and rise of right-wing nationalism and associated racial discourses. In Britain and other advanced imperial states, the

New Imperialism was a unifying project that counterbalanced new political challenges of socialism, feminism and trade unionism, 'enemies within' that challenged the hegemony of the powerful and undermined empire.

To what extent was imperial culture, in colony and imperial centre, modern or atavistic, that is, influenced by pre-modern 'feudal' values? In 1919, Schumpeter conceptualized imperialism as 'dark and irrational' compared with capitalism that was 'progressive and rational'. It served the needs of certain classes and was motivated by a 'feudal atavism', an 'objectless disposition' to dominate as a continuation of ancient imperial feudal states, such as Japan and pre-industrial European states (Schumpeter, 1919, p. 95). Empire thus became an outlet for old landed interests under pressure from new social groups and also provided employment for the expanding middle classes who now abandoned trade and industry in favour of 'aristocratic' values. Hobson acknowledged that imperialism was negative and parasitic but argued that the late nineteenth century witnessed a merger of the aristocratic and middle classes who rejected business in favour of finance capitalism and the 'service' sector, the most modern forms of capitalism (Cain, 2002). This new class of 'gentlemanly' capitalists, crucial to understanding the dynamics of late-imperialist expansion, was centred on London and South East England and represented an amalgam of old wealth united by a common culture of empire based on bourgeois, but 'gentlemanly', values. It was this class who also provided the imperial administrators, redefining the imperial mission as the 'export version' of the 'gentlemanly' order (Cain and Hopkins, 1993, pp. 25–6, 131–2, 201, 233). Expatriate cultures did develop atavistic tendencies, clinging on to values which had become outmoded in the modern metropolitan centre and characterized by anomie and decadence. But it was modern bourgeois, not feudal, values that informed the culture of empire (Stoler and Cooper, 1997) and, in the informal empires in Latin America and China, the values of bourgeois 'gentlemanly capitalism' predominated. This given, modern bourgeois values were melded with atavistic values of racial and cultural superiority. Imperial culture was thus characterized by tensions between the forces of atavism and the progressive vision associated with modern empires.

The contradictions between imperialism and modernity intensified in the interwar years when Western liberal democracy was threatened by both fascism and communism. The progressive and liberal British Empire was now defined in opposition to Marxist and fascist totalitarianism. The position of the communist Soviet Union was complex. In the 1930s, when rapid modernization through industrialization was taking place, the Soviet Union represented itself as the future state, the post-capitalist modernity that benefited the masses, not the few. Radical anti-colonialists regarded the Soviet Union as an ally in the struggle against imperialism. Conversely, to French and British imperialists, Stalin was a new and tyrannical tsar bent on imperial expansion and communism represented the major threat to their empires. Fascism posed different dilemmas. A complex blend of modernity and archaic culture, fascism embraced science and modernism in architecture, used complex technologies and bureaucracies, and perpetuated capitalism, but suppressed the liberal democratic culture associated with modernity. For Zygmunt Bauman the Holocaust was predominantly a product of modernity (Bauman, 1989). Eugenic policies associated with German racial policies were also justified by modern science and endorsed in the USA and Scandinavia (Black, 2004).

In the view of radical analysts the progressive modernity of democracy was universally in retreat by the 1930s. Democratic European governments became more reactionary, fascist tendencies were evident in Britain and France and the old imperial powers of Spain and Portugal became fascist dictatorships. Colonial civil liberties declined and the international human-itarianism of the League of Nations was undermined as Italy, Germany and Japan all contravened the League's resolutions in embarking on their imperial projects (Bush, 1999, p. 262). Fascist Italy and Germany made new colonial claims and Italy invaded Ethiopia in 1935; plans for the expansion of the continental German Empire eastwards took shape. In Japan a new style 'Emperor fascism' emerged, blending Japan's drive towards modernity with atavistic tendencies which renewed imperial expansion (Case study 2). These developments highlighted the essential incompatibility between empire and democracy first commented on by American anti-imperialists in the 1890s (Ninkovich, 2001, p. 45; Barnes, 1939), but also stimulated anti-colonial challenges to the Eurocentricism inherent in the concept of modernity, whether expressed through liberalism or socialism.

Modernity and the ambiguities of development in the postcolonial world

After the First World War a combination of factors, including the anti-democratic nature of colonial rule, intensification of economic exploitation, Western racism, the fascist threat and the socialist promise of a more equal world, stimulated anti-colonial nationalist movements. During and after the Second World War, the influence of socialism was marginalized by the Western powers and most newly independent nation-states initially adopted the Western political model and the dominant model of development was modernization theory, 'following in the footsteps of the West' (Rostow, 1960). Ludden (1992) argued that development was a legacy of colonialism that demonstrated the dualism between modernity and tradition. Yet it became 'such a secure category of the modern' that it has disguised its own colonial roots as well as its ongoing and intimate relationship with Western hegemony. The idea developed out of colonial concerns with managing the economy, collecting data and revenue but also from government initiatives to tackle the poverty and backwardness that impeded the modern imperial mission (for instance, Anstey, 1929).

The emergence of ex-colonial, independent Third World nations regenerated discussion of the link between capitalism, imperialism and modernity and the nature of its impact on the ex-colonized. Radical theorists argued that development on Western lines secured the ongoing domination of capitalism and continuing neo-imperialist relations in the postcolonial world (Amin, 1973; Dos Santos, 1970). The very term 'Third World' suggested a continued hierarchy of modernist development. The First World constituted the rich, developed countries mainly in the West (but including Japan, Australia and 'white' South Africa); the Second World embraced the more 'backward' socialist states, with China and the Soviet Union at the centre; and the Third World included all those parts of the globe that had been colonized (Worsley, 1964). The terminology arguably concealed the ongoing combined but uneven development of Western capitalism that persisted when these 'worlds' dissolved with the end of socialism (Chapter 6).

But is the impact of capitalism on the development of the non-Western world always negative? Marx argued that capitalism revolutionized social relations in the colonies and gave the oppressed peoples the means and method of achieving their own liberation. Bill Warren returned to Marx in his provocative critique of dependency theory and the concept of neo-colonialism, which, he argued, simply regurgitated in modern form the Leninist argument that parasitic capitalism held colonies in a dependent thrall. Criticizing 'anti-capitalist romanticism', he argued that colonialism was both 'Dr Jekyll and Mr. Hyde'. Imperialism, as a 'pioneer' of capitalism, acted as a 'powerful engine of progressive social change' and, as capitalism advanced, dependency and imperialism declined. Western education, in particular, was 'deeply subversive' of traditional outlooks and pre-capitalist structures facilitating individualism, rationalism and democracy (Warren, 1980, pp. 3, 9, 125, 135). Marx ultimately saw capitalism as a destructive force, a transitory phase that would lead to communism. For Warren, modernization through capitalism brought uneven, but positive, modern development.

When Warren's *Imperialism: Pioneer of Capitalism* was published in 1980 it was criticized for being Eurocentric and reiterating a revised form of modernization theory – a process of one-way transfer that took no account of the dialectics or resistance to Western hegemony (Pieterse, 1990, p. 11). Additionally, Warren's arguments may have had relevance to the experiences of the new Asian economies, such as Korea, but were far less relevant to Africa, the focus of his book, where the development of the 1970s had gone into reverse by the 1980s. With the imposition of neo-liberal economic policies that arguably reflected a 'new' imperialism, as distinct from the New Imperialism of the c. 1880–1914 era, global inequalities deepened. Neo-liberal globalization involved rolling back the state, reducing subsidies, promoting privatization and developing export sectors to integrate developing economies more fully into the global capitalist free market system. China and India may have witnessed spectacular growth but class inequalities within states in both the developed and less developed world widened. Aid to poorer countries was made contingent on 'good governance', democratization and improved human rights. Critics argued that this constituted a new form of modernization theory that promoted individual enterprise and the removal of barriers to progress, including 'tradition', to spread the universal, 'superior' values of Western liberal democracy. Yet as Amin (2001) noted, ironically, democracy was formerly regarded as a luxury of the developed states who had delivered material benefits to the majority – hence Western support for autocratic regimes in Africa and for Latin American dictators. Additionally, the modernizing economic 'miracles' in the Far East (Korea, Taiwan) were achieved with strong state intervention under military dictatorships. Finally, although democracy and the market were supposed to mutually reinforce one another, in effect, the market promoted wider inequalities (pp. 7–9).

Imperialism: Pioneer of Capitalism stimulated a re-evaluation of development theory, Marxist, neo-Marxist and liberal – in particular the over-prioritization of economic and political factors at the expense of culture. Development studies, both Marxist and liberal, were rejected as universalizing or West-centred (Amin, 1990) and, argued Wolfe (1997), neither modernization nor underdevelopment theories questioned the concept or value of development *per se* (Wolfe, 1997, p. 395). There was also a backlash from the right in defence of modernity against the 'ethic of Third Worldism', allegedly promoted by 'left-wing intellectuals and journalists' from the 1960s, that implicated Western 'civilization, science and modernity' in the 'imperialistic oppression' of the non-West (Kimball, 2001, pp. 1–3). Bruckner (1986) argued that political correctness and liberal guilt were a form of 'Western masochism' that resulted in a distorted Western pity for the non-West, but also in glorification of the simplicities of primitivism. It was these 'passionate Third Worldists' who were really holding poor nations back from development by exploiting them for their own ideological purposes: such compassion for the suffering poor was really a form of contempt. Roger Sandall (2000) also criticized Western 'designer tribalism', or glorification of the primitive in the tradition of Rousseau's 'Noble Savage', arguing that most traditional cultures are repressive and economically and artistically backward (Sandall, 2000). Certainly, the return to cultural essentialism and prioritization of cultural difference and diversity have done little to challenge widening economic inequalities. Nonetheless, as Furedi (1995) points out, we must be wary of such reassertions of superior Western values over the 'backward and primitive' as they have done much to justify the 'new' imperialism (Chapter 6).

There is a case to be made for modernity: peasant lives are harsh, impoverished and precarious and poorer societies should have as much right to the benefits of modernity as those in the West. The problem is that modernity was spread through Western imperialism and involved a cultural and economic power relationship. Without such intervention non-Western societies would arguably have embraced modernity but on their own terms and timescale. Indeed, as already emphasized, the West never had a monopoly on modernity and gained much from more advanced Asian cultures in its own development (Hobson, 2004). Universalizing aspects of modernity, such as democracy and technological and economic development, can have a positive impact in conjunction with a conscious effort to understand what is common across different cultures. What we must disassociate from, argues Hogan (2000), is absolutism, the ethnocentricism of the West, an unselfconscious assumption that one culturally particular set of values and practices applies to everyone and everyone thinks (or should think) the same way.

Imperialism, modernity and Eurocentrism: challenges to Western knowledge

Imperialism and colonization constructed a model of the world that placed Europe at the centre and resulted in Eurocentric histories (Blaut, 1993). Modernity has produced a polarized, linear, universalist narrative of the civilized West versus the backward 'Rest', as represented in William McNeill's *Rise of the West* (1960). The influential early-nineteenth-century German liberal philosopher, Hegel, argued that, given the continuing upward progress of the West towards liberal democracy and civilization, it was the necessary fate of Asiatic empires (including China) to be subjected to Europeans (Hegel, 1956, pp. 142–3). Marx, for differing reasons, also believed that Asia was held back by the 'Asiatic mode of production' and 'oriental despotism' and could only be brought into the history of modernity though contact with Western culture. Western knowledge produced a hierarchy of progress that gelled into a scientific racism exemplified in the following quote by the eminent Victorian explorer, Sir Richard Burton:

> I believe the European to be the brains, the Asiatic the heart, the American and African the arms and the Australian the feet, of the man-figure . . . the negro ranks between the Australian and the Indian – popularly called Red – who is above him . . .
>
> (Burton, 1863, p. 12)

The idea of time and history as located in the dynamic West has had a particularly profound influence on conceptions of African history (Feierman, 1995, p. 41). For Hegel (who based his evidence on 'copious' second-hand missionary accounts) Africa was the 'unhistorical' only on the 'threshold' of the world's history:

> Africa Proper as far as history goes back . . . has remained – for all purposes of connection with the rest of the world – shut up: it is the Gold-land compressed within itself – the land of childhood . . . beyond self-conscious history . . . enveloped in the dark mantle of night.
>
> (Hegel, 1956, pp. 91–9)

The 'sensual' negro represented man in his 'completely wild and untamed state' and was therefore incapable of development or progress (ibid.). On the eve of independence this view still prevailed. 'In the race for progress', asks Elspeth Huxley, chronicler of white colonization of Kenya, 'why alone among the races of mankind did [the Bantu] stand still . . . building . . . no permanent houses, finding no means to improve their soil, evolving no industries, above all inventing no written word and creating no form of art?' (Huxley, 1941, pp. 16–17). The Hegelian 'myth' of Africa, argued Said (1993, p. 168), proved powerful and enduring and was absorbed into Western liberalism and Marxism.

There has been a mounting academic challenge to this Eurocentrism. At each major turning point in its development up to 1800, argues Hobson (2004), Europe benefited from the assimilation of Eastern technologies and ideas. After that date Asia contributed land, labour and resources to building

European empires. Rather than passive and marginalized, Asia was crucial to the rise of the West. From a different perspective, postmodernist and post-colonial theorists have challenged the grand narratives of liberalism and Marxism that privileged the West. Eurocentric conceptions of history, assuming an irreversible and progressive linear progress unleashed by the dynamic of modernity and related concepts of temporality, have been subjected to critical scrutiny. Although at times obscurantist, over-theorized and jargon-ridden, developing tortuous and circular arguments, their critique of the epistemological foundations of modernity and interrogation of its relationship to colonial power has some validity. Yet, as Dipesh Chakrabarty (2001) conceded, postcolonial histories that prioritize the view from the margins can never transcend the influence of European epistemologies as a framework for analysis. Europe both liberated and constrained colonial development and European (Western) thought and modernity have become everybody's heritage through the globalizing impact of imperialism.

The non-West is still doomed to be never quite modern. What is needed, argued Chakrabarty, is the freeing of European thought from Eurocentrism and a renewal from the margins through blending the analytical tradition of Marxian thought, the universal narrative of the historical development of capital (and its 'intimate handmaidens', imperialism and colonialism) and Heidegger's hermeneutic traditions that produce 'affective histories'. Such histories stress human belonging, diversity and difference and modify and disrupt the universalizing tendencies of Western historicism, liberal and Marxist. Such histories subvert the chronological straitjacket of what Walter Benjamin termed the 'secular, empty, and homogenous time of history'. Thus to 'provincialize' European thought is 'to hold in permanent tension a dialogue between two contradictory points of view': Western intellectual thought and historicism must be engaged with in a more positive sense, 'decolonized' and reclaimed, rather than simply critically deconstructed and dissolved into cultural relativism and spatial and chronological fragmentation (Chakrabarty, 2001, pp. 16, 23, 254).

The ambiguities embedded in modernity suggest a continuous but shifting relationship between the modern and the archaic. Western modernity was far from monolithic and there is no coherent and stable modernity resulting in 'upward, ever upward' progress, the liberal view of history. New perspectives on modernity, influenced by postmodernism, have emphasized the importance of the colonial periphery and multiple centres of modernity. Recent literary works on *creolité* have reversed the origins of modernity in exploring how new/modern hybridized cultures emerged in the Caribbean. Creole cultures have been reconceptualized as dynamic, new and unique, forged through, and in conflict with, European modernity (Dash, 1998). Caribbean slavery created new, 'modern' people who had to negotiate many of the contradictions, dualities and ambiguities that faced the postcolonial migrant (David Brion Davis, 1984, p. 14). The African slave trade and other diasporic migrations, free and coerced, associated with imperial expansion, were crucibles of cultural modernity and created new diasporic cultures. Slaves, sailors and poor European migrants to the Americas also made a significant contribution to the political struggles for citizenship and democracy stimulated by the Enlightenment (Linebaugh and Rediker, 2000). As the people of the periphery migrated into the imperial centres, metropolitan cities like Paris and London took on the 'creolised multi-ethnic look' of a nineteenth-century colonial centre (Wolfe, 1997, p. 401). New perspectives on modernity have thus challenged the primacy of the West in defining what constitutes 'modern'.

***

As the world reached the year 2000, the link between modernity and imperialism remained unresolved. In Richard Drayton's words: 'Our world is still in shock from the great "modernising" projects of capital, government, science and imperialism' (Drayton, 2000, p. 274). In the long line of modernizers stretching back to the Enlightenment, Western politicians continued to see modernity as a unilinear, and inevitably good, historical process, but the inherent contradictions in modernity also persisted. Some ways of being 'modern', suggested John Gray (2003), are monstrous, as in Hitler's use of new technologies to commit genocide and Stalin's use of terror in the name of creating a modern economy. Islamic fundamentalism, like Nazism, also reflected the paradoxes of the modern. al-Qaida's anti-Western terrorism, argued Gray, combined the use of modern technology with 'non-rational' mystic or religious beliefs. But, equally, the ultramodern USA in effect became a less secular regime than Turkey, controlled by right-wing fundamentalist Christians who refuted scientific evidence for evolution and saw the 'clash of civilizations' stimulated by Islamic fundamentalism as a new Crusade of Christians against Islam (Ali, 2003).

Contradictions inherent in the spread of modernity and democracy through imperialism also persisted. The justification of the invasion of Iraq in 2003 was to bring the benefits of modernity to the Middle East according to the neo-conservative vision of free markets and democracy. Yet, at the same time as the USA was promoting democracy in Iraq and elsewhere, it was supporting ruthless tyrants in Kazakhstan to secure future oil interests. As in the past, the USA has adopted different policies depending on shifting imperial interests. Democracy is a defining characteristic of modernity but, concluded Samir Amin (2001), neither modernity nor democracy has reached the end of its potential development. Democratization is a better term as this denotes a dynamic, unfinished process in the spread of a more enabling form of modernity, which will bring the promise of greater equality. Democratic rights were never the spontaneous result of capitalist development but a product of the struggles of victims of the system, men and women (pp. 8, 10). In the imperial context, these struggles for democracy and autonomy from Western dominance have been complex and protracted. The following Case study explores these complexities through the response of Japan and China to the intrusion of modernity, capitalism and Westernization through imperialism.

Case study 2
China and Japan: modernity, imperialism and anti-Westernism

China and Japan provide useful case studies to demonstrate the relationship between capitalism, imperialism and modernity. Understanding the contemporary positioning of both states in the global economy demands a long view of their responses to Western culture. Reactions to modernity, as represented by predatory European and US imperialism, were seminal to the collapse of the Chinese Empire and the rise of Japanese imperialism. In the scramble for the Far East in the latter part of the nineteenth century, imperialist powers took advantage of the relative weakness of China and Japan. Both societies had declined because of economic failures that resulted in demographic, and other social, pressures. In China, this led to internal migrations and group conflict, an inability of peasants to pay taxes and an overextended and inefficient bureaucracy. With underfed, demoralized troops, the Chinese imperial state was unable to resist the superior military might of the French and British, failed to bring in reforms and was further weakened by Western imperial penetration that stimulated domestic rebellion (W. R. Thompson, 2000, p. 94). Initially vulnerable, state-led modernization programmes enabled Japan to join the Western imperial 'club'. Why did China decline into chaos in response to Western imperial penetration and Japan become an imperial power in its own right? Why did Chinese and Japanese cultures interact differently with Western modernity? To what extent did engagement with imperialism stimulate modernization but also anti-Westernism, resistance and nationalism in both China and Japan?

China: imperial decline and political turmoil

At the point of the 'great divergence' in the eighteenth century, China was, in many respects, more advanced than Europe in relation to key features of modernity: the use of labour and land that conformed to a market economy; commercialization; commoditization of goods; demographic and proto-industrial growth and urbanization (Pomeranz, 2000; Wong, 1997). Medicine was not very effective anywhere in the world but Asian cities, argues Pomeranz (2000), were far ahead in public health, sanitation and the provision of clean water. Smallpox prevention seems to have been independently developed in the eighteenth century in Europe, China and India (p. 46). Why, then, did China become vulnerable to European penetration? A key reason is China's isolation from international markets. Between 1405 and 1433, Zheng He (Cheng Ho), appointed Admiral of the Western Seas by the emperor, embarked on a number of epic voyages. Whereas Columbus had only three vessels, Zheng He had over 60 and sailed some 35,000 miles, visiting 30 countries (Levathes, 1996). China could have acquired a seaborne empire in East Africa and Asia but, instead, the Chinese imperial rulers closed the 'Middle Kingdom' off from the outer world, leaving the field open to the predatory European seaborne empires. Economic factors are also relevant. Because of the very labour-intensive, year-round multi-cropping, enormous amounts of work were needed to preserve a fragile economy: 'Old World cores' like China could not create a factory labour force in the same way as in Britain; gender relations were more 'progressive' in the West in that women were more able to move into factory work (Pomeranz, 2000, pp. 288–9; Goldstone, 1996).

European contact with China went back more than a thousand years (Cameron, 1989), but by the end of the eighteenth century, whilst China's achievements in the imperial period were recognized, knowledge of the country remained scanty. As interest increased, an East India Company-sponsored embassy to China extended British knowledge of the region but failed to achieve desired trade treaties and the establishment of a diplomatic mission (Singer, 1992). In the early nineteenth century increasing contact with Europeans compounded internal problems. Between 1800 and 1840 there was local resistance to *Gaijin* (foreigners), accompanied by further decline of the Qing (Manchu) imperial dynasty. Chinese culture was increasingly viewed as decadent and a blockage to economic development. The turning point in relations between Britain and China were the 1839–40 'Opium Wars', so called because the British gained a monopoly on the growth of opium in India and control of the opium trade. This was British gunboat diplomacy to force the Chinese to open up to trade and allow the British to penetrate the lucrative opium, silk, tea and silver trade. The wars were a 'clash of two cultures with differing world views' and demonstrated the failure of Chinese to resist British imperial expansion. In addition to the expansion of free trade, the 'Opium Wars' were justified as a fight against 'backwardness' and by the belief that China should be opened up for its own good by modern agents, merchants and missionaries (Marchant, 2002, pp. 43, 47). Rather than an 'Opium War', Britain's conflict with China can be interpreted as an assertion of British cultural and economic superiority (Gelber, 2004). Whatever the underlying reasons, under the grossly unequal Treaty of Nanking, 1842, the Treaty Ports were established and Britain acquired a 150-year lease on Hong Kong. With British control of the trade, opium addiction achieved crisis levels and undermined the Chinese capacity to fend off imperialism and achieve the modernization that would enable it to match Japanese development.

Europeans became increasingly preoccupied with facets of Chinese culture they regarded as barbaric and an affront to civilized, modern values, such as foot binding of women, female slavery and the practice of concubinage, the murder of girl children and opium smoking. If Orientalist constructs of the Chinese increasingly defined the relationship between Europe and China (Bickers, 1999), the Chinese had their own 'Oriental racism'. To the Chinese, Europeans were the barbarians and white 'foreign devils' or ghosts, who smelled of raw chicken and whose women had tails (Han, 1972, 1965). The period 1840–1900, however, witnessed more intense cultural penetration through missionaries, who saw the Chinese as backward, heathen and decadent (see Figure 3.1). The evangelical China Inland Mission pushed far into 'untouched' China to save souls (Porter, 2004). Defeat by the British showed that Confucian China was in need of reform and scientific and technical development and the Chinese intelligentsia engaged increasingly with the ideas of modernity. But deepening strains were reflected in the anti-Qing Taiping rebellions (1850–64).

By 1885 other European powers had joined the scramble for Asia and China had lost important territories formerly in her sphere of influence: Indochina to France, Burma to Britain, the Northern Frontier to Russia's 'civilizing mission' in Asia and, in 1895, the Ryukyu Islands, Formosa (Taiwan) and Korea to a now-resurgent Japan (see Map 5, p. xxii). In China imperialist penetration was reflected in acquisition of treaty ports, trading concessions and increased foreign investment and control of the economy. Expatriate communities – European and Japanese in Chinese cities, particularly Shanghai – expanded (Bickers, 1999). International free-trade open door policies (formulated by the USA to protect its own interests) facilitated the 'golden age'

Figure 3.1   Representations of 'heathen' and 'native' China: 'A Chinese
opium den'

of 'gentlemanly capitalism', 1905–11, a 'cooperative financial imperialism'
centred on a British programme of foreign-financed infrastructure (Petersson,
2002, p. 109). China maintained nominal political sovereignty but had
become what Lenin termed a 'semi colony', dominated by a combination of
formal and informal imperialism.

Was imperialist penetration of China benevolent or malevolent? Jürgen
Osterhammel (1986) emphasizes the exploitative role of economic imperialism

in China and its link with the two Chinese revolutions (1911 and 1949). By 1911, argued Bailey (1988), China was a 'demoralised ruin' characterized by the corruption and fragmentation of the state. Two-thirds of businesses and 41 per cent of railways were foreign-owned. As the state disintegrated into warlordism after 1916, even more concessions were sold to foreigners and, in the 1920s, 25 per cent of the national income went to pay off foreign loans. Foreign investment increased and the Japanese imperial presence expanded. Eighty per cent of Chinese were peasants and imperialism intensified poverty and distress (ibid.). Ch'en agrees that, although traditional attitudes were 'indefensible', imperialism had mostly negative consequences and did little to fulfil the humanitarian mission of modernizing and raising the Chinese standard of living. From 1842 to 1942, he argues, China was treated by the West with 'distrust, ridicule, and disdain, mingled . . . with pity and charity, only occasionally with sympathy and friendliness' (Ch'en, 1979, pp. 33, 377–8). Bailey (1988) and Bickers (1999) also cite the humiliation of the Chinese by Westerners, including the 'Apartheid' in Shanghai. Conversely, revisionists like Jack Gray (2002) and Marchant (2002) reject the concept of informal empire and argue that the Western powers made a positive contribution to growth in China.

The penetration of Western modernity had both positive and negative consequences, intensifying internal fissures between traditional and modern elements that weakened China's capacity to resist imperialism but also catalysing change. Modernizers, often young men educated in Britain and the USA, rejected modernization imposed through imperialist control of the economy but advocated Westernization through the emancipation of women, adoption of Western mathematics, science and technology and democracy (Ch'en, 1979). They wanted to cherry-pick the best from Western culture in the interests of building a strong China whilst rejecting 'trivial and vulgar' elements such as Christianity (Feng Kuei-Fen 'On the Adoption of Western Learning', c.1860, cited in Snyder (ed.), 1962). The republican nationalists of the *Kuo-min-tang* (revolution of the people of the country) or KMT, led by Sun Yat Sen, gave political voice to this modernizing faction. The KMT admired Japan's successful modernization (below) and this deepened the conflict with the Confucian conservatives, who wished to preserve the traditions of the Chinese Empire.

Hostility to both 'Western devils' and Chinese 'Westernizers' intensified during and after the Boxer Uprising, 1899–1900. Xenophobic revivalism was encouraged by the Qings, who still refused to make reforms and this further stimulated the modernizing nationalist faction. The *I-ho-ch'uan* (righteous harmony fists) was a secret society of Boxers, which made its appearance in

Shandung Province in North China in 1899. Every Boxer was assured that he was immune from death since his body was protected by magic, and looting, burning, robbing and killing were soon out of control. The initial targets were Roman Catholic missionaries and converted Chinese who refused to participate in the rituals needed to save local communities from famine. Boxer placards also accused Christians of poisoning wells. Christianity was resented by modernizers and traditionalists and, as Che'en observed, the Chinese Empire posed 'the greatest challenge' to Christians. There were only a few Protestant converts but Catholicism, present since the eighteenth century, was firmly rooted in the rural areas. By 1914 there were 1.5 million Catholics in China, although many were allegedly 'rice Christians' who had converted for material gain, and there were no influential converts (Ch'en, 1979, pp. 92, 101).

The Boxer Uprising drew widespread support as it developed into wider opposition to Western 'foreign devils' who disturbed the Middle Kingdom and urged the Chinese to 'turn their backs on Heaven' and forget their ancestors. Boxers were exhorted to attack the intrusion of Western power, to 'Push aside the railway tracks . . . Pull out the telegraph poles . . . destroy the steamers' so that 'the great France will grow cold and downhearted' and the English and Russians 'disperse'. This would revive the prosperity of the 'whole Elegant Empire of the Great Ching [Qing] Dynasty' (Boxer placards cited in Snyder (ed.), 1962). The rebellion culminated in the siege of the foreign legations in Beijing, June–August, 1900, that precipitated an international crisis and intervention by the imperialist powers. China, a main supplier of cheap labour to meet the demands of expanding Western imperial economies now represented the 'Yellow Peril', a threat to modern civilization. The expatriate British community regarded the attacks on Europeans, deaths of missionaries and the siege of the legations as the equivalent of the 1857 Indian Mutiny, although historical amnesia has now erased the more negative impact of Britain in China (Bickers, 2000, p. 17). A debate, however, continues in Chinese history as to whether the Boxers were a patriotic movement or simply an unruly uprising of xenophobic peasants who failed to drive out the foreigners. To modern nationalists the Boxers embodied the very characteristics that they believed had led to China's weakness. Later, Communist historians represented the Boxers as a peasant rebellion against foreign imperialism. The Boxer Uprising was subsequently revised as the 'Invasion of the Eight Allied Armies', shifting the focus to the foreign response (Cohen, 1997).

After the rebellion was put down with the help of the West, the Qings were forced to make reforms. In 1905, the National Army established a military government that aimed 'to cleanse away two hundred and sixty years of barbarous filth [and] restore our four thousand year fatherland'. This was the beginning of national revolution. The target of hostility was the Manchus, the Tartar descendants of the 'Eastern barbarians beyond the Great Wall'. Restoring China was to make 'China the China of the [Han] Chinese'. KMT nationalist ideology was based on equality and political rights. The aim was to create a 'socialist state' through 'social improvements' and reform of land ownership. 'Evils in social customs' – keeping slaves, foot binding – 'the poison of opium' and 'the obstructions of geomancy' – *feng-shui* – were to be prohibited (Sun Yat Sen's Early Revolutionary Program, 1905, in Mason (ed.), 1977, pp. 134–8). The Empress Tzu (Cixi) died in 1908 and was succeeded by Pu Li. In the 1911 revolution the emperor was deposed and the KMT leader, Sun Yat Sen, became prime minister of the new Republic of China.

The Republican era, 1911–49, was a period of upheaval and change. There was an influx of White Russians after 1917 and the Japanese presence was further raised when Japan was given Germany's Chinese concessions at the Treaty of Versailles in 1919. Tensions between the Chinese and Japanese in Shanghai and the increasing insecurity of the expatriate community during the turbulent interwar period are sensitively explored in Kazuo Ishiguro's novel, *When we were Orphans* (2000). China disintegrated into warlordism and, after 1929, civil war between communists and nationalists. Chaos worsened with the Japanese invasion in 1936. Ch'en (1979) argued that dynamic Soviet modernity now became more attractive than the stagnating modernity of the old imperial powers threatened by economic instability and fascism (p. 31). In popular left analyses of the 1960s and 1970s this communist vitality was contrasted with nationalist decline.

In a provocative revisionist study, Rana Mitter (2000a) has argued that the Republican era of the 1920s saw some of the most innovative and exciting social and cultural experiments ever seen in China and claims that some of the warlords dismissed in communist historiography as bandits helped to create an infrastructure for modern China. In effect, this was a pivotal period in the problematic transition towards modernity, epitomized by the May 4th Movement in 1919, a protest against imperialism and concessions given to Japan at the Treaty of Versailles and a rejection of tradition in favour of modernity, including the emancipation of women. China was now outward-looking, liberal and progressive, with a possibility of moving towards democracy and industrialization; it was 'a more intellectually varied period . . . than the stifling conformism of Maoist China' (pp. 30–31). This progress, argues Mitter, was blocked by Japanese aggression and, subsequently, the diversion of communism, with its erasure of the past, although the ethos of May 4th has now returned to post-Maoist China (Mitter, 2004). Gray (1990) and Marchant (2002) also argue that the Nationalists inherited the empire intact in 1911, with the framework of a modern state, and that the main barrier to progress was communism, which represented the continued defeat of Enlightenment values in China.

Effectively, the interwar years were shaped by struggles between the conflicting modernities of liberalism, socialism and fascism, complicated by continuing imperialist Japanese penetration. The nationalist leadership admired Japan and Germany and Chiang Kai Shek actively approved of the fascist Blueshirts formed in the early 1930s who founded the New Life Movement in 1935. This blended the Nazi concept of the state as embracing the whole of life and the ascetic tradition of Confucianism, regarded as the vitalizing force that would restore past glories to a new Chinese nation (Ch'en, 1979, pp. 86–7, 194). It was the communists who co-ordinated the War of Resistance (Sino–Japanese War) 1937–45, although Mitter (2000b) argues that this myth of heroic resistance was promoted (and exaggerated) by the Chinese Communist Party after 1980, when earlier policies were abandoned and the leadership needed new unifying themes (p. 228).

The turn towards cultural histories in the 1990s has refocused debates and more priority has also been given to the complex cultural processes involved in the movement from feudal empire to modernity. Ruth Rogaski (2004) has explored how imperialism introduced new Western scientific concepts, including the link between public health and hygiene, national sovereignty and race fitness. Foreign observers and the modernizing Chinese elites regarded the Chinese masses as lacking the modern virtues of cleanliness and therefore acting as a brake on modernization. Yet hygiene and public health were important concepts in Chinese consciousness before the arrival of Europeans and became crucial elements in the formulation of Chinese modernity (Rogaski, 2004). The relationship between imperialism, modernity and cultural identities, including gender identities (Brownell and Wasserstrom (eds), 2002), has also been investigated. As in Japan, imperialism and modernity constructed new Chinese identities, including belonging to the 'imagined community' of nation (Gerth, 2003). Modern nationalist identities were forged through crises precipitated by Western penetration and Japanese invasion that challenged China's self-perception as an empire at the centre of world civilization, bonded by a common universal culture (Mitter, 2000b, pp. 11–12). Contemporary Chinese identities are still influenced by memories of imperialism and 'national humiliation' in the nineteenth century (Bickers, 2000, p. 12). How different were Japan's experiences?

Japan: modernization and imperial expansion

On the eve of Western intrusion in 1853, the emperor of the 2000-year dynasty had become a mere figurehead and real power lay in the Togugawa family shogunate (1603–1867). Commodore Matthew Perry and four US warships forced Japan, isolated under a feudal system, and weakened by internal fissures, to open to the West. The USA negotiated unequal treaties that opened up ports to foreigners and Japan to Western influence. The complex interaction between modernity and 'tradition' and gender and race identities of Westerners and Europeans was evoked in Puccini's opera, *Madame Butterfly*, based on a story by the American John Luther Long (1898). Cho-Cho-San, a geisha who has a child by an American naval captain, is abandoned by him for a 'modern' American woman. He returns to Japan with his wife, who then expresses maternalist concern for the poor abandoned girl. *Madame Butterfly* and representations of Japanese women in similar popular Orientalist texts (Honey and Cole, 2002) became metaphors for Japan's weakness and lack of masculine strength to resist Westernization. After a period of conflict and upheaval in 1868, the military power of the Shogunate was curbed and the ancient form of imperial rule restored under Emperor Meiji. Meiji Japan, 1866–1912, was defined by the slogan 'civiliza- tion and enlightenment' and a determination to resist Western power through modernization and reform (Buruma, 2003, pp. 10–20). In Western eyes, Japanese strength now contrasted with Chinese weakness and decadence; modernity versus stagnant pre-modernity. (See, for instance, the contrasting images of Chinese decadence in Figure 3.1 (p. 103) and Japanese strength and vigour in Figure 3.2.). Japan's defeat of Russia in the war of 1904–5 that culminated in the fall of Port Arthur and the destruction of the Russian Baltic fleet was interpreted by anti-colonial activists as the first challenge to white Western power. Conversely, Britain and the USA now regarded Japan as a buffer and ally against Russian expansionism in the East. This was the pre- condition for putting together the rudiments of a Japanese Empire.

From 1905 to 1930 a more assertive Japanese Empire emerged and demands for equality of esteem with the West intensified. Japan attended the 1919 peace conference in Versailles as an honorary white power, evidence of acceptance into Western modernity as a member of the new League of Nations. But conference delegates refused to accept the Japanese on racially equal terms (Lauren, 1996, p. 73). Japan's response to these racial humilia- tions was the expansion of its own empire and an emergent ideology of racial superiority linked to the growth of patriotism (Jansen, 2000; Horne, 2004). Pre-1931 Japan moved into a new phase of defensiveness against the West

Figure 3.2 A Japanese bayonet attack during the war with the Russians in 1904–5

through the acquisition of a formal empire where the Japanese emulated administration of the British Empire, which Japanese imperial strategists particularly admired. Japan's imperial mission was to develop and transform decaying Asian civilizations and policies of Japanization were introduced in occupation colonies like Korea (Myers and Peattie, 1984, pp. 1–10, 40–44). After 1930 economic imperialism akin to that of Western powers became more important and resulted in the expansion of an informal empire in China (Duus, Myers and Peattie, 1989).

Japan now claimed the right to assert its own Asian Monroe Doctrine and establish peace through a 'co-prosperity sphere' based on a Pan-Asian or 'Asia is one' ideology (Beasley, 1987; Iriye, 1987). In effect, this was an assertion of racial superiority over the peoples it dominated, emphasizing the link between race and imperial power in justifying modern imperialism (Chapter 1). Racism against the Chinese went back to the Sino–Japanese War. The terrible Japanese atrocities in China after the invasion in 1936, particularly the Nanking massacre of up to 300,000 in December 1937, have been attributed to such negative representations of the 'inferior' Chinese in government propaganda and a jingoist popular press (Buruma, 2003, pp. 84–6). More widely, the New Order in Asia, declared in November 1939, confirmed the need for Asian people to be guided by Japan; Western materialist culture was rejected in favour of the Confucian principle. After openness to Western ideas and assimilation there was a return to Japanese roots and a militant nationalism cemented by the new Pan-Asian ideology. Before the Japanese invasion of China in 1937, Britain appeased Japan in order to protect informal economic interests in China threatened by the rise of nationalism (Kibata and Adamthwaite, 1986). After 1937, Japan became a major threat to Western interests in Asia and during the war, 1941–5, the old imperial order, represented by Britain, was replaced by the New Order, led by Japan. The legacy of this 'Holy War' against the West, and the aggressive imperialism that degenerated into exploitation and cruelty, have reverberated into the present with demands for apologies and reparations. Nationalist revisionist history of the 'Great East Asian War', however, has reasserted the contemporary representation of Japan as a victim of Western imperialism forced to stand up for Asian peoples (Buruma, 2003, p. 84).

Was Japanese imperialism fuelled by atavistic feudal elements, modernity, internal tensions in Japanese society, protection of ruling interests, reactions against the West and nationalism, or a combination of all these factors? Jansen (2000) suggests that Japanese imperialist expansion was a logical response to living in an imperialist world and the threat of being engulfed. Beasley (1987) favours economic explanations of Japanese imperialism as a product of modernity, but Western theories of imperialism do not completely explain Japan, and cultural and political contradictions within Japanese society, stimulated by modernity, must also be considered. Martin (1986) and Bix (2000) explore Schumpeter's 'atavism of the ruling aristocracy' and the preservation of feudal structures as a plausible explanation. In the Meiji era, energies of the 'restless samurai class' were deflected in the modernizing project to attain equality with the West (Martin, 1986, p. 78). Economic development was rapid and resulted in the formation of the big corporations, or *zaibatsu*, but social tension and conflict surfaced as social and political changes lagged behind. Older, militaristic values within the modernizing state resurfaced after 1914 and, despite the more liberal 'Weimar period' in the 1920s, when modern left and liberal elements expanded, democracy remained fragile. In 1928 Emperor Hirohito was reborn as a living god, there was a resurgence of Shintoism and the period named Showa (illustrious peace) began. In May 1932 the prime minister was assassinated opening the epoch of 'Emperor fascism' (Bix, 2000). An imperialism based on 'mythical vainglorious [military] nationalism', was now 'in symbiosis' with the need for overseas expansion as a safety valve for domestic tensions (Martin, 1986, p. 71).

As in Germany, fascism intensified the contradictions between modernity and archaic culture. More recently, however, historians have suggested that expansionism in the 1930s was the result of Japan's maturing modernity, not feudal atavism. Louise Young (1998) has argued that Japan's empire in Manchuria (Manchukuo), 1932–45, was a modern phenomenon based on a modern mass society, not an autocratic imperial rule. There has also been more interest in the relatively unexplored territory of the culture of Japanese imperialism and the ways in which Japanese identities changed and traditions were reinvented with modernity, forging a modern culture with its own modern unifying national myths (Vlastos (ed.), 1998; Minichiello (ed.), 1998). What, then, are the key comparisons and contrasts between China and Japan?

China and Japan: a 'special relationship'?

Were China and Japan interconnected in their humiliation by the West? Did a special relationship between China and Japan develop in the counteracting of Western modernity, as exemplified in the influence of Japanese modernization on China? How and why did their responses differ? Key similarities between China and Japan include a history of feudalism and a culture based on interconnections in the religions and philosophies of Shintoism, Buddhism,

Confucianism and Taoism. Both experienced internal weaknesses prior to Western penetration, resulting from lack of social and political reform. Vulnerable to Western aggression, they were forced to open up to the modern world through war and/or diplomacy at the end of a superior Western gun barrel. Reactions to imperialism in both countries were a complex combination of anti-Westernism, hatred of foreigners and feudal atavism, but also enthusiasm for modernization promoted through a Westernized and Westernizing elite. Modernity also stimulated nationalism, socialism and patriotism that had enduring consequences for both China and Japan. The convolutions of imperialism and modernity intensified internal instability and poverty, creating diasporas whose racial exclusions and victimization further nourished animosity towards the West.

There were also significant differences that determined responses to Western imperialism. Japan was a collection of islands on the fringes of the continent, occupying a position in Asia similar to that of Britain in Europe. Lack of resources was an important stimulus to ingenuity and expansionism. Ethnically, it was relatively homogenous. China, on the other hand, was a huge and ethnically diverse empire with potentially rich resources. Socio-politically, Japanese society was based on the military feudalism of the Samurai as opposed to Chinese bureaucratic feudalism. In Japan there was a merging of feudal and new bourgeois interests during the Meiji era of rapid modernization. In China conflict between Confucian conservatives and modernizers intensified, culminating in the 1911 nationalist revolution. Japan's imperial status in Asia was negligible before the late nineteenth century, in contrast to the ancient Chinese Empire, yet this position was reversed by the twentieth century. China became vulnerable to a mixture of formal and informal penetration and lost parts of its empire. Japan initially experienced some informal imperialism, but quickly reversed the balance of the relationship with the West, expanded empire in China and overran the European Asian empires, accelerating decolonization. Thus China experienced imperial decline and internal conflict while Japan, after a seemingly successful modernization, joined the imperial power clique.

Imperialism and modernity thus had a differential impact on China and Japan. What have been the long-term consequences? John K. Fairbank (1998) argued that imperialism in China was both oppressive and stimulating and had an important impact on Chinese economic and political development. Jack Gray (2003), in his survey of a huge span of Chinese history, emphasizes the positive impact of Western modernity. A supporter of the pro-democracy movement in China, Gray argues that contemporary China is moving, with much of the rest of East Asia, toward a new 'Confucian corporatism', having finally achieved a synthesis between East and West that has resulted in a successful modernization (2003). Japan avoided the imperialist interventions and civil wars that afflicted China, but always demonstrated an uneasy relationship with the West. Japan had spectacular successes in modernizing, but not without creating social tensions within Japanese society. In the interwar years the rise of trade unionism, the influence of communism and feminism were all in conflict with the anti-Western atavistic factions who wanted to return to imperial traditions.

The Japanese Empire was destroyed by the ultimate in modern Western technology, the atom bomb. Japan's aggressive militarism in 1941–5, and its cruel and barbaric treatment of other Asians and white prisoners of war was regarded by the West as a consequence of its feudal culture, weak democratic institutions and failure to modernize. Fascism in Germany was seen as a perversion of German culture, whereas Japanese culture needed to be completely transformed (Buruma, 2003, pp. 108–10). The conquering USA now adopted a paternalistic, civilizing mission to 'guide an immature people with backward institutions to maturity [and] eliminate what was primitive, tribal and ritualistic', echoing earlier colonial attitudes towards the Philippines (Dower, 1996, p. 280). Citizenship education for democracy (including women's rights), new school syllabuses centred on democracy and the transformation of 'backward' agriculture through modern scientific farming were the key strategies in reconstruction during the US occupation, 1945–52. These policies and the interaction between American 'modernity' and Japanese 'tradition' in the period of occupation were humorously and perceptively explored in *Tea House of the August Moon* (1958), starring Marlon Brando.

Kazuo Ishiguro's novel, *Artist of the Floating World* (1986) narrated by a traditional artist, explores changing identities during the occupation and the ways in which the Japanese enthusiastically embraced American culture, rejecting a past now associated with defeat and national humiliation. However, the end of the occupation was marked by anti-American protests. New tensions between modernity and tradition surfaced and opposition to the spread of modern Americanized culture revived Samurai traditions and new nationalist sentiments rooted in protection of traditional culture (Dower, 1999). The novelist Yuki Mishima (Kimitaka Hiraoka) founded a private army, based on Samurai codes, mounted a failed coup d'état in Tokyo in 1970 and then committed *seppuku* or ritual disembowelment (Scott-Stokes, 1975).

***

After the Second World War both China and Japan were firmly committed to modernization, but by different paths. Japan had a spectacular recovery, embraced the ultramodernism we now associate with Japanese urban cultures and, as a successful capitalist economy, rejoined the rich West, meshing in with the new networks of global economic power defining the postcolonial era. With the Communist revolution in 1949, China adopted an alternative Maoist mode of development, informed by anti-Westernism, which involved decoupling from the international system. Ultimately, the Chinese Communist Party brought in reforms which encouraged capitalist enterprise and reintegrated into international markets. Is China now fulfilling the arrested development promised before the nineteenth century? Growth has been spectacular – does this imply that capitalism is really the only road to a prosperous society? As China has opened up to Western markets, young Chinese have enthusiastically adopted Western fashions and the culture of capitalism has percolated through urban centres. Shanghai and other Chinese cities are becoming more like Hong Kong, now returned to China from Britain. Conventional interpretations of Western Asia's development as a response to Western penetration have now been challenged as Eurocentric. Asian scholars have stressed the importance of interregional developments and networks in industrialization and the ways merchants and migrants exploited inter-imperial conflicts. Modernization was thus autonomous and not simply a matter of catching up with the West (Sugihara (ed.), 2005). Will the twenty-first century be the Asian century and the focus of modernity shift from Europe and restore the parity that existed before the 'great divergence'?

Culture and imperialism

Cultural transformations have characterized all empires, ancient and modern, but it was the modern empires that developed the most sophisticated 'technologies of governance' and/or 'cultural technologies' (Dirks, 1992, p. 3), a 'scientific' colonialism directed at transforming 'traditional societies' into modern productive colonies. Stoler and Cooper (1997) propose that colonies need to be analysed as 'laboratories of modernity' but also sites of the 'other', against which Europeanness could be defined. In the late imperial and neo-imperial era, when development discourse began to replace colonial discourse, the spread of Western culture and civilization heralded modernization. But how neutral were modernization and Westernization? To what extent can they be conceptualized as Western cultural imperialism?

Culture is here defined as a shared set of values linking language, religion, kinship, work and the individual's conception of the world around them. It is adaptive and dynamic and linked to power relations and can thus generate tension, conflict and resistance. Culture has been increasingly prioritized in research into imperialism since Edward Said's influential *Orientalism*, first published in 1978. In *Culture and Imperialism* (1993), Said pioneered analysis of 'narratives of empire in fiction and history' as they influenced culture in the imperial centre. He analysed the power of representation in constructing colonial subjects but also demonstrated the importance of anti-imperialist challenges to this culture of imperialism. Influenced by Said, the 'new' imperial and postcolonial histories increasingly emphasized the indivisibility of the 'civilizing mission' in metropole and colony in creating a bourgeois imperial culture. There was greater focus on the nature of colonial societies and the impact of colonial rule on colonizer and colonized (Dirks (ed.), 1992; Stoler and Cooper (eds), 1997; Hall, 2000). Culture became central to debates about the nature of colonial knowledge. Empire, emphasized Cohn (1996), was as much a cultural and intellectual as a political/economic phenomenon and colonial knowledge facilitated conquest and rule. Postcolonial theorists thus reconceptualized modern colonialism as 'a form of relocation and renegotiation of opposites and boundaries', as opposed to 'a narrative framed by the hierarchical knowledge and subjects instituted by western domination', a narrative of the binary of self/other, colonized and colonizer, occident and orient, civilized and primitive (Prakash, 1995, pp. 1, 4).

This chapter reflects on this reorientation in imperial studies towards cultures of colonialism. The main areas focused on will be the nature of the colonial encounter, the culture of the imperial rulers, including the relationship between gender and empire, and the impact of colonialism on colonizer and colonized. Tensions between colonial power, imperial hegemony and cultural resistance are also examined. A key concept here is cultural imperialism, which operated in both colony and metropole (Van de Veer, 2004, p. 4). Cultural imperialism and popular imperialism constituted two prongs of the same hegemonic processes, but arguably served different functions. Problems of defining cultural imperialism on the periphery, as distinct from popular imperialism in the imperial heartland (discussed in Case study 4) will be expanded on in the Case study 3 on colonial Africa that follows this chapter.

The colonial frontier and the nature of the colonial encounter

Interest in the colonial encounter between Europe and its others, initiated in 1492, was stimulated by the 'cultural turn' in imperial history. Studies have revealed this encounter as unequal but complex in terms of cultural interactions between colonizer and colonized (Hulme and Whitehead, eds, 1992; Daunton and Halpern (eds), 1999; Pagden, 1993). In the Roman Empire the frontier (*limes*) was initially a road separating terrains in the empire, but came to denote routes of penetration and a fortified frontier between Romans and the 'others' still not subjugated. The Roman Empire was open-ended geographically and conceptually, a constantly shifting frontier (Lintott, 1993, p. 42). From early to late empires the frontier constituted a shifting border, physical but also metaphorical, between two or more cultures, and all frontiers were seminal in forging the new identities of colonized and colonizer. Cultural fluidity and the creation of mestizo populations associated with colonization have a long history going back to the empires of late Antiquity (Chapter 1).

Sexual relations between colonizer and colonized (miscegenation) created mixed-race minorities, *métis* in the French colonies or *mestizos* in the Spanish Empire (Klor de Alva, 1995; White, 1999). Such minorities often prospered but were also in an ambivalent position. Their position worsened with the development of scientific racism and they experienced identity problems in colonial and postcolonial societies (Aldrich, 1996, pp. 161–2).

The colonial encounter and the nature of the colonial frontier are important concepts and have enabled historians and anthropologists to develop new insights into the nature of early colonial societies and, in particular, white settler societies (which include the United States) that shared much in common in terms of culture and history. Lynette Russell argues that:

> Cross cultural encounters produce boundaries and frontiers. These are spaces, both physical and intellectual, which are neutrally positioned, but are assertive, contested and dialogic. Boundaries and frontiers are sometimes negotiated; sometimes violent . . . the frontier is an intellectual construct which has little . . . salience to those people involved in its construction and maintenance.
>
> (Russell, 2001, p. 1)

Europeans on new colonial frontiers had to engage in reciprocal relations with indigenous peoples on whose help they initially depended (see Figure 4.1). If this mutual relationship deteriorated their lives could be endangered and/or they could be killed, as was Captain Cook in 1779 by the Hawaiians. The Pilgrim Fathers who founded the Plymouth Colony, Massachusetts, in 1620, could not have survived their first winter in New England without the turkey and squash provided by friendly locals, hence Thanksgiving (which has became a more important celebration than Christmas in the United States). Without Aboriginal knowledge and help, the ill-equipped first convict labour settlement in Sydney would not have survived. The British, French and Spanish all needed indigenous allies in expanding and defending their empires. Subsequently, indigenous peoples were cheated out of, or killed for, their lands and collaboration with certain indigenous groups to suppress resistance intensified ethnic tensions. Mary Louise Pratt has described the colonial encounter as:

> . . . a space in which peoples geographically and historically separated come into contact with each other and establish ongoing relations, usually involving coercion, racial inequality and intractable conflict.
>
> (Pratt, 1992, pp. 6–7)

Figure 4.1 The colonial encounter during the exploration of the Pacific prior to colonization; circa 1770s: 'Captain Cook presenting pigs to the Maoris'

Violence, as well as collaboration and cultural interchange, characterized the colonial encounter. Indigenous peoples resisted but were ultimately subjected to European power, although this was a long and uneven process; in parts of North America this subjection was not completed until the late nineteenth century.

The colonial encounter centred on new frontiers. There are important debates relating to the nature of the frontier in both Australian and South African historiography, derived from a critique of Frederick Turner's conceptualization of the American frontier. The 'Turner thesis' (1921) proposed that the consolidation of the frontier involved a process where the 'unsettled' became 'settled'. It was a meeting place between 'savagery' and 'civilization' and, in the USA, brought progress, democracy and allied liberal values. In South Africa, liberal historiography located the origins of the Apartheid state in the 'frontier' racial attitude of Afrikaners (Boers) that lacked the civilizing elements of the Enlightenment (Penn, 2001). Marxist historiography argued that the liberal 'frontier thesis' prioritized race and ignored class and capitalism. More recently, Mostert (1992) and Crais (1992) returned to the frontier but claimed that it was the British government, British settlers and the British army expanding the Eastern Cape frontier that were responsible for racial segregation.

It has been claimed that the colonial frontier represented 'the rejuvenation of the lone white male in the wilderness' through control over and separation from 'a feminized and racialized landscape' (Kaplan, 1993, pp. 4, 9–10). In Australia, romanticized myths of the heroic frontier, consisting of a line dividing culture from nature, which included Aboriginal society, helped to construct white Australian masculinities. Feminist historians, however, have challenged conceptualizations of the Australian frontier as masculine, arguing for the importance of gender in understanding frontier culture (Schaffer, 2001; Lake, 1998). Both white and indigenous women shaped the colonial encounter. In most initial contact situations between Europeans and indigenous peoples, indigenous women were the cultural conduits through their sexual relationships with white men. White customs that they learned were passed on to sons: in this sense they were 'agents of civilization' (Schaffer, 2001, p. 137). But as more white women came to the frontier to 'civilize' the men, the position of indigenous women deteriorated (Bell, 1984). These debates have broader relevance to all settler frontiers.

Reynolds (1987) prioritized indigenous resistance on the frontier, in which Aboriginal peoples were active agents in resisting white intrusions, but such resistance studies have been criticized for exaggerating indigenous agency and autonomy. There has been greater emphasis on collaboration on the frontier, with the hybridization of cultures and incorporation of whites into indigenous cosmologies and world views (Russell, 2001, p. 12). Interaction also occurred through trade, exchange and sexuality and, whilst old identities were undermined, new identities were created. The whole concept of the frontier has been challenged and the shifting and ephemeral nature stressed. It has been argued that the physical frontier loses meaning after the closing of the frontier and becomes a 'cultural space' between two (or more) cultures that still exist (Wolski, 2001). This reconceptualization has fostered research into new 'frontiers' in postcolonial European and North American cities inhabited by migrants and, in Australian cities, urban Aboriginal peoples. Such frontiers or borders are sites of resistance but also of the contestation and negotiation of identities, and foster 'cultural hybridity' (Bhabha, 1994). Thus Lynette Russell (2001) claims that, as a concept, the frontier lacks 'temporal and geographic specificity' (p. 13), although this is perhaps too sweeping a generalization. The initial colonial encounter was undoubtedly complex but physically defined by place and time and constituted a specific stage in colonial expansion and colonization. It was a space where colonial culture was first articulated.

Culture and colonialism

From the early colonial encounters, the nature of colonial rule was never static and changed over time. Many colonized peoples experienced changes in the colonial ruler. Examples here include the transfer of the Philippines from Spain to the USA, the acquisition of the former German colonies by France, Britain and other imperial or sub-imperial powers after the First World War. What remained constant was the colonial situation, 'the unchanging complex of rule, exploitation and cultural conflict in ethnically heterogeneous political structures that had been created by influence from without' (Osterhammel, 1997, pp. 64–5). Imperial administrations, civilizing missions and cultures of colonialism were shaped by the interactions between colonizer and colonized in diverse cultural, political and economic contexts. In the early imperial era, the Spanish demonstrated almost total indifference to the cultures they encountered in Latin America and the Philippines (Kamen, 2002) yet they were less averse to race-mixing than the French and English who, by the early twentieth century, possessed extensive anthropological and ethnographical knowledge of their colonial subjects. British indirect rule effectively resulted in racial segregation and the subtle racism underpinning French policies of assimilation was the focus of Frantz Fanon's influential analysis of the psychological affects of colonialism, *Black Skin, White Masks* (1952).

Before the 1960s, studies of colonial rule focused on administrative and political systems. They were written within the discourses of power and contributed to colonial knowledge in helping to manage the colonial subjects. Early challenges to this genre, emphasizing the importance of neglected 'cultures of colonialism', came from the colonized, for example, Fanon, Albert Memmi and Aimé Césaire, who explored what Nandy has termed the 'colonial consciousness of colonizer and colonized' (Nandy, 1983, p. 1). 'Colonization of the personality', argued Fanon (1952), resulted in the internalization and acceptance of the European superiority. In the Western academy studies of these psycho-social affects of colonialism were pioneered by Octave Mannoni in his analysis of the 'dependency complex' of the colonized created through paternalism (Mannoni, 1956). Presaging future historiographical developments, the sociologist George Balandier (1970) argued that previous studies based on economics, political administration or race relations provided only a limited, fragmented view of colonial societies. What was needed was a deeper understanding of colonial ideologies and a 'complete conspectus' of the 'colonial situation', pre- and post-conquest, that adopted an interdisciplinary approach and reconceptualized the relationship between colonizer and colonized as dynamic and marked by tension and conflict (pp. 21–7).

Since the 1980s, research has questioned the dualism that divided colonizer and colonized in former studies and focused on the interrelationships. Edward Said (1994) argued that imperialism consolidated a mixture of cultures and identities on a global scale and imperialism was as much a formative element in development of metropolitan cultures as it was for colonized societies. His ideas were incorporated into new imperial histories that explored the cultures of colonized and colonizers and explored how cultural imperialism helped to legitimize imperial power. Under the influence of the ideas of Marx, Benjamin, Gramsci, Foucault, Derrida and Said, colonialism was reconceptualized as a 'metaphor for the subtle relationship between power and knowledge . . . culture and control' (Dirks (ed.), 1992, p. 11). New analyses of the nature of colonial rule embraced strategies of power, the link between colonialism and identity formation of rulers and ruled, and interconnections between the public institutions of the colonial state and the intimate domestic lives of colonizer and colonized. To what extent have these new conceptual frameworks helped to advance our understanding of the relationship between culture and imperialism?

Imperial power and cultural oppression

Cultural strategies to legitimize imperial power, including co-option of local elites, can be traced back to earlier empires. Roman emperors lacked any grand design to spread the culture of Rome but the imperial centre was sustained through Romanization, the fusion of imperial and local institutions and cultures. Roman culture was itself a blend of indigenous and foreign elements and was receptive to other cultures, especially Greek. This given, widespread diffusion of the traditional gods of Rome: Jupiter, Juno and Minerva, particularly under the later emperors, became an essential element of imperial propaganda and ideology. Religious cults and social practices that 'civilized' Romans regarded as barbarous, such as human sacrifice, or that threatened the advance of empire, such as customs practised by the druids of Gaul and Britain and the prophetesses of Germany, were suppressed (Garnsey and Saller, 1987, pp. 178–81). Garnsey and Saller conclude, however, that, in the main, Rome's contact with alien religions was marked by peaceful penetration rather than coercion. Roman gods were syncretized with indigenous gods: in Britain, for instance, the goddess Minerva found local counterparts, such as Sulis, the water goddess of Bath (ibid., p. 181).

The cultural impact of Rome was, in some ways, not dissimilar to that in later empires. Roman *coloniae* were an extension of Rome, a community of Roman citizens. Rank and clothing in the empire were visual symbols of power, as were spatial definitions of seating in amphitheatres, with enormous fines for violation. Such visual symbols of power affirmed the imperial social structure and were calculated to impress the subordinated populations of the empire. Adoption of Roman culture by the local elites, including a villa, strengthened pre-conquest social divisions and superiority over the masses. Roman culture had less influence in the countryside, but peasants did become Romanized through the army, the main instrument of exposure to the dominant culture. Romanization in the Western Empire (see Map 1, p. xvi) was deep-rooted and long-lasting but it was less successful in the East, where the elites, influenced by Jewish, Egyptian and evolving Oriental cultures, were less zealous in embracing Roman culture (Garnsey and Saller, 1987, pp. 116–17, 167–9, 202).

In later European empires similar cultural strategies were employed, but modern racial ideologies and economic priorities arguably resulted in more extensive cultural oppression/suppression. The histories of colonized peoples, argues Cohn (1996), were shaped through cultural technologies of dominance. Colonial and imperial domination operated through mechanisms of cultural imperialism that resulted in cultural oppression, that is, a debasement and negation of the values of colonized peoples that undermined their cultures. Cultural imperialism was essential to legitimizing colonial rule and the racial orders that sustained it, muting the essentially exploitative nature of colonial administration and fudging conflicts of interests between colonizer and colonized. The concept of cultural imperialism, however, is diffuse and difficult to define. As Tomlinson (1991, p. 7) stresses, it is a composite of two highly problematic concepts which cannot be reduced to a single meaning, but a key feature is that:

> [Cultural imperialism] operated through disrupting and changing the context within which people give meanings to their actions and experiences and make sense of their lives.
>
> (Thomas, 1994, pp. 2–3)

Cultural imperialism involves a dominant power imposing aspects of its culture on a society which is 'weaker' or 'backward' in some military, economic or technological sense (Meade and Walker (eds), 1991, p. 80). Allied to, but not synonymous with, cultural hegemony, the concept implies a more conscious process of suppression of inferior cultures. Cultural strategies were more subtle than other forms of colonial control, such as policing and the law, and had some success, in that the colonized internalized inferiority. But cultural oppression also fostered resentment and challenges to scientific racism and linguistic imperialism were vital to psychological survival and resistant political action (LaCapra (ed.), 1991; Bush, 1999).

The links between culture and imperialism raise fundamental questions about the operation of power and knowledge in colonial societies, the ways in which the values and culture of the dominant power are spread at the expense of the dominated, and the degree to which colonized subjects were actively engaged in complex cultural choices, interacting with the dominant culture although 'not in conditions of their own choosing' (Tomlinson, 1991, p. 3). The ideology and practice of imperialism were the domain of powerful groups and vested interests for which empire brought tangible benefits. Material power was expressed through economic, military and technological superiority, but equally important was the cultural power of dominant discourses which represented colonial subjects in a way that reinforced their inferiority, justified imperial rule and secured legitimacy for imperialism in both colony and imperial heartland (Chapter 5). Cultural power may be defined as the will to dominate and not be dominated, to impose change whilst remaining unchanged (Von Laue, 1989). It operates at the level of the individual and collective consciousness and is transmitted through cultural mediums. In

Foucaultian analysis culture itself becomes a mechanism of repression through the operation of powerful discourses. In the colonial context these generate representations of individuals and groups which have the power to include and exclude, to police and control every area of life, including sexuality (Stoler, 1996).

Cultural imperialism is thus premised on the relationship between knowledge production and control and imperial power. Power is maintained through hegemonic ideologies (or discourses of power), the dominant or ruling set of ideas in a society, that worked in the interests of powerful groups in metropole and colony. Gramsci defined hegemony as 'the predominance, obtained by consent rather than force, of one class or group over other classes . . . the spontaneous consent of masses to the general direction imposed on social life by the dominant . . . group' (Hoare and Newell Smith (eds), 1971, p. 12). In conjunction with other, more tangible, forms of power, hegemonic ideologies were utilized by the state to legitimize, and ensure the continuation of, imperial regimes. In India, for instance, the Raj was represented as modernizing India, emphasizing the weak, 'backward' and disunited nature of Indian society and the superiority of British institutions and legal systems. British rule depended on Indian acquiescence to this ideology (Cohn, 1996).

Colonizers, argued Chatterjee (1994), were involved in a 'hegemonic project' that was powerful and long-lasting (p. 79). To be successful, imperial hegemony had to come to terms with, incorporate and transform the values of the colonized. Direct violence, defined as state violence through soldiers and policemen, was the exception rather than the rule in the history of British imperialism in India and Africa. Control was maintained through 'gentle violence' that changed the 'day to day reproduction of life under colonial rule in the name of civilization and reason' and transformed colonial peoples' consciousness (Engels and Marks, 1994, pp. 1–2). Domination, observes Osterhammel (1997), was based on the threat of force, but also 'communication imperialism', the collection, processing and dissemination of information about colonized society by centralized institutions. Important here were collaborators, not colonial soldiers or puppet native rulers, but 'semi-autonomous agents', middlemen with a foot in both camps, whose interests were best served by helping to sustain the colonial state (pp. 64–6).

Nicholas Dirks, however, has queried the use of hegemony in relation to colonial power as it implied consent and political participation absent in the colonial context (Dirks (ed.), 1992, p. 7). Gramsci's ideas were developed for modern Italian society, where there was a substantial civil society (interest groups, trade unions, political parties) and an educated, literate population facilitating the dissemination of hegemonic culture. These aspects of modernity were not present in colonial societies, or, if emergent, as in the period from 1918 up to the end of European empires, were suppressed and/or steered by the colonial powers in an attempt to neutralize the potential danger to the imperial status quo. Effectively, hegemony, in metropole and colony alike, could never secure complete ideological and political control; this was central to Gramsci's interest in the active resistance of 'subalterns' against the 'officer' class. In the colonial context resistance was generated through dynamic tensions between the hegemonic ideologies of the colonizers, pre-colonial cultures and the oppositional discourses of African and Asian nationalism. As Daunton and Halpern (1999) emphasize, elites are dominant, but rarely hegemonic, and autonomous domains for indigenous resistance and politics have always existed (p. 10). Certainly, we need to query the passivity implied in the concept of a monolithic Western cultural imperialism and acknowledge the active agency of colonized peoples. Autonomous action, however, was continuously constrained by powerful cultural strategies employed by the colonial governments. How did cultural power operate in practice?

Transforming colonial cultures: cultural power in practice

Conduits of cultural imperialism included Western medicine, science and technology, Christianity, European education and languages and Western principles of business, law, taxation and accountancy. These impacted on religion, language, education, family/kinship/gender relations, political systems and customary law. European legal systems underpinned colonial administrations and were fundamental in ordering colonial society (Benton, 2002; Kirkby and Coleborne (eds), 2001). Western medicine conflicted with indigenous knowledge and disrupted cultural practices (Meade and Walker (eds), 1991). Work culture and notions of Western time were also imposed on colonial workers, with ambivalent consequences (Cooper, 1997). As in England during industrialization, the linear time of modernity replaced the circular time of the rural communities linked to the seasons, but both co-existed, for instance, in the consciousness of African migrant workers. In the late imperial era, the mass media – radio, film, and advertising – became powerful new cultural agents representing the imperialist's vision of empire to both colonizer and colonized (Chapter 5). The British Broadcasting Corporation (BBC) Empire service developed a global reach on to which the present-day BBC World Service was mapped.

Language was a powerful tool of cultural assimilation and coercion (as noted in Case study 1 on Ireland). In the Roman Empire, Latin was imposed as the official language and subordinated local languages were ignored. Local urban elites had a Roman education (Garnsey and Saller, 1987, p. 186). Later British and French empires utilized language in a similar way. 'To speak a language is to . . . assume a culture' wrote Frantz Fanon (1993, 1952, pp. 17–18). Colonial culture, however, was characterized by 'linguistic dualism'. As Memmi observes, the difference between native language (mother tongue, dialect) and cultural language (standard, national, official) is not peculiar to the colonized, but colonial bilingualism cannot be compared to standard linguistic dualism:

> Possession of two languages is not merely having two tools, but actually means participation in two psychical and cultural realms. Here the two worlds symbolized and conveyed by the two tongues are in conflict: they are those of the colonizer and colonized.
>
> (Memmi, 1990, 1957, p. 173)

In the British colonies English became the official *lingua franca* and this was essential to forging consolidated states in multi-ethnic colonies like India and Nigeria. French and Portuguese had a similar role in bonding the Francophone and Lusophone empires. Recognized *lingua francas* were central to colonial control and 'nation building' during the transition from colonialism to independence. But dominant indigenous languages were also prioritized over minority languages, exacerbating post-independence ethnic conflict. In the Philippines, the US colonial government promoted the regional language, Tagalog, as a national language to forge identity in an ethnically and linguistically complex archipelago (Osterhammel, 1997, pp. 102, 103).

Linguistic imperialism was inseparable from the introduction of Western education, but educational policies varied. In the Philippines the USA made a greater priority of national education than any other colonial power. This contrasted with Indonesia, where only a mere 0.32 per cent could read Dutch, and where, in general, the colonial authorities actively discouraged Indonesians from speaking Dutch (Osterhammel, 1997, p. 102). In the French colonies there was a rudimentary public education system to promote policies of assimilation, but in the British, Belgian and German colonies education was left primarily to missionaries. Education in European languages was an apparently successful strategy in securing the ideological consent of the educated elites but, as we shall see in Case study 3, Europeanization also resulted in ambiguous and conflictual responses.

Missionaries were crucial to the civilizing mission and have been targeted as prime agents of Westernization through education. The missionary project was also directed to transforming family life, gender relations and sexuality, often with adverse consequences for women in many indigenous cultures from Canada (Anderson, 1991), Spanish America (Guttierrez, 1991), Australia (Choo, 2001) and Africa (Vaughan, 1991). Recent historiography, however, has challenged the image of missionaries as simply agents of imperialism (Maxwell and Lawrie, 2001; Porter, 1999, 2004). 'Religion and empire frequently intermingled', wrote Porter (1999), 'but were as likely to undermine each other as they were to provide mutual support' (p. 245). Osterhammel (1997) concluded that missionary activities often had unintended repercussions that developed their own dynamics outside the missionary remit, and the spread of Christianity had an ambiguous impact. Thus, suppression of native cults and the establishment of a state-supported Christian monopoly in Spanish Latin America and the Philippines resulted in interesting syncretic blends where elements of indigenous religions lived on in Catholic practices (Osterhammel, 1997, pp. 97, 197–8; Rafael, 1992, pp. 65–89). In Cuban Santeria, for instance, Roman Catholic saints have their African equivalent; thus, St Barbara, patron saint of firemen, is also the Yoruba Orisha of thunder, Shango.

The process of Christianization was complex and Catholicism was more able to absorb pre-Christian traditions than Protestantism (reflecting perhaps the powerful link between the Protestant Reformation and modernity). But African and Protestant beliefs also syncretized in the African or 'Ethiopian' churches that emerged in the late nineteenth century. In Africa and the Caribbean a fusion of evangelical Christianity with African belief systems stimulated resistance movements (Turner, 1982; Comaroff and Comaroff, 1997). The success of the Christian project was dependent on particular cultural configurations: Protestantism or Catholicism interacting with Hinduism, Buddhism, Islam or animism ('paganism' in colonial discourse). Christian penetration linked to imperial expansion provoked anti-Christian resistance as in the Maji Maji rebellion in East Africa, 1905–7, the Boxer Uprising (Case study 2) and Islamic revivals in Malaya, the Dutch East Indies, India and Algeria. The threat of European imperialism in nineteenth-century Africa inspired a *jihad* that spread Islam in North and West Africa in direct competition with Christian missions. By 1880 Islam was making more converts in Africa than Christianity. In the Sudan the millenarian Muslim sect, the Dervishes, grew rapidly, inspired by the Mahdi. Moslem armed resistance culminated in the siege of Khartoum in 1885, in which General Gordon died – one of the most humiliating defeats the British experienced (Rotberg and Mazrui (eds), 1970, pp. 146, 166). The British in India and elsewhere ultimately came to an accommodation with Moslem subjects, cultivating them as a conservative force. French universalism undermined religious institutions in an attempt to assimilate Muslims into French culture (Clancy-Smith (ed.), 2001, p. 4).

Most studies of missionaries focus on the period before 1914. Missionaries remained important during the twentieth century, but their role changed in line with new imperial priorities. Cultural interventions were now increasingly supported by knowledge of colonial 'others' derived from the new social sciences of ethnography, anthropology and linguistics. The establishment of an International Institute of African Languages and Culture in 1926 represented a powerful alliance between anthropologists, missionaries and colonial officials concerned with the problems of 'culture contact'. The School of African and Oriental Studies (1938) and the Colonial Social Science Research Council (1944) became the authoritative arbitrators of British colonial knowledge. The London School of Economics, founded by British Fabian socialists in 1898, trained both colonial administrators and social administrators, and strong links were forged between the colonial and domestic social policy agenda. Similar efforts to place colonial knowledge on a scientific footing were evident in other European imperial centres. Additionally, American philanthropic foundations such as the Laura Spellman Foundation, established by Rockefeller in 1918 in memory of his wife, became influential in funding sociological and anthropological research into 'the more dangerous social concerns', reflecting their own hidden agendas (Berman, 1980, pp. 185–7; Goody, 1995, pp. 17–18).

These initiatives lend support for Edward Said's arguments that Western scholarship is deeply implicated in the perpetuation of Western power. Academic Orientalists focused on the 'civilized' who needed modernity to drag them out of cultural and economic stagnation. Anthropologists directed their researches to the 'primitive' and colluded with the colonial authorities in the creation of tribalism and ethnic consciousness. As Vail (1989) emphasizes, 'tribalism' is not rooted in the precolonial past but is a twentieth-century ideological construct. Anthropologists and post-Second World War political scientists captured ethnicity at a moment in time, with no concern for historical roots or the dynamics of African cultures. The Western media continue to represent 'tribalism' as irrationality, an atavistic leftover, emphasizing its contribution to African backwardness, war and civil conflict. As Barratt Brown (1997) has pointed out, this has led to consistent Western misunderstanding of indigenous culture and its potential strength in African development.

Similar arguments have been made about anthropological and Orientalist constructions of caste in India, which, claims Dirks (1992), is a 'product of rule' rather than a predecessor of it (p. 8). In Orientalist discourse, caste was assumed to be the 'essence' of Indian civilization; people were not autonomous agents but products of a backward caste system (Inden, 2001, pp. 117, 125–6). Such representations of caste and village society were challenged by post-independence anthropologists but, argues Prakash (1995), implicit in these developments was a search for 'authenticity'. Old ideas appeared in new guises, reproducing a concept of 'caste driven, other worldly India' which modernization theory reformulated as 'traditional India' in the 1960s (p. 237). Following the pioneering work of Bernard Cohn, anthropology as a form of 'colonial knowledge' supporting the colonial project was challenged, but caste is still viewed as a major obstacle to Indian modernity.

There are thus strong arguments in support of the view that anthropology supported rather than undermined the structures of knowledge and racial discourses which underpinned imperial power. 'The anthropological concept of culture', argues Dirks, might never have been invented without a 'colonial theatre' that 'necessitated the knowledge of culture' for control and regulation (Dirks (ed.), 1992, p. 3). Kuklich (1991, pp. 50–52) argues that British anthropology was simply a 'child of colonialism' and constructed a distinct identity dependent on its relationship with imperialism. It encouraged colonial officers to make more systematic studies of the language and culture of the peoples they administered, which were subsequently embodied into administrative strategy. Conversely, Goody (1995), a 'second-generation' African anthropologist, defends his mentors as detached empiricists who judged all cultures equally, according to their relative value systems, and were often at odds with the more reactionary missionaries and administrators. Some, who were 'Left and Red', sought to modify or even abolish colonial rule and were not welcome in the colonies.

From the African perspective, however, anthropologists, like missionaries, were an intrusive element intensifying the cultural conflicts generated by colonial rule. The nationalist leader, Jomo Kenyatta, trained as an anthropologist but became one of the leading critics of anthropological interference in Kenya (Kenyatta, 1979, 1938). Eslanda Robeson, the wife of the African-American singer and political activist, Paul Robeson, studied anthropology at London School of Economics in the 1930s and her fieldwork in Uganda was conducted from an African, rather than a Eurocentric perspective. Why, she asked, should the colonized reveal their 'sacred histories' and intimate details of their lives to whites who failed to show them the respect of learning their language and were part of a more generalized oppressive white presence? Such considerations, she concluded, cast serious doubt on the validity of 'scientific data' (Robeson, 1946, pp. 10–12, 163). Criticisms of European anthropology and other forms of cultural intervention, however, constituted a minority view and the evolving social sciences, missionaries and medicine became crucial to the modernizing mission in the colonies after the First World War. The modernizing mission also brought more white women into the colonies as wives, nurses, doctors, teachers and missionaries. Gender thus became more central to defining the culture of modern colonialism.

Cultures of modern colonialism: gender, race and sexuality

Since the 1980s research has established the centrality of gender to articulating and sustaining sex/race frontiers (Stoler, 2002; Burton (ed.), 1999; Pierson and Chaudhuri (eds), 1998; Stasiulis and Yuval-Davis, 1995). Strict policing of marriage, sexuality and racial boundaries in European colonial societies made empire respectable through 'moral rearmament' and sustained difference, and distance, from the subordinated culture (Stoler, 1990). Women regulated imperial male sexuality and were the guardians of moral and physical health and hygiene in the expatriate home (Collingham, 2001). They were seminal in the construction of whiteness and superior gender identities which legitimized and sustained imperial power at a time when white prestige was threatened as never before. Only a minority of upper- and middle-class white women were actively involved in empire, but, asserts Haggis (1998), all white women in the colonies and the metropolitan centre were privileged by the racialized gender orders that sustained imperialism. White women's engagement with empire was arguably more diverse than these generalizations suggest (Bush, 2004). Nevertheless, their presence was essential to securing race discipline, uniformity, normalcy and order in colonial societies.

The increase in numbers of white women in the colonies after 1900 resulted in the domestication of former colonial frontiers. White women were vital to the regulation of sexuality through preventing men from 'going native' and keeping native mistresses. Domesticity and marriage stabilized white expatriate cultures, creating class-based communities which conformed to shared values and demonstrated a remarkable similarity across European tropical empires (Clancy-Smith and Gouda, 1998; Bush, 1999; Bickers, 1999; Procida, 2002). Bourgeois respectability and discipline, as conceptualized by Foucault, were integral to the development, stability and future prosperity of progressive modern empires and involved the parallel domestication and moralization of colonizing and colonized society. Gender relations in other cultures were interpreted from the perspective of Western patriarchal and

moral values. Colonized women were now seen as the key to the domestication and modernization of colonized societies. Christian conversion would
'moralize' and tame 'primitive' women, who would become good, subservient
wives and mothers (Vaughan, 1991). Such policies emphasize how the
construction of domesticity and gender identities in public discourse is
historically fluid and intimately linked to socio-economic developments in
metropole and colonies.

Since the 1980s more attention has been paid to gender as an analytical
concept in the study of imperialism (Levine (ed.), 2004). Gender-sensitive
historiography challenges the assumption that imperialism was essentially
a masculine project, but also focuses on the gendered experiences of the
colonized (Bush, 1990; Anderson, 1993; Choo, 2001; Coquery Vidrovitch,
1997). Engels and Marks (1994) have emphasized how questions of class
and gender were important in manufacturing consent in the colonies: African
and Indian women as a focus of colonial hegemonic strategies 'stood at
the intersection of colonial and indigenous notions of coercion, consent and
gender'. Colonial rulers and their male subjects may have shared commitment
to the colonial project but also held 'not dissimilar ideas about the subordination of women' (p. 11). Other areas of study include the relationships between
feminism, racism and imperialism (Vron Ware, 1992); masculinity and empire
(Dawson, 1994; Alderson, 1998; McDevitt, 2004); homosexuality (Aldrich,
2003); gender, sexuality and empire (Levine, 2003; Stoler, 2002; Burton
(ed.), 1999) and constructs of gender in colonial discourse, including travelogues (Mills, 1991; Melman, 1995; Lewis, 1996; Grewel, 1996). There have
also been studies of gendered perspectives on anti-colonial and anti-imperial
activism (Bush, 1998; Chaudhuri and Strobel, 1992) and Commonwealth
feminism in Britain's white dominions, including white feminists' relations
with indigenous women (Lake, 1993; Paisley, 1998; Woollacott, 1998).

Gender analysis interrogates the impact of imperialism on gender relations
and identities and the ways in which colonial policies intersected with the
private domestic lives of colonizers and colonized. In colonial discourse the
colonized were arguably conceptualized as feminine, submissive, pleasure-
giving, accommodating and, ultimately, metaphorically screwed (Said, 1978;
Glissant, 1981). Imperial heroes were fighters, adventurers and proponents
of 'muscular' Christianity, a glamorized image of 'real men' forcing inferior
colonized men into submission. Superior white masculinity was defined by
rational thought, a sense of duty and 'gentlemanly values', qualities lacking
in childlike or 'effeminate' colonized men (Sinha, 1995). Similarly, plucky,
adventurous, emancipated white women were superior to downtrodden
African and Asian women, but also to colonized men (Bush, 1999; Procida,
2002). 'I am a woman', wrote the West African 'imperial adventuress', Mary

Kingsley (1862–1900) in 1899, 'but a woman of masculine race' (cited in Birkett, 1992, p. 150). Superior imperial female identities were also expressed through women's role in racial and cultural reproduction as 'Mothers of Empire', breeders of a 'pure race', who were vital to the domestication (and thus 'civilizing') of empire and the preservation of race purity in the colonies (Davin, 1978; Wildenthal, 2001; Alessio, 1997).

These constructs of superior masculinity and femininity defined European cultures of colonialism. Superior white gender identities were linked to middle- or upper-class status. Lower-class and poorer whites – the 'servants' as opposed to the elite agents of the British and other empires – also contributed to the culture of colonialism, but were regarded by the elite classes as a potential threat to the colonial order. European prostitutes and poorer European men, petty traders and skilled workers, did not meet the standards expected of Europeans abroad and were more likely to engage in mixed-race relationships, posing a threat to the racial borders that sustained white prestige and power. Levine (2003), Stoler (1996, 2002) and others have emphasized the relationship between colonial power and discourses of sexuality expressed in concrete terms in the colonial management of sexuality. They have challenged Hyam's depiction of colonialism as a model of aggressive heterosexual desire (Hyam, 1990) and provided a more complex reading of the relationship between empire and sexuality. Control of sexuality and superior white gender relations, demonstrated through Christian marriage and domesticity, maintained social hierarchy and distance between ruler and ruled. The gendered culture of the colonizers was thus central to the articulation of colonial power and expression of cultural superiority. What was the impact of the culture of colonialism on colonizer and colonized?

Colonizer and colonized: power, resistance and cultural change

Colonialism simultaneously shaped the culture of the colonized and metropolitan colonizing society. From the late eighteenth century the 'Indians', the nabobs of the East India Company, influenced English culture with their 'Oriental' ways. In nineteenth-century Britain Indian cultural influences were reflected in food, jewellery and Indian shawls, or cheap imitations known as 'Paisley prints', architecture and the arts (Chaudhuri, 1992; Crinson, 1996; Mackenzie, 1995). European artists, writers and architects appropriated elements of the cultures of the colonized whilst, simultaneously, colonized

peoples intervened in Orientalist discourse, subverting stereotypes in constructing their own world views of imperial power (Codell and MacLeod
(eds.), 1998). In a less positive vein, Nandy (1983) emphasizes the continuity
between the oppressor and the oppressed and the way in which the subjugation of the ruled also involved the subjugation of the ruler. In the case of India,
he argues, the impact of colonial rule was tremendous in terms of economic
exploitation, psychological uprooting and cultural disruption but the long-
term cultural damage to British society was greater (pp. 31–2, 39).

As Curtin (2000) has pointed out, many studies of colonialism provide
a uniformly negative view of its cultural impact on the colonized, but if
colonialism did promote homogenization no general pattern emerged. People
threatened by the rise of Western power chose to borrow selectively from the
West. This 'culture change by intent' was not Westernization of one's own
culture but an 'optimum mix of the two' and applied particularly to religion
(pp. 109–10). Cultural and other consequences of colonialism were contingent on the nature of the societies of both colonizer and colonized and
the character of alien rule. The impact of Western culture was two-edged,
involving cultural oppression but also a dynamic fusion of cultures. 'Never did
imported modernity and local tradition merely clash or coexist', concludes
Osterhammel, 'instead new blends evolved' (1997, p. 97). Some elements of
Western culture, such as democracy and civil liberties, were viewed as positive
and used by nationalist organizations in their struggles against imperialism.
The imposition of Western political and bureaucratic structures weakened
and undermined pre-colonial practices, but also influenced political culture
during and after nationalist struggles for independence.

Additionally, postcolonial writings have emphasized resistance to, and
subversion of, dominant cultures and the ways in which colonized subjects
actively appropriated aspects of 'Western' culture and melded them into their
own subordinated cultures, creating new, hybrid forms. An example here
is how imperial languages also stimulated cultural resistance in revivals of
indigenous languages and the creation of creole languages. Such resistance
also embraced the subversion of dominant cultural codes through mimicry,
that is, utilizing the tools of the dominant, such as written English, in non-
standard forms (Bhabha, 1984). Mimicry undermines the colonial project
to 'civilize' the colonized by presenting the colonizer with a distorted reflection, rather than a confirmation, of him/herself. Thus cultural imperialism
resulted in cultural and racial oppression but also acted as a stimulus to
anti-imperialism and race consciousness. Reassertion of positive precolonial
cultural identities became an integral part of oppositional discourses to
imperialism, such as Pan-Africanism and Pan-Arabism, that were linked to

independence struggles. Irish nationalism was accompanied by a Gaelic revival
of Irish culture and language, suppressed under colonial rule and Islamic anti-
Westernism inspired the Iranian revolution in 1979.

A key criticism of the concept of cultural imperialism, then, is that it implies
a conscious, one-way process of cultural imposition. Neither the imperial
project nor the response of the colonized was monolithic. Moreover, there was
no mono-directional colonial hegemony, but 'different historical trajectories
... of contest and change ... with lags and disjunctures along the way'
(Breckenridge and Van de Veer, 1993, p. 10). Much depended on the type of
colony – settler or non-settler – and the balance between the indigenous and
colonizing population. The Europeanization of societies was much more
successful where the indigenous populations were all but wiped out, as in
Australia and North America. Where white settlers were in the minority, as
in Kenya, Algeria, Vietnam, Malaya and South Africa, cultural struggles were
more intense. Minority expatriate societies were sometimes decadent, cruel
and violent, as in the upper-class 'Happy Valley' set in Kenya in the interwar
years. This is what Aimé Césaire called the 'decivilization' of the colonizer
(Césaire, 1972, pp. 20, 57–8). Expatriate communities developed their own
culture directed to maintaining cultural and racial segregation emphasizing
distance, difference and superiority. Physical and sexual segregation and colour
bars strengthened the white enclaves in Africa, India and China that defined
minority white settler societies (Bush, 1999; Collingham, 2001; Bickers,
1999; Kennedy, 1987).

In non-settler societies, small numbers of Europeans administering large
tracts of land encountered resistance, despite the co-option of indigenous
local elites and other agents of colonial control (police, clerks, soldiers), and
the colonial cultural project was imperfect, to say the least. Imperial hegemony
was never complete and many rural parts of empires had little exposure to the
imperial culture, although even remote areas experienced imperial authority
through taxation, law and policing. Resistance to colonial rule was a constant
feature of the colonial relationship. In India vast tracts of land were never
visited by the district officer and were under British rule in name only. Some
areas in the Purnia district, Bengal, an area of river plains and jungle, were
renowned for their lawlessness. Officers sent to the district regarded it as a
form of punishment or 'censure' and were ignorant of local languages and conditions. They would be subject to 'flood, famines and epidemics of enormous
proportions' and experience a 'prison-like atmosphere' enhanced by lack
of co-operation of the indigenous population in revenue collecting. They had
little control over the local landlords (*Zamindars*) and also failed to rein in
the independent European indigo planters, hated by the indigenous popu-

lation, who wielded enormous power as 'perfect little kings' in their own village clusters (Hill, 1997, pp. 51–85). The planters thus retained autonomy from the British administration similar to that of Jamaican sugar planters in the eighteenth century and developed a similar decadent culture, a wild lifestyle of drunkenness and sexual exploitation of local women. Poverty and oppression pushed the peasants into banditry (*dacoity*) and uprisings as cruelty and enslavement stimulated slave resistance.

The cultural contact zone was often messy, fluid and unpredictable and cultural interaction on the 'borders' was promoted by a variety of agents, colonizing and colonized. Complicated links existed between colonizer and colonized; no absolute or mono-directional colonial hegemony existed, nor was there a unified imperial cultural project. Colonial agents often had conflicting visions of the role of Western culture in colonial societies: some wished to preserve tradition, others to modernize (Chapter 3). Missionaries and colonial officials clashed over cultural interventions in colonized societies.

But such critiques can downplay the very real imbalance of power between the 'West' and the 'Rest', past and present. Culture was, and remains, an indispensable weapon in maintaining hegemony without violence. Colonial discourses and cultural strategies ensured divisions between, for instance, educated, Westernized elites and 'native' masses and 'primitive' Africans and 'civilized' West Indians: upper- and middle-class South Asians, whose consciousness was firmly shaped by class as well as culture and race, regarded themselves as superior to other colonized peoples, including the South Asian peasant and working classes. These fissures have had important consequences for postcolonial societies. Colonialism also undermined traditional technologies and economies, with implications for gendered identities and widening gender and class inequalities. As Dirks observes:

> Cultural forms in newly classified 'traditional societies' were reconstructed and transformed by and through colonial technologies of conquest and rule, which created new categories and oppositions between colonized and colonized . . . modern and traditional, West and East . . . male and female.
>
> (Dirks, 1992, p. 3)

Imperialism not only had socio-economic consequences for the colonized but generated psychological and cultural conflicts which remain unresolved. Cultural oppression left a lingering psychology of inferiority and dependency, a problematic internalization of Western superiority. This 'colonization of the mind' was arguably one of the most intractable and damaging legacies of colonial rule. As the late Julius Nyerere, ex-president of Tanzania, pointed out, Africans did not only need political independence but also 'mental liberation'. This is echoed in Bob Marley's song 'Liberate Yourself from Mental Slavery' and Ngugi Wa Thiong'o's arguments for the need to decolonize the mind through reclaiming African languages as a medium for literature (Ngugi, 1991). The Indian context was different but 'loss . . . of self' had implications for recovering identities during and after colonial rule (Nandy, 1983). The legacy is 'internal Orientalism' whereby it is difficult for both Indians and outsiders to think of India outside of Orientalist categories; the very cultural base of public life was affected by ideas of difference and division that have colonial and Orientalist roots (Breckenridge and Van de Veer, 1993, p. 11).

Anti-colonial nationalism promoted cultural renaissance and the demands of the newly independent Third World bloc in the UN in the 1970s for a New International Order directly addressed the legacy of centuries of Western cultural oppression. In addition to a fairer global economic system, Third World states wanted a new cultural order and an end to Western dominance of information flows and media production. Independence was asserted, for instance, through the Third Cinema movement, promoting Third World film makers in order to challenge the hegemony of Hollywood. But colonial culture and Western colonial power persisted into the postcolonial era, undermining these challenges. Cultural imperialism became more powerful and sophisticated as the twentieth century progressed and now operates primarily through powerful multinationals like the Coca-Cola Corporation. These corporations assert 'soft power' through marketing techniques to change culturally determined consumer tastes (Klein, 1999). The focus of this chapter has been on formal colonialism in the nineteenth- and twentieth-century experiences which, concluded Dirks, 'remade the world' (Dirks, 1992, p. 23). Compartmentalizing colonialism in this way can, however, erase important continuities from pre- to postcolonial societies and detract from continuing imperial relationships (Chapter 6).

***

This chapter has demonstrated the combined, but uneven, impact imperialism had on the cultures of the colonizers and colonized. It has highlighted key links between imperialism, race, culture, power and resistance. The case study that follows will explore these themes in more depth in relation to British Africa. In analysing the intersections of the cultures of colonizer and colonized, however, we should not forget the material reasons for Western power and the intimate connections between imperialism and capitalism highlighted in Chapters 1 and 3. As Albert Memmi pointed out, although colonial privilege was not exclusively economic and racial and cultural humiliations were also fundamental to the self-esteem and superiority of the colonizer,

> The idea of privilege is at the heart of the colonial relationship, and that privilege is undoubtedly economic . . . deprivations of the colonized are almost directly the result of the advantages secured to the colonizer.
>
> (Memmi, 1990, 1957, p. 10)

Material and cultural power were, and remain, two interrelated prongs of Western hegemonic power. Additionally, cultural change cannot be divorced from violence, psychic or physical, and here the history of colonialism arguably equates with the Nietszchean definition of history as a 'barbarous narrative of debt, torture and revenge, of which culture is the blood-stained fruit' (Nietzsche, cited in Eagleton, 2000, p. 108).

Case study 3
Culture and imperialism in British Africa

> 'It is Empire Day at Bukoba [Tanganyika] . . . on the ground marches a sequence of eight processions, each headed by a flag and a smart band, while at the rear the primitive is represented in the tribal dancers and mummers, grotesque in dress and action. Well in front of each procession strides one man. Seven wear tropical suits and sun-helmets; the eighth has a German Hussar uniform . . . These are the big chiefs of Bukoba . . . now leading their tribes to the great event of the year, the inter-tribal sports'.
>
> (Margery Perham, *The Times*, 27 November, 1930)

These observations of a British colonial expert provide insight into key cultural processes central to legitimizing colonial rule, including African observance of the traditions and rituals of the colonizers (in this case, the former German rulers of Tanganyika, now Tanzania). Colonial incorporation was similar in Africa and India, involving pacification by force, economic exploitation and the policing of rigid racial boundaries, but also cultivation of collaborative elites and cultural imperialism. There were, however, import-ant differences related to the specific cultural/historical configurations in African societies, their relationship with the West and the nature of race dis-course. Orientalist perceptions of Indian culture were more positive until the evangelical and utilitarian civilizing missions of the early nineteenth century. With the expansion of the slave trade, Africans were relegated to the lowest position in the racial hierarchy and the primitive and barbaric nature of African societies provided the rationale for European colonial annexation after 1880.

Cultural interactions between Africa and Europe were ongoing from early contact but cultural encounters intensified in the nineteenth century (McCaskie, 1999). At first, Africans were confident that they could resist colonization by the strength of culture and religion, military prowess developed in expanding their own kingdoms, and diplomacy. Some African states, the Asante of what is now modern-day Ghana, for instance, wanted to develop and modernize through European education and development of cash-crop production, but on their own terms (Boahen, 1990). Africa needed 'modernization', but this came in an unfortunate way which distorted development and undermined African societies. Africans underestimated the power of European technology, the railways, telegraph, Maxim gun and medical technology that helped to secure European hegemony. Moreover, contact between Africa and Europe over a long period, beginning with the slave trade, had led to adverse social changes. As these changes accelerated with colonial annexation, some Africans did very well out of collaborating with Europeans and divisions between Africans deepened, weakening opposition. The impact on Africa was profound. As Basil Davidson (1978) observed:

> Generally the pre-colonial, pre-nationalist African community offered the individual a moral and psychological identity within his world and a guide to reality that was rounded and complete, encompassing past, present and future. In a decisive cultural sense, this was the basis on which the Africans met the colonial experience.
>
> (Davidson, 1978, p. 51)

This world, adds Davidson, was turned upside down as colonial annexation undermined African culture and sense of community, although this did not occur without resistance. The complexities of cultural encounters and interaction on the African 'frontier', specifically Southern Nigerian society, are evoked in Chinua Achebe's classic novel *Things Fall Apart* (1962).

The main aims of colonial rule were the maintenance of order, avoidance of heavy financial expenditure, exploitation of economic resources and management of labour as Africa's 'chief asset' (Beer, 1923). Colonial rule was sustained through use of force and violence – colonial policing was an important element in the psychology of colonial control – and technological advantage. But equally important was the hegemonic ideology of the benevolence and invincibility of British rule, the 'higher ideals' of empire that concealed the uglier, exploitative elements of colonialism. 'Native administration' was thus premised on paternalistic indirect rule, Lord Frederick Lugard's 'dual mandate' whereby the British ruled in trust through Native Authorities until such a time as Africans could stand on their own feet (Lugard, 1922).

Despite the British commitment to preventing the erosion of traditional culture through indirect rule (discussed in Chapter 3), colonial administration undermined socio-cultural structures, including African gender relations. Medicine and religion were particularly disruptive to African world views and identities. Megan Vaughan (1994) has argued that medical discourse had a powerful impact in 'pathologizing' Africans mentally and physically and contributed to the generation of new racial discourses about Africans after 1930. Missionaries assumed that African 'pagan' religions were inferior and failed to understand the nature of African religions and their centrality to African life. 'Muscular Christianity', expressed through sacrifice and endeavour on the pagan 'frontier', persisted up to the end of empire. In Bathhurst, the Holy Ghost Fathers had to contend with 'paganism in its most depraved form and . . . the venomous hostility of Mohammedanism'. Even in the 1950s the life of a missionary was purportedly hard 'in a land more backward, more steeped in paganism and misery than the lands the Apostles trod two thousand years ago'. Yet, 'God's promise' of rewards to the missionary were ample and thus:

> His mind is focused on the salvation of souls and for that he is prepared to face . . . climate . . . fevers, long treks on foot, anxieties of every kind, for the sake of a few uncomprehending blacks.
>
> (Robinson, 1952)

Most studies of Christianity have focused on the evangelizing British or American Protestant missionary societies, but Catholic missions were also important. The Society of the Missionary Fathers of the Holy Ghost was founded in 1848 and pioneered Catholic missions in Africa, the Caribbean and Oceania. Before that date there was 'no missionary society' in the Catholic Church devoting itself 'entirely to the salvation of the Black' from 'paganism, superstition and immorality'. The Holy Ghost Fathers allegedly 'penetrated darkest Africa before Livingstone, Brazza and Stanley'. By 1874 they were organizing missions and mission seminaries for 'the Blacks in America' and then moved from Ireland and France into England. Evangelizing in 'hard' missions was represented as an epic of 'suffering and sanctity'. Nuns were also involved and Irish nuns settled in Freetown in 1822 and in the 1950s still ran 'several flourishing schools and orphanages' (Robinson, 1952).

As noted in Chapter 3, there is a keen debate about the relationship between missions and empire. Indeed, in the African context missionaries were not always in harmony with the colonial administration, as in the conflicts over female circumcision in Kenya in the 1930s (Berman and Lonsdale, 1992, pp. 340–5). Africans reworked Christianity in ways that sometimes inspired resistance (Isichei, 1994). Nevertheless, missionary interventions in African belief systems compounded the psychic and social stresses induced by colonialism. Such stresses were sensitively explored by Wulf Sachs in *Black Hamlet* (1937), a study of the mind of a traditional South African healer who defends his world view against the alien beliefs of Christianity. A bitter critique of Christianity in Kenya is also found in Ngugi wa Thiongo's story, *Wedding at the Cross* (1975). The main character is humiliated by the model Christian African, 'Douglas Jones', when he asks to marry his daughter. His manhood is 'diminished' and he rebels against pressures to become 'respectable' according to European mores and marries according to African customs. Ultimately, he conforms and becomes a Christian himself, but when he forces his wife into a Christian 'wedding at the cross' it is she who refuses, reflecting a more general female resistance to missionary attempts to 'moralize' African men and women (Vaughan, 1991). The story also illuminates issues relating to naming and identity reflected in the imposition of Christian names divorced from the African cultural context.

Colonialism also introduced the concept of private land and property rights, individual rather than collective ownership based on kinship bonds. This led to the emergence of a cash economy and the commercialization of everyday life. Demand for new commodities, rising expectations and ideas of individual freedom undermined indigenous social relationships. Interaction between colonizers and colonized produced new classes of rich farmers, Western-educated elites and an urban and rural migrant working class. Emphasis on encouraging male cash-crop production also eroded women's economic activities that stimulated resistance against both colonial authorities and collaborative African chiefs (Coquery-Vidrovitch, 1997, p. 31). Informed by European patriarchal values, colonial administrators ignored women's institutions and bolstered African patriarchy to police 'unruly' women. Only men were educated in Western knowledge; women were the epitome of the 'primitive', all that was 'dark and evil' (Vaughan, 1991, pp. 22–3) and thus symbolized the backwardness of Africa that impeded the liberal modernizing agenda. After 1918 colonial policies were increasingly directed towards stabilizing societies undermined by migration and urbanization through the promotion of Western domesticity, marriage and gender roles. Missionaries became more central to the colonial project in promoting this modern

Christian morality and related values of motherhood and marriage. Modern Western methods of childbirth, however, conflicted with traditional practices and women were still largely excluded from Western education except for domestic science and mothercraft (Hunt, 1999; Tranberg Hansen (ed.), 1992; Allman, 1994).

Gender and class are thus important variables in evaluating white cultural power. New social cleavages in African societies aided legitimization of colonial rule but also inspired new forms of resistance. It was the male, educated Africans who experienced the most intense impact of cultural imperialism. Western education inculcated European cultural values and was directed to securing elite loyalty to colonial governments but also stimulated race consciousness and nationalism. Colonial administrators recognized early on the need to accommodate the developing bourgeoisie and safely channel their aspirations. Education, warned Lugard, 'has not brought happiness and contentment' to educated Africans and should be for the advancement of the community rather than 'the subversion of constituted authority'. To avoid the problems that had emerged in India, the primary object of education should be the 'formation of character and habits of discipline'. Religious and moral instruction was essential and 'reading books for girls' should be drawn up by 'a thoroughly qualified [white] lady'. Boys' education should inculcate 'morals, truthfulness, and courage, love of fair play and justice, respect for authority, cleanliness and the dignity of labour'. Biographies of 'good men' of 'character' like General Gordon and David Livingstone were recommended reading (Lugard, 1922, pp. 130–6).

Scouting philosophy was also seen as a valuable weapon in the 'moralization' of African boys. Warren (1986) suggests that scouting in the 1920s offered a unifying multi-racialist ideal and the reasons for local involvement were not primarily imperial. This may have had some relevance for the 'white dominions' but, as Evelyn Waugh cynically observed (if through his somewhat warped racist lens), the 'ten rules' of the Scouting movement emphasized notions of white masculinity and bourgeois Victorian virtues, such as thrift, trust and 'cleanliness in thought, word and deed', that were clearly inappropriate in different cultural settings (Waugh, 1946, pp. 141–2). African Cubs and Scouts, together with children at government schools, attended Empire Day celebrations where they saluted the flag, sang 'Rule Britannia', paraded, marched in their best uniforms and played competitive games. Patriotism was instilled in schoolchildren from an early age. When Princess Marie Louise visited a convent of the White Sisters in Cape Coast, the children had been carefully coached for her visit and most of their writings consisted of 'simple explanations of the words Empire, Citizenship, Patriotism, and a really excellent description of the origins of the Union Jack' (cited in Bush, 1999, p. 98).

Whilst the educated bourgeoisie were the most vulnerable to cultural imperialism, the majority of colonized subjects also experienced rituals promoting the 'higher ideals' of empire that were crucial in bonding them to the empire. Terence Ranger (1996) has convincingly explained the importance of the invention of rituals and 'tradition' in gaining consent for empire from both colonizer and colonized through creating a 'shared framework of pride and loyalty'. Whist this was arguably most successful in the colonial military and public school system, it was extended into the rural areas in the interwar years. Pomp and ceremony accompanied all important imperial occasions, such as the arrival and departure of governors and VIP visits. English traditions, such as Empire Day, St George's Day and Poppy Day, were celebrated with parades of ritual power and enforced even in the bush, where Africans reputedly wore 'poppies on their loincloths' although oblivious to their significance (Colonial officer, cited in Bush, 1999, p. 93).

The motif of loyalty was impressed on chiefs who were bought off with ceremonial badges of office bearing the British king's head. This reflects Lugard's vision of an ordered Africa where chiefs were hierarchically organized on military lines from first down to fifth grade and sworn in by oaths of allegiance and insignia. Lugard also warned that 'official etiquette and ceremonial' were to be strictly adhered to as matters of 'great importance' to African chiefs (all assumed to be male). Colonial administrators were thus warned to study 'native etiquette carefully [and] prohibit the assumption of privileges . . . by those not entitled to them by Native custom'. On the other hand they were to 'exact all proper courtesy' and should take prompt action on any signs of 'discourtesy' towards whites, such as 'a contemptible present', dispatch of a 'low-grade or dirty' messenger, or lack of punctuality (Lugard, 1922, pp. 307–11).

Palavers (from the Portuguese, *palabra* or word, a reflection of early Portuguese influence on West African coastal creole) were central to this bonding of imperial and 'traditional' authority. The pomp and ritual of the palaver continued well into the 1950s. Elspeth Huxley argued that in the uncertain years following the Second World War, palavers retained a 'mystical significance' and, although 'out of fashion' and supplanted by the 'doctrine of equality', appealed to some 'profound and enduring African emotion'. Writing of the Gambia, she evokes a vivid image of colonial ceremonial 'traditions':

> On a dais sits a phalanx of officials in shining topees . . . constrained by
> high collars most unsuited to the tropics . . . beneath a Union Jack, flanked

by two policemen, stands the Governor, addressing a gathering of chiefs
... A curiously old-fashioned, Sanders of the River scene of British
imperial power staging its little pageant beside this ancient, inimical water-
way into the alien heart of Africa, and staging it well, with immaculate white
men, loyal chiefs, orderly spectators; flags, bunting, bugles; the oath of loyalty, the Queen's message, the sense that this remote and uneventful little
cluster of huts and bush is part of a greater fellowship from which it can
draw nobility and purpose.

(Huxley, 1955, pp. 37–8)

Royalty had a central function in cementing the 'shared' traditions of empire
that forged an 'imagined community' of imperial belonging. The mythic
benevolence of the 'Great White Queen', Victoria, was crucial to representations of the 'good' empire. Throughout British Africa, Queen Victoria
became an icon to the colonized, representing the higher imperial ideals
of justice and fairness that would be carried on through the British monarchy.
This is in spite of the fact that when the queen (and subsequent monarchs)
were petitioned over genuine grievances, petitioners were snubbed. Loyalty,
obedience and allegiance to king and empire were paramount to bonding the
'imperial family' after 1918 and secured through royal tours of the empire.
Princess Marie Louise, heavily promoted as a granddaughter of Queen
Victoria, toured the Gold Coast in 1926 opening roads, bridges and hospitals
and visiting colleges and schools. As the first royal to trek around the Gold
Coast, her tour extended the bounds of this imperial bonding.

While on trek (itself an important ritual in confirming white presence,
power and racial superiority) with Governor Guggisberg and his wife,
the princess attended numerous palavers where the natives turned out in all
their exotic finery and offered presents to the honoured white guests. Her role
was to thank the chiefs for their welcome and offer to take back 'a message
of homage and loyalty to their King'. The trope of the 'loyal subject' was
invoked as evidence of the fact that most Africans welcomed British rule. The
First World War was cited as a crucial catalyst in securing this loyalty. This
was demonstrated when Princess Marie Louise unveiled a war memorial to
the 'very war-like and turbulent' Fra Fra of the Northern Territories, who were
only 'curbed' by the English after 1911. In her letters home she observes
that the First World War had transformed the Fra Fra into 'peaceful and
obedient people' who showed their loyalty by fighting for the British in
the Cameroons and Togoland. Loyal war veterans were focal points of imperial ceremonies in the interwar years when ex-servicemen were routinely
inspected by the governor and other white dignitaries (cited in Bush, 1999,
pp. 93–5, 98).

For the 'Westernized' elites, loyalty to king and country (Britain) was secured through an English education 'suited to an English gentleman' that denigrated African culture and where any language other than English was strictly forbidden (Chief Enahoro, Nigerian nationalist, cited in Bush, 1999, p. 95). Adopting the language of the colonizer was central to wearing the white mask which suppressed African culture and resulted in psychic stress and internalization of racial inferiority. Educated Africans experienced the most intense cultural transformations as well as the racial humiliations of being 'white' but not white. The ambiguous responses of Africans 'in between' two cultures are explored in Joyce Carey's novel *Mr. Johnson* (1939). 'I am a true Englishman at heart', declares Mr. Johnson, yet his inability to act so baffles and infuriates the white colonial officer for whom he works as a clerk.

Such 'semi-educated natives' were much despised by white residents. Yet even Africans in official positions who had the vote and were invited to parties in Government House were a target of derision to the 'heartless perfect eye' of Europeans, scornful of their attempts to ape Western manners (Greene, 1962, 1936, p. 34). The racially excluded African bourgeoisie, based mainly in the coastal towns, thus created its own parallel society which ironically mimicked the culture of these denigrating Europeans. The Lagos bourgeoisie, for example, created a superficially Western lifestyle, with net curtains at the windows and tennis courts. Churches were filled each Sunday with this Black elite, who also attended literary clubs and social functions where evening dress was worn (Margery Perham, cited in Bush, 1999, p. 99). As Bill Freund points out, ardent Christianity, Western names and capitalist values promoted through missionary education became part of the cultural baggage the African bourgeoisie carried through to independence (Freund, 1998, pp. 156–7).

***

British colonial Africa was ruled by a small minority of whites and consent could not have been secured purely by force. Cultural strategies varied from non-settler to settler colonies and colonial rule was much harsher in the latter. Nevertheless, throughout British Africa (and other European colonies), the constant affirmation of cultural superiority was essential in sustaining the mystique of power. The 'culture of colonialism', premised on intermeshing class, race and gender orders, was fundamental to the workings of imperial power. 'Prospero and Caliban', colonizer and colonized, were locked in complex spirals of power and dependence, collaboration and resistance. The colonizer's 'reality' was shaped by dominant discourses generated at the heart of the empire, individual personality and class position but also through interaction with the colonized. Conversely, African 'reality' was shaped by white racism and cultural oppression but also refusal to become the compliant colonial subject of white imagination. The penetration of Western culture undermined and divided African colonial society, but it also stimulated new forms of organized protest against colonial rule and oppositional nationalist discourses through which African dreams of freedom were more forcefully articulated.

Chapter 5

Representing empire

Representations of the colonized became central to postcolonial literary and cultural studies and 'new' imperial histories. The preceding chapter focused on the imperial periphery and the role of culture in the legitimization of the imperial project. The focus here is on evaluating new conceptual frameworks prioritized in historiographical developments since the 1980s that explore representations of empire and the colonial 'other' in metropolitan culture. Such representations in colonial discourse, the visual media, popular culture and imperial propaganda were vital to securing mass consent for empire in the imperial centre and have been significant in shaping superior national identities since the 'first global age' centred on the supremacy of the British Empire (Bayly, 1989; Wilson, 1998; Colley, 1992a). After 1880, imperialism and national identity were interlinked in the official propaganda of all Western European empires. Popular imperialism reflected Eurocentrism, a powerful discourse of white racial and cultural superiority, and worked through myriad cultural channels to secure consent for empire in the imperial heartland (Mackenzie, 1984). Four main areas will be considered: dominant discourses and representations of imperial power; the relationship between such representations and the legitimization of imperial power; 'Orientalized' representations of the Oriental and African 'other' and the reverberations of these powerful discourses and representations in shaping perceptions of the imperial past in present national histories. I also consider how such white representations have been challenged and subverted by colonized/Orientalized subjects and postcolonial minorities in ex-imperial centres. The case study of representations of the British Empire c. 1890–1939 that follows provides a more in-depth examination of the relationship between imperialism, popular culture in the imperial centre, and national identities.

Representing empire: dominant discourses

Prioritizing representation has refocused study of the imperial past towards the power of discourse and analysis of imperial control as organized via knowledge-producing systems (Richards, 1993). Economic and political histories were criticized as too determinist, separating metropole and colony, a materialist view that ignored the history of power which also embraced culture (Van de Veer, 2004, p. 4). There is a lively debate amongst historians about the nature of representation and my interpretation of the relationship between representation and reality will not be shared by all historians. Ankersmit (2001) and Munslow (2003), for instance, consider that all history is positioned and historical interpretation is not the 'truth' as we only have the historians' representation of the past. Yet, the prioritization of culture and 'imagining' empire through deconstructing language, semantics, symbols and literary and visual representations can obscure or marginalize 'real' structures of power. Discourses and representations, like theory, do not exist independently of the material world. Imperial discourses informed practical policies of governance and, in turn, such discourses were shaped by shifting economic and political conditions. Cultural, political and economic power are thus inseparable. As Amy Kaplan points out in discussing the nature of American imperialism:

> [Imperialism is] . . . Not just about foreign diplomacy or international relations, [but] also about consolidating domestic cultures . . . To foreground cultures is not only to understand how they abet the subjection of others or foster their resistance, but also to ask how international relations reciprocally shape a dominant imperial culture at home, and how imperial relations are enacted and contested within the nation . . . If the importance of culture has gone unrecognised in historical studies of American imperialism, the role of empire has been equally ignored in the study of American culture . . . Imperialism as a political or economic process abroad is inseparable from the social relations and cultural discourse of race, gender, ethnicity, and class at home.
>
> (Kaplan, 1993, pp. 14–16)

Such discourses are neither monolithic nor static and are determined by the changing relationship between the imperial centre and periphery. We can chart these important changes through the imperial discourses of the two dominant twentieth-century empires, Britain and the USA. In British imperial discourse between 1918 and 1945 semantic shifts from empire to

Commonwealth flagged important changes in colonial policy and representations of the colonized. As one empire propagandist put it, the British imperial
mission was now '. . . a great experiment in progressive civilisation based on
tolerance and a sympathetic and helpful trusteeship . . . of natives' (Hurd,
1924, pp. 5–6). In the unstable milieu of the interwar years, empire strengthening was a key aim. During the War the 'empire family' had stood together
in defence of the 'motherland', fostering 'empire intimacy', a new domestic
motif of empire. The mass democratization of Britain and its five 'white'
Dominions, now equal partners in the movement for empire self sufficiency,
engendered a new sense of (white) 'empire citizenship'. Visions of more
participatory and inclusive empire were articulated through popular culture
and politics (Case study 4). In imperial policies there was a 'move from [mas-
culine] power to [feminine] service' (Perham, 1944).

By the 1930s scientific racism had been superseded by race relations discourse that prioritized cultural as opposed to biological difference (Barkan,
1992). Mounting challenges to empire transformed imperial discourse. During
the Second World War the discourse of a humanitarian Commonwealth
committed to racial equality and equal partnership of all members of the
Commonwealth became essential to gaining the consent and loyalty of the colonized and aided the manipulation of nationalism to secure ongoing imperial
interests. Developments in the language of empire reconstructed representations of the colonial subject from barbaric 'other' to modern, civilized, equal
citizen. But discourses are also internally inconsistent and commitment to
racial equality was more rhetoric than reality. Caribbean migrants to postwar
Britain found no welcome in the motherland, only racial exclusions. The
colonial 'others' were no longer 'out there' but remapping the imperial
centre with their physical presence and challenges mounted to imperial
representations of the colonial subject (Bush, 2005).

The discourse of humanitarianism also defined American self-representation
as an ascendant power during the Second World War. The USA now took over
the mantle of global 'champion of the oppressed', claimed by Britain since
the abolition of slavery in 1838, and adopted an anti-imperialist rhetoric
dedicated to spreading democracy, freedom and prosperity to oppressed
colonial peoples. American exceptionalism was re-articulated as inherently
anti-imperialist, in opposition to old European empires. Exceptionalism
emerged out of the American Revolution and implied that the USA was
exemplary, a model and a superior point of reference for the rest of the world.
In effect, this assumed (and still assumes) cultural superiority and universalism of values. American imperial discourse provides another example of
the internal inconsistencies in the logic of such discourses of power and the

linguistic slippages that fudge reality and rhetoric. Since the 1940s, argues Kaplan (1993), a 'double dynamic' has developed in US self-representation whereby linguistic displacement accompanies denial: 'World Power' not 'American Empire'; 'discovery' not 'imperium'; 'unipolarity' not 'hegemony'. Imperial politics is thus something others do abroad, not Americans. In the 1980s Cold War environment this displacement occurred in the demonization of the Soviet 'Evil Empire' (pp. 12–13).

Such inconsistencies and subterfuges in imperial discourses did not deflect from their power at any one point in history. What the language of imperialism, articulated through official discourse, provides is a general metaphor for the age that informs every cultural medium. This is applicable to ancient and early modern as well as modern European empires. But modern media and communications fostered a language of Western power that straddled the national boundaries of individual imperial states and infiltrated literature, advertising, academic discourse and pedagogy. National cultures introduced some specificities but the overriding metaphor was of Western cultural, economic, military and technological superiority, of modernity and progress. Thus, from the mid-nineteenth century, the language of empire was influenced by scientific racism, eugenics, patriotic nationalism and supreme confidence in the imperial mission. After the First World War, the era of bellicose, expansionist imperialism was superseded by the progressive, humanitarian imperialism articulated at the League of Nations, which prioritized development, modernization, welfare and reform. We now turn from the self-representation of empire in imperial discourses to explore how such representations strengthened imperial power and gained consent for empire in both colony and metropole.

Representation and the legitimization of imperial power

Mapping the empire

Central to representing empire and subjugated colonies is cartography, the physical and metaphorical mapping of empire and boundaries. The Greek, Roman and Chinese Celestial Empires created maps that placed their empires at the heart of the known world, but by the sixteenth century the world had been mapped according to the global European vision. With the exception of the Peters projection, conventional mappings of the world prioritizing Europe and North America remained largely unchallenged, even after the red of formal empire had been erased (Crow and Thomas (eds.), 1983). Maps, like photographs, constructed what Said (1985) called an 'imaginative geography' that legitimated 'a universe of representational discourse' and drew 'dramatic boundaries' that reflected the interests of the West (pp. 71–4). This inspired postcolonial deconstructions that challenged such colonial mappings (Huggan, 1991, pp. 125–38). Such studies emphasized that geography was the 'queen' of European imperial sciences, the key to imperial power and the ideal subject to teach empire in schools. The map was the principal geographical tool and state support was often provided for the exploration and mapping of Africa, Asia and Latin America from the eighteenth century (Bell, Butlin and Hefferman (eds), 1995, p. 4). The importance of mapping to empire is evident in the resourceful disguises used by colonial cartographers to map the disputed North West boundaries of British India to secure territory from a predatory Russia (Meyer and Brysac, 2001).

To map was to possess, to tame and order *terra nullis*. To fly over what were once the great prairies of the US Midwest provides a vivid aerial view of such mappings – neat square plots of private property and orderly roads and towns. Maps could also exclude and erase the inferior culture and create 'landscapes of progress where order replaced chaos' (Bell, in Bell, Butlin and Heffernan (eds), 1995, p. 200). In Apartheid mappings of South Africa, the shadow cities of the African townships were omitted, creating the illusion of a 'white man's country'. Maps thus created colonies that reflected European ambitions, rivalries and diplomatic agreements rather than natural ethnic or cultural spaces of shared identity and recognition. Sub-Saharan Africa, the 'dark', 'unmapped' continent, was particularly vulnerable to carving up and the imposition of artificially created boundaries. In India, princely kingdoms retained elements of precolonial mappings but place names were anglicized and the railway network created a European mapping of the subcontinent. Colonial mappings also shaped events in the postcolonial era. In sub-Saharan Africa artificial boundaries drawn up by Europeans divided ethnic groups between different colonies or forced different ethnic groups to live together in one colony. This has contributed to postcolonial ethnic and religious conflicts from the Biafran civil war in the 1960s to the genocide in Ruanda in the 1990s. East and West Pakistan were British creations of the bloody partition that accompanied independence in 1947; separated by great distance, the two halves of Pakistan had no future as a viable entity and, after another bloody war in 1971, East Pakistan became Bangladesh.

We must also consider the 'imaginary mappings' of empire in colonial discourse. Inspired by Said, postcolonial theorists have argued that such discourses created symbolic mappings, landscapes and 'spaces' interpenetrated by sets of representational relations – class, gender, race, nation and sexuality – that created the 'borders' of imperial power. Such 'discursive terrains' are 'spatial' and composed of a variety of differently inscribed and imagined locations. Foucault has been influential here in his definition of 'heterotopias' or 'spaces of otherness', including enslavement or colonialism, that are the opposite of utopias (Lowe, 1991, p. 15). Thus the heterotopia/colony also creates 'spaces' of resistance to dominant discourses in empire and metropole. Geographers have enthusiastically embraced such postcolonial conceptualizations in wresting their discipline from its imperial/Eurocentric traditions. Despite the rather off-putting language, this reconceptualization of space and contested borders extends our understanding of the power of representation and dynamics of power and resistance. Such reconceptualizations have emphasized how empires, ancient and modern, created 'imaginary' landscapes. Yet empires also created 'real' landscapes, concrete representations of power that provided tangible evidence of imperial power in colony and metropole. Together with visual and other representations of empire in popular culture these shaped the consciousness of both colonized and colonizers.

Public representations of imperial power

Cultural affirmations of power, designed to impress the subordinated populations, have been central to self-representation from the ancient empires onwards. The Romans inscribed power on colonized landscapes through roads, military camps, villas and towns. They built monuments and triumphal arches throughout the empire and, as in China, empire 'personalized' was visible everywhere in the bodies and lives of individual emperors and the coinage that bore their image. The world inhabited by both Roman subjects and citizens of empire was shaped by such visions of empire (Woolf, 2002, p. 321). This was paralleled in the later British Empire. The iconography of royalty was evident in the mundane and ceremonial throughout the empire and statues of Queen Victoria abounded (Steggles, 2001, p. 44). In the Roman Empire imperial superiority and rank were expressed through clothing and spatial divisions of seating in theatres and amphitheatres. Gladiatorial spectacles, plays, festivals and praise songs to Roman military might symbolized Roman power; the cult of the emperor, associated with diffusion of the Roman gods, was an essential element of imperial ideology and propaganda (Garnsey and Saller, 1987, pp. 116–17, 167, 190). In later European empires, segregated housing, pomp and ceremony, and dress styles were central to white prestige. Throughout European tropical colonies the sola topi (pith helmet) became the visual symbol of the ruling caste, whilst 'native' dress emphasized subservience. Clothing, argued Cohn (1996) was a vital element in the self-representation of the British in India but also became central to the creation of new nationalist identities as Gandi and Nehru refashioned Indian dress as a visual symbol of the nationalist struggle (pp. 143–60).

In the imperial centres superior imperial identities were confirmed through colonial and empire exhibitions that celebrated economic and political power and aimed to secure popular support for empire. The 1931 Colonial Exhibition held in Paris was designed to make imperialism 'an integral part of French consciousness' and was a huge success. There were displays of 'native' troops and the Great Hall contained 'sumptuous frescoes glorifying empire'. The Paris Metro was extended especially for the exhibition and commemorative stamps and postcards were produced. At the same time, the imperial message was reinforced in French state schools where every classroom had a map with the empire in pink (Evans, 2000, pp. 19–25). British empire exhibitions are discussed in more depth in Case study 4. Such exhibitions also reinforced the message of imperial greatness for colonial visitors and enabled them to view white representations of themselves and their culture. Thus at the 1931 Paris exhibition, Egyptian visitors saw exotic but sanitized representations of Egyptian culture that edited out contemporary political realities (Mitchell, 1988, p. 11).

Exhibitions and ceremony were also central to representations of American imperial power before and during the First World War (Rydell, 1984). Christopher Columbus was appropriated as quintessentially American and Columbian traditions were invented in 1892, capitalizing on the 400th anniversary of the 'discovery' of America to unite the nation in an era of US imperial expansion. Huge celebrations in New York City involved parades, floats, fireworks, naval marches and the unveiling of a statue of Columbus in Central Park. Columbus 'served as the embodiment of the nation and excuse for nationalistic fervour' and the World's Columbian Exposition in Chicago in 1893 was the 'most elaborate and extensive yet undertaken' (Sale, 1992, pp. 350, 352). Opened by President Cleveland, the exposition began with the 'Halleluiah Chorus' providing an uplifting background to a display of machinery driven by electricity, demonstrating US technological power. Columbus Day was promoted by the Knights of Columbus after 1898 and by 1934 had become an official national holiday. Columbus became a common place name, only surpassed by Washington and, outside the USA, Queen Victoria (ibid., pp. 359–60).

Central to representations of US power were technological triumphs. A mechanized reproduction of the Panama Canal provided the centrepiece of the San Francisco Panama-Pacific Exposition in 1915 that celebrated the completion of the project. Inspiring awe in the spectators, the exhibit shaped perceptions of the USA's developing imperialist persona based on technological and scientific, as well as cultural, superiority. The guidebook to the fair announced it as a 'celebration of a "race of people in the making" that can be traced back to Athens . . .'. This referred to the 'whole world' but was led by specific 'Great American Achievements' (cited in Brown, 1993, pp. 140–9). More recently, the technological triumph of the 'computer game' destruction of Baghdad in 2003 was beamed globally and the US 'logo' emphasized imperial power at press briefings. Operation Iraqi Freedom, argues Gregory (2004), unfolded like a film script, projecting America as superpower, and President Bush surrounded himself with the trappings of Hollywood to declare victory. In an 'aestheticization' of politics (and violence) for the domestic audience, Washington's 'script' saw Iraq as 'an empty screen on which America could project its own image'. But Iraqis were not 'extras in a silent movie' and disrupted the 'production' through anti-occupation resistance (pp. 216–17). Contemporary representations of imperial power are strengthened by allusions to past empires. For instance, the film, *Gladiator* (US, 2000) portrays a Roman Empire defined by cultural and ethnic diversity, mobility, and globalizing tendencies. In this sense it may also be interpreted as a reflection of the twenty-first century world centred on the USA.

Popular imperialism: selling empire to the masses

Visual and written representations of the empire and the colonial 'other' are fundamental to understanding the power of 'popular imperialism' in metropolitan centres. The dominant official discourse of empire in official texts and propaganda infiltrated popular fiction, journalism and travel writing. There were agents of colonial propaganda in all European colonial powers, whose influence filtered down into the provinces, familiarizing citizens with the colonial idea and mission (Goerg, 2002; Wildenthal, 2001; Spurr, 1995). The Japanese media and government propaganda popularized the Japanese imperial mission in Manchuria in the 1930s (Buruma, 2003; Young, 1998). In the USA and Europe, empire was sold on the basis of philanthropy and missionaries, national destiny and implicit belief in racial/cultural superiority. Positive benefits emphasized in European colonial propaganda reflected national priorities, but common themes included colonial settlement, a better life and economic and commercial gain. In Germany and Britain before the First World War 'social imperialism' rationalized empire on the basis of wealth creation to improve the social conditions and welfare of the masses. Empire consolidated nationalism cultivated through the 'mass producing traditions' that emerged throughout Europe and in the USA after 1870 (Hobsbawm, 1983).

Working-class whites experienced empire as popular entertainment and spectacle and benefited as settlers in the colonies and through cheap products of empire. Such 'carrots', asserts Pieterse (1992), served to 'neutralise class struggle' and transform class solidarity and political unrest into national and racial solidarity (p. 70). Advertising became more sophisticated from the 1890s and the frequency of imperial motifs and racial imagery in the marketing and packaging of consumer goods throughout imperial Western Europe ensured that European consumers were also 'consuming the subjection of the colonised' (ibid. p. 84). From the beginning, mass advertising worked through images and text with which the public could easily identify and the empire and the colonized were perfect (and profitable) images throughout Europe during the imperial era. As Goerg has demonstrated in her study of advertisements in provincial Strasburg in the period 1877–1930, clichéd representations of Africa were popular but representations went far beyond the world colonized by France and embraced the mythical Orient (Goerg, 2002, pp. 95–7). This begs the question of the extent to which advertising, as a commercial medium, reflected current imperial discourse or simply appealed to a broader interest in the exotic 'other' in European popular culture. Did advertising create images of the 'other' or simply reproduce powerful representations of the colonial subject created through Orientalist and racialized discourses? Such representations located in dominant colonial discourses were fundamental to all popular imagery of the colonized.

Constructing the colonial/Orientalized subject: race and cultural difference

All cultures read signs about people to categorize them and locate them in terms of social relationships, cultural differences and structures of power. The difference with representations constructed through colonial knowledge is their power to facilitate the concrete repression/exploitation of the colonial subject/'other' and to confirm imperial superiority and gain consent for empire in the imperial heartland. Representations of the 'other' legitimizing imperial power are not exclusive to the West. The Japanese were constructed as culturally different and implicitly inferior, particularly after defeat in the Second World War, but Japanese imperialist ideology also constructed negative representations of peoples Japan wished to subjugate. After the Sino-Japanese War, 1894–95 the Japanese were portrayed in government propaganda and in the popular media as a tall, white, vigorous and divine race compared with the cowardly, cretinous, yellow Chinese. This, argued Buruma (2003), justified atrocities towards the Chinese and other Asian peoples, including the Nanking massacre in December 1937 when up to 300,000 may have died, an event which still affects relations between China and Japan (pp. 85–6). Most studies, however, focus on Western representations of the non-Western 'other'.

Postcolonial theorists have argued that, in Eurocentric myths of the civilizing mission, 'colonial reality' appears only in its 'estranged representation' (Prakash, 1995, p. 4). Clichéd images and racial stereotypes of the colonized emerged through persistent replication, constructing powerful representations of colonial subjects that retained enduring features. Yet such representations were not estranged from reality. As 'colonial knowledge' they informed colonial policies and thus impacted in a concrete way on the lives and identities of the colonized. We must also avoid universalizing generalizations. Constructions of the colonized 'other' were differentiated by gender and class positions and multiple representations existed simultaneously, depending on the perspective of the (Western/European) observer and their specific relationship to the colonized subject at any given moment in time. An example here is the 'fabulous fiction' of slave women's identities; in pro-slavery discourse they were simultaneously anonymous workhorses, promiscuous or exotic sexualized women and resistant 'she devils'; abolitionists conceptualized them as exploited victims in need of the civilizing influence of Christianity (Bush, 2000). Additionally, as with imperial/colonial discourses, representations of the colonized are not static and reflect the changing nature of the colonial mission, developments in the metropolitan centre and changing power relations between the West and non-Western peoples. Hence the emergence of more negative representations of the Chinese as China succumbed to Western imperialism. When power is threatened by resistance stereotypes become uglier, as in the 'black brute' and 'ape-like Irish', a process of 'Negroization' to emphasize inferiority (Pieterse, 1992).

Visual representations of empire and the colonized 'other' were particularly powerful, positioning Europeans at the 'apex of universal history' (Wolfe, 1997, p. 405). Recent studies of race and representation in art, influenced by postcolonial theory, have prompted us to look in new ways at European art (Pollock, 1993). When I was in Melbourne in 1996, I went to a fascinating exhibition, curated from all over the world, dedicated to representations of the frontier by European artists in Australia and the USA. The American paintings conveyed a bright and utopian New World to which European colonization would bring progress and prosperity, and Native American Indians were represented as the pure 'noble savage' of Enlightenment thought. As Brown (1999) points out, Native American Indians were regarded as less culturally malleable than Africans, but also less physically distant from whiteness, and aesthetic representations of 'Red' Indians were contrasted with crude racist stereotypes of African-American slaves (pp. 94–5). Conversely, in the Australian paintings, Europeans were portrayed looking outwards to the ocean with their backs towards the fearful interior. Such white fears of the wild, primitive and dangerous Australian interior were later evoked in Australian films such as *Walkabout* (Nicholas Roeg, 1970) and *Picnic at Hanging Rock* (Peter Wier, 1975) and have produced the white suburban cities clinging to the coastal rim. Artists submerged such fears by taming the alien landscape with the imprint of old Europe: Hobart, Tasmania in the style of Canaletto, bucolic scenes of Victoria derivative of Constable. Aboriginal peoples were painted in permanent shade, whereas white settlers were always bathed in the sunlight of 'civilization', validating the dispossession of Aboriginal lands in the name of redemption and progress. As civilization advanced indigenous peoples and their 'prehistoric', timeless Australian landscape were 'brushed out' of landscape images and, thus, Australian history (MacNeil, 2001).

Museums, ethnography, anthropology and popular travelogues, aided by photography, were also seminal in shaping superior white racial identities (Maxwell, 2000). Ethnographic displays date back to the early nineteenth century when what Bernth Lindfors (1999) termed 'ethnological show business' became lucrative and popular in British cities; African villages and exotic architecture reached the French provinces (Goerg, 2002). In the United States, the collection of Carl Akeley, the American scientist, explorer and hunter who went on a series of collecting exhibitions to British Somaliland and British East Africa between 1896 and 1926, formed the basis of the African Hall at the American Museum of Natural History which opened in New York in 1936 (Harraway, 1993). The photograph became a powerful way of representing the colonized 'other' through the imperial lens and reinforced anthropological representations (Edwards, 1994). Photography is not an innocent 'eye of history': photographs are culturally constructed 'moments in broader discourses' that require historical contextualization. Photographs are combined with linguistic messages, titles, captions and text and 'photographing the natives' was linked to racial science and confirmed the discourse of inferiority and superiority that justified empire (Ryan, 1997).

After 1918, the new visual medium of popular film disseminated imagery of Western superiority to an even wider mass audience. 'Euro-colonial cinema', as the 'Eye of Empire', could transform white spectators into 'armchair conquistadors', affirming a sense of vicarious power. Simultaneously, colonized spectators viewed offensive representations of themselves that emphasized their inferiority but deepened ambivalence to colonial rule (Shohat and Stam, 1994, pp. 303–4). Empire also became more associated with leisure and visual colonial spectacle. Tourism displaced live ethnographic displays, as people could travel in greater numbers to gaze on the colonial 'others'. The tourist consumed exotic or different experiences and souvenirs, photos and postcards that reproduced ethnological representations and affirmed his/her own superior imperial identity (Phillips, 1995). From the 1920s Cunard Line started to run short cruise breaks to supplement revenue from Atlantic liners. Caribbean cruises offered exoticism, winter sunshine and, for Americans, escape from Prohibition. Cunard 'White Star' and 'New World Rivieras' cruises visited Nassau, Florida, Jamaica and California. Lascar seamen, from coasts of India and the Maldives, used by P&O Line since the 1840s, lent an 'exotic' air on deck with uniforms of dark blue, knee-length, embroidered tunics over white trousers, red sashes and brimless cap-like turbans of the same red material (National Maritime Museum, London). The Caribbean was now a tame tropical playground; in contrast, the 'wild' African and Indian 'jungle' lured adventurous white men and emancipated white women and generated a new genre of travelogue such as Delia Akeley's *African Jungle Portraits* (1930) and Ethel Mannin's *Indian Jungle Journey* (1940). For adventurers from a tamed Europe and United States, the African continent was the ultimate wilderness, a vast reserve for hunting game, where African peoples were erased from the landscape. What are the origins of such Western representations of Asia and Africa?

Orientalist discourses

Edward Said defined 'Orientalizing' as the process whereby the 'other' is represented in an 'essentialized' form, emphasizing difference and distance between the familiar (Europe, We, Us) and the strange (Orient, East, Them). For Said the Orient was 'less a place than a *topos*, a set of references, a congeries of characteristics', the location of one of the West's 'deepest and most recurring images' of the 'other' (Said, 1985, pp. 43, 177). This 'Orientalizing' intensified (and continues to intensify) the West's sense of itself. The Orient is now used to define the 'non-West' but this generalization obscures how and why different representations of the 'Orient' and Africa emerged. It is thus important to try to define the 'Orient'. As Inden observes, different meanings have existed over time and perhaps we should speak of 'Orients' – the Near East, the Far East, South Asia – rather than 'Orient' (Inden, 2001, p. 97).

Changing perceptions of the Orient are reflected in the fortunes of the Oriental Club, founded in London in 1824 to meet the growing needs of those serving in the 'extensive . . . British Empire in the East' (Forrest, 1968, pp. 226–7). Initially directed to individuals who had served in the military or the East India Company in India, membership was broadened to include those who had resided or travelled in the East. By the 1840s the club had 'honorary Indian gentleman members' (pp. 66–7). Malaya hands were included after 1880. By the 1950s, however, the name evoked a sleazy club in Soho, reflecting just how the meaning of the word 'Orient' had changed.

During the Cold War the 'East' implied the Communist East. The Orient as 'other' was re-appropriated by the French Left in the 1970s when they embraced Maoism after the failures of 1968. The Chinese became the 'revolutionary others' but, argues Lowe (1991), this new Orientalizing perpetuated much of the discourse, relationships and structures that these radicals had wanted to topple in 1968 (p. 199). In academic discourse the Orient fell out of favour, replaced by area and 'third world' studies (Inden, 2001, p. 97). In the Western imagination, however, it continued to evoke exotic tourist locations and imperialist nostalgia, as in the commercial renovation of the Orient Express. Yet the recent war in Iraq has demonstrated how deeply a damaging Orientalism has infiltrated into Western consciousness. As Said (1985) observed, since the growth of Arab resistance in the Middle East intensified after the First World War, representations have focused on the 'oversexed degenerate . . . capable of devious intrigues [and] treacherous'. But, he adds, 'lurking behind all these images is the menace of the jihad' (p. 286). How did these Western representations of the Orient emerge and were they always so negative?

Western ambivalence to the Orient, reflected in admiration combined with fear and related cultural denigration, was evident from early cultural contact between Muslims and Christians. In his classic study of the Crusades, written before the postmodern debates about Orientalism, Runciman (1965) observed that when pilgrims and crusaders visited the Frankish colony of Outremer (Palestine) they contrasted the sophistication of Eastern culture, enhanced by Roman sewerage systems, with the simple, often harsh feudal life in Western Europe. The 'luxury [and licence] of . . . life' both impressed and shocked Occidentals (p. 323). Christians believed that they were heirs to Rome and its superior civilization and Moslem Saracens were represented as devils in contemporary imagery. But Frankish settlers were seduced by Moslem culture, particularly luxurious clothes and furnishings. When not in armour, knights wore silk burnouses and turbans; their ladies adopted the traditional Eastern fashion of a long under robe and a gold-embroidered short tunic or coat. Outside they were veiled like Muslim women, although allegedly this was to protect their skin from the sun. As with all colonists, the Frankish settlers had to adapt to 'native' ways and employ 'native' servants and rely on 'native' medicine to treat the strange diseases with which they were afflicted (pp. 317, 322–3).

Yet beneath the seduction, fear of 'otherness' was also evident. Settler women, for all their 'airs of delicacy and languor', had to be tough, and noble-women led the defence of castles in the absence of husbands. Settlers also had to live with the threat of the Assassins, a religious sect organized by the Persian, Hasan as-Sabah, in the late eleventh century (Runciman, 1965, pp. 323–4). This medieval al-Qaida set up secret lodges in Syria, murdered in the name of religion and were a thorn in the side of the mainstream Muslim opposition to Christian colonization. Such threats reflected Muslim humiliations during the First Crusade, c. 1099–1101, although Muslim pride was redeemed in the Second Crusade when Saladin reclaimed Jerusalem in 1187. The tolerance and sophistication of Arab culture contrasted with the 'intolerance and barbarity' of the Crusaders (ibid., pp. 473, 323). Yet the negative representations of the Islamic Near Eastern world, derived from Crusader rationales for their Holy War, have threaded down through history. At the cusp of modernity in the eighteenth century, Europeans grudgingly recognized the influence of Near Eastern Islamic culture on the development of their own culture, but regarded continued Ottoman rule over parts of Eastern Europe as a threat. Contemporary sources described the 'Ottoman' as a 'potentially dangerous alter ego of the European', whose religion, Islam, was a 'false, fanatical cousin of Christianity' (cited in Inden, 2001, p. 112). Fear of fanatical Islam has persisted; the fact that in the early twenty-first century the word 'crusade' was once more applied to a new Western 'war' on Islamic terrorism testifies to the durability of negative Orientalist discourses about the Middle East.

From the sixteenth century and the expansion of European travel to Asia, however, more positive representations of the Orient also emerged. The eighteenth-century Enlightenment, and associated debates about the nature of civilization and progress, were pivotal in the development of modern Orientalist thought. Initially, the Orient was used to describe everything in Asia, but particularly the Middle East and the Ottoman Empire. With European expansion into North Africa, India and the Far East, argues Inden (2001), there was greater differentiation. As British power in India expanded, so knowledge about the subcontinent came to dominate conceptualizations of the Orient. The Enlightenment had both positive and negative consequences as India became a focus of academic enquiry. Early Orientalists like Sir

William Jones (1746–94), who founded the Asiatic Society of Bengal, were romantic admirers of Oriental culture. Some East India Company officials and traders also took a positive interest in Asian culture, embraced 'Oriental' dress and customs and married into good local families (Dalrymple, 2002).

In the early nineteenth century the anti-romantic, positivist utilitarians and evangelical missionaries, the two key prongs in British modernity, with their belief in progress and the civilizing mission, displaced the earlier romantics. In effect, both romantics (idealists) and modernizing positivists gave a hegemonic account of Asian culture that represented themselves as superior: romantics were critical of Western values and institutions and aspects of emergent modernity but did not accept Eastern equivalents as substitutes (Inden, 2001). But, as Majeed (1992) has demonstrated, developments in British culture influenced the evolution of Orientalist discourse and more negative perceptions of Asian society. Influential here were Thomas Babbington Macaulay's *Minute on Indian Education* (1835), which made a strong case for Anglicization of Indian culture, and *History of India* (1817), where James Mill argued that Western knowledge should replace Eastern and that the increasingly powerful East India Company should 'push' Indians into history. Now, the prevailing view was that the 'Chinaman and the Hindu were the true others', whose civilizations were 'irrational [and stagnant] formations' (Inden, 2001, pp. 211–13). This was the foundation of Indology, a positivist or empirical/realist and privileged discourse that denied Indians the power to represent themselves. The West's depictions of India as a land dominated by imagination, rather than reason, allowed the West to appropriate and dominate the region (Inden, 1990). By the end of the nineteenth century knowledge was collected through official ethnography and photography and statistics replaced older forms of representation. The British, writes Cohn, had not only invaded and conquered India but 'through their [Orientalist] scholarship, had invaded an epistemological space [and] reordered the nature of Indian knowledge' (Cohn, 1996, p. 53).

By the ninteenth century Orientalist knowledge of India had become a tool of governance (Bayly, 1996) and the more negative perceptions of China facilitated European expansion (Case study 2). From 1870 the French had a desire to conquer and dominate the Orient and promoted an image of superior French masculinity, forcing the feminized Orient into submission and hence protecting Europe from the decadent influence of Islam (Lowe, 1991). In popular European representations, however, the Orient had also become a location of fantasy and imagination. In British culture Oriental motifs were connected with pleasure and entertainment, as in the Brighton Pavilion and later Alhambra Palaces of popular working-class entertainment

(Mitchell, 1992). An idealized 'Orient' was exhibited in metropolitan centres like Paris. Europeans, argued Timothy Mitchell (1988), were disappointed by the unruly, dirty and backward Orient they confronted in their travels but the 'imagined Orient' held promises of escapism and eroticism. The exotic *Thousand and One Nights* or *Arabian Nights Entertainment* in a sanitized version was popular with Victorian 'young ladies'; Sir Richard Burton's erotic, unabridged translations (1882–6) reflected the growing obsession with the Orient as a location of sexual promise (Melman, 1995, p. 63). In Gustave Flaubert's novels the Orient is associated with sexual escapism, a site of freedom from the repressed sexuality of bourgeois France and in *Voyages en Orient* (1850) Flaubert revealed his own desires (Lowe, 1991, pp. 8–9). By the early twentieth century North Africa, the Middle East and India had also became a site of erotic fantasy for French and British homosexuals, of whom T. E. Lawrence – 'Lawrence of Arabia' – is one of the best known (Aldrich, 2003, pp. 14–15).

Central to male heterosexual fantasies of the Orient was the seraglio (harem) which represented the hidden sexual delights behind 'the veil', covers of modesty which needed to be 'penetrated'. French Orientalist painters, of whom Delacroix is the most famous, specialized in representing this female Oriental sexuality – as nude women in the hammam (Turkish baths) or women unveiled in their interior world of the harem. His 'Odalisque', a Turkish servant, became the definitive concubine in European imagery (Stevens (ed.), 1984). From the earliest contact between Christians and Muslims, argues Melman (1995), the harem evoked two essential Oriental characteristics: violence (the oppression of women) and sensuality (polygamy and promiscuity) and thus represented a white male fantasy. European representations of the Orient were clearly gendered and white women's travel writings on the Orient differ from those of men and were not always racist (Lewis, 1996). For some women the Orient represented freedom as well as exotic adventure, although this clearly differentiated them from subordinated Oriental women. Melman suggests that Lady Mary Wortley Montagu, who travelled to Turkey with her diplomat husband in the late eighteenth century, may have found escape from her unhappy marriage by immersing herself in Turkish culture. She adopted Turkish women's dress and visited harems, which she domesticated and normalized in her writings (pp. 59–61). In the twentieth century white women also experienced the Orient as liberated women, trekking through the Sahara desert and adopting Oriental dress (Motley, 1961).

After 1918 erotic representations of the Orient filtered into popular culture, where the reproduction of gendered stereotypes of the colonial

'other' reinforced superior white gendered identities. The Orient was constructed around representations of women's sexuality, in allusions to veiling
and unveiling, and the effeminacy and decadence of men. But representations of the Oriental male as inherently bestial – the sexualized pasha and sheik
as a threat to white womanhood – also appeared in popular culture. Oriental
men were crucial in the moral panics over the white slave trade prior to
the First World War. After the war popular film and fictional romances had
'desert' themes centred on handsome, brutal 'Oriental' men forcing white
women into the submission and sex slavery associated with oppressed,
inferior colonized women (Melman, 1986, p. 137). Emblematic here is *The
Sheik* (1919), starring Rudolph Valentino, which reflected both the seductive
and threatening aspects of Oriental sexuality and culture. Chinese men in
London's Limehouse were also represented as a sexual threat to white womanhood, luring girls into their 'opium dens' and thus undermining the morality
and racial integrity of white society (Bickers, 1999). Such representations
reflected the increasing threat of Chinese, Arab and Egyptian nationalism to
imperial interests. In 1920 there was a major rebellion in Iraq and in 1922
Egypt became nominally independent. Pan-Arabism and resurgent Islam
were challenging the real and discursive power of the West. The Oriental
male threat had to be neutralized through emasculation and the belief that
homosexuality was endemic amongst 'depraved' Oriental and Arab men
(Aldrich, 2003, pp. 14–15). In popular culture, negative representations
of the colonized helped secure consensus in the metropolitan heartland
around internal threats to imperial stability. Simultaneously, Orientalism as an
academic discipline became more sophisticated to meet these new challenges
to empire. However, these cracks in the structures that supported Orientalism
post-1918, argues Lowe (1991), also stimulated critiques of Orientalist discourse reflected, for instance, in the writings of E. M. Forster.

Contrasting representations of the Orient over time demonstrate how
constructions of the colonized 'other' in text or visual image are fluid and
metamorphose, depending on imperial priorities and the degree of colonial
resistance. Elements of the gendered and racialized Orientalist discourse
refined over the imperial era have persisted into the postcolonial era. Take,
for instance, the feminization of the colonized/inferiorized whose passivity
and subjection is emphasized by emasculation through conquest. Shohat
and Stam (1994) referred to the 'phallic vigour' of the 1992 Gulf War where
America recovered from the 'traumatic impotence' suffered in Vietnam
(p. 128). Writing of US torture of Arab prisoners in Iraq, Jonathan Raban
(2004) observed that in the US media before the Second Gulf War, the Iraqi
people were pictured as 'yearning, femininely, childishly, with one voice for

. . . democracy and would greet their liberators with . . . flowers'. To Paul Wolfowitz ('Wolfowitz of Arabia'), US Deputy Defence Secretary and a key policy maker for the 2003 war, Iraq was a 'comely' bride imprisoned by her wicked stepfather who needed liberating. Here, argued Raban, were parallels with the language used by T. E. Lawrence, who was also devoted to 'liberating' Arabia.

By the time of the invasion, concluded Raban, Iraq had been so exhaustively Orientalized that it had lost almost all connection with reality. In the US-controlled prisons 'Arabia' was 'nude and under a hood'. America was on an 'Orientalist rampage' in which Arabs were 'systematically denatured, dehumanised, stripped of all human complexity, reduced to naked babyhood [and] feminised in women's panties' (p. 6). With growing resistance harsher images emerged and the victim bride was replaced by the barbaric 'rag head' who must be ritually humiliated. As Lisa Lowe (1991) stressed, the 'newly configured Orientalisms' that emerged in the 1980s also demand critical attention, as do the resistance and dissent that exposed tensions and conflicts in dominant discourses about the 'other'. As in the colonial era, violence and repression continue to be justified by Orientalist discourse but also to stimulate 'practical' resistance (pp. x, 25). This demonstrates that Orientalism is not simply on abstract discourse but determined policies and practices that impacted, and continue to impact, adversely on the lives of non-Western peoples. This is true of Orientalizing discourses applied in a more general sense, but significant differences also existed in representation of Oriental and African peoples that affected imperial policies towards different colonial subjects and impacted on postcolonial experiences.

Constructing the African subject: racialized discourses

Orientalism was powerful in the way it constructed subordinated Oriental subjects but exoticisization of Oriental culture constituted a more subtle and complex form of racism than the crude scientific racism that defined African identities. From the era of the slave trade and the beginnings of the African diaspora, white representation of Blackness conflated 'the negro race' and Africans. By 1900, Africa, 'conquered, and dismembered', had become an object of contempt. Even the 'thick massive nature of its shape' was contrasted in contemporary representations with the 'slender elegance' of Europe (cited in Sibeud, 2002, pp. 160–1). This had, and still has, a seminal influence on the economic and social position of Africans in the American and European diasporas. In the Western imagination Africa became a hinterland 'at the back of once upon a time', a 'mirage', a timeless world of adventure and exotic stimulation, outside modernity (Hoyningen-Huene, 1938, pp. 16–17). Wealthy travellers, male and female, revelled in the animal-like beauty of 'savages', their exotic customs and the emotional appeal of 'uncivilized' Africa, whilst colonial rule was justified on the grounds that natives were 'a thousand years away' from civilization (Mills, 1929).

Anthropological representations were influential in shaping popular images of Africa. As an academic discipline Orientalist discourse was about the decaying 'civilized', whereas the focus of anthropologists was the 'primitive' (Inden, 2001, p. 99). Academic anthropology had the same approach to 'Darkest Africa' as to 'Darkest England'. Both were represented as alien territories with a perceived different, and inferior, culture. The impoverished inhabitants of Britain's urban 'jungles' were racialized as primitive 'others', a 'heart of darkness' in the civilized metropole. This linkage was patently expressed in General William Booth's *In Darkest England and the Way Out* (Salvation Army, 1890). Booth drew on Henry Morton Stanley's best-seller *In Darkest Africa*, published in the same year. 'The intrepid explorer', he wrote, 'ploughed' his way into the 'inner womb of the tropical forest':

> The mind of a man with difficulty endeavours to realize this immensity of wooded wilderness . . . where the rays of the sun never penetrate, where in the dark, dank air . . . human beings dwarfed into pygmies and brutalized into cannibals lurk and live and die.

Stanley, continued Booth, conveyed the 'full horror of that awful gloom'; he added that 'it seemed to me only too vivid a picture of many parts of our own land'. In both cases, there is 'a light beyond' where the weak and barbaric are rescued by the interventions of 'the best in manhood and womanhood of our land' (Booth, 1890, pp. 15–23). Booth's book generated considerable interest and spin-offs such as Frederick Tucker's *Darkest India* (Bombay, 1891). Social investigators, and later, anthropologists, thus both equated the 'other' within, the urban poor, and, in the twentieth century, Black minorities, with the colonized 'other'.

Anthropological research did little to challenge existing conceptions of Africa, validated the cult for the primitive in avant-garde European art, initiated by Picasso's 'borrowings', and informed popular amateur anthropological writings and ethnographic film, an important new medium which snapped societies supposedly as they were. The film *Sanders of the River* (1935), made by the American director Zoltan Korda, and starring the African-American actor Paul Robeson as the 'loyal' chief, provides insight into popular representations of colonial Africa that reached mass audiences.

Ethnographic documentary film provided the 'authentic' African setting for the studio shots and images of the natural 'primitive'. 'Real members of the Acholi, Tefik, Juruba (*sic*), Mendi and Kroo tribes' were used but Africa is still transformed into a fantastic and unreal continent. The District Officer, Sanders, is responsible for some 'quarter of a million cannibal folk' in West Central Africa, which he polices on his little steamer, *Zaïre*, evoking images of Conrad's *Heart of Darkness*. Based on the book of the same name by Edgar Wallace, 'Lord Sandi's' Africans are 'illogical', immersed in an alien, forested, spirit world of 'violent death and horrid happenings', far from the civilized society 'beyond the lazy, swelling, blue sea' (Wallace, n. d., pp. 14–15, 48–61). Accused by the Black nationalist Marcus Garvey of selling out out on his race in accepting a role that reproduced demeaning stereotypes, Robeson never took such parts again and he and his wife, Eslanda, devoted themselves to redressing negative representations of Africa (Bush, 1999, pp. 215–16).

There are important similarities in British and French colonial discourse; representations of Africa in French popular culture had a similar role to Stanley's *In Darkest Africa* in justifying aggressive expansion before the First World War (Schneider, 1982). Both British and French discourse reflected the increasing influence of scientific racism, and the eclipse of the earlier paternalist civilizing mission associated with anti-slavery discourse on Africa. The Congrès de Sociologie Coloniale, held in association with the 1900 Universal Exhibition criticized the principles of assimilation that informed French republicanist colonial policy and the missionary civilizing mission. Sibeud (2002) concludes that where earlier assimilationists, as 'negrophiles', saw pathos, colonial sociology – in effect, racial psychology – revived negro-phobia and hierarchies of civilization, envisaging only 'monstrosity and the impossibility of assimilation' (p. 163). There are clear parallels here with con-trasting positions demonstrated in British segregationist and assimilationist discourse dicussed in Chapter 3. But, adds Sibeud, by 1900 the French Anti-Slavery Congress also made use of outdated stereotypes, such as cannibalism, and endorsed forced labour as the first step to civilization (pp. 157–60). Throughout Europe clichéd representations of Africans had degenerated to the level of caricature, a longstanding feature of European representations of blackness stemming back to the era of slavery.

These debates before the First World War, however, resulted in challenges to such clichéd representations. In 1901, Maurice Delafosse outlined the basic rules for ethnography and paved the way for an emergent 'Africanism' and the radical ethnography of the 1920s and 1930s, marked by cultural stud-ies by Africans as well as Europeans (Sibeud, 2002). This new ethnography informed with anti-colonial challenges to colonial race discourse. Examples include the contributions to Nancy Cunard's unique *Negro Anthology* (1934) and the ethnographical fieldwork carried out by the African-American, Kathleen Dunham, on African-Caribbean dance forms. The two world wars in the twentieth century also resulted in new types of contact between colonial soldiers based in France and Britain and local populations, rural and urban. Caricatured images of savagery were replaced by more recognition of 'person-hood' of Africans and African-Americans, and even praise for their 'good-natured' side (Goerg, 2002; Smith, 1986). As more of the colonized migrated into the 'heart of empire', however, representations once again became uglier. In Britain, the 'good' Caribbean and African 'old timers' of the Second World War years were supplanted in popular representation by the dangerous criminal pimps and drug pushers of emergent racialized ghettos, ghettos that also blight French postcolonial cities (Bush, 2005).

Despite challenges from Black intellectuals and pan-Africanist activists, negative representations of Africa – effectively an elision of paternalistic representations of Africans as victims, cruder images of indelible savagery, and Africa as the last wilderness for European adventurers – have proved highly durable. Images of Africa as the savage 'heart of darkness' retained a persistent resonance in Hollywood films. In the comic duo, Abbott and Costello's *Africa Screams* (1946), rereleased on video in the 1980s as a 'Cinema Classic', Africa is represented as a big game adventure park, a source of easy riches (diamonds) and inhabited by dangerous cannibals. The cannibal with a bone through the nose cooking the white man in a large black pot remained a popular trope in post-Second World War European cartoons (Pieterse, 1992). The alleged savagery of the Kenyan Mau Mau against white settler families also filled the media in the 1950s. Alternatively, the vision of Africans as passive victims combined with Africa as a wilderness for the pleasure of whites was replicated in the film *Out of Africa* (1985) based on the book by the Danish writer and Kenyan settler, Karen Blixen (Isak Dinesen).

Joseph Conrad's *Heart of Darkness* (1902) remains an essential literary text in understanding the complexities of white representations of Africa and has become a particular focus of postcolonial discourse analysis. Was Conrad implicated in constructing a powerful racialized discourse or was his novel an anti-colonialist exposé of the horrors in the Congo basin which 'decivilized' the Europeans who perpetrated them? For the Nigerian author, Chinua Achebe, Conrad's writing was blatantly racist but the Black British writer Caryl Phillips has argued that Conrad was using colonialism to explore universal questions relating to man's capacity for evil. *Heart of Darkness* was thus exploring the dark side of European culture as much as the primitive and threatening Africa encountered in the Congo 'jungle' (Phillips, 2003).

Conrad's novel is certainly too complex to be dismissed as racist but, in essence, does not challenge the dominant image of Africa in the Western imagination. Such representations of Africa and generic 'hearts of darkness', real and metaphorical, have endured into the postcolonial era. As in Conrad's era, contemporary constructs of the 'other' and the primitive continue to reveal as much about the nature of the 'civilized' as the 'uncivilized'. The ambiguities in representations of the 'heart of darkness' explored by Conrad persist into the present, metamorphosed into a generalized primitive 'otherness' that masks the dark heart of Western civilization.

In Francis Ford Coppola's *Apocalypse Now* (1979), Conrad's Congo is transposed into the Mekong River during the Vietnam War. In the film, Captain Willard (Martin Sheen) goes up river to 'the beginning of time'; to a 'heart of darkness', of barbarism and anarchy, that has become the personal fiefdom of the rogue Colonel Kurtz (Marlon Brando). 'The horror, the horror', declares Kurtz, and visions of this timeless, terrible world are given additional force by the soundtrack of The Doors' song, 'The End'. In the spirit of Conrad, Coppola was exploring the American psyche of the 1970s as much the American encounter with the colonized 'other'. *Apocalypse Now*, argues Kaplan (1993), can thus be interpreted as a critique of the horrors of American imperialism and, implicitly, French colonialism in Vietnam (addressed more directly in the uncut version *Apocalypse Now: Redux*, released in 2001). But, like Conrad, Coppola also reiterated dominant representations of the colonized 'other'. Coppola's 'Congo', adds Kaplan, was neither Africa nor Vietnam. *Apocalypse Now* was made in the Philippines, an ex-US colony, at that time ruled by the repressive Marcos regime propped up by the USA. 'By turning the Philippines into a timeless "jungle" backdrop', she argues, 'Coppola denied . . . the present dynamics of empire' (pp. 18–19). The imperial past and present thus still blend in contemporary popular culture, reflecting Western representations of the non-Western others. This raises the important question of how the imperial past is remembered in the West.

Representations of empire in post-imperial culture

Sites of memory

Today, monuments, street names and other physical reminders of empire constitute what Pierre Nora (1998) has called *Les Lieux de Mémoire*, or tangible 'realms of memory'. Imperial memory in Britain is triggered by war memorials and monuments to the dead in cathedrals that commemorate the Indian Mutiny, the defeat of General Gordon at Khartoum and other imperial markers. Westminster Abbey is a veritable temple of empire. Names of places and buildings – West India Docks, India House, Mafeking Street – evoke the imperial past. In Rome major thoroughfares named Somalia and Addis Ababa in the 'African quarter' recall Italy's African colonies and brief occupation of Ethiopia after its violent annexation in 1935. In France, too, the imperial past is visible in the landscape (Aldrich, 2002). War monuments also evoke memories of empire. At Vimy Ridge in Northern France, North Africans who died fighting for France in the First World War are commemorated in the main monument and Indian troops are listed on the Menin Gate at Ypres, but other colonial troops and non-combatant workers are generally relegated to hidden corners in war cemeteries. It is only in recent years that there has been recognition in Britain of the need for a monument commemorating colonial troops who died in the two world wars.

As demonstrated in Case study 4, the way in which empire is remembered remains a significant element in debates about the nature of postcolonial British identities. Henry Kamen's *Road to Empire* (2002), which challenged myths of heroic conquistadores, caused a furore in Spain, indicating the importance of memories of the Spanish Empire, despite the fact that this ended with the Spanish–American War (1898) (Tremlett, 2003, p. 17). Memory of empire has also been kept alive through migration from the ex-colonies into the old imperial heartlands of Europe, creating multicultural cities. The French Right have interpreted this as 'colonization in reverse' and warned that migration is an attempt at domination and 'revenge for the past' (Flood and Frey, 2002, p. 205). The 'empire within' evoked fears of swamping and regenerated discourses of racial and cultural superiority associated with the imperial era. Academic disciplines also continued to reproduce forms of colonial knowledge produced in the colonial era to legitimize continuing Western domination (Breckenridge and Van de Veer, 1993, pp. 1–3). In Western popular culture 'Orientalist' representations of the 'primitive other' were reworked into a romanticized, sanitized form as an adjunct to consumerism, in fashion or adverts.

How is the imperial past remembered and represented in public (as opposed to academic) history? Aldrich (2002) emphasizes the 'amnesia' and 'disinheritance' in French 'colonial memory' (p. 211). But does such 'amnesia' reflect a wish to forget the darker aspects of the past and the humiliations of decolonization? Historical amnesia and the construction of national memory in heritage and media retain selective visions of the imperial past, perpetuate Eurocentrism, reproducing dominant discourses, and deny the marginalized a voice in the past. As Rosaldo (1989) observed, postcolonial culture is pervaded by an 'imperialist nostalgia' that promotes a childlike 'innocent yearning' for the past, captures people's imaginations and conceals more brutal aspects of the imperial past (Rosaldo, 1989, p. 108). Thus representations of empire in contemporary Western culture sustain a continued national mythology about the benevolence or heroics of empire. Such romanticization of the imperial mission began during the imperial era proper and has a long history: the Romans created a history that satisfied their own pride and impressed and enlightened foreigners and/or imperial subjects (Lintott, 1993, p. 176). This justificatory narrative was rooted in a mythical past age and was important in identifying and confirming a superior Roman ethnicity (Woolf, 2002, p. 321). Similarly, histories of the British Empire written during the late imperial era, when its power was increasingly challenged, drew on a mythologized past going back into Anglo-Saxon times, which emphasized the superiority of the English character (for instance, Wilkinson, 1944). Myth and metaphor informed the language of the British Empire to justify and secure popular support (MacDonald, 1994). Yet a myth is not unreal or purely fictional, but can be defined as:

> . . . a system of beliefs accepted by a group concerning its own living past, even though all that is believed is, in the narrowest sense 'historical' [it is] not what things are but what they are believed to be that really matters.
>
> (McCrone, 1937, p. vii)

'Mythical history' flows backwards rather than forwards in time and is thus characterized by nostalgia accompanied by amnesia in the public memory, whereby subjects that are a threat to the 'national imaginary' are suppressed or obliterated (Wright, 1985, pp. 145–6). Thus public memory in relation to the imperial past is selective. This has stimulated interrogation of how the imperial past is represented in public history displays, in museums and heritage centres. How significant are such displays in shaping contemporary national and ethnic identities?

Public history: museums and heritage

In the 'museum age' – 1840–1930 – exhibits, ethnographic displays and colonial exhibitions in Europe were designed around the preservation and commoditization of 'native cultures': empire was presented as popular spectacle in the imperial centre and this shaped popular consciousness of the colonized 'other' (Coombes, 1994). Such displays sometimes included live anthropological exhibits and became spaces where the dead were exhibited 'as if they are alive' and the living 'as if they were dead' (Kirschenblatt-Gimblett, 1991, p. 398). Ethnographic displays and material objects were presented as separate from (and thus unrelated to) history, implying a static authenticity of colonized cultures that reinforced dominant discourses. Indigenous peoples, argues Phillips (1995), quickly grasped the material value of artefacts and thus were proactive in defining the 'authentic' in selling to Western collectors. Nonetheless, indigenous objects that suggested a dynamic cultural flow across the static tradition/modernity boundary and provided evidence of 'negotiation with Western artistic and economic systems', such as tourist art, were excluded from museum displays (pp. 99–100, 107).

Museum displays entertain as well as inform, but this raises problems in the postcolonial era as to how human experiences, living cultures and complex and abstract concepts such as empire can be condensed to an eye-catching, themed visual display of material objects. Wider context is lost and familiar representations of empire and the colonized are dealt with uncritically. Heritage and museum displays, argue Bloxham and Kushner (1998), have provided a hierarchical and racist legacy for the contemporary world. In such displays there are clearly problems of contextualization and how spectators identify with the objects on display. What 'story' do the visual exhibits convey? How does the exhibit reinforce the spectator's own identities and familiar, shared history with other spectators? Who is excluded from the story? Challenges to negative representations in ethnographic display, museums and heritage, and the media are fundamental to the struggles of indigenous peoples and of racialized Black and Asian minorities in the West for equality and respect. For instance, as part of the post-Apartheid cultural realignments, the Khoi San people (depicted in colonial discourse as 'Hottentots') organized a conference in July 1997, affirming their previously suppressed culture and identity. The conference was held in the Natural History Museum in Capetown, where an ethnographic display of their culture could still be viewed, and provided a powerful critique of the museum's displays, emphasizing the need for change.

Protests from racialized minorities in the West about their marginalization in national histories or distorted representations of their cultures in public history prompted challenges to existing museum practice within the relatively new discipline of museum studies. Museums, it was argued, constituted an 'imperial archive', a surviving token or souvenir of imperial power and certain ideological assumptions rooted in the imperial past informed selection and display of artefacts. What was needed was a postcolonial museology that integrated the culture of colonizer and colonized and prioritized the excluded (Barringer and Flynn (eds), 1998, pp. 4–7). The challenge was to deconstruct the colonial discourse that constructed primitive cultures as pre-modern and static. An example here is the transformation of dead colonial displays into the revamped National Museum of the American Indian at the Smithsonian in Washington that 'celebrated the living, dynamic cultures' of First Nation peoples (Phillips, 1995, pp. 99, 117). In Australia, too, more attention was paid to the representation of a positive Aboriginal past in museums and the inclusion of Aboriginal art in galleries. The 'black armband view' of Australian history promoted recognition of the uglier aspects of white settler society in the oppression of Aboriginal peoples (Hall, 1998). The histories of Aboriginal peoples and migrants from multicultural backgrounds have been brought into a national history formerly represented as the Anglo-Saxon heritage. In Britain and North America there have been demands for museums to tell the history of, and monuments to commemorate, the slaves who died in the transatlantic trade or on plantations. After much pressure from the Black community, the gallery of transatlantic slavery was opened at Liverpool Maritime Museum in 1994, challenging Liverpool's amnesia about its past as a premier slaving port.

Such initiatives, however, have not been without controversy and accusations of political correctness from those who wish to preserve the white and/or whitened version of the colonial past. Criticisms are not restricted to those who retain a white settler/imperialist mentality. Liverpool's transatlantic slavery gallery was condemned as patronizing and paternalist, motivated by white guilt and lacking an Afrocentric perspective (Kogbara, 1994). Bloxham and Kushner (1998) argue that the efforts of museums to reassess the role they should play in postcolonial societies in the 1990s met with only limited success. Prioritizing historical and cultural relativism in displays does not necessarily solve the problems of ethnic minority marginality, nor does it erase popular stereotypes:

> The post-modern ideal of global citizenship and its romantic interest in ethnic minorities in representing such a model is far removed from the day-to-day reality of such groups. Racism still shapes their experiences and legislation, not amended representations, is needed.
>
> (Bloxham and Kushner, pp. 351, 356)

Contemporary Australia provides an apt example here. Despite initiatives to include the history of indigenous peoples in museums and art galleries, and white middle-class Australian love of a commoditized and financially lucrative Aboriginal art, the majority of white Australia still wanted to erase the indigenous minority from the national story (Ramussen, 2004). A minority of Aboriginal peoples may have benefited from such initiatives but the majority have continued to struggle against poverty and marginalization and anger erupted in the 'race' riots in inner-city Redfern, Sydney, in February, 2004 (Chapter 6). Located on the borders of prestigious Sydney University, Redfern demonstrated the intensity of alienation and the movement of the 'frontier' to the white cities, but also confirmed dominant contemporary white representations of Aboriginal peoples as criminals, scroungers and a morally polluting threat to the affluent white Australian dream. Struggles to challenge and/or subvert dominant representations of the colonized and non-Western 'other' of the postcolonial era are thus ongoing.

The view of the subaltern: challenges to Western representations of non-Western societies

Today and in the imperial past, powerful representations are/were the outcome of a dynamic dialogue between those who construct(ed) the subordinated 'subject' through text and visual representation and the subordinated who contest(ed) such essentialist and denigrating representations. Such representations were, and remain, rooted in concrete relations of economic and political power and the preservation of class and race boundaries in both colonial and postcolonial societies. Yet through struggle, the colonized/neocolonized 'other' shaped new, self-determined identities. Additionally, they turned their own critical eye on the powerful, creating their own 'representations' and thus engaging in a process of consciousness raising about dominant societies.

So far the emphasis has been on how 'we' in the West saw 'them'. How did they see us? It is easily forgotten in postcolonial preoccupation with deconstructing Western discourse that the colonized also had their representations and stereotyped images of the colonizer. The end of the nineteenth century saw the beginnings of travelogues written through the eyes of the colonizer rather than the colonized. As Antoinette Burton notes, the 'eye' of the colonized, like that of the colonizer, was clearly gendered and class-based but provided an interesting counterbalance to Western representations. Visitors to the imperial metropoles subjected the imperial culture to their own critical gaze, demystifying the essence of imperial power. Through their travel writings they asserted themselves as an 'I' rather than the 'colonial subject' constructed through colonial discourse, the object of colonial rule. Indian travellers were impressed by the crowds and the size and energy of London, but also noted the poverty and dirt that disappointed them. They were disconcerted by the sexual overtures of white women and observing the condition of the London poor demystified the imperial centre (Burton, 1996, pp. 127–32). Letters home written by Indians fighting for the British Empire in World War I also provided a critical view from the colonized (Omissi (ed.), 1999).

But 'counter-representations' and dominant representations share similar problems relating to how individuals interpret their world. Travelogues, Western or non-Western, say as much about the traveller as about the object of the traveller's gaze and we need to read the subtext to disentangle the 'real' from the 'imaginary'. Visual and literary impressions of the non-Western traveller, like those of the Western traveller/artist are culturally mediated. How the writer/artist interprets his/her subject is inseparable from the influences which shape his/her own identity. The European artists in Australia imposed a romantic European landscape on the Antipodean 'wilderness'. Chiang Yee, a Chinese artist from Shanghai travelling through the Yorkshire Dales and Lake District areas of England in the 1930s and 1940s, viewed the landscape through the eye of a 'homesick Easterner'. His sketches of local beauty spots nostalgically evoke a mountainous Chinese landscape of his youth (Chiang Yee, 1937, 1941). As Herbert Read observed in the preface to *The Silent Traveller in the Lake District* (1937), Chiang Yee, 'dared to enter our national shrine . . . and challenge our complacency'. He wrote about difference and otherness but also attributed 'certain oriental modes of thought and feeling' to the poet Wordsworth and highlighted 'the universality of all true modes of thinking'.

With the increase in colonial migrants coming into the imperial heartlands in the twentieth century, more works were produced on how 'they see us'. In *La Noire de . . .* or *The African Girl* (1967), the Senegalese writer and film director, Sembène Ousmane, who worked as a docker in Marseilles, evoked the pressures of life in the metropole through the eyes of a Senegalese girl who accompanies her white employers home. The Caribbean writers George Lamming and Samuel Selvon encapsulated migrant impressions of London in *The Emigrants* (1954) and the *Lonely Londoner* (1955) respectively. Literature and film from the perspective of the colonized have critically dissected and subverted white representations, providing interpretations of their cultures free from the gaze of the white man. India, Turkey and Iran all have thriving film industries that provide a different angle on culture, migration and relations with the West. But in a world dominated by Hollywood such films are marginalized by media representations that continue to prioritize the West and a superior whiteness (Dyer, 1997).

***

Orientalized representations of the colonized 'other' were challenged by anti-colonial nationalist movements (Said, 1994). Post-independence, the simple binaries between East and West, primitive and civilized were transformed into the discourse of the Third World and development. But the dreams of progress and modern development that would render Orientalist representations anachronistic were not fulfilled, particularly in Africa. Representations of Africa as primitive and backward resurfaced but this time defined against the 'rest', including the 'East' (Inden, 2002, p. 107). Historical images of Blackness continued to influence racist constructs and impact on contemporary Black identities (Lively, 1998; Low, 1996). Orientalizing of the 'other', contrasted with Occidentalist constructs of the civilized, rich and powerful West, persisted in corporate advertising and logos, Hollywood film and the Western media. In the ex-metropolitan centres, myths of empire constructed through imperial discourse and related representations of the colonized have also reverberated into the postcolonial era. The following case study on representations of empire in British culture expands in more depth on the impact this had, and continues to have, on national identities.

The marginalized subjects of Eurocentric representation have pressed for recognition in the public displays of the past. There have been promising developments. Heritage, argues Jacobs (1996), has been transformed into a 'dynamic process of creation' in which a 'multiplicity of pasts' jostle for recognition. Literature and cartoon representations containing racist stereotypes have been challenged and suppressed. Race equality policies have resulted in more positive representation of Black and Asian minorities in the Western media. But important as these challenges have been in the reconstitution of positive postcolonial identities, they have not been sufficient in themselves to tackle issues of poverty and exploitation that have continued to define the experiences of millions globally, in postcolonial Western cities and throughout the ex-colonized parts of the world. In analyses of representation, the material basis of, and reasons for, the 'Orientalizing' of subordinate peoples in popular and official discourse should not be forgotten. The following chapter explores the continuities in global structures of power fundamental to continued global inequalities in the post-imperial era.

Case study 4
*Representing empire in British culture in the imperial and
post-imperial era*

> There is only one thing more staggering than the pace and scale of the
> British Empire and that is the pace and scale with which the British have
> sought to elevate it to the level of myth or denigrate it with historical amnesia.
>
> (Younge, 2002)

How did Britain acquire an imperial culture and identity? Armitage (2001)
stressed the role of the ideology of early empire in shaping conceptions of
what it meant to be British. From the late eighteenth century, representations of empire in popular culture were vital to securing support for empire:
national identity and race, class and gender differences in British society
were articulated in reference to colonized subjects (Hall, 2002; Burton,
1994b; Wilson, 2003). With decolonization, imperialism became deeply
unpopular; museums shelved their imperial artefacts and school curricula
shifted towards liberal multiculturalism, redressing the racism and ethnocentricism in orthodox texts on empire. But with the New Right's challenge to
the liberalism that had shaped the postwar world, the deep-seated nature
of British imperial identities resurfaced. Postcolonial studies of the 'empire
within' emphasized how the imperial heritage continued to influence British
Black and Asian lives and identities and the contours of the postcolonial city
(Gilroy, 1987; Jacobs, 1996).

Conventional historians have queried whether there was a hegemonic
'imperial project' shaping British culture, arguing that the concept of, and
enthusiasm for, empire was more diffuse (Marshall, 1995, pp. 385–6). Prior
to the seminal studies in John Mackenzie's *Imperialism and Popular Culture*
(1986) historians believed empire had no relevance to domestic developments, particularly after the First World War. Such scepticism persists (Porter,
2004b). Yet, as Peter Marshall concedes,

> The neglect of the imperial dimension in the writing of British political,
> social and cultural history is hard to refute . . . general histories of Britain
> rarely leave readers with much sense of what it meant for Britain to have
> been at the centre of a world-wide empire.
>
> (Marshall, 1995, p. 379)

As David Cannadine points out, empire was as much an 'imaginative construct' in the minds of men and women as maps and territory (Cannadine,

1995, p. 194), and John Mackenzie (1984) demonstrated that imperialism was a significant element in shaping British identities. Britain's empire, argues Andrew Thompson (2005), had a significant impact on Britain's domestic history in the nineteenth and twentieth centuries. This case study will demonstrate that imperial discourse and related representations of the colonized were embedded in the popular psyche through a variety of media. This produced a powerful consensual culture of imperialism where voices of dissent were shaded out. Representations of empire changed with the evolving imperial mission, but perceptions of white superiority that shaped British national identities persisted in British culture into the postcolonial era. What, then, is the evidence for these arguments?

Empire and British domestic culture

Empire became more prominent in British politics and royal ceremonials after 1880 (Thomson, 2000; Cannadine, 1996) and infiltrated popular consciousness through the active involvement of migrants to the colonies, missionaries and soldiers. As Marshall (1995) points out, for most of the nineteenth century and up to the Second World War the British army was essentially a colonial army and missions involved huge mobilizations of men and women, home and overseas (p. 392). Such involvement strengthened xenophobia and a sense of superiority over non-European peoples. Additionally, argued Mackenzie (1986), working-class autobiographies, memoirs and oral evidence testified to the power of popular imperialism and the imperial/racial content of geography lessons. Popular imperialism was not simply jingoism and xenophobia – a morbid hatred of foreigners – as implied by the contemporary critic of empire, J. A. Hobson. 'Moral' or liberal imperialists promoted a more benevolent imperial mission, particularly after the First World War. Nonetheless, all representations of empire created a world view that shaped British people's consciousness and constituted a united set of ideas, reflected not only in official propaganda but through diverse mediums of popular culture (pp. 2–7).

Consent for imperialism, then, was gained through popular representations of empire that reproduced stereotypes of colonial subjects, provided images of the superior, white, male imperial archetype, and reinforced a strong sense of consensual national identity linked to pride in the British race. Even if the working-class majority were ignorant of empire, as sceptical historians like Bernard Porter suggest, it entered their subconscious and shaped social reality and identities. A recent Glasgow website posted reminiscences of the 1938 Glasgow Empire Exhibition, opened by the newly crowned King George VI and Queen Elizabeth (the late Queen Mother). Childhood memories had remained strong after 60 years and 'never dimmed'. Respondents (some who had migrated to Canada, the USA and Australia after the First World War) still owned memorabilia and recalled the new 'Coronation trams' that carried people to the exhibition, the imposing modernist Exhibition Tower, the military parades and streets jammed with spectators. They recalled 'the Maori from New Zealand, Canadian Mounties and the rosiest apples from the far-flung reaches of the Empire'; particularly memorable were the exotic 'exhibits' such as the 'giraffe-necked women from Burma' (The Glasgow Website, 2004).

Empire filtered into the everyday mundane ephemera and artefacts found in people's homes. Working-class families had links with empire through family who had migrated or through relatives in the military or colonial police. When I was a child in the 1950s, BBC Radio's *Two-Way Family Favourites* still echoed round the far-flung reaches of Britain's presence overseas; images of empire suffused my education and provided the motif for pageants and projects. Like the majority of the British working class whose families had no vested interests in empire and whose day-to-day preoccupations were deeply parochial, I remained largely oblivious of my 'imperial world view' until I went to live in the Caribbean. Why did empire continue to hold a strong, if incoherent, grip on British culture and national consciousness for so long, reinforcing a sense of superior 'Britishness'?

Representations of empire and imperial consciousness

The importance of imperialism in popular culture increased after Disraeli's Crystal Palace Speech in 1872 that revived the imperial ideal and its centrality to British power. The 1870s were a vital decade in melding patriotism and the new nationalist, imperialist and royalist ideology (Cunningham, 1981). 'Traditions' were invented, such as Empire Day, Mafeking Night and royal events like Queen Victoria's Jubilees in 1887 and 1897. The consumption of imperial products and exhibitions in British metropolitan centres and imperialist subcentres, such as Australia, generated imperial consciousness (Hoffenberg, 2001). The propaganda role of exhibitions became more important after 1880 as 'complacent pride' in empire was transformed into concern for defence as imperial competition intensified (Greenhalgh, 1988, p. 58). Imperial propaganda was disseminated through official and non-governmental agencies, commercial agencies and academia. The Empire Day Movement

(1903), Royal Colonial Institute (1868) and the British Empire League (1895) were established to promote empire. The Imperial Institute was set up under the instigation of the Society of Arts on the eve of Queen Victoria's 1887 Jubilee to celebrate 'the marvellous growth' of the British Empire during her reign (*Journal of the Society of Arts*, vol. XXXV, no 1779, 24 December, 1886, p. 90). The elite London *Times* became 'vigorously imperialist', but empire also provided numerous exciting and sensationalist stories for the new popular press of the 1890s that had a much wider readership (Snyder (ed.), 1962, p. 81). Representations of the colonial 'other' in popular literature and travelogues confirmed the superior, essentially masculine, character of the empire (Phillips, 1997; Bristow, 1991). Popular theatre, music hall and music in general were also important cultural channels celebrating empire and confirming superior identities (Mackenzie (ed.), 1986; Richards, 2001).

Visual representations gave coherence to an empire that was a more incoherent phenomenon. Images of royalty, the military, the Union Jack and John Bull symbolized the indivisibility of empire and nation and took symbols of colonial adventures into every home (Mackenzie, 1984, p. 5). Stamps provided ubiquitous references to empire and colonial 'others' and commemorated imperial events such as the Boer War and the 1924 Wembley Empire Exhibition (Hamilton, 1941). In 'empire advertising' images of African and Asian people were popular in selling tea, biscuits, cocoa, coffee, tobacco and soap (Ramamurthy, 2002). Soap was equated with spreading civilization to Africa and was thus central to Britain's new imperial commodity culture by the end of the nineteenth century. Soap advertisements suggested an affinity between empire and domesticity and symbolized racial hygiene and imperial progress (McLintock, 1995, p. 207). Images of empire and race were also conveyed through ephemera such as souvenirs, postcards, Christmas cards, cigarette cards issued by Players, Wills and the Imperial Tobacco Company, *bric-à-brac* and the packaging of popular empire products. The craze for picture postcards from the turn of the century drew heavily on the 'splendour of colonial life' and photographic explorations of empire charted the progress of the 'civilizing mission' (Ryan, 1997, pp. 11, 183). Photography also captured events like the 1897 Jubilee through the 'imperial lens' and reinforced the indivisible bond between Queen Victoria, the empire and British national identities (ibid., p. 224).

Imperial sentiment and the notion of 'citizens of empire' were spread through youth movements and the imperial curriculum taught in schools (Mangan (ed.), 1988). Empire Day, 24 May, founded by the Earl of Meath in 1903 as a day of patriotic celebrations, became a school holiday and was celebrated into the 1950s (Mackenzie, 1986a, p. 165). The Boy Scouts and

Girl Guides movements were seminal in capturing the minds of the young for empire and cultivating superior imperial identities. Baden-Powell's *Scouting for Boys* (c. 1908) drew on the traditions and ethos of 'moral musculature' (Boehmer (ed.), 2004). In *Boy Scouts Beyond the Seas: My World Tour* (1913) Baden Powell emphasized that Scouts were to 'be prepared' for warlike natives or going out to some 'oversea Dominion'. Similarly, the Girl Guides provided opportunity for young girls to join in the work of empire and exercise their 'moral muscles' (Agnes Baden-Powell, 1912). J. A. Hobson was critical of such malign influences on the minds of the young:

> Most serious of all is the persistent attempt to seize the school system for Imperialism masquerading as patriotism, to capture the childhood of a country, to mechanise its free play into the routine of military drill, to cultivate the savage survivals of combativeness, to poison the early understanding of history by false ideals of pseudo heroes and by a constant discouragement and neglect of the really vital and elevating lessons of the past, to establish a 'geocentric' view of the moral universe in which the interests of humanity are subordinated to that of the 'country' . . . to feel the overweening pride of race . . . and by necessary implications to disparage other nations . . . to call it patriotism is as foul an abuse of education as it is possible to conceive.
>
> (Hobson, 1988, 1902, p. 26)

Retrospective studies support this view. Motifs of imperial and racial superiority and imperial successes that infiltrated children's comics, books and the school curriculum were important in shaping working-class imperial identities (Castle, 1996). African 'yarns' and heroic tales of 'colonial butcheries', diffused racial ideas and were highly popular (Mackenzie, 1986, pp. 6–7). Henry Morton Stanley's best-selling *In Darkest Africa* (1890) was marketed in a simplified version with a jigsaw puzzle, reaching a wide, younger audience (Youngs, 1994). The public school 'games ethic' cultivated 'moral musculature', preparing young men to 'play the game' in the battlefields of empire (Mangan, 1986). Certain public schools, particularly in towns where there were what Buettner (2004) calls 'transplanted empire fragments' of Anglo-Indians, had strong links with empire. Curriculums were designed to train imperial leaders and equip them with the 'gentlemanly' virtues of character: courage, compassion and fair play, but also cultivated superior white, masculine identities. In public school stories in popular comics, the British children were heroes, tolerant and helpful to poor Africans and Indians, and the real racists were other foreign nationals: Germans, Italians, Mexicans. Such images continued to reinforce the relationship between race, hierarchy and nationality (Castle, 1996, p. 115). Cruder stereotypes were conveyed through 'Sambo' head money boxes and children's games like 'Aunt Sally', where the aim was to try to throw a ball in the mouth of the caricatured head of an old, smiling Black woman with a hat.

The growing 'empire within' also shaped British attitudes to empire and race. By 1900 London was the imperial metropolis *par excellence*, the greatest city on earth, with a growing resident population of South Asians, West Africans, West Indians and Chinese (Schneer, 1999; Lahiri, 2001; Burton, 1998). Wealthy Indian travellers attended the 1886 Colonial and India Exhibition in London and in 1895 three kings from Bechuanaland visited London, led by King Khama, to petition for British protection from South African expansion under Cecil Rhodes – a visit that was heavily reported in the press (Parsons, 1998; Burton, 1996). Positive impressions of Indian and African royalty may have existed, particularly of the former, who were paraded out in their princely finery at empire bonding occasions like Queen Victoria's Jubilees, but an increase in poorer colonial residents and associated mixed-race relationships enhanced fears of racial degeneration and intensified hostility to emergent Black and Asian minorities, exemplified in the 1919 race riots in Cardiff, Liverpool and other British cities. The empire within expanded further after the First World War and generated important debates, some informed by eugenics, about the 'race problem' in Britain (Bush, 1999).

A dominant assumption in conventional historiography is that after the First World War, the empire began to decline. It has been argued that before the First World War imperialism was important in defining a superior Englishness that influenced national identities (Tidrick, 1990), but after 1918 a more insular, feminized, domestic Englishness emerged (Light, 1991). In effect, argues Bernard Porter (2004b), the British Empire expanded after 1918 and engaged in a more 'predatory' imperialism. Empire continued to shape Englishness and Englishness to shape empire. It was this Englishness, built on assumptions of racial and cultural superiority since the early empire, that defined the culture of imperialism in the imperial centre and colonies. British national/imperial identities were defined by Englishness and this submerged regional and ethnic differences that might have undermined the empire. Retaining this coherent identity became more imperative as threats to empire mounted.

'Empire Strengthening' and popular imperialism, 1918–39

Weakened by war, the empire became even more important to Britain's economic survival and international prestige. Intensification of imperial competition, combined with challenges to empire from international communism, socialism and anti-colonial protest, resulted in a policy of imperial economic protectionism. Britain became increasingly dependent on imperial markets and there was more direct state intervention in both imperial policy and propaganda. The British Left dubbed these policies 'Empire Strengthening' (Bush, 1999). Empire was actively promoted through the British Broadcasting Corporation (BBC), the Empire Marketing Board (EMB), Empire Exhibitions, Empire Day and royal visits to colonies. Members of the royal family had actively participated in the imperial project since before the First World War, the men as soldiers, the women as patrons of good works. After the war royalty became even more central to the imagery of benevolent empire. As Cannadine (1983) stresses, the 'outstandingly successful [royal] tours' cemented bonds between Britain and her empire and royal rituals, particularly the coronation of George VI in 1937, provided public displays of the greatness, wealth and power of empire, generating emotive imperial sentiment across the political spectrum.

British national identities continued to be profoundly shaped by reference to the imperial hinterland and its colonial subjects. Public awareness was heightened and extended by new media – film and radio – that became fundamental to imperial 'propaganda' in Britain and its colonies. For commercial film-makers, the empire was good business and the British cinema and Hollywood were seminal in projecting imperial and racial superiority (Bourne, 1998; Richards, 1984). Cinema involved a world view explicitly and implicitly rooted in imperial perceptions (Mackenzie, 1984, pp. 68–9). Any films whose content threatened to undermine white prestige were censored in the colonies (Smyth, 1983). Crucial in fostering empire consciousness at home and in the colonies was the BBC, which gave unswerving support to 'monarch and empire' and inaugurated an Empire Service in 1932 (Mackenzie, 1986a, p. 173). The EMB became the centre for Imperial film production until it was axed in 1933 due to government cuts. In 1935 the Imperial Institute took over the Empire Film Library, whose audiences – mostly schoolchildren – reputedly totalled over 4,700,000 (Smyth, 1983, pp. 78–94).

The EMB was central to the government's strategy to secure popular support for, and enhance consciousness of, empire. The EMB, argues Constantine (1986), was trying to sell the concept of empire itself, not simply empire products. Billboards were posted throughout Britain with four to five posters that were changed every week, and there were 490 individual posters. The EMB also organized shopping weeks around Empire Day. The image conveyed though advertisements was of a modern, egalitarian empire, beneficial to masses in Britain and colonies, where consumers represented the constructive driving force. This changed the connotation of the word 'empire' (ibid.). The advertisements reflected the new domestic imagery of empire, now represented as a family bonded to the motherland. The unity of this benevolent empire was symbolized by the Empire Christmas Pudding, made 'According to a recipe supplied by the King's Chef, Mr. Cedard, with their Majesties' Gracious Consent'. Ingredients from all over the Empire were included: brandy from Australia, South Africa, Cyprus or Palestine; sugar from the British West Indies or British Guiana; cloves from Zanzibar and beer from England, Wales, Scotland or Ireland (London, National Maritime Museum: Wolfson Empire and Trade Gallery). This recipe provided a symbolic blending of empire into one, and evoked a harmonious domesticity endorsed by the King Emperor.

Key events in popularizing empire were the empire exhibitions held in London and elsewhere. The 1924–5 British Empire Exhibition cost the government and colonies £2.2 million and covered a 50-acre site in Wembley, London with a specially built Empire Stadium (subsequently the Wembley Football Stadium) and multiple pavilions and walkways where you could 'walk around the empire' for 6d. The opening ceremony was broadcast on the radio, cabled to all parts of the empire, and HMV pressed a record. Massed bands, conducted by Sir Edward Elgar, played tunes with an imperial, patriotic or religious theme, including Elgar's new Empire March (Richards, 2001, pp. 194–6). In his opening speech the King Emperor George V described the exhibition as a 'living picture of the history and structure of the British Empire' ('The King Opens the Great Exhibition', *The Manchester Guardian*, 23 January, 1924). In recognition of women's more prominent role in empire after 1918, the Queen was patron of the exhibition's women's section. Emphasis was placed on the promotion of the 'white empire' and the Dominions had prime sites. The 'tropical' colonies remained in a subordinate position, reinforced by 'Native displays'.

The Wembley exhibition was a huge spectacle that attracted 27 million visitors, including visitors from the empire, although we can only speculate as to what those from the 'tropical' – that is, 'coloured' – colonies made of this celebration of the white empire. The exhibition was promoted by souvenirs such as tea caddies and plates and Players' British Empire series cigarette cards. A *Game of the British Empire* or *Trading with the Colonies* was produced for the 1924–5 exhibition, embedding in children's minds the economic importance of empire. The 1924–5 and subsequent Wembley empire exhibitions adopted the lion logo as the symbol of empire, representing the qualities of 'honesty, simplicity and strength' that defined the British character. In 1927 the lion logo was sold to the Imperial Tobacco Company as a registered trademark (Museum of London). Such initiatives, however, lost steam in the 1930s, as economic depression, international instability and the growth of anti-colonial resistance undermined the imperial vision. The Second World War would accelerate the disintegration of empire. The 1938 exhibition reflected these changes. Promoting Glasgow as the second city of empire, the exhibition cost £11 million and was visited by 13 million visitors. However, for the first time India did not take part (Museum of Empire and Commonwealth). In 1940, the exhibition infrastructure was used to accommodate French Alpine troops evacuated from Norway and then, from 1943, German prisoners of war (The Glasgow Website, 2004).

Empire consciousness and British identities

What was the impact of these popular representations of empire and the colonized on the self-identification of British people? The middle and upper classes, products of public schools, benefited most in terms of careers and returns from imperial investments (Cain and Hopkins, 1993, pp. 25–6, 131–2). This 'gentlemanly' elite had a much firmer sense of being part of empire than did the working classes. Working-class involvement with empire came through migration to the white Dominions, through military service, or as seamen. The majority had minimal involvement and/or interest in the colonies but, as the liberal anti-imperialist critic, J. A. Hobson, pointed out, empire had an important social/psychological impact, stimulating nationalism and patriotism. Imperialism also deflected the masses from 'gaining the substance of power' promised with the spread of democracy (Hobson, 1988, 1902, pp. 141–2). Working-class identities became more 'conservative, insular and nationalistic' than during the mid-nineteenth century as empire shaped their sense of national identity. Although self-interest remained focused on domestic preoccupations, the working classes absorbed the subliminal messages about empire and racial superiority that permeated British culture (Stedman-Jones, 1983). Additionally, the working classes benefited from cheap empire products and the subordinated Tropics were represented by popular fruits of empire, such as bananas (Hobsbawm, 1989, p. 195). Class differences are thus important in understanding individual and group relationships to empire but a superior imperial consciousness cut across gender and class divisions and secured majority consent for Britain's imperial mission. With the growth of the mass media, this imperial consciousness was arguably more pervasive after, than before 1918.

The empire remained deeply embedded in popular consciousness during and after the Second World War. As Mackenzie (1986a) observes, during the War the BBC heavily promoted Empire and Commonwealth, a Festival of Empire was held in 1946 and 1,000 schools remained affiliated to the Empire Day Movement up to the 1950s. The coronation of Elizabeth II in 1953, observes Cannadine (1983), continued the imperial motif of great state occasions; regiments of Commonwealth and colonial troops marched in the procession, emphasizing that Britain was still a great imperial power. Even during the period of decolonization, empire remained central to defining British national and racial identities and influenced the ways in which Britishness was constructed in popular culture (Webster, 2005). What are the implications of this for post-imperial Britain?

Echoes of empire and British national identity

There was an assumption that, with the end of empire, imperial consciousness dissipated, particularly among the younger generation. Imperial decline resulted in loss of global status but also presented a formidable challenge to the key assumptions, ideas and values that had shaped imperial culture. Yet, decline was met with ambivalence and denial, though also with nostalgia. These conflicting responses were reflected in popular culture, coupled with a refusal to embrace a multiracial society as migration from the new Commonwealth increased (Ward (ed.), 2001). This failure of British society to confront the imperial past and to challenge powerful myths of empire echoed into the 1990s. A Gallup poll conducted in 1997 revealed that, although British people did not know much about empire, they remained proud of it and a substantial proportion regretted its demise. A kind of 'imperial afterglow' – a belief that the empire was good and mutually beneficial to Britain and her colonies – was reflected in responses to the poll from young and old alike. The main difference between the 'imperial generation' (born before 1947) and the later 'post-imperial' generation was in factual memory of imperial events, with the former scoring much better (King, 1997). What this suggests is that although names and places of empire had become a hazy memory, the idea of empire, the myth of benevolent empire, as promoted through imperial discourse, retained some power and influence in defining national identities.

Contemporary representations of empire in the public realm consist of generalized abstractions framed in an explanatory framework for public consumption. Examples here are the modern exhibits of material objects and imperial ephemera in the Wolfson Empire and Trade Gallery at the National

Maritime Museum, Greenwich, London and the British Empire and Commonwealth Museum in Bristol. Relevant to understanding the role of these museums is the discussion of material representations of empire in Chapter 5. How do we chart the path from the imperial past to the multicultural present without romanticizing the past or condemning it? The new British Empire and Commonwealth Museum was finally located in Bristol, a city with strong links to the slave trade and empire, and was funded substantially by private donation. The more conservative advocates for the museum were concerned about loss of imperial knowledge and the fact that the 'story of empire' was being eroded from the national consciousnesses. Commentators like Neil Darbyshire (1997) rightly pointed out that the history of the British empire was indivisible from that of British society. But the museum's advocates wanted to present a sanitized history that reiterated the greatness and essential humanitarianism of the British Empire as a counterbalance to the Left, who emphasized racism and exploitation.

On balance, comments on the new museum have been positive. The museum trustees, arguably, managed to steer a middle course. Although some of the backers were accused of holding conservative and patriotic views, the museum succeeded in telling the story of empire 'with caution but not embarrassment' (Younge, 2002). Exhibition rooms include 'Exploration and plunder', 'Empire at home', 'Humanitarian impulse', 'Commonwealth ideal' and 'The Commonwealth comes to Britain'. The museum aims to be inclusive; its publicity literature claims 'multicultural Britain' as 'perhaps the richest legacy of the colonial experience' and stresses that the empire is everyone's history in Britain and the Commonwealth (publicity brochure, 2003). A radio station, Commonwealth FM, was launched, broadcasting from the museum to demonstrate its commitment to multiculturalism and to working with local ethnic minority groups. It could be argued, however, that the museum still prioritizes the essential humanitarianism of the empire and the virtues of the modern Commonwealth. Debates about representations of empire and its heritage in British culture and curriculums will undoubtedly continue.

More critical reappraisal of the imperial legacy dovetailed with growing angst in the 1980s over how British national identity, history and culture should be defined in postcolonial Britain (Colley, 1992b). Empire, it was argued, remained residual in the collective memory but in a multicultural society the question of which empire became more pertinent. Was it the empire of racial hierarchies, whose legacy still impacted on the identities of Black British citizens, or the benevolent empire that, on balance, did more good than harm? Or is this binary polarization too simplistic? It may, indeed, be argued that the imperial legacy is no longer relevant in an era of globalized culture and British citizens can now claim an inclusive and ethnically diverse identity. But to what extent is British, and indeed Western, society liberated from the powerful cultural hegemony that legitimized imperial power and fused national identities with imperial and racial superiority? These issues are addressed more fully in the concluding chapter.

Postcolonial perspectives: imperialism or globalization?

> There is a real danger that the world economy will evolve into the biggest
> world empire yet, and there will be those on the winning side who will hail
> it, as [some] did the Roman Empire, for the peace it will bring and the
> limitless prospects for propagating particular ideologies. But in our world
> of many cultures we need a more flexible model . . . that will suppress the
> strife of nation states but also nourish our religions, languages and customs.
>
> (Fowden, 1993, p. 172)

Will imperialism continue in the future or are we moving towards a globalized world where respect for cultural diversity is combined with peace through greater equality? Alternatively, is globalization simply a euphemism for contemporary imperialism? With the collapse of communism in the late 1980s, more positive appraisals of the imperial past and contemporary globalization emerged that celebrated the apparent triumphalism of Western democracy and capitalism (Fukuyama, 1992). Imperialism in history was now interpreted by some 'as little more than the opening up of closed economies' (Blackburn, 2001). Thus, in *Empire: How Britain Made the Modern World* (2003), Niall Ferguson emphasized the benefits of 'Anglo-globalization' in furthering the spread of liberal capitalism and opening up global markets. Conservatives attacked liberal political correctness for encouraging a negative view of the imperial past and a blaming and shaming that exonerated the victim (Bruckner, 1986; Kimball, 2001). The colonial era, observed Frank Furedi (1995), was increasingly portrayed as a 'golden age' and blame attributed to the Third World: 'backwardness' stemmed from corrupt, undemocratic regimes. The changing intellectual and political climate since the 1980s has also informed the 'new racism' and 'new imperialism' (Balibar, 1991; Furedi, 1995). In Africa these developments have justified recolonization by the West.

In the postcolonial era, argues Jürgen Osterhammel (1997), forms of manipulation, exploitation and cultural appropriation associated with the imperial era were retained (p. 119). Revisionist histories can be criticized for sanitizing the negative aspects of imperial history and ignoring the inheritance of racism and global inequalities. In effect, the gulf between the West and the 'non-Western' world is widening. What part does Western economic, political and cultural power play in perpetuating inequalities? Are such inequalities evidence of ongoing imperialist relations? How do we draw up the balance sheet on the imperial past and assess its impact on the contemporary world? This chapter will thus consider whether the term 'imperialism' still has relevance in the postcolonial world. It will critically evaluate the concepts of globalization and Westernization, the role of corporate capitalism in these processes, and examine evidence for and against the claim that the USA is now the only imperial power. The ways in which the imperial past intrude into the present are also considered in relation to ongoing struggles to redress Western domination past and present.

A post-imperial world?

Independence or neo-imperialism?

With decolonization of the European empires, the world supposedly entered the post-imperial era. In the 1970s, the newly independent Third World asserted a new identity, defined through political non-alignment from either capitalist 'first' or communist 'second' worlds. This was the decade of hope and action against racism with the establishment of a UN Committee on the Elimination of Racial Discrimination. A Third World bloc began to change the composition of the United Nations and lobbied for a new international economic and information order (to develop independent Third World media). 'Third Cinema' emerged, celebrated at the Havana Film Festival. Films like *Blood of the Condor* (Bolivia, 1969, Jorge Sanjines) reflected ongoing political and cultural struggles but also a new liberationist culture opposed to 'mental' colonization: the Americanization of Latin America. But independence was queried by neo-Marxist and dependency theorists who argued that neo-colonialism and informal imperialism perpetuated dependence (Baran, 1957;

Frank, 1969; Galtung, 1968). Andre Gunder Frank (1969) proposed that capitalism induced a process of 'developing underdevelopment' in poorer regions, including Latin America, supposedly independent since the mid-nineteenth century. This was the result of three interrelated processes: the drain of surplus wealth from periphery to centre; the conservation of precapitalist modes of production arresting modern development on the periphery; the creation of an international division of labour that widened inequalities between the developed 'first' and underdeveloped 'third' world but also *within* both rich and poor states.

Effectively, US-dominated international organizations such as the International Monetary Fund (IMF) and the World Bank restructured the world economy to ensure a continued flow of wealth to the West, creating debt and dependency in the Third World. Inequalities between the rich West and poor non-Western world (now also called North and South) widened with the collapse of communism, which took the steam out of any Third World initiatives. Additionally, the concept of the 'three worlds' had emerged with the Cold War and decolonization, and was no longer relevant after the collapse of communism. The Third World lost its battle to achieve a new international economic order and became increasingly marginalized in the global media (McGrew, 1992; Pilger, 1995). Inequalities within the developing world also widened. South Asian economies were rapidly developing. In Africa development went into reverse and the continent became vulnerable to recolonization as 'smart white boys' working for the IMF were sent out to run failed postcolonial states (Klitgaard, 1990).

The fall of the last great empire, the Soviet Union, arguably opened up the post-imperial age proper, an era of conflicts and identity struggles in newly independent multi-ethnic states delayed by the continuation of imperial power relations throughout the twentieth century (Barkey and von Hagen, 1997). Haynes (1993) argued that, with the end of communism, the 'empire of brute force' was no longer necessary. However, this explains neither the military aggression of the United States from the early 1990s nor the power a dominant Russia still wielded over its former empire. As Furedi (1995) observes, we may be in a postcolonial, but not a post-imperial era and thus imperialism as a concept remains relevant. Wider global struggles, centred on religious, political, economic and cultural problems rooted in the imperial era, have persisted. Continuing echoes of empire – cultural oppression, economic exploitation, genocides, racial exclusions and inequalities – disrupt visions of a postcolonial world and lend support to arguments that globalization is simply a new stage in Western imperialism. To critically evaluate such arguments we need to examine definitions of globalization.

The nature of globalization

There is a huge and complex social science literature on globalization and it is not within the scope of this study to address debates in detail. These have been covered comprehensively elsewhere (Held and McGrew (eds), 2003). Globalization refers to the processes whereby the world becomes one place, based on new concepts of time and space (Axford, 1995). It is defined by a growth of interconnectedness of economic and political activities, culture and migrations across national boundaries and continents. The speed of cultural communications accelerated to unprecedented levels after the Second World War and the locus of political power has shifted from national governments to international organizations and forums. The volume of migration has increased and richer states now demonstrate an unprecedented level of ethnic diversity. Cosmopolitanism has replaced bounded political communities (Held *et al.*, 1999). World culture theorists like Roland Robertson (1992) have stressed the interchange of cultures that has led to a 'compression of the world and the intensification of global consciousness' (p. 8). For the Left, true globalization presupposes global citizenship, democracy, equity and peaceful co-existence (Galtung, 2005).

Radically opposed positions have emerged. Critics of neo-liberal global-ization have argued that it has imposed a violent postcolonial imperialism, deepened race, class and gender hierarchies, undermined vulnerable com-munities, adversely impacted on the economies and cultures of those lower down in the hierarchy and created a system of global apartheid (Axford, 1995; Alexander, 1996; Bauman, 1998; Mittleman, 2000). Zillah Eisenstein (2004) has defined globalization, from the era of slavery onwards, as a 'systematic patriarchal structuring of racialized, sexualized, global exploitation' (p. 183). Conversely, for Thomas Friedman (2000), globalization could be empower-ing or coercive but has had many good consequences. Globalization was the 'inexorable integration of markets, nation states and technologies', was driven by new technology – particularly the Internet – and confirmed that capitalism now had no serious rivals (p. 7). Reiterating old arguments about the 'non-aggressive' nature of capitalism, Friedman has proposed the 'Golden Arches Theory of Conflict Prevention'; that is, when a country is sufficiently economic-ally developed to support a McDonald's chain and integrate into the global network of goods and services its inhabitants will never want to fight a war again. Thus global is good (Friedman, 2005)! The international business com-munity has also made strong arguments for the positive benefits of globalization.

Other debates centre on globalization's impact on politics and the nation-state. 'Hyperglobalists' argue that a new world order is emerging that is eroding and fragmenting states; sceptics refute these claims as exaggerated (Held *et al.*, 1999). The global economic system, observes Andrew Gamble (2002), may display a greater tendency to cohesion and interconnectedness, but as a polity it remains fragmented and has never been transformed into a world system (p. 129). Hirst and Thompson (1996) dispute claims of a unified global economy and argue that the world is breaking into blocs where different forms of capitalism flourish; the post-Cold War world has reverted to neo-imperialism and the nation-state retains a vital role in securing social justice. David Held (1999) recognizes deep problems in globalization but argues that it has not foreclosed options for democracy and has transformed political action, uniting communities across borders in struggles against new, common, globalized problems. Some have queried the whole concept of globalization. Samuel Huntington (1997) claims that the world is fragmenting into conflict based on religious and cultural differences. Benjamin Barber (1995) envisages a world torn between globalism and tribalism, *Jihad* or 'McWorld'.

What we must beware of are ahistorical analyses that ignore the impact of imperialism and colonialism in shaping global cultures, identities and economic structures. Hyperglobalists regard the present global system as different from what went before, whereas world systems theorists argue that globalization is not new and is as old as the origins of capitalism. In the twentieth century, however, this world system was completed but simultaneously moved into a crisis that would bring about its end (Wallerstein, 1998). Historians have emphasized important links between imperialism and globalization (Bayly, 2003; Hopkins (ed.), 2002). Jan Nederveen Pieterse (2004) also prioritizes the long-term historical development of globalization and the multiple, varied and complex processes that have contributed to it. Held *et al.* (1999) explored the political, economic, cultural and environmental impact during different eras. They distinguished between pre-modern, early modern (1500–1850), modern (c. 1850–1945) and contemporary globalization. Neo-liberal globalization, emerging in the late 1970s, promoted global markets, privatization and Western democratic culture.

Globalized diversity or Western cultural hegemony?

The cultural impact of globalization has generated similar polarized debates. Globalization is linked to the spread of modernity. Has this resulted in homogenization of local cultures that has undermined cultural identities and threatened cultural diversity (Latouche, 1996)? Or, have globalization and modern communications accelerated a more positive convergence and/or hybridization of cultures (Pieterse, 2004)? Some elements of Western culture have always been regarded as desirable and selectively incorporated, as in the Japanese response to Western imperialism discussed in Case study 2. But such choice is not always possible and, as argued in Chapter 4, cultural strategies have always been central to sustaining imperial power. In the postcolonial era, then, does the concept of cultural imperialism still have relevance? Tomlinson (1991) has argued that the concept of an all-pervasive cultural imperialism is outmoded and monolithic. It assumes passivity whereas the diffusion of Western culture is mediated by local cultures, class and gender differences that have ensured cultural diversity. Local cultures have thus actively impacted on the global. Homogenization of cultures (global) and heterogenization (local) can intertwine in what Roberston (1995) has called 'glocalization'. Creative hybridizations of cultures also occur. An example here is world music, which has become increasingly popular among Western consumers and musicians and can promote positive globalization through fusion of different cultural genres. Such cultural fusions, suggests Middleton (1992), query simplistic readings of cultural imperialism.

Perhaps this is an appropriate point to extend definitions of culture addressed in Chapter 4. Terry Eagleton (2000) defined four types of culture: culture as civility; culture as identity; culture as commercialism; culture as radical protest. All these are relevant to understanding ongoing processes of, and responses to, globalization and Westernization. Problems, argued Eagleton, emerged from the fact that postmodern culturalism simultaneously promoted cosmopolitanism and a universalizing hybridization of cultures but also an anti-universalist cultural relativism that prioritized difference and diversity and a culture of solidarity, based on shared identities. There was growing evidence on a global scale of conflicts between 'culture as identity' and culture as a commodity reflected in local resistances to global capitalism and the Western culture that it promoted (pp. 72, 75–7, 129). Additionally, capitalism cynically manipulated cultural relativism and 'diversity', which became a new euphemism to avoid tackling real inequalities. 'Culturalism', claimed Amin (2001), divides the world into 'races', 'communities' and 'cultural groups', imposes West-defined hierarchies on the international system, and locks the disadvantaged within these communities. Moreover, the postmodern emphasis on culture and diversity has obscured American military domination and the ongoing globalization and concentration of economic, culture and political power (Jameson, 1984; Harvey, 1990).

What evidence is there, then, for continuing Western cultural hegemony? The 'world revolution in Westernisation' (Von Laue, 1989) was, and remains, premised on ethnocentricism and racism. Cultural oppression and racism arguably constitute the most damaging postcolonial heritage (Davies, Nandy and Sardar, 1993), as highlighted by the reggae icon, Bob Marley, in 'Emancipate yourselves from mental slavery'. Western domination is still legitimized by cultural superiority. After the collapse of communism in the 1980s, the postcolonial world and the underdeveloped parts of the ex-USSR were expected to follow in the footsteps of the West, in terms of economic organization (capitalism and integration into the global markets); individualism and enterprise; moral and political values (Christianity and liberal democracy) and popular culture (mass consumerism, music, films, food). Western ideals of modernity, democracy and human rights were presented to the non-West as universal, although Asian critics pointed out that these were (and remain) culturally specific (Ching, 1993). Such 'universal' values were promoted through powerful government aid agencies and the US-dominated IMF and World Bank. Aid was made conditional on democratization, improved human rights and 'structural adjustment', privatization and integration into global markets. This has had important implications for the national sovereignty of weaker states, particularly in Africa. But are we talking about Westernization or Americanization?

Westernization or Americanization?

John Tomlinson suggests we must distinguish between economic globalization and cultural globalization, which should not be conflated with Americanization (Tomlinson, 2003). Taylor (2002) distinguishes between Americanization, which emphasizes the liberatory aspects of American culture and offers the promise of a better life, and globalization, which operates as a threat (p. 301). But can the economic and political aspects of global Western power, centred on the USA, be separated? Accelerating technological developments since the Second World War have ensured that Western media and information industries have a global reach. The dominant US media have arguably reinforced an ideological framework that works in the interests of US business (Hamelink, 1994). The mass media waged cultural wars against movements that threatened US imperialist interests. Global propaganda penetration was facilitated by the US Information Service, satellite TV networks and the radio station Voice of America. This cultural power, interpenetrating, and supported by, economic and political power, secured Western cultural hegemony.

In the 1980s, during the Reagan administration, the US government mass media became a major growth industry and one of the largest TV networks to emerge was the Christian Broadcasting Network (CBN). The spread of Christian fundamentalism was viewed as crucial to US government/CIA strategies to counteract social movements demanding greater justice and equality for the poor. Central America, the Caribbean and Africa all became prime targets for evangelism concealing political motives (Marishane, 1991). Since the invasion of Iraq, US-style satellite programmes have been beamed to the Arab world (Burkeman, 2003). The 'information superhighways' of the Internet, of course, have been used to extend access to information, promote grass-roots democracy and co-ordinate anti-globalization and other protests. But information technology is dominated by US systems and, as Nelson Thall, chairman of the Marshall McLuhan Center on Global Communications, observed the power of the Internet is that it 'makes you think [and write] like a North American' (Thall, 1995).

Film production, promotion and distribution and cinema ownership are also dominated by US companies. Since the 1920s, the US film industry has been uniquely successful in defining popular culture and projecting the 'American dream', shaping cinema audiences' world views. Films that challenge this have limited circulation in the West. An example here is *The Voyage* (1992 Argentina, dir. Fernando Solanas) that explored the negative impact of US-imposed neo-liberal policies in Latin America and asserted American identities distinct from 'Norte [North] Americans'. Music production is also dominated by multinationals and the flow of influence in popular music since the 1970s has been overwhelmingly from the rich to the poor countries. Despite the fact that cultural hybridization is most marked in relation to music, 'third world' musicians have continued to be exploited or 'internationalized' by multinationals and their styles homogenized and sanitized. Not surprisingly, strong links persisted between music, politics and resistance in the non-Western world (Middleton, 1992).

Neo-liberal globalization since the Reagan/Thatcher era also accelerated further penetration of US consumerist and business cultures. US credit card and debt culture that has proved highly lucrative to US-dominated businesses has spread globally as US markets have become saturated (Ritzer, 2003). 'Coca-Cola' imperialism and the 'McDonaldization' of the world have changed tastes and economic organization of labour. George Ritzer (1993) defined McDonaldization as efficiency, rationalization, a 7-day, 24-hour, no time society. It promotes predictability and uniformity, emphasizes quantity, not quality, and uses non-human technology to control people. As the US economy has moved from dominating industrial production to the 'malling' of America, added Ritzer, this new culture of malls, amusement and theme parks, and Internet shopping channels has spread globally. In the 1990s, argued Naomi Klein (1999), global branding brought together marketing and consumerism to recapture flagging markets, increasing the wealth and cultural influence of corporations like Nike and Microsoft. This 'sneakerization' of society emphasized choice and diversity, but in reality imposed another aspect of capitalism's relentless uniformity. Additionally, 'dollar imperialism' rendered local currencies worthless in the ex-Soviet Union, the besieged socialist world (Cuba), and poorer states with collapsing economies. Inequalities widened between those who had access to dollars and other Western currencies and those who did not. Local currencies thus withered, but corruption and crime increased.

Cultural imperialism still operates at the level of popular culture, but also intellectual culture, in the control of scientific and academic knowledge and the definition of dominant academic discourses. US universities and textbook publishers, backed up by US aid programmes, have penetrated educational systems and played a crucial role in shaping elites. With aid packages Western technologies have been 'sold' to developing countries as superior to local technologies, often with negative consequences. Such technologies change work practices, transform social and gender relations and conflict with belief systems and traditional forms of medicine. They are thus inappropriate, and/or not sustainable, in poorer countries. As under formal imperialism, religion, education and language remain important to strategies of cultural dominance. Linguistic imperialism persists in the hegemonic dominance of English (Ngugi, 1993). Local languages, dialects and cultures have become increasingly threatened. Additionally, global language and culture are now dominated by American business language and

> Nation states are no longer interested in ideology ... Politicians look like businessmen and talk like businessmen ... They compete ... for exports, inward investment and tourism and are acutely aware of the national brand.
>
> (Overell, 1999)

But is this evidence of continuing imperialist relations or the dominance of capitalism through globalization?

Capitalism, imperialism and globalization

Debates about the relationship between modern capitalism, imperialism and globalization go back to the early twentieth century. For Lenin modern imperialism was the highest stage of capitalism when the world was carved up and informal imperialism extended. Schumpeter, however, argued that imperialism represented feudal atavism and aggressive militarism that would disappear as capitalism, with its non-militaristic imperatives of capitalist accumulation, expanded (Schumpeter, 1919). Kautsky (1914) developed his theory of an ultra (informal) imperialism stimulated by advanced capitalism but, like Schumpeter, believed that an 'inter-imperialism', characterized by co-operation of capitalists, would promote peace. Unfortunately Kautsky's theories were refuted by the outbreak of the First World War which, argued Lenin, was a direct consequence of imperial/capitalist competition.

World systems theorists like Immanuel Wallerstein place capitalism rather than imperialism *per se* at the centre of global dynamics. In this context globalization and imperialism are not synonymous and globalization is a new phase in capitalism. Giovanni Arrighi (1994) stressed the need to analyse the dynamics of global capitalism in the *longue durée* in order to explain how it has structured relations between the poorer and richer nations of the world. For Eric Hobsbawm (1994), modern imperialism lasted no longer than a lifetime, but globalization wrought great changes from 1914, endorsing Marx's view that capitalism was a permanent and revolutionizing force (pp. 15–16). Lenin had envisaged a world carved up by great corporations, extending and strengthening economic imperialism, but, argued Richard Sklar (1976), capitalism, not imperialism, was responsible for the oppression of Third World peoples.

Central to understanding contemporary economic globalization are the multinational corporations (MNCs). The powerful global corporation, argued Barnet and Müller (1974), had the potential to integrate production on a global scale and realize the 'ancient capitalist dream of One Great Market' (pp. 18–19). Anthony Sampson wrote of the oil corporations:

> With their complexity, range and resources, they were institutions that had appeared to be part of a world government. Their executives could fly between Pittsburgh and Kuwait, San Francisco and Saudi Arabia, as casually as across their own state. Their computers could analyse the supplies and demands of half the countries of the world. Their boards could allocate [huge sums of money] to bring into being a new oilfield . . . or a new trade route. . . . Their sky scraper headquarters . . . seemed to evoke a new world where nations themselves were obsolescent.
>
> (Sampson, 1975, p. 12)

From the 1970s polarized positions on the nature of MNC activity and their role in the globalization of capital emerged. On the positive side, the beneficial contributions multinationals made to Third World development were emphasized. Critics of this view pointed out the neo-imperialist, exploitative nature of MNCs and the fact that their activities were protected by US military power. Sklar (1976) concluded, however, that MNCs undermined imperialist relations by uniting local and corporate interests that transcended national boundaries and diminished the power of the nation-state. They thus promoted a global culture of the transnational capitalist class. These debates continued as MNC activity intensified. The post-imperial world, wrote Haynes (1993), was run by an international oligarchy wielded by a 'managerial bourgeoisie' whose aims were to guarantee the interests of corporate capitalism. But capitalism still needed powerful states, in particular the USA, which controlled the global military order and communications networks. To what extent is global capitalism premised on imperialist relations of power, formal or informal? If we accept that imperialism still exists, how does it differ from what went before? It is useful here to bear in mind categories used for comparing empires in Chapter 1: justificatory ideologies and myths; economic exploitation; cultural and racial superiority; strategies to secure power.

Contemporary neo-liberal globalization controlled knowledge production and created new imperial 'myths' of the inevitability and beneficial nature of neo-liberal economics (Gills, 1997). As during the imperial era, in the post-imperial age shared ideology secured the consent of ruling groups and collaborators to the system (Wallerstein, 1974). De la Campa, Kaplan and Sprinkler (1995) argued that imperial culture persisted even if it had moved into a new 'late' phase underpinning global initiatives such as the General Agreement on Tariffs and Trade (GATT) and the North America Free Trade Association (NAFTA). After decolonization, imperialism consolidated its power, affirming Lenin's position on the dynamics of capitalism and creation of informal empires. This 'imperialism without colonies' demonstrated 'enormous vitality' around the world (pp. 2–6). Jeff Haynes (1993) emphasized the primacy of capitalism over imperialism but conceded that the collapse of communism created conditions that favoured a revival of classic and/or ultra-imperialist relations. For Derek Gregory (2004), the occupation of Iraq in 2003 represented the 'colonial present' as it flagged continuities between past and present and demonstrated that 'active constellations of power, knowledge and geography' continued to colonize lives all over the world (p. xv). In contrast, Hardt and Negri (2000) have reconceptualized globalization as empire, 'a universal order that accepts no boundaries and limits' (p. 5). This unified global empire differs from earlier European empires and capitalist expansion. It dominates and runs the world but is not geographically

specific. Incorporating American traditions of hybrid identities, constitution-
alism and expanding frontiers, this empire promotes new forms of racism and
creates a new imperial world order defined by the power of MNCs. For them,
globalization is the latest stage in imperialism. What evidence supports such
arguments?

Corporate power has now reached an unprecedented level. In the 1990s
MNCs accounted for an estimated 70 per cent of world trade and their power
relative to national governments had substantially increased (Held *et al.*,
1999). At the end of the twentieth century Bill Gates possessed more money
than 135 of the UN member states and the Ford Motor Company had a greater
global sales total than the combined GDP of Greece, Ireland and Luxemburg
(Overell, 1999). Globalization has affected workers in poor and wealthy
countries alike. Since the end of formal empires, inequalities of wealth have
intensified between and within nations and only the centres of global capitalism in both rich and poor nations benefit (Amin, 2001). In *Roger and
Me* (1989), Michael Moore, an American patriot in the populist tradition,
explored the impact of MNC relocation (in this case General Motors) to
developing countries on the working classes, black and white, in his home
town of Flint, Michigan.

Additionally, neo-liberal globalization has stimulated new labour migrations, leading to fears of swamping by white Europeans and increased racism
and xenophobia. Illegal migration has increased concern over modern
slavery, where slavery is defined as working for no money under the threat
of violence (Bales, 1999). Slavery still exists in human trafficking for the sex
trade, domestic and agricultural labour, including child labour (Van den
Anker, 2003). In Europe and the USA, globalization has resulted in a resident
underclass, a transient, insecure and exploited workforce and a 'gangmaster'
work culture. The lucrative trade in illegal migrants to richer countries is
facilitated by the globalized connections of international criminal organizations, which have also globalized drug markets. Exploitation of the poor
has 'diversified' into an invidious trade in body parts to service the health
and well-being of the rich. In India and Brazil this 'market' is well developed
and the film *Dirty Pretty Things* (UK 2003, dir. Stephen Frears) exposed
the vulnerability of illegal migrants in Britain to this expanding market.
Transnational globalization, argues Zilla Eisenstein (2004), retains gendered
and racialized structures of power that reproduce inequalities.

Cultural differences have also been encouraged as part of a global strategy
for world management, to fragment any forces of opposition. These new divide
and rule tactics work against universalist values of democracy (Amin, 2001).
In Ruanda, Bosnia, Kosovo and Sudan, ethnicity and economic conflict,

combined with the aftershock of history, resulted in ethnic cleansing and genocide. In developing countries, argued Amy Chua (2003), neo-liberal globalization has concentrated wealth in the hands of market-orientated ethnic minorities, widening disparities of wealth between such minorities and the majority ethnic group and creating political instability. In the Philippines, for instance, the Chinese account for one per cent of the population, but own over half the wealth. But the causes of ethnic conflicts are also rooted in the divide and rule tactics used in the era of formal imperialism. The colonial powers, adds Chua, encouraged ethnic minorities to migrate and settle. In contrast to disadvantaged minorities in the West, such collaborative minorities often enjoyed economic privilege and they have continued to collaborate in the post-colonial project of neo-liberal globalization.

Regardless of whether these developments constitute globalization or imperialism, there is a wealth of evidence relating to the negative impact of what Richard Falk (1999) referred to as a seemingly unstoppable, 'predatory' globalization. Neo-liberal policies imposed on the developing world have increased poverty and inequality. Global poverty has shifted from the countryside to the cities as privatization has pushed peasants off their land (UNDP Report, 1999). Joseph Stiglitz, Senior Vice President and Chief Economist of the World Bank in the late 1990s, argued that IMF liberalization policies have resulted in unemployment, hyperinflation, recession and state collapse, as in Argentina. Globalization has its benefits, he conceded, but operates predominantly in American and wider Western capitalist interests; international institutions needed to be more responsive to the poor, the environment and broader political and social concerns (Stiglitz, 2002). George Ritzer (2003) sees globalization as tantamount to Americanization of the world to profit US companies. But is Americanization effectively a reflection of US imperial power? At this point we need to examine debates over the nature of US imperialism.

'Pax Americana': an exceptional nation or a world empire?

Myth and reality

Most studies of imperial and postcolonial culture omit discussions of the USA as an imperial power. The USA, argues Army Kaplan (1993), is either absorbed into a general notion of the West or it stands for a monolithic West. US continental expansion is treated as an entirely separate phenomenon from nineteenth-century European colonialism rather than related to it. In conventional historiography, the assumption endures that the American struggle for independence from British colonialism resulted in an anti-imperialist culture in the USA (p. 17). The concept of American 'exceptionalism' has defined the USA as a unique nation. Proponents of this view argued that, after the brief imperialist era before the First World War (Chapter 1), external interventions were not sanctioned by anti-imperialist administrations from Woodrow Wilson (1912–21) onwards, or by the US public (Kaplan, 1993, pp. 12–14; Lipset, 1997). After the First World War, the 'anti-imperialist' USA championed the 'self determination of nations' and this myth of US anti-imperialism strengthened during the Second World War.

As stressed in Chapter 5, mythology and history have always sustained an intimate relationship, particularly in self-representations of empires. Challenging such myths is a leitmotif which runs through *Narratives of Empire*, Gore Vidal's multi-volume fictionalized history of the USA since the revolution. 'Manifest destiny' was premised on the superiority of protestant Anglo-Saxon culture, and westwards expansion involved the imposition of power over the indigenous inhabitants. Bernard Porter (2005) has challenged American 'exceptionalism' on the grounds that there were important similarities between British and US imperialism. Many parallels have also been made between British and US strategies to suppress protest and opposition to the 2003 invasion of Iraq (Dodge, 2003; Ali, 2003; Sluglett, 2006). Chomsky (1994) argued that both empires represented themselves as the freest of nations within their own boundaries, but used oppressive coercion outside against those who will not, or cannot, comply with economic liberalism. Additionally, in Britain and the USA, imperialism has played an important role in shaping a strong sense of national identity and internal cohesion and justified the need to suppress internal threats to capitalism, such as class conflict and oppositional movements.

Keylor (1992) challenges myths of isolationism and argues that the American state was expansionist from the time of the Monroe Doctrine (1823) which claimed hegemony over Latin America. US informal empire in Central and Latin America was extended in what Keylor terms the 'era of direct domination', 1914–32, with military interventions in Nicaragua, Haiti and the Dominican Republic. During the depression years, the USA became more insular and protectionist, but 'indirect hegemony' persisted (pp. 22, 72, 206–17). US cultural influence was also extended through US philanthropic foundations such as the Carnegie Trust and Rockefeller Foundation (Arngrove (ed.), 1980). Developments in the Second World War also challenged myths of anti-imperialism. Humanitarian rhetoric of human rights and self-determination concealed a bid for global hegemony. In 1945, the

USA controlled 50 per cent of the global GNP and dominated new international organizations such as the IMF, the World Bank and the UN (Ambrose, 1983; Cox, 1984). After the war the USA reneged on commitment to self-determination as applied to colonies that were strategic to the new Cold War order; energies were now directed to counteracting anti-colonialist communist movements in Indonesia, the Philippines, Vietnam, Japan, Latin America, Africa and the Caribbean. The US helped to reinstate French colonial rule in Vietnam as a buffer against the communist nationalists led by Ho Chi Minh (who ironically, had worked with the Americans in fighting the Japanese during the war), and supported continued French and British colonial rule in Africa. In what Robinson and Louis (1994) called the 'imperialism of decolonization' the British Empire was not decolonized but neo-colonized under new management.

Up to the late 1970s, argued Haynes (1993), the USA exercised imperialist control in the Philippines and Nicaragua and, in Iran and Egypt and Latin America states, informal imperial domination (Kautsky's ultra-imperialism of capitalist domination). Marxist critics argued that the USA had defined a New World Order in its own interests, supporting neo-colonialism in the ex-European empires and ensuring continued dependency of the poor on the rich countries (Owen and Sutcliffe, 1972, p. 254). Yet the USA remained an empire in denial, defining itself as a 'world power' (Kaplan, 1993, p. 12). International relations analysis, which replaced academic discourse about imperialism with the end of formal imperialism, strengthened this analysis of the nature of US power. American foreign policy was interpreted as a response to Cold War threats, the 'containment of communism', rather than an imperialist strategy to expand power (Smith, 1986; Schwabe, 1986). In the *New York Times* in 1960, the Soviet Union was represented as the last great imperial state, engaged in a 'new imperialism' in Cuba, the Congo and elsewhere (Snyder (ed.), 1962, pp. 594–5). After Castro came to power in 1959, President Kennedy reasserted the Monroe Doctrine and Cuba was subjected to intense US imperialist interference (displayed in the exhibition on 'Yankee imperialism' in the National Museum of the Revolution in Havana). Cuba, dominated by the USA since 1900, represented all that the USA hated – a small, weak, but defiant Third World country vehemently opposed to US imperialism and advocating socialist, as opposed to capitalist, development. After 1989 the US blockade on Cuba was tightened in the hope that the Cuban economy would collapse. Cuba experienced a harsh 'special period' of rationing but to date, the regime has held firm.

It was the war in Vietnam that galvanized debates about the nature of US imperialism. Neo-Marxists and other radical critics emphasized the political/cultural base of US imperialism and its connection with capitalism and militarism. Imperialist intervention in Vietnam, they claimed, made huge profits for the military–industrial complex and advanced the technologies of modern warfare, reflected in the perfection of napalm by Dow Chemicals (Chomsky, 1973). Critics disputed this link between capitalism, the military power of states and imperialism, first articulated by Lenin in 1916, on the grounds that the costs of the Vietnamese and other interventionist wars exceeded any economic gain (Shaw, 1984). Indeed, the Vietnam War seemed to work against US interests. Between 1965 and 1970, the USA experienced plummeting growth rates, a decline in its share of total world exports and internal opposition to the Vietnam War was widespread. Cuba and Vietnam had become symbols of resistance in the developing world and the USA faced mounting challenges, culminating in the Iranian Revolution in 1979 (Swingina, 1989). Yet, argued Petras and Rhodes (1976), in reality the USA had strengthened imperial control. Cracks in the system appeared after 1970 but the rate at which Third World countries, 'even those with relatively nationalistic governments', were becoming incorporated into the US *imperium* accelerated. Even the Vietnamese victory was pyrrhic. The war resulted in enormous loss of life and ecological destruction, but the USA refused any compensation and Vietnam was arguably 'recolonized' after the collapse of communism (Pilger, 1995).

The Reagan administration reversed national humiliations of the 1970s in a resurgent Cold War against the Soviet 'evil empire'. Costly direct US intervention was replaced by the arming and training of surrogate forces to fight proxy wars in Third World socialist states in Nicaragua, Angola and El Salvador. New policies of 'low-intensity conflict' included manipulating food aid and promoting Christian fundamentalism through expanding global radio stations. This era saw the emergence of what are now termed 'the neo-cons and theo-cons' and the growing influence of right-wing ideologues, think-tanks and 'independent' foundations in shaping US policy. The neo-cons became more prominent with the demise of the Soviet Union and the consolidation of the USA as the only global power. Crucial to the neo-con cultural agenda was the mission to spread Protestant fundamentalism (hence the use of the term 'theo-cons'). The *Voice of America* increased its global output of religious programmes. American fundamentalist leaders openly identified their understanding of Christianity with US imperial values, seeing the USA as a 'chosen nation' with a destined mission to save and evangelize the world (Marishane, 1991). The 'new' imperialism, argued Frank Furedi (1995) began with the collapse of communism and the First Gulf War, 1991–2. The invasion of Iraq opened up a new phase of direct US intervention and represented a shift of interest to the Middle East. Interest in Africa initially declined but the USA is now a major player in the recolonization of Africa to secure its valuable resources, particularly oil, given the growing instability in the Middle East.

A hegemonic power?

Hegemony, in particular the Gramscian concept, has been analysed at various points in this book. O'Brien (2002) defines it as:

> . . . the deployment of power and persuasion by a dominant state to defend the planet, avoid warfare and to promote economic stability, commerce and cultural exchanges on a global scale.
>
> (p. 4)

Manuel Ugarte (1995), Chalmers Johnson (2003) and others have equated the USA with the 'new Rome', on the basis that no hegemonic power since Rome has existed comparable in scope, scale and intensity to the USA since 1941. O'Brien and Clesse (2002) suggest that comparisons with Britain are more fruitful in understanding the nature of US hegemonic power. Conversely, John Hobson (2002) argues that American hegemony has proved to be a unique institutional form and very different from the imperial structures that Britain created in the nineteenth century (p. 321). For Giovanni Arrighi (1990), hegemonic states are not just great powers but have something extra that marks them out as unusual and special. Both Arrighi and Wallerstein (2002) conclude that there have only been three hegemons in world systems analysis: the United Provinces, the United Kingdom, and the United States. Power was based on Dutch mercantilism, British industrialism and American consumerism respectively.

America may now have become the sole hegemonic power yet, as Noam Chomsky (2002) pointed out, the USA has remained an empire in denial and suffering from historical amnesia, an amnesia in which even liberal American intellectuals and journalists have colluded. Chomsky has been consistently one of the most outspoken critics of US imperialism, which he regards as a continuity of the expansion of world systems through imperialism that began in 1492 (Chomsky, 1993). Questioning the motivation for, and consequences of, the 'war on terror' since the 9/11 attack on the World Trade Centre in New York in 2001, he argued that the American elite have frequently bombed and terrorized in the name of freedom and the defence of their economy (Chomsky, 2003). The invasion of Afghanistan and Iraq after 9/11, however, produced a new generation of writings on American imperialism. Reasons given for the invasion include the rise of the neo-cons to positions of influence and/or links between Christian fundamentalism, the Bush administration and support for Israel, and US desire to control oil resources (Johnson, 2003; Vidal, 2004; Khalidi, 2004). New geo-global priorities have been emphasized, particularly US oil strategy in the Caspian region (Kleveman, 2003), justified by the need to combat the 'axis of evil' from Iraq to North Korea. Reflecting this post-Cold War shift in strategy, US military bases in Western Europe have been closed and new bases opened in more strategic locations.

The USA, argues Chalmers Johnson (2003), has used humanitarianism and the concept of 'lone superpower' as euphemisms to conceal harder imperial motives supported by aggressive militarism. In Iraq, a war was launched with no legal justification and against worldwide protests. Arguably, the US mission is to transform the world and establish cultural, political and economic frameworks that will help to sustain the hegemony of the elite minority who are in power. US companies like Haliburton were deeply supportive of action in Iraq and Afghanistan. 'Privatization' of the armed forces and reconstruction of 'failed' states offer lucrative profits and have strengthened links between government and business. Corporate power was the driving force behind US foreign policy and the war in Iraq (Galbraith, 2004), but American neo-cons have defended such military interventions and 'shock and awe' tactics as essential to spreading free trade and democracy globally and, thus, peace and prosperity. Leading neo-cons like Paul Wolfowitz, Dick Cheney and Richard Perle believe that American leadership is good for America and the world and that this justifies the use of force and an increase in military expenditure. The 2004 presidential elections strengthened the hand of the neo-cons. As Todd (2004) points out, we can be optimistic about the spread of democracy but can the USA only achieve this by coercion and military interventions?

David Harvey (2003) argues that the rise of the neo-cons has moved the world closer to fulfilling Lenin's prediction of economic collapse and endorsed his arguments linking the dynamics of capitalism, creation of informal empires and global conflict. The USA is moving towards 'endless war', an imperialism motivated by the inherent failures and contradictions in the US economy and the need to control the global economy. Imperialism, concedes Chalmers Johnson (2003), also has sorrows – a loss of democracy as the US government is transformed into a 'military junta'; the replacement of truth with propaganda and disinformation, glorifying power and war; and, finally, bankruptcy as social programmes are eclipsed. US citizens are neglected in favour of 'endless war' against terrorism that promotes a state of perpetual fear. Johnson concludes that America has entered one of its worst periods, worse than the paranoid excesses of McCarthyism and, unless the people reclaim Congress, nemesis awaits. Emmanuel Todd (2004) and Vernon Coleman (2003) arrived at similar conclusions.

Imperialism, argued Michael Rogin (1993), impacted negatively on American culture, generating a discourse centred on the defence of morality and family values that deflected attention from poverty and other serious social problems. For Anatol Lieven (2004), this imperial culture was shaped by the instability of American national identity. Americans, he concluded, were driven by patriotism rather than nationalism and, after 9/11, this degenerated into intolerance and national paranoia about the terrorist/Islamic threat. Tensions sharpened between humanitarian concerns that provided the justification of imperial interventions and contempt and indifference towards non-Americans. The neo-cons and the business elite determined the politics and culture of the USA and liberals and foreigners were scapegoated for undermining family, religion and nation. The rise of the neo-cons has eclipsed the liberal values of civic nationalism and social equality associated with the foundation of the Republic and later moderating influences. Rather than the mature nationalism of a secure dominant state, American nationalism is thus more akin to that which developed in pre-1945 Germany. Lieven's assessment raises a crucial question. If the USA reaches its nemesis by imploding will the dominance of the West and Westernization be reversed?

The imperial legacy: ongoing struggles in a 'postcolonial' world

The more aggressive phase in American imperialism since the 1980s re-energized struggles against Western domination that have their roots in the earlier era of European formal empires and stimulated new resistances against global systems of power (Wallerstein, 2002; Amin, 2001). In Europe McDonald's has been under attack from anti-globalization protestors and the 'slow movement' in Italy has challenged the American '24/7' global culture that leads to overwork, eating on the hoof, fragmented families and societies and cultural and social impoverishment. The Global Justice Movement has organized protest against the IMF and the World Bank, including tax revolts, and has campaigned against 'global apartheid'. Anti-globalization protest has brought together activists in the World Social Forum and focused on unequal trade promoted by the WTO and G8 economic power and control of markets. Coca-Cola's monopoly has also been challenged, predominantly in Arab states, where their own brands of soft drinks have had marketing success as a result of the growth of anti-Americanism. Peasants in India involved in disputes over water with Coca-Cola have started using it as an insecticide.

Such developments offer hope for a better new world order that promotes global justice (Monbiot, 2004). As Barry Gills (1997) has observed, in the contemporary global era, as in the past, people will challenge 'wild' or 'savage' capitalism based on exploitation and denial of human rights. Thus, Linebaugh and Rediker's 'many headed hydra' of resistance has continued to disturb and threaten the powerful. Such struggles constitute new social movements focused on grass-roots democracy, including women's movements, and ecological issues promoting globalization from below (Falk, 1999). Resistance is resurfacing in Africa; grass-roots movements, in which women are often prominent, are challenging both the forces of neo-liberal globalization and local collaborators. As Zilla Eisenstein (2004) points out, the 'greatest struggles of resistance' may be located with 'anti-racist feminisms against empire', although these have been silenced, past and present (p. xix).

In Latin and Central America, where neo-liberal policies have been a disaster for peasants and urban workers, opposition is mounting. In Mexico, the Zapatistas fought for the rights of peasants in impoverished rural areas and gained popular support. They revived indigenous languages, challenged neo-liberal policies and subverted Western technology through the use of the Internet. Struggles for land rights and livelihoods against rapacious capitalism are ongoing in Brazil. In Venezuela, the left-wing president, Hugo Chavez, was re-elected in 2004, despite attempts by the USA to destabilize the government (Venezuela is one of the USA's main suppliers of oil). In the same year, popular protest resurfaced in Bolivia. Richard Gott (2005) has argued that, not since the eighteenth century, has such a 'seismic upheaval' occurred amongst the indigenous peoples of Latin America, the majority population who have been consistently marginalized and impoverished since the days of the conquistadores. In Africa, also, there are unfinished struggles to redress the racist heritage and, in the ex-white settler heartlands in Southern Africa, to reclaim land expropriated by white settlers. In Zimbabwe a legacy of bitterness from the era of white supremacy has resulted in extreme and, unfortunately, counterproductive policies. The jury is still out on what will happen in post-Apartheid South Africa in relation to the sensitive issue of land redistribution and the move to a more equal, multiracial society.

Indigenous peoples' struggles

In the postcolonial world oppressed indigenous peoples, estimated to number 370 million in over 70 countries worldwide, have also found a new voice.

These include First Nation struggles for recognition in Australia, South Africa, Siberia, Amazonia, South East Asia, North and South America, Northern Norway, Sweden and Finland, the homeland of the Sami peoples. Such struggles have been catalysed by the discourse of universal human rights and the multiculturalism and identity politics that have also been central to postcolonial challenges to the racist/imperial heritage in the USA and Britain. Identity formation is at the heart of indigenous politics and an emergent sense of nationalism (Dean and Levi (eds), 2003). A 'pan-Indian' identity in the USA and Canada has crossed ethnic and national boundaries, and communal gatherings have celebrated a positive identity, not simply a shared victimhood (King, 1999). More Australians, Canadians and North Americans are now claiming indigenous ancestry, resulting in growing populations with a higher political profile. Common grievances and identities in a globalized world are now voiced in forums such as the annual World Festival of Indigenous Cultures, held in Norway (Burnside, 2003).

Assertions of indigenous identities have also extended to critiques of Western museums and 'ethnographic' displays (Chapter 5). There have been requests for the return of sacred objects taken back to Europe by travellers, scientists and officials that are now festering in museum basements. The return by the French government in 2002 of the remains of Saartje Baartman 'the Hottentot Venus', to the Khoi-San peoples of the South African Cape, is a good example here. The Khoi-San (Hottentot) peoples were the first to inhabit the Cape. Baartman was displayed in London and Paris in the early nineteenth century as a sexual freak on account of her 'unusual' genitals. On her death in Paris, her remains were carved up, her genitals and brain pickled and her skeleton put on display in the Musée de l'Homme until 1976. The return of Baartman's remains was important because she epitomized the suffering of all Khoi-San peoples under colonialism. Now numbering approximately 100,000, and represented by the National Khoi-San Consultative Conference embracing all indigenous peoples of Southern Africa, the Khoi-San remain marginalized in the new democratic South Africa (McGreal, 2002). The traditional homelands of the San peoples of the Kalahari desert have also been threatened by the Bostwana government, which allegedly wants to secure diamond and other resources and has forcibly relocated the San, despite protest from San and Western-based human rights groups (Meldrum, 2004).

In the West there is now more recognition that the culture and knowledge of indigenous peoples, formerly despised by Europeans, have much value. This includes sustainable management of the environment and the derivation of drugs from plants. Scientists have recognized the value of Australian Aboriginal peoples' weather knowledge (Young, 2003, p. 9). White settler historiography has also been critiqued and revised to incorporate history from the indigenous peoples' perspective. With the rebirth of Maori political aspirations in the 1970s, academics began to explore their position as descendants of colonial migrants, their 'Pakeha' identity and relationship to the Maori peoples (King, 1985). Though controversial, initiatives like National Sorry Day in Australia have given recognition to the former white oppression of Aboriginal peoples. Yet there is also a backlash against what some see as the politically correct romanticization of the 'primitive' (Chapter 3).

Indigenous peoples are still faced with the dilemma of incorporating elements of modernity that they need to prosper whilst retaining their culture and identity. New problems have also resulted from contact with modern culture and urbanization. In Canada, the Innu (Innuit) were forced to settle in towns as part of a government modernization project; they had houses, central heating and snowmobiles, but dislocation from their old homelands and way of life resulted in alcoholism and substance abuse. Treaties protecting indigenous peoples' way of life as the frontier expanded have been consistently breached, particularly when valuable resources such as oil and gas were at stake (Brody, 1986). Indigenous art and culture have become fashionable and some indigenous peoples can capitalize on this, as with the demand for Navaho and other Native American jewellery in the USA, but most indigenous peoples remain poor and marginalized from the mainstream culture. Inequalities between indigenous populations and the majority European populations persist. Social and economic deprivation in New Zealand was graphically explored in the film *Once were Warriors* (New Zealand, 1995, dir. Lee Tamahori) about the lives of urban Maoris. In Australia statistics of deprivation are even starker and Aboriginal peoples suffer higher death rates than other indigenous minorities, including New Zealand Maoris and Native American Indians. Aboriginal life expectancy is 20 years less than the general population and 50 per cent of Aboriginal men are dead by the age 50. Aboriginal peoples constitute only two per cent of the population but 20 per cent of the prison population (Ramussen, 2004).

A common grievance of indigenous peoples is police/state violence. This protest from the Mohawk nation to the prime minister of Canada and the premiers of British Columbia and Ontario in 1995 was triggered by the deaths of several young men, one aged 15 who was allegedly unarmed but 'executed' by a bullet to the head. The letter complained that:

> We have remained silent for some time now in the hope that your governments could finally come to terms honorably with our rights and sovereign control over our lands and destiny. You have always said that all you needed

was a little more time – as if 500 years was not enough. And what have you given to our people with that little more time? You have given us more guns, more bullets, more violence, more threats, more empty . . . rhetoric about your law and order, all at the expense of justice for our people.

(Signed Rotiskenakatch, Mohawk Nation,
Six Nation Confederacy, Kahawake Territory,
www.spunk.org/texts/colon/sp00107.txt. accessed 11.06.02)

The 2004 riots in inner city Redfern, Sidney, in February, 2004 were also triggered by the death on a bicycle of an Aboriginal teenager while being chased by the police. Located on the borders of prestigious Sydney University, the riots demonstrated the intensity of alienation, the movement of the 'frontier' to the white cities and continued 'frontier fighting' against social inequalities and injustices (Russell, 2001, p. 4). These race riots were the worst experienced in Australia and reminiscent in context, actions, cause and events to defensive riots of racialized minorities in Los Angeles, Liverpool and the London borough of Brixton in the 1980s and 1990s. Common threads include the 'postcolonial' legacy of racism and hostility to 'non-white' migrants in white cities and attribution of blame by the white majority to 'agitators' who incited violence. After the Redfern riots it was claimed that such 'agitators' had damaged the Aboriginal cause (Editorial, *Herald Sun*, Melbourne, 17 February, 2004). Despite acknowledgement that the Aboriginal population suffered 'crippling social disadvantage', the riots were blamed on 'failed social engineering' and alienated, intractable, unemployable youngsters who had 'contempt for society' (Piers Akerman, *The Daily Telegraph*, Sydney, 17 February, 2004). For Aboriginal peoples, however, the riots represented '. . . a powerful collective will to struggle against imperial forces that continue to interfere with [and] to reinterpret our history, our identity, and our future prospects' (Ray Minniecon, *Sydney Morning Herald*, 17 February, 2004).

Land remains at the heart of indigenous people's struggles against private multinationals who want to exploit resources and against governments who fail to protect indigenous land rights (see Figure 6.1). In 2004, the South American Mapuche Indians won a case against Benetton, the Italian clothing manufacturer, which is the biggest landowner in Patagonia, the source of 10 per cent of its wool. Benetton was criticized over the eviction of a Mapuche family and the Mapuche accused the company of having the same mentality as the conquistadores and colonists who forcibly seized their lands in the nineteenth century. Benetton finally agreed to give up some of its land to end a dispute that was undermining its image as a caring, culturally sensitive company that had invested money in a museum dedicated to Mapuche history and

Figure 6.1 Postcolonial struggles: protest against the Jabiluka uranium mine, Sidney, 1998 (author's own photograph)

culture (Hooper and Baldock, 2004). Not all struggles are against dominant Westerners. In postcolonial states in Africa and Asia, indigenous movements for self-determination have been crushed as a threat to the unity of the state and the interests of the powerful (Dean and Levi, 2003). The postcolonial elites have thus perpetuated inequalities established in the era of formal empires.

Religion, culture and resistance

In the postmodern world, religion and belief have become more central, in contrast to the secularity of the modern period. This is related to the chaos unleashed by the 'New World Order' (or disorder) ushered in with the fall of communism and the ending of the certainties of the Cold War era. As the neo-cons gained more power, Protestant evangelical religion increasingly defined US political culture and was promoted in potentially disruptive areas as a counterforce to radicalism. As Robertson (1992) has noted, religion became a strong site of cultural conflict resulting from globalization. Global conflicts and non-Western resistances now reflect a new blending of politics and religion. The failure of socialism to bring about a secular millennium has also resulted in a new religious millenarianism in poorer countries.

The most powerful challenges to Western hegemony have come from a resurgent Islam. After 1918, the collapse of the Turkish Empire resulted in the expansion of imperialism (French, British and US) in the Middle East. Palestine under a British mandate witnessed increased Jewish immigration and the origins of the contemporary Israeli/Palestinian conflict. Islam was apparently weakened and in retreat but was revived in the Iranian revolution in 1979 and in the more widespread Islamic fundamentalism that constitutes the 'terror' of the West. Bernard Lewis (2003) has argued that the anti-Americanism, as opposed to anti-Westernism, that has fuelled this Islamic threat, constitutes a 'rejection and condemnation . . . of all that America is seen to represent in the modern world' and can be traced back to the Iranian revolution (p. 87). The revival of Islam as a political force has evoked fears in the West of the 'clash of civilizations', a conflict between the West and Islamic fundamentalism conceptualized as the 'New Crusades' (Ali, 2003).

Western hegemony is now increasingly defined as Christianity (civilized) versus Islam (fanatical, irrational) and since 9/11 there has been a reassertion of Western moral and cultural superiority. Recent targets of US intervention – Afghanistan, Palestine, Iraq – are all parts of the ancient Turkik and Persian empires (Gregory, 2004). Orientalist scholars such as Bernard Lewis still generalize about the 'Arab mind' and blame the problems of the Arab/Moslem

world on poverty, tyranny and failure to embrace modernity. Islamic fundamentalism is thus simplistically dismissed as 'anti-modern' and understanding such weaknesses in Islamic culture and society is seen as vital to defeating
Islamic terrorism (Lewis, 2003, pp. 57–8, 87). Stereotypes of passive Oriental
women persist and one rationale for interventions in undemocratic Islamic
states is to 'liberate' such women from oppression. Thus Laura Bush's concern for the plight of women under the Taliban was important in humanizing
George Bush's intervention in Afghanistan. In effect this can be seen as a contemporary version of 'imperial feminism' (Chapter 3) that remains in tension
with the interests and aspirations of women outside the powerful West
(Eisenstein, 2004, p. 149). In the preface to the 2003 edition of *Orientalism*,
Edward Said argued that general understanding of the Middle East, Arabs and
Islam had not improved since his book was first published. Pentagon advisers
still use the same old clichés suggesting a continuity of imperialist discourse.
Such neo-Orientalist discourse and Western intervention in Iraq have further
stimulated Islamic fundamentalism and dissent. Resistance in Iraq, blamed
on outsiders and links with al-Qaida, is largely indigenous and ongoing
(Ali, 2003).

Conclusion: future trends

This chapter has established a close, and often confusing, link between capitalism, globalization and imperialism. It has demonstrated how the imperial
past echoes into the 'post-imperial' present and that key concepts dealt with in
earlier chapters – racism, cultural imperialism, Westernization, Orientalism,
poverty and inequality, and resistance struggles – remain relevant to interrogating the life experiences of non-Western peoples and Black, Hispanic and
Asian minorities in Europe and North America. I have focused particularly
on the United States as the dominant hegemon, exploring links between
Americanization, globalization and imperialism. There are positive developments but Leviathan is still crushing the Hydra of resistance that began in
the first age of European imperialism. In Africa and Latin America, resistance
has been weakened by the decimation of the organized working class through
neo-liberal economic policies. In Africa, in order to survive, peasants have had
to sell land and assets and migrate to the cities. Western consortia are buying
up land to expand commercial plantations. Africa is once more being carved
up by the rich nations for its valuable resources. AIDS is taking its toll of the
young and thus the future of the continent. In South Africa and Botswana

up to 30 per cent of the population are HIV-positive. Apart from AIDS, infant mortality rates are also rising (Nugent, 2004). Elites, formerly leaders of nationalist struggles, now identify once more with Western centres like Washington, London and Paris rather than their own rural areas. Collaboration intensifies corruption, which facilitates recolonization and reinstates neo-colonialist relations.

In relation to global power relations there is no room for complacency. A global girdle of military power – bases, secret intelligence centres, and Star Wars defences – now protects and defends the interests of the powerful. Large Western companies still have inordinate power to determine the fate of the less privileged. GM technology is an example here, although this has been a focus of strong global resistance. Similarly, pharmaceutical companies have disproportionate power over health in control of vital medicines, such as the antiretrovirals needed to combat HIV, that are too expensive for sufferers in the developing world. There is little evidence that inequalities produced by neo-liberal globalization are diminishing. Poverty and exploitation also remain highly gendered. As the eminent economist, J. K. Galbraith (2004), has stressed, there can be no international stability without peace and prosperity in the developing world and this can only be promoted if the world's resources are more fairly shared out.

What impact will the 2004 Asian tsunami and subsequent disasters have on relations between the developing world and the West? Will reconstruction divert funds from the proposed 'Marshall Plan' for Africa that is favoured by the British government? The 2004 Asian tsunami highlighted the dependence of many parts of the developing world on tourist 'colonization' where the pleasure and the profits mainly benefit the West. Paradise, writes George Monbiot, is the founding myth of the colonist (Chapter 1) but is now transformed into the exotic holiday location of the Western tourist (Monbiot, 2003). Such attitudes echo back to colonial times and the European re-inscribing of African and Asian tropical 'wildernesses' as adventure and hunting playgrounds for Europeans. Will the poorer parts of the world continue to be the West's Garden of Eden (as opposed to the locals' hell) or will tourists be put off by growing dangers? The example of the speedy return to 'tourism as normal' after the Asian tsunami suggests not.

Central to my arguments is the role of the USA as the new imperial hegemon. Robin Winks predicted in 1993 that 'world events will force upon us a reinterpretation of imperialism that is far more sweeping than anything we have seen since the fall of modern empires'. There would be an increase in the 'imperialism of aid', more cultural imperialism and the supremacy of American technology. The USA, the 'imperial giant', would increasingly be called to intervene in conflicts (Winks, 1994). Winks predicted this would be through the language of the United Nations, whereas since the breach over Iraq, the USA has, effectively, claimed this language of rights and peace to justify unilateralist imperial policies. Such US interventions have their supporters; in *Colossus* (2004) Niall Ferguson argued that many parts of the world would benefit from direct US rule, taking over the role of Britain in the nineteenth century. But, there are dark and disturbing developments. The White House is now committed to market-orientated 'reconstruction and stabilization' and has plans for countries that, as yet, are not in conflict, a predatory form of 'disaster capitalism', a sophisticated colonialism differentiated from the 'vulgar colonialism' of the past (Klein, 2005).

The situation is changing, however. America, argued Donald White (1996), dominated the twentieth century – the American century – but was already in decline. The European Union is now expanding and threatens to rival the USA. Developments in the USA also threaten its position as global hegemon; the dollar has fallen and the USA is the largest debtor nation (Johnson, 2003). The ethnic balance is tipping towards the Hispanic population: Mexican, Puerto Rican, Cuban and other minorities from Central and Latin America, who are rapidly overtaking African-Americans as the largest minority. What implications does this have for the American 'Western' culture that is promoted globally? As Andrew Gamble (2002) has pointed out, hegemony exercised by a single state is 'a rare and transient phenomenon' in the history of the world system: states find it difficult to retain hegemony for long and, once lost, it cannot be regained (p. 127).

On the prospects for the non-Western parts of the postmodern world as the post-1945 global order collapsed in the 1990s, Davies, Nandy and Sardar (1993) concluded:

> In this . . . remaking of a new world, the others, as real people of the non-West, have a major role . . . It is their experience of wrestling with their own ambiguous identity that contains the kernels of resistance and defiance on which a genuine plural future can be created . . . The non-West must learn to talk to itself and of itself; through its own language. . . . Only when [its debates] are grounded in its own conceptual universe can it hope to create a new relationship with the Western world and author its own postmodern reality.
>
> (Davis, Nandy and Sardar, 1993, pp. 92–3)

Can the chasm between the West and the non-West be bridged? Or will this be rendered insignificant by the decline of Western civilization? Is the future ultimately in a revived Islam and/or renaissance of the East, particularly China and India, in retreat since the eighteenth century and the British-dominated 'first age of globalization'? There are powerful arguments that the West is gradually losing control and the centre of the world system will revert back to East Asia (Frank, 1998). Will the twenty-first century witness conflicts between the USA, Europe and Asia for global hegemony, centred on oil wars and other struggles for diminishing resources and defended by 'Star Wars' global security systems? Alternatively, will the world become more extensively globalized, with greater concentrations of wealth and more consolidated power of the rich that transcends former West/non-West divisions? More optimistically, will such globalization foster successful struggles for a fairer, more sustainable world?

Recommended reading

This list is by no means comprehensive. In the past two decades many interesting, rich and detailed studies have been published, covering all aspects of empires, imperialism and postcolonialism. Given the wide-ranging nature of my study in charting theoretical and conceptual trends I have also employed multidisciplinary perspectives, where relevant, embracing the social sciences, anthropology and archaeology as well as history. I have had to be brutally selective, indicating key historiography and seminal studies that will provide entrées into more specialist areas of study and this guide to recommended reading should be used in conjunction with the fuller Bibliography of sources consulted in writing this book.

General works on world history, empires and imperialism

For **world history** a classic and significant starting point is Fernand Braudel, *The Perspective of the World* (1984) that challenged the Eurocentricism of existing world histories as represented by William H. McNeill, *The Rise of the West* (1962) and their uncritical acceptance of expanding capitalism. Braudel's work opened up fresh debates about the nature of world systems, their link to capitalism and whether they predated the modern world system which began with the expansion of European imperialism in the sixteenth century. In *The Emergence of the Global Political Economy* (2000), William R. Thompson utilizes systems analysis and social science models to analyse the development of the global system from *circa* the eleventh century. Andre Gunder Frank and Barry Gills in *The World System* (1993) go back even further. Economic developments are also addressed in David Abernethy, *The Dynamics of Global Dominance* (2000). For an accessible summary of world systems theory, see Immanuel Wallerstein, 'The Rise and Demise of the World Capitalist System', reprinted in Cain and Harrison's *Imperialism* (2001), vol. 2, and for application in a less Eurocentric context, Chase Dunn and Hall's *Rise and Demise: Comparing World Systems* (1997). In *Empire: A Very Short Introduction* (2002) Stephen Howe provides a clear, general overview, galloping across time and empires in less than a hundred pages. A more detailed comparative perspective is provided in Michael Doyle, *Empires* (1986). Philip Curtin, *The World and the West* (2000) focuses on interactions and non-Western responses and in *Colonization* (1997) Marc Ferro provides a critique of the European impact on the rest of the world. For a classic Marxist study see Harry Magdoff, *Imperialism from the Colonial Age to the Present* (1978). For a useful collection of relevant maps, see *Collins Atlas of World History* (London, HarperCollins, 2004).

Chapter 1: Untangling imperialism: comparisons over time and space

The study of **ancient, classical and non-European empires** is a specialized area, often new to modern historians. I found the following texts illuminating and helpful in gaining a grasp of the historiography. For rich detail and stimulating interdisciplinary comparisons, employing conceptual frameworks developed for modern empires, see Susan Alcock *et al.* (eds), *Empires* (2002); articles here range from Persia and China to Central and Latin America and the Near East. Michael Wood's *In the Footsteps of Alexander the Great* (2004, 1997) provides a lively and accessible introduction to the Greek Empire and, for the Roman Empire, I recommend Garnsey and Saller, *The Roman Empire* (1987). Giles Fowden, *Empire to Commonwealth* (1993) is good on the rise and decline of Roman, Byzantine and Islamic empires from the second to ninth centuries, as is Patricia Crone's *Meccan Trade and the Rise of Islam* (1987) on the rise and influence of Islam. For economies of pre-European Asian empires, see Chaudhuri's *Asia Before Europe* (1990) and, for the Ottoman Empire, Inalcik and Quateart's *An Economic and Social History of the Ottoman Empire* (1994).

A classic study of **European empires before 1800** is Scammel's *The World Encompassed* (1981), which covers the Mediterranean city states that pioneered long-distance trade, and the companion volume, *The First Imperial Age* (1989). Also recommended is Parry's *The Establishment of European*

Hegemony (1961) and, for more recent historiographical developments, Sanjay Subrahmanyam, *The Portuguese Empire in Asia* (1993); George Raudzens, *Empires, Europe and Globalization* (1999) and James Tracy (ed.), *The Political Economy of Merchant Empires* (1991). Anthony Pagden's *Lords of All the Worlds* (1995) provides insight into the ideological mood of the times. For an accessible introduction to the conquest of the Americas see Michael Wood's *Conquistadors* (2003) and for more detail, Hugh Thomas, *Rivers of Gold* (2004). In *The Conquest of Paradise* (1992) Kirkpatrick Sale provides a lively assessment of the legacy of Columbus. For more controversial debates, see Henry Kamen, *Spain's Road to Empire* (2002) and Matthew Restall, *Seven Myths of the Spanish Conquest* (2004). For a comprehensive study of the European slave trade see Robin Blackburn, *The Making of New World Slavery* (1997). Michael Conniff and Thomas Davis, *Africans in the Americas* (1994) provides a useful overview of slavery in the Americas and the creation of the African diaspora. The history of slavery from ancient to modern times is clearly charted in James Walvin's *Atlas of Slavery* (Harlow, Pearson Education, 2006).

For general and comparative studies of **later European empires** see Andrew Porter, *European Imperialism 1860–1914* (1992); H. L. Wesserling, *Imperialism and Colonialism* (1997); D. K. Fieldhouse, *The Colonial Empires* (1982) and Rudolf von Albertini and Albert Wirz, *European Colonial Rule* (1982). For global dimensions, Christopher Bayly, *The Birth of the Modern World* (2003) is essential reading, as is Eric Hobsbawm's *The Age of Empire* (1989) for the impact of empire on European politics, cultures and economies. For accessible and informative studies of specific empires, see Robert Aldrich, *Greater France* (1996); Wolfgang J. Mommsen, *Imperial Germany* (1995) and Adam Hochschild, *King Leopold's Ghost* (1999), a controversial book that challenged contemporary Belgian amnesia about empire. Dominic Lieven's *Empire* (2000) provides a lively comparative analysis of Russian and other European empires, including the Austrian-Hungarian Hapsburg Empire.

Historiography of the epoch of formal European imperialism is dominated by the **British Empire** for the simple reason that Britain was the global hegemon. The best overview texts are Denis Judd, *Empire* (1996); Bernard Porter, *The Lion's Share* (2004) and Cain and Hopkins, *British Imperialism, 1688–2000* (2001). Combining political, cultural and economic insights, these texts are complementary even if they do not always agree on key debates. For a controversial revisionist position see Niall Ferguson, *Empire: How Britain Made the Modern World* (2003). A must for deeper understanding of the early empire is David Armitage, *The Ideological Origins of the British Empire* (2001) and, for the emergence of Britain as the premier modern imperial power, Christopher Bayly, *Imperial Meridian* (1989). A seminal work that explores empire from the perspective of individuals omitted from dominant narratives is Linda Colley's *Captives* (2002). James Walvin provides a clear and accessible introduction to the slave system in *Britain's Slave Empire* (2000). For erudite, authoritative but orthodox detail spanning the emergence, rise and decline and historiography of the British Empire, the five-volume *Oxford History of the British Empire* (*OHBE*), published 1998–9 is essential. The *OHBE* was inspired, in the main, by the work of an older generation of imperial historians centred on the Oxford–London–Cambridge axis, extending to the Ivy League American universities. With its orthodox historical style, the *OHBE* was criticized for marginalizing gender, Ireland and newer postcolonial perspectives. For a good summary of the main criticisms, see Dane Kennedy, 'The Boundaries of Oxford's Empire' (*International History Review*, vol. 23, 2001). These criticisms resulted in a series of companion volumes, including Philip D. Morgan and Sean Hawkins (eds), *Black Experience and the Empire* (2004); Philippa Levine (ed.), *Gender and Empire* (2004) and Kevin Kenny (ed.), *Ireland and the British Empire* (2004). For a useful overview of historiographical developments, see Linda Colley, 'What is Imperial History Now?' in David Cannadine, ed., *What is History Now?* (2002).

Very few works deal explicitly with **race and imperialism**. For a wider perspective, a classic study is Victor Kiernan's *The Lords of Human Kind* (1972). In *Race and Empire* (2005), Jane Sampson provides an accessible, short overview from the early modern period to decolonization. For a more focused study on British Africa and Britain's colonial empire 'within', see Barbara Bush, *Imperialism, Race and Resistance* (1999). Essential reading for American racism and imperialism is Reginald Horsman, *Race and Manifest Destiny* (1981). Ann Laura Stoler's influential *Race and the Education of Desire* (1996) utilizes anthropological and Foucaultian insights to explore the complexities of race, class, gender and sexuality in shaping colonial cultures. In *White Identities* (2000), Bonnett addresses the contribution of empire to shaping white 'ethnic' identities. George Frederickson's *Racism: A Short History* (2002) provides a good general introduction to the concept of race. Essential reading for twentieth-century developments is Paul Gordon Lauren's *Power and Prejudice* (1996) and for a provocative analysis of the 'new' racism and imperialism see Frank Furedi's *The Silent War* (1998).

Resistance was similarly neglected in orthodox studies of imperialism. For a magisterial study of slave resistance see Robin Blackburn, *The Overthrow of Colonial Slavery* (1988) and, for a unique and stimulating study of resistance struggles across the 'black Atlantic', see Peter Linebaugh and Marcus Rediker, *The Many Headed Hydra* (2000). In *Empire and Emancipation* (1990),

Jan Nederveen Pieterse explores the dialectic between power and resistance. For resistance in Africa, the African diaspora and British anti-imperialism, see Barbara Bush, *Imperialism, Race and Resistance* (1999). Pioneering works on critics of empire in the imperial heartlands include: A. P. Thornton, *The Imperial Idea and its Enemies* (1959); Bernard Porter, *Critics of Empire* (1968) and Stephen Howe, *Anti-colonialism in British Politics* (1993). For interesting and wide-ranging studies of anti-colonial resistance and European anti-colonialism informed by postcolonial theoretical perspectives, see Edward Said, *Culture and Imperialism* (1994) and Robert Young, *Postcolonialism* (2001).

For a general survey of **European decolonization**, see John Springhall, *Decolonisation since 1945* (2000); and for an overview of conventional historiography, Murial Chamberlain, *Decolonization* (1987). In *Decolonization: the British, French, Dutch and Belgian Empires, 1919–1963* (1978), Henri Grimal prioritizes the role of the colonized and anti-colonial nationalisms. Conflict in the ending of empires is addressed in Anthony Clayton, *The Wars of French Decolonization* (1994); Frank Furedi, *Colonial Wars* (1997) and Susan Carruthers' seminal study, *Winning Hearts and Minds: British Governments and Colonial Insurgency, 1944–60* (1995). For British decline in the context of the US rise to power and Cold War politics see Wm Roger Louis' classic *Imperialism at Bay* (1977) and seminal article (with Ronald Robinson) 'The Imperialism of Decolonisation' (*Journal of Imperial and Commonwealth History*, 1994, vol. 22, no. 3). A longer view is provided in Anne Orde, *The Eclipse of Great Britain* (1996). Recent historiographical developments in decolonization studies are addressed in R. F. Betts, *Decolonisation* (1998); Prasenjit Duara (ed.), *Decolonization: Perspectives from Now and Then* (2004) and James D. Le Sueur (ed.), *The Decolonisation Reader* (1997). For a good summary of new debates, see Stephen Howe's review article 'When – If Ever – Did Empire End? (*Journal of Contemporary History*, vol. 40, no. 3, 2005). For comparative perspectives, see Sebastian Balfour, *The End of the Spanish Empire, 1898–1923* (1997); Justin McCarthy, *The Ottoman Peoples and the End of Empire* (2001) and Michael Grant, *The Fall of the Roman Empire* (1990).

Chapter 2: Untangling imperialism: theories, concepts and historiography

Highly recommended as an accessible, but coherent and authoritative, overview is Osterhammel's *Colonialism* (1997, updated and expanded, 2006). A classic text exploring economic theories of imperialism and critics is Roger Owen and Bob Sutcliffe's *Studies in the Theory of Imperialism* (1972), which reproduced seminal revisionist articles published in the 1950s and 1960s by Ronald Robinson and others. These debates are also addressed in Norman Etherington, *Theories of Imperialism: War, Conquest and Capital* (1984); W. J. Mommsen, *Theories of Imperialism* (1980) and Anthony Brewer's short but succinct *Marxist Theories of Imperialism* (1982, 1990). For a comparison of the French and British empires see Winfried Baumgart, *Imperialism* (1982). Wolfgang Mommsen and Jürgen Osterhammel (eds), *Imperialism and After* (1986) is an excellent collection of seminal articles on twentieth-century imperialism. In *Empire and Emancipation* (1990) Jan Nederveen Pieterse critiques the limitations of political/diplomatic and economic explanations and makes an argument for the inclusion of culture and race. A most useful article that takes in the whole sweep of theoretical conceptual developments in the twentieth century is Patrick Wolfe's 'History and Imperialism: A Century of Theory, from Marx to Postcolonialism' (1997) reproduced in Cain and Harrison's *Imperialism* (2001) vol. 3. For detailed study of theoretical developments from Lenin, Schumpeter and Hobson to postcolonial theorists Peter Cain and Mark Harrison's three-volume reader, *Imperialism: Critical Concepts in Historical Studies* (2001) is indispensable. For developments in economic theories of imperialism, see Peter Cain and Anthony Hopkins, *British Imperialism Vol. 1: Innovation and Expansion, 1688–1914* (1990) and *British Imperialism Vol. 2: Crisis and Decolonization, 1914–1990* (1993). Debates these studies stimulated are addressed in Ray Dummet (ed.), *Gentlemanly Capitalism and British Imperialism: the New Debate on Empire* (1999) and Shigeru Akita (ed.), *Gentlemanly Capitalism and Global History* (2002).

Essential reading for **Orientalism and postcolonial theory** is Edward Said, *Orientalism* (1978) and, for the debates it generated, A. L. MacFie, *Orientalism: A Reader* (2002). In *Orientalism: History, Theory and the Arts* (1995) John Mackenzie provides a lively riposte to Said, arguing that Western approaches to the Orient were more ambiguous and interactive than he implied. Accessible introductions to postcolonial theory include Ania Loomba, *Colonialism/Postcolonialism* (1998) and Leela Gandhi, *Postcolonial Theory: a critical introduction* (1998). For good definitions of complex terminology, see John MacLeod, *Beginning Postcolonialism* (2000). In *Deconstructing History* (1997) Alun Munslow provides a useful glossary of concepts and theories that have informed the postmodern turn in history. Patrick Williams and Laura Chrisman's *Colonial Discourse and Postcolonial Theory: A Reader* (1993) provides a definitive survey of key developments and theorists. More detailed reading of key postcolonial theorists and their critics can be found in

Cain and Harrison, *Imperialism: Critical Concepts in Historical Studies*, (2001) vol. 3. For the influence on South Asian studies and imperial history, see Ronald Inden, *Imagining India* (1990), Carol Breckenridge and Peter Van de Veer, *Orientalism and the Post-Colonial Predicament* (1993) and Gyan Prakesh (ed.), *After Colonialism* (1995). For developments in subaltern studies see Saurabh Dube, *Postcolonial Passages* (2004) which concludes with a 'cyber conversation' with Dipash Chakravarty on the theme of India's encounter with modernity through empire and nationalism. Articles in Dirlik, Bahl and Gran's *History After the Three Worlds*, make the case for post-Eurocentric histories.

In 'Orients and Occidents' (*OHBE*, Vol. V, 1999) David Washbrook articulates a robust defence of orthodox imperial historians and, in a seminal article: 'Back to the Future: from National History to Imperial History' (*Past and Present*, no. 164, 1999), Anthony Hopkins also critiques the postcolonial turn, arguing for a greater confluence of economic and cultural perspectives. Dane Kennedy's 'Imperial History and Post-Colonial Theory' (*Journal of Imperial and Commonwealth History* 1996, vol. 24, no. 3) provides a balanced and constructive appraisal of the impact of postcolonial theory. For appraisal in hindsight and critical evaluation of theories, critiques and ongoing developments see David Theo Goldberg and Ato Quayson (eds), *Relocating Postcolonialism* (2002), which includes conversations between key postcolonial theorists – Gayatri Spivak, Edward Said, Homi Bhabha – and sceptics such as Benita Parry.

Case study 1: Ireland

A good starting point in untangling Ireland's relationship with the British Empire is Nicholas Canny, *Making Ireland British* (2001). For a provocative and stimulating entrée into revisionist, anti-revisionist and postcolonial perspectives see Stephen Howe's *Ireland and Empire* (2000). Essential for historiographical debates is Kevin Kenny (ed.), *Ireland and the British Empire* (2004), which includes an article by Joe Cleary on postcolonial perspectives. For the ambiguities of Irish colonization see David Fitzpatrick's excellent article 'Ireland and the Empire' (OHBE, vol. 111, 1999). Links between India and Ireland are explored in Michael and Denis Holmes (eds), *Ireland and India* (1997) and Keith Jeffery's edited collection, *'An Irish Empire'* (1996) that focuses on the Irish as agents of empire. The nationalist argument that colonial conquest was a dominant factor in Irish history and nationalism is articulated by Anthony Carty in *Was Ireland Conquered?* (1996) and Liz Curtis, *The Cause of Ireland* (1996). For revisionist critiques see James Boyce and Alan O'Day (eds), *The Making of Modern Irish History* (1996). In *Modern Ireland* (1996) Liam Kennedy mounts an attack against the influence of postcolonial theory in Irish historiography. For a defence against revisionism, see David Lloyd, *Ireland After History* (Cork, 1999). For the most nuanced studies of the famine, revising both nationalist and revisionist positions, see Christine Kinnealy, *This Great Calamity* (1994) and *The Great Irish Famine* (2002) and Cormac Ó Gráda, *Black '47 and Beyond* (1999).

Chapter 3: Imperialism and modernity

For a challenging critique of Eurocentric interpretations of global developments see J. M. Blaut, *The Coloniser's Model of the World: Geographical Diffusionism and Eurocentric History* (1993). John Hobson, *The Eastern Origins of Western Civilization* (2004) makes a forceful argument for contribution of Asia to the West's development. In contrast, in *The Dynamic Society* (1996) Graeme Snooks adopts an evolutionary approach that prioritizes Western industrialization as the major force in globalization. For the importance of Europe's unique industrialization in securing global dominance see David Landes' classic text, *The Unbound Prometheus* (1969). Michael Adas' *Machines as the Measure of Man* (1989) provides an incisive critique of the impact of Western technology on dominated parts of the world. Roy Porter's *Enlightenment* (2000) and David Brion Davis, *Slavery and Human Progress* (1994) provide illuminating insight into intellectual developments during the Enlightenment. The nature of modernity is also explored in Marshall Berman's thought-provoking study *All That is Solid Melts into Air* (1993). Zygmunt Bauman's *Modernity and the Holocaust* (1989) provides conceptual insight into understanding tensions between progressive modernity and atavistic brutality. For tensions between modernity and colonial power, Stoler and Cooper's influential collection, *Tensions of Empire* (1997) is essential reading. The uncomfortable elision of modern Western knowledge and thought with South Asian culture and knowledge is explored in Dipesh Chakrabarty's *Provincialising Europe* (2000). Gendered perspectives are addressed in Antoinette Burton (ed.), *Gender, Sexuality and Colonial Modernities* (1999) and the role of imperial feminism in the modernizing project in Burton's *Burdens of History* (1994) and Lora Wildenthal's *German Women for Empire* (2001). A classic text advocating that newly independent nations should 'follow in the footsteps of the West' is Walt Rostow's *The Stages of Economic Growth* (1960). For critiques of post-independence development along Western lines see Arturo Escobar, *Encountering Development* (1993) and Andre Gunder Frank, *Capitalism and Underdevelopment in Latin America* (1969). In *The Tears of the White Man*, Pascal Bruckner (1983) put forward an influential defence of the positive benefits of Western modernity.

Case study 2: China and Japan

For **Chinese history** an authoritative general text is John King Fairbank, *China: A New History* (1998) and, for relations with Britain, Jürgen Osterhammel, 'Britain and China, 1842–1914' (*OHBE*, vol. III, 1999). In *Rebellions and Revolutions* (2003) Jack Gray adopts a revisionist position, emphasizing the more positive impact of Western imperialism. For an opposing viewpoint, see Jürgen Osterhammel's seminal article 'Semi-Colonialism and Informal Empire in Twentieth Century China' in Mommsen and Osterhammel (eds), *Imperialism and After* (1986). Rana Mitter's *A Bitter Revolution* (2004) and *The Manchurian Myth* (2000) are essential reading for historiographical revisions on the relationship between imperialism, modernity and nationalism. In *The Great Divergence* (2000), Kenneth Pomeranz provides stimulating arguments as to why China declined and in *China Transformed* (1997) Roy Bin Wong criticizes Eurocentrism in analyses of China's development. Essential reading for the Japanese in China is Ramon Myers and Mark Peattie (eds), *The Japanese Informal Empire* (1984). Kazuo Ishiguro's novel *When we were Orphans* (2000) provides vivid insight into relations between the Japanese resident in China, other expatriate groups, and the Chinese before the Second World War.

There is an extensive literature on **Japan**, representing Western and Japanese scholarship. For a comprehensive and magisterial work see Marius Jansen, *The Making of Modern Japan* (2000). Ian Buruma, *Inventing Japan* (2003) provides an accessible and interesting overview with a useful glossary. For Japanese imperialism, a classic and accessible study is W. G. Beasley's *Japanese Imperialism, 1894–1945* (1987) whilst Peter Duus, Ramon Myers and Mark Peattie provide an authoritative and detailed analysis in *The Japanese Colonial Empire* (1989). In *Japan's Total Empire* (1998) Louise Young provides an interesting revisionist study. For the Second World War and after, see Akira Iriye, *The Origins of the Second World War in Asia and the Pacific* (1987) and John Dower, *Embracing Defeat* (1999). In *Artist of the Floating World* (1986), Kazuo Ishiguro provides fictionalized insight into the Japanese perspective on this period.

Chapter 4: Culture and imperialism

A seminal text prioritizing the central relationship between culture and impe-rialism in shaping both colonized and colonizing societies and stimulating further studies is Edward Said's *Culture and Imperialism* (1993). Nicholas Dirks (ed.), *Colonialism and Culture* (1992) is also indispensable reading. Catherine Hall's *Culture and Imperialism: A Reader* (2000) addresses the impact of British imperialism in both colonies and metropolitan centre. Peter Garnsey and Richard Saller, *The Roman Empire* (1987) facilitates interesting comparisons between the Roman and later empires. For the complexities of the **colonial encounter** see Mary Louse Pratt, *Imperial Eyes* (1992), Anthony Pagden, *European Encounters with the New World* (1993) and Martin Daunton and Rick Halpern, *Empire and Others* (1999). For revisions of the concept of the **colonial frontier**, see Lynette Russell's *Colonial Frontiers* (2001). Key works on the **cultural dynamics of colonialism**, addressing complexities of race, gender and sexuality include Stoler and Cooper, *Tensions of Empire* (1997) and Julia Clancy Smith and Frances Gouda (eds), *Domesticating the Empire* (1998). For US imperialism, the challenging art-icles in Amy Kaplan and Donald Pease, *Cultures of United States Imperialism* (1993) are recommended. Bernard Cohn's influential *Colonialism and its forms of Knowledge* (1996) combines historical and anthropological insights into colonial discourse. For the debates over the relationship between **anthro-pology and colonialism** see Henrietta Kuklich's critical *The Savage Within* (1991) and Jack Goody's defensive response in *The Expansive Moment* (1995). In *Settler Colonialism and the Transformation of Anthropology* (1999), Patrick Wolfe develops a passionate and convincing critique of anthropolo-gical knowledge. The nature of **colonial power** is effectively explored in Dagmar Engels and Shula Marks (eds), *Contesting Colonial Hegemony* (1994) and, for a convincing critique of Western cultural impositions, see Megan Vaughan, *Curing their Ills* (1991). In *Religion versus Empire* (2004) Andrew Porter provides a moderated criticism of undifferentiated use of the concept of cultural imperialism in relation to missionaries. For **relations between colonized and colonizer** and the impact of colonial rule on the identities of the colonized, Albert Memmi's *The Colonizer and the Colonized* (1990, 1957) and Frantz Fanon's *Black Skin, White Masks* (1993, 1952) are classic and essential texts. Postcolonial perspectives are explored in Ashis Nandy, *The Intimate Enemy* (1993) and Homi Bhabha, 'Of mimicry and man: the ambi-valence of colonial discourse' (*October*, 28, Spring, 1984).

Since the 1980s more historical research has focused on the centrality of **gender** in understanding relations between colonizers and colonized.

For insight into the range of topics and debates in this area, see Philippa Levine (ed.), *Gender and Empire* (2004) and Clare Midgley (ed.), *Gender and Empire* (1998). Also recommended is Ruth Pierson and Nupur Chaudhuri (eds), *Nation, Empire, Colony: Historicizing Race and Gender* (1998). Key debates are summarized in Angela Woollacott, *Gender and Empire* (Palgrave, 2006). For a provocative and critical polemic on white women and racism see Vron Ware's *Beyond the Pale* (1992). Masculinities are explored in Mrinalini Sinha's pioneering study *Colonial Masculinity* (1995). Highly recommended for the relationship between **sexuality, race and gender** in defining boundaries of power between colonizer and colonized is Ann Laura Stoler, *Carnal Knowledge and Imperial Power* (2002) and Philippa Levine's *Prostitution, Race and Politics* (2003). In the light of these studies, Ronald Hyam's *Empire and Sexuality* (1991) appears deterministic and lacking a sophisticated gender analysis. Gender is also central to studies of **white settler societies and expatriate cultures**. Recommended here are Dane Kennedy, *Islands of White* (1987); John Butcher, *The British in Malaya* (1979); Robert Bickers, *Britain in China* (1999); Mary Procida, *Married to the Empire* (2002) and Elizabeth Buettner, *Empire Families* (2004).

Case study 3: Culture and imperialism in British Africa

For accessible overviews critical of British imperialism and emphasizing the active agency of Africans in resisting colonialism, see Basil Davidson, *Africa in Modern History* (1978) and A. Adu Boahen, *Africa under Colonial Domination* (1990). A different perspective on the nature of colonial rule is provided in Andrew Roberts, *The Colonial Moment in Africa* (1986). In *Imperialism, Race and Resistance* (1999), Barbara Bush also addresses cultures of colonialism in West Africa and resistance strategies. For the later period, Frederick Cooper, *Africa Since 1940* (2002) is essential reading. For gender perspectives I would recommend Catherine Coquery-Vidrovitch, *African Women* (1997) and Nancy Rose Hunt *et al.* (eds), *Gendered Colonialisms in African History* (1996). Karen Transberg-Hansen (ed.), *African Encounters with Domesticity* (1992) is essential reading for gendered colonial policies. A seminal article on strategies to legitimize colonial rule is Terence Ranger's 'The Invention of Tradition in Africa' in Hobsbawm and Ranger's *The Invention of Tradition* (1996). Chinua Achebe's *Things Fall Apart* (1962) provides illuminating fictionalized insight into African responses to colonialism and in *Decolonizing the Mind* (1991) Ngugi wa Thiong'o provides a provocative and robust challenge to European cultural dominance.

Chapter 5: Representing empire

Significant general works include John Mackenzie, *Propaganda and Empire* (1984); William Schneider, *An Empire for the Masses* (1982); Tony Chafer and Amanda Sackur (eds), *Promoting the Colonial Idea* (2002) and Jan Nederveen Pieterse, *White on Black* (1992). Ella Shohat and Robert Stam's *Unthinking Eurocentrism* (1994) is a seminal text on Eurocentrism in the media. Fruitful cross comparisons with representations of the Roman Empire are found in Peter Garnsey and Richard Saller's *The Roman Empire* (1987). On visual representations see Ann Maxwell, *Colonial Photography and Exhibitions* (2000) and James Ryan, *Picturing Empire* (1997). For exhibitions and the promotion of empire, see Peter Greenhalgh, *Ephemeral Vistas* (1988) and Peter Hoffenberg, *An Empire on Display* (2001). One of the best critical studies of museums and representations of the colonial subject is Annie Coombes, *Reinventing Africa* (1994). For **representations of the Orient** Edward Said's *Orientalism* (1978) is foundational reading. In *Imagining India* (1990) Ronald Inden provides a seminal analysis of Orientalist knowledge and India. For a critique of contemporary Orientalism, see Deborah Gewertz and Frederick Errington, 'We Think, therefore They Are? On Occidentalising the World' in Kaplan and Pease (eds), *Cultures of United States Imperialism* (1993). For gendered representations, see Reina Lewis, *Gendering Orientalism* (1996) and Billie Melman's *Women's Orients* (1992). Orientalism in European popular culture is explored in Timothy Mitchell, 'Orientalism and the Exhibitionary Order' in Nicholas Dirks (ed.), *Colonialism and Culture* (1992). For travel writing, **colonial discourse** and representations of the colonized and colonizers, including gendered perspectives, see George Robertson *et al.* (eds), *Travellers' Tales* (1994); Sarah Mills, *Discourses of Difference* (1991) and Inderpal Grewel, *Home and Harem* (1996). For the viewpoint of the **colonized in the heart of empire**, see David Omissi (ed.), *Indian Voices of the Great War* (1999) and Antoinette Burton, *At the Heart of Empire* (1998). For postcolonial perspectives on race and representation, see Gail Chiang-Liang Low, *White Skins, Black Masks* (1996).

Case study 4: Representing empire in British culture

A key work stressing the indivisibility of imperial and domestic culture is Andrew Thompson's *The Empire Strikes Back?* (2005). In *The Absent Minded Imperialists* (2004), Bernard Porter argues from the sceptic's viewpoint. Essential for representations of empire in British culture are John

Mackenzie's *Propaganda and Empire* (1984) and *Imperialism and Popular Culture* (1986) and, for racist imagery, Katherine Castle's *Britannia's Children* (1996). In *Ornamentalism* (2001) David Cannadine develops a provocative argument that class, not race, defined the culture of empire. For seminal studies interrogating the role of empire in shaping British national identity from the eighteenth century, see Kathleen Wilson, *The Sense of the People* (1998); Linda Colley, *Britons* (1992) and Catherine Hall, *Civilizing Subjects* (2002). The relationship between postcolonial British identities and empire is explored in two seminal articles, Linda Colley, 'Britishness and Otherness: An Argument' (*Journal of British Studies*, 31, 1992) and Shula Marks, 'History, the Nation and Empire: Sniping from the Periphery' (*History Workshop,* Spring 1990, no. 29). For the 'empire within' and problems relating to British national identities in the postcolonial era, see Paul Gilroy, *There Ain't no Black in the Union Jack* (1987). The impact of the decline of empire on British culture and politics is explored in Stuart Ward (ed.), *British Culture and the End of Empire* (2001) and Wendy Webster's *Englishness and Empire, 1939–1965* (2005).

Chapter 6: Postcolonial perspectives: imperialism or globalization?

Recommended works on historical perspectives on globalization and imperialism are Anthony Hopkins (ed.), *Globalization in World History* (2002) and Christopher Bayly, *The Birth of the Modern World* (2003). In *The Twentieth Century World* (1992), William Keylor provides a good overview of international developments. A complementary text with a different approach and emphasis is Eric Hobsbawm, *The Age of Extremes* (1994). For debates about the **continuity of imperialism** after the ending of empires, seminal critiques from the left include Paul Baran's *The Political Economy of Growth* (1957) and Samir Amin's *Neo-Colonialism in West Africa* (1973). Contrasting views are found in David Fieldhouse's *The West and the Third World* (1999) which challenges the concept of neo-colonialism. Forceful cases for continuing imperialist relations are made in Frank Furedi's *The New Ideology of Imperialism* (1995), David Harvey's *The New Imperialism* (2003) and Derek Gregory's *The Colonial Present* (2004). For debates over the nature of postcolonial development see Tim Allen and Alan Thomas (eds), *Poverty and Development in the 1990s* (1992) and, for a comprehensive study of postcolonial problems in Africa, Paul Nugent, *Africa since Independence* (2004).

There are authoritative and extensive websites devoted to **globalization**: try *YaleGlobal Online*, http://yaleglobal.yale.edu. Articles in *The Global Transformations Reader* (2003) edited by David Held and Anthony McGrew, provide an essential and comprehensive survey of key debates about the nature of contemporary globalization. Influential studies challenging the concept of globalization include Samuel Huntington's *The Clash of Civilizations* (1997) and Ben Barber's *Jihad vs. McWorld* (2003). For ethnic conflict, see Amy Chua, *The World on Fire* (2003) and for the new slavery, Christien van den Anker, *The Political Economy of New Slavery* (2003). Giovanni Arrighi in *The Long Twentieth Century* (1994) analyses the role of capitalism in shaping the modern global order and Naomi Klein in *No Logo* (1999) critiques the multinational corporations. For cultural perspectives, see Roland Robertson's *Globalization* (1992) and Jan Nederveen Pieterse's *Globalization and Culture* (2004) that rejects polarized arguments for or against cultural uniformity (homogeneity) and/or diversity (heterogeneity) in favour of hybridization. Also relevant here is John Tomlinson's *Cultural Imperialism* (1991). For a critical study of the impact of **Westernization,** see Serge Latouche, *The Westernisation of the World* (1996) and, for **Americanization**, George Ritzer's influential and persuasive *The McDonaldization of Society* (1993). For critiques of Eurocentrism see Ngugi wa Thiong'o, *Moving the Centre* (1993) and Merryl Wyn Davies, Ashis Nandy and Zia Sardar, *Barbaric Others* (1993). For critiques of neo-liberal globalization, from a left and liberal viewpoint respectively, see Samir Amin 'Imperialism and Globalization' (*Monthly Review*, vol. 53, no. 2, 2001) and Joseph Stiglitz, *Globalization and its Discontents* (2002). In *The Condition of Postmodernity* (1989) David Harvey provides a trenchant critique of postmodern capitalism and globalization. Titus Alexander analyses deepening inequalities in *Unravelling Global Apartheid* (1996). For the link between globalization and imperialism see Michael Hardt and Antonio Negri, *Empire* (2000).

For the history of **US imperialism** Frank Ninkovich's *The United States and Imperialism* (2000) is a useful starting point. The American and British empires are compared in Patrick Karl O'Brien and Armand Clesse (eds), *Two Hegemonies* (2002). For the impact of imperialism on US culture, Amy Kaplan and Donald Pease (eds), *Cultures of United States Imperialism* (1993) is essential reading. Key works dealing with the nature of imperialism post-1990 and its negative impact on the world and US culture and politics include Noam Chomsky, *Hegemony or Survival* (2003), Chalmers Johnson, *The Sorrows of Empire* (2003), Anatol Lieven, *America, Right or Wrong* (2004) and Emmanuel Todd, *After the Empire* (2004). In *Colossus* (2004) Niall Ferguson provides a controversial argument that is more sympathetic to

America's global role. Tariq Ali, *Bush in Babylon* (2003); Rashid Khalidi, *Resurrecting Empire* (2004) and Tony Dodge, *Inventing Iraq* (2003) provide critical perspectives on US interventions in Iraq and emphasize historical continuities between British and US imperialism in the Middle East. In contrast, Bernard Lewis in *The Crisis of Islam* (2003) argues in support of interventions. For ongoing **resistance**, see Barry Gills (ed.), *Globalization and the Politics of Resistance* (1997) and for a useful overview of resistance against capitalism and imperialism past and present, Immanuel Wallerstein's 'New Revolts against the System' (*New Left Review*, 18, Nov–Dec, 2002). For links between past and present in **indigenous peoples' struggles** see Ken Coates, *Global History of Indigenous Peoples* (2004) and for ongoing struggles Bartholomew Dean and Jerome Levi (eds), *At the Risk of Being Heard* (2003). In *The Age of Consent* (2004), George Monbiot proposes a blueprint to challenge neo-liberal globalization and in *ReOrient* (1998) Andre Gunder Frank critiques Eurocentricism in Western knowledge and social sciences and makes an argument for the ultimate decline of Western supremacy.

Bibliography

Note: The *Oxford History of the British Empire* will be abbreviated to *OHBE* followed by the volume number.

Abernethy, David *The Dynamics of Global Dominance: European Empires Overseas, 1415–1980* (New Haven and London, Yale University Press, 2000)

Achebe, Chinua *Things Fall Apart* (London, Heinemann, 1962)

Adam, Ian and Tiffin, Helen (eds) *Past the Last Post: Theorizing Post-Colonialism and Post-Modernism* (Hemel Hemstead, Harvester Wheatsheaf, 1991)

Adas, Michael *Machines as the Measure of Man: Science, Technology and Western Dominance* (Ithaca, New York, Cornell University Press, 1989)

Adas, Michael 'Imperialism and Colonialism in Comparative Perspective', *The International History Review*, xx, 2, June 1998

Ahmad, Aijaz 'Postcolonialism: What's in a Name?' in de la Campa, Kaplan and Sprinkler (eds), *Late imperial Culture* (1995)

Ahmed, Leila *Women and Gender in Islam: Historical Roots of a Modern Debate* (New Haven, Yale University Press, 1992)

Akita, Shigeru (ed.) *Gentlemanly Capitalism, Imperialism and Global History* (London, Palgrave Macmillan, 2002)

Alcock, Susan E. and Morrison, Kathleen D. 'Imperial Ideologies' in Alcock *et al.* (eds), *Empires* (2002)

Alcock, Susan E. *et al.* (eds) *Empires: Perspectives from Archeology and History* (Cambridge, Cambridge University Press, 2002)

Alderson, David *Mansex Fine: Religion, Manliness and Imperialism in Nineteenth-Century British Culture* (Manchester, Manchester University Press, 1998)

Aldrich, Robert *Greater France. A History of French Overseas Expansion* (London, Macmillan, 1996)

Aldrich, Robert 'Putting Colonies on the Map: Colonial Names in Paris streets' in Chafer and Sackur (eds), *Promoting the Colonial Idea* (2002)

Aldrich, Robert   *Colonialism and Homosexuality* (London, Routledge, 2003)

Alessio, Dominic D.   'Domesticating "the Heart of the Wild": Female Personifications of the Colonies, 1886–1940', *Women's History Review*, VI (1997), pp. 239–71

Alexander, Titus   *Unravelling Global Apartheid: An Overview of World Politics* (London, Longman, 1996)

Ali, Tariq   *Bush in Babylon: The Recolonization of Iraq* (London, Verso, 2003)

Ali, Tariq   *The Clash of Fundamentalisms: Crusades, Jihads and Modernity* (London, Verso, 2003)

Allen, Tim and Thomas, Alan (eds)   *Poverty and Development in the 1990s* (Oxford, Oxford University Press, 1992)

Allman, Jean   'Making Mothers: Missionaries, Medical Officers and Women's Work in Colonial Asante, 1924–1945', *History Workshop Journal*, Autumn 1994, Issue 38

Ambrose, Stephen   *The Rise to Globalism: American foreign policy since 1938* (Harmondsworth: Penguin, 1983)

Amin, Samir   *Eurocentrism* (London, Zed, 1990)

Amin, Samir   'Imperialism and Globalization' *Monthly Review*, vol. 53, no. 2, 2001, www.monthlyreview.org/0601amin.htm

Amin, Samir   *Neo-Colonialism in West Africa* (Harmondsworth, Penguin, 1973). Trans. Francis McDonagh

Anderson, David   *Histories of the Hanged: Britain's Dirty War in Kenya and the End of Empire* (London, Wiedenfeld and Nicholson, 2005)

Anderson, Karen   *Chain Her by One Foot: The Subjugation of Women in 17th Century New France* (London, Routledge, 1991)

Andrews, George Reid   *Afro-Latin America 1800–2000* (Oxford, Oxford University Press, 2004)

Ankersmit, Frank R.   *Historical Representation* (Stanford, Ca., Stanford University Press, 2001)

Anstey, Vera   *The Economic Development of India* (London, Longmans, Green & Co., 1952; 4th edn; first published, 1929)

Archer, Léonie (ed.)   *Slavery and Other Forms of Unfree Labour* (London, Routledge, 1988)

Armitage, Andrew   *Comparing the Policy of Aboriginal Assimilation: Australia, Canada and New Zealand* (Vancouver, UBC Press, 1995)

Armitage, David   *The Ideological Origins of the British Empire* (Cambridge, Cambridge University Press, 2000)

Arngrove, R. F. (ed.)   *Philanthropy and Cultural Imperialism: The Foundations at Home and Abroad* (Boston, G. K. Hall, 1980)

Arrighi, Giovanni   'The three hegemonies of historical capitalism', *Review*, 13, 1990, pp. 365–408

Arrighi, Giovanni   *The Long Twentieth Century: Money, Power and the Origin of Our Times* (New York, Verso, 1994)

Ashcroft, Bill, Griffiths, Gareth, Tiffin, Helen   *The Empire Writes Back: Theory and Practice in Colonial Literature* (London, Routledge, 1989)

Atlan, Catherine and Jézéquel, Jean-Hervé   'Alienation or Political Strategy? The Colonised Defend the Empire' in Chafer and Sackur (eds), *Promoting the Colonial Idea* (2002)

Axford, Barrie   *The Global System: Economics, Politics, Culture* (Cambridge, Polity Press, 1995)

Baden-Powell, Agnes   *The Handbook for Girl Guides or How Girls Can Help Build the Empire* (London, 1912)

Bailey, Paul, J.   *China in the Twentieth Century* (Oxford, Basil Blackwell, 1988)

Balandier, Georges   *The Sociology of Black Africa: Social Dynamics in Central Africa* (London, Deutsch, 1970); trans. Douglas Garman

Bales, Kevin   *Disposable People: New Slavery in the Global Economy* (Berkeley, UCLA Press, 1999)

Balfour, Sebastian   *The End of the Spanish Empire, 1898–1923* (Oxford, Clarendon Press, 1997)

Balibar, Etienne   'Is there a Neo-racism?' in Balibar and Wallerstein, *Race, Nation and Class* (1991)

Balibar, Etienne and Wallerstein, Immanuel   *Race, Nation and Class: Ambiguous Identities* (London, Verso, 1991)

Ballantyne, Tony   *Orientalism and Race: An Aryan Empire* (London, Palgrave Macmillan, 2001)

Baran, Paul A.   *The Political Economy of Growth* (New York, Monthly Review Press, 1957)

Barber, Benjamin R.   *Jihad vs. McWorld* (London, Corgi, 2003; first published, 1995)

Barfield, Thomas J.   'The shadow empires: imperial state formation along the Chinese-Nomad frontier' in Alcock *et al.* (eds), *Empires* (2002)

Barkan, Elazar   *The Retreat from Scientific Racism: The Changing Concepts of Race in Britain and the United States between the World Wars* (Cambridge, Cambridge University Press, 1992)

Barkan, Elazar   'Post-Anti-Colonial Histories: Representing the Other in Imperial Britain', *Journal of British Studies*, 33, 1994

Barkey, Karen and von Hagen, Mark (eds)   *After Empire: Multi-Ethnic Societies and Nation-Building: the Soviet Union and the Russian, Ottoman and Hapsburg Empires* (Boulder, Colo., Westview Press, 1997)

Barnes, Lionel L.   *Empire or Democracy: A Study of the Colonial Question* (London, Victor Gollancz Ltd, 1939)

Barnet, Richard J. and Müller, Ronald E.   *Global Reach: The Power of the Multinational Corporations* (New York, Simon and Schuster, 1974)

Barraclough, Geoffrey   *An Introduction to Contemporary History* (Harmondsworth, Penguin, 1973)

Barratt Brown, Michael   *After Imperialism* (London, Heinemann, 1963)

Barratt Brown, Michael 'An African Road for Development: Are We All Romantics?', *Leeds African Studies Bulletin*, December 1997, no. 62

Barrell, John and Chrisman, Laura (eds) *Colonial and Post-Colonial History* (Oxford, Oxford University Press, 1993). Special issue of *History Workshop Journal*, Issue 36, Autumn 1993

Barringer, Tom and Flynn, Tom (eds) *Colonialism and the Object: Empire, Material Culture and the Museum* (London, Routledge, 1998)

Bauman, Zygmunt *Modernity and the Holocaust* (Cambridge, Polity Press, 1989)

Bauman, Zygmunt *Globalization: The Human Consequences* (Cambridge, Polity Press, 1998)

Baumgart, Winfried *Imperialism: The Idea and Reality of British and French Colonial Expansion, 1880–1914* (Oxford, Oxford University Press, 1982)

Bayly, Christopher A. *Imperial Meridian: The British Empire and the World, 1780–1830* (London, Longman, 1989)

Bayly, Christopher A. *Empire and Information: Intelligence Gathering and Social Communication in India, 1780–1870* (Cambridge, Cambridge University Press, 1996)

Bayly, Christopher A. 'The First Age of Global Imperialism c. 1760–1830', *Journal of Imperial and Commonwealth History*, vol. 26, no. 2, May 1998

Bayly, Christopher A. *The Birth of the Modern World, 1780–1914: Global Connections and Comparisons* (Oxford, Blackwell, 2003)

Bayly, Christopher A 'Writing World History', *History Today*, vol. 54 (2), February 2004

Bayly, Susan 'The Evolution of Colonial Cultures: Nineteenth Century Asia' in Porter (ed.), *OHBE*, vol. III (1999)

Beasley, William G. *Japanese Imperialism, 1894–1945* (Oxford, Clarendon, 1987)

Beer, George Louis *African Questions at the Paris Peace Conference* (London, Dawsons of Pall Mall, 1968; first published, 1923; ed. and Intro. Louis Herbert Gray)

Bell, Dianne *Daughters of the Dreaming* (London, Allen and Unwin, 1984)

Bell, M., Butlin, R. A. and Heffernan, M. J. *Geography and Imperialism, 1820–1920* (Manchester, Manchester University Press, 1995)

Benedictus, Leo 'London: The World in One City: A Special Celebration of the Most Cosmopolitan Place on the Earth', *The Guardian*, G2, London, 21 January 2005

Benn Michaels, Walter 'Anti-Imperial Americanism' in Kaplan and Pease (eds), *Cultures of United States Imperialism* (1993)

Benson, John and Matsumura, Takao *Japan, 1868–1945* (London, Longman, 2000)

Benton, Lauren *Law and Colonial Cultures* (Cambridge, Cambridge University Press, 2002)

Berlin, Ira *Many Thousands Gone: The First Two Centuries of Slavery in North America* (Cambridge, Mass., Harvard University Press, 1998)

Berman, Bruce and Lonsdale, John   *Unhappy Valley: Conflict in Kenya and Africa* (Oxford, James Currey, 1992), Book 2, 'Violence and Ethnicity'

Berman, E. H.   'Educational Colonialism in Africa: The Role of American Foundations, 1910–1945' in Arngrove (ed.), *Philanthropy and Cultural Imperialism* (1980)

Berman, Marshall   *All That is Solid Melts into Air: The Experience of Modernity* (London, Verso, 1983)

Bethell, Leslie (ed.)   *Colonial Spanish America* (Cambridge, Cambridge University Press, 1987)

Betts, Raymond F.   *France and Decolonization* (London, Macmillan, 1991)

Betts, Raymond F.   *Decolonization* (London, Routledge, 1998)

Bhabha, Homi and Comoroff, John   'Speaking of Postcoloniality in the Continuous Present: A Conversation' in Goldberg and Quayson (eds), *Relocating Postcolonialism* (2002)

Bhabha, Homi   'Of mimicry and man: the ambivalence of colonial discourse', *October*, 28, Spring 1984

Bhabha, Homi   *The Location of Culture* (London, Routledge, 1994)

Bhadra, Gautam, Prakash, Gyan and Tharu, Susie (eds)   *Writings on South Asian History and Society* (Delhi, Oxford University Press, 2002)

Bickers, Robert   *Britain in China: Community Culture and Colonialism, 1900–1949* (Manchester, Manchester University Press, 1999)

Bickers, Robert   'Chinese Burns: Britain in China 1842–1900', *History Today*, vol. 50, 8, August 2000

Birkett, Dea   *Mary Kingsley: Imperial Adventuress* (Basingstoke, Macmillan, 1992)

Birmingham, David   *The Decolonisation of Africa* (London, UCL Press, 1995)

Bix, Herbert P.   *Hirohito and the Making of Modern Japan* (New York, Harper Collins, 2000)

Black, Edwin   *War Against the Weak: Eugenics and America's Campaign to Create a Master Race* (New York: London, Four Walls Eight Windows, 2004)

Blackburn, Kevin   'How can we understand globalization?', *http: //www. milkbar.com.au/globalhistory.html* (2001)

Blackburn, Robin   *The Overthrow of Colonial Slavery, 1776–1848* (London, Verso, 1988)

Blackburn, Robin   *The Making of New World Slavery: From the Baroque to the Modern* (London, Verso, 1997)

Blaut, J. M.   *The Coloniser's Model of the World: Geographical Diffusionism and Eurocentric History* (New York, The Guildford Press, 1993)

Blaut, J. M.   'Evaluating Imperialism', *Science and Society*, vol. 61, no. 3, 1997

Bloxham, Donald and Kushner, Tony   'Exhibiting racism: cultural imperialism, genocide and representation' in *Rethinking History*, vol. 2, no. 3, 1998

Boahen, A. Adu   *African Perspectives on Colonialism* (Baltimore, Johns Hopkins University Press, 1987)

Boahen, A. Adu   *General History of Africa, vol. 7: Africa Under Colonial Domination, 1880–1935* (Oxford, James Currey, 1990)

Boehmer, Elleke   *The Empire, the National and the Postcolonial, 1890–2002* (Oxford, Oxford University Press, 2002)

Boehmer, Elleke (ed.)   *Scouting for Boys by Robert Baden Powell* (Oxford, Oxford University Press, 2004; first published, 1908)

Bonnett, Alistair   *White Identities: Historical and International Perspectives* (Harlow, Prentice Hall, 2000)

Bose, Sugata and Jalal, Ayesha   *Modern South Asia* (London, Routledge, 1998)

Bourne, Stephen   *Black in the British Frame: Black People in British Film, 1896–1996* (London, Cassell, 1998)

Boxer, Charles R.   *The Dutch Seaborne Empire* (London, Hutchinson, 1965)

Boxer, Charles R.   *The Portuguese Seaborne Empire* (London, Hutchinson, 1969)

Boyce, George D. and O'Day, Alan (eds)   *The Making of Modern Irish History: Revisionism and the Revisionist Controversy* (New York, Routledge, 1996)

Braudel, Fernand   *The Perspective of the World* (Berkeley, UCLA Press, 1984, trans. Sian Reynolds)

Breckenridge, Carol A. and Van de Veer, Peter   *Orientalism and the Post-Colonial Predicament: Perspectives on South Asia* (Philadelphia, University of Pennsylvania Press, 1993)

Brewer, Anthony   *Marxist Theories of Imperialism: A Critical Survey* (London, Routledge, 1990; first published, 1982)

Bristow, Joseph   *Empire Boys; Adventures in a Man's World* (London, Unwin Hyman, 1991)

Brody, Hugh   *Maps and Dreams: Indians and the British Columbia Frontier* (London, Faber and Faber, 1986; first published, 1982)

Brown, Bill   'Science Fiction, the World's Fair and the Prosthetics of Empire, 1910–1915' in Kaplan and Pease (eds), *Cultures of United States Imperialism* (1993)

Brown, Judith M. and Louis, Wm. Roger (eds)   *The Oxford History of the British Empire: vol. V, The Twentieth Century* (Oxford, Oxford University Press, 1999)

Brown, Kathleen   'Native Americans and early modern concepts of race' in Daunton and Halpern (eds), *Empire and Others* (1999)

Brownell, Susan and Wasserstrom, Jeffrey N. (eds)   *Chinese Femininities: Chinese Masculinities: A Reader* (Berkeley, UCLA Press, 2002; foreword by Thomas Lacquer)

Bruckner, Pascal   *The Tears of the White Man: Compassion as Contempt* (London and New York, The Free Press/Collier Macmillan, 1986; first published, 1983; trans. and Intro. William R. Beer)

Brunschwig, Henri   *French Colonialism, 1871–1914: Myths and Realities* (London, Pall Mall Press, 1966)

Buell, Robert Leslie   *The Native Problem in Africa* (New York, Macmillan, 1928, 2 vols)

Buettner, Elizabeth   *Empire Families: Britons and Late Imperial India* (London, Oxford University Press, 2004)

Burkeman, Oliver   'Arab World now faces invasion by American TV', *The Guardian*, London, 12 April 2003

Burnside, John   'Journey to the Centre of the Earth', *The Guardian*, London, 18 October 2003

Burroughs, Peter and Stockwell, A. J. (eds)   *Managing the Business of Empire: Essays in Honour of David Fieldhouse* (London, Frank Cass, 1998)

Burton, Antoinette   *Burdens of History: British Feminists, Indian Women and Imperial Culture, 1865–1915* (Durham, N. C, Duke University Press, 1994a)

Burton, Antoinette   'Rules of Thumb: British History and "imperial culture" in nineteenth and twentieth century Britain', *Women's History Review*, vol. 3, no. 4, 1994b

Burton, Antoinette   *At the Heart of Empire: Indians and the Colonial Encounter* (Berkeley, UCLA Press, 1998)

Burton, Antoinette   'Making a Spectacle of Empire: Indian Travellers in *Fin de Siécle* London', *History Workshop Journal*, 45, 8, 1996

Burton, Antoinette (ed.)   *Gender, Sexuality and Colonial Modernities* (London, Routledge, 1999)

Burton, Sir Richard   *Wanderings in West Africa* (Dover Publications, 2 vols., 1992, 1863)

Buruma, Ian   *Inventing Japan, 1853–1964* (London, Wiedenfeld and Nicholson, 2003)

Bush, Barbara   *Slave Women in Caribbean Society, 1650–1838* (Oxford, James Currey, in conjunction with Heinemann Caribbean and Indiana University Press, 1990)

Bush, Barbara   'Britain's Conscience on Africa: White Women, Race and Imperial Politics in Inter-war Britain' in Midgley (ed.), *Gender and Imperialism* (1998)

Bush, Barbara   *Imperialism, Race and Resistance: Africa and Britain, 1918 to 1945* (London, Routledge, 1999)

Bush, Barbara   ' "Sable Venus", "She Devil" or "Drudge"? British Slavery and the "Fabulous Fiction" of Black Women's Identities', *Women's History Review*, vol. 9, no. 4, 2000

Bush, Barbara,   'Gender and Empire: The Twentieth Century' in Levine (ed.), *Gender and Empire* (2004)

Bush, Barbara   'The Dark Side of the City': Racialised Barriers, Culture and Citizenship in Britain c. 1950–1990s' in Werner Zips (ed.), *Rastafari: A Universal Philosophy in the Third Millenium* (Kingston, Jamaica, Ian Randle Publishers, 2005)

Bush, Barbara and Maltby, Josephine   'Taxation in West Africa: transforming the colonial subject into the "governable person" ', *Critical Perspectives on Accounting*, 15, 2004

Bush, Julia   *Edwardian Ladies and Imperial Power* (Leicester, Leicester University Press, 1998)

Butcher, John G.   *The British in Malaya, 1880–1941: The Social History of a European Community in Colonial South East Asia* (Oxford, Oxford University Press, 1979)

Cain, Peter   *Hobson and Imperialism: Radicalism, New Liberalism and Finance, 1887–1938* (Oxford, Oxford University Press, 2002)

Cain, Peter and Harrison, Mark (eds)   *Imperialism: Critical Concepts in Historical Studies* (London, Routledge, 2001) 3 vols

Cain, Peter and Hopkins, Anthony G.   'Gentlemanly Capitalism and British Expansion Overseas, 11: New Imperialism, 1850–1945', *Economic History Review*, 40, 1987

Cain, Peter and Hopkins, Anthony G.   *British Imperialism Vol. 1: Innovation and Expansion, 1688–1914* (London, Longman, 1990)

Cain, Peter and Hopkins, Anthony G.   *British Imperialism Vol. 2: Crisis and Decolonization, 1914–1990* (London, Longman, 1993)

Cain, Peter and Hopkins, Anthony G.   *British Imperialism, 1688–2000* (London, Longman, 2001; 2nd edn)

Cameron, Nigel   *Barbarians and Mandarins: Thirteen Centuries of Western Travellers in China* (Oxford, Oxford University Press, 1989)

Cannadine, David   'The Context, Performance and Meaning of Ritual: The British Monarchy, c. 1820–1977' in Hobsbawm and Ranger (eds), *The Invention of Tradition* (1996)

Cannadine, David   'British History: Past, Present and Future?', *Past and Present*, 116, 1987

Cannadine, David   'The Empire Strikes Back', Review Article, *Past and Present*, no. 145, May 1995

Cannadine, David   *Ornamentalism: How the British Saw their Empire* (London, Allen Lane/Penguin, 2001)

Cannadine, David   'What is History?' British Academy Centenary Lectures, 2002

Canny, Nicholas P. (ed.)   *The Oxford History of the British Empire*: vol. I: *Origins of Empire* (Oxford, Oxford University Press, 1998)

Canny, Nicholas   *Making Ireland British* (Oxford, Oxford University Press, 2001)

Carey, Joyce   *Mr. Johnson* (London, Methuen, 1939)

Carrier, James   'Occidentalism', *American Ethnologist*, 19, 1992

Carroll, Clare and King, Patricia (eds)   *Ireland and Postcolonial Theory* (Cork, Cork University Press, 2003)

Carruthers, Susan   *Winning Hearts and Minds: British Governments and Colonial Insurgency, 1944–60* (London, Cassell, 2004)

Carty, Anthony   *Was Ireland Conquered? International Law and the Irish Question* (London, Pluto Press, 1996)

Castle, Gregory (ed.)   *Postcolonial Discourses: An Anthology* (Oxford, Blackwell, 2001)

Castle, Katherine   *Britannia's Children: Reading Colonialism through Children's Books and Magazines* (Manchester, Manchester University Press, 1996)

Césaire, Aimé   *Discourse on Colonialism* (New York and London, Monthly Review Press, 1972; trans. John Pinkham)

Ch'en, Jerome   *China and the West; Society and Culture, 1825–1937* (London, Hutchinson, 1979)

Chafer, Tony and Sackur, Amanda (eds)   *Promoting the Colonial Idea: Propaganda and Visions of Empire in France* (London, Palgrave Macmillan, 2002)

Chakrabarty, Dipesh   *Provincialising Europe: Postcolonial Thought and Historical Difference* (New Jersey, Princeton University Press, 2001)

Chamberlain, Muriel E.   *Decolonization: The Fall of the European Empires* (Oxford, Blackwell, 1987)

Chase-Dunn, C. and Hall, T. D.   *Rise and Demise: Comparing World Systems* (Boulder, Co., Westview Press, 1997)

Chatterjee, Partha   *Nationalist Thought and the Colonial World: A Derivative Discourse?* (London, Zed, 1986)

Chatterjee, Partha   'Was there a Hegemonic Project of the Colonial State?' in Engels and Marks (eds), *Contesting Colonial Hegemony* (1994)

Chaudhuri, K. N.   *Asia Before Europe: Economy and Civilization of the Indian Ocean from the Rise of Islam to 1750* (Cambridge, Cambridge University Press, 1990)

Chaudhuri, Nupur   'Shawls, Jewelery, Curry, and Rice in Victorian Britain' in Chaudhuri and Strobel (eds), *Western Women and Imperialism* (1992)

Chaudhuri, Nupur and Strobel, Margaret (eds)   *Western Women and Imperialism: Complicity and Resistance* (Bloomington, Ind., Indiana University Press, 1992)

Ching, Frank   'An Asian View of Human Rights', *Far East Economic Review*, 29 April 1993

Chomsky, Noam   *The Backroom Boys* (London, Fontana, 1973)

Chomsky, Noam   *Year 501; The Conquest Continues* (London, Verso, 1993)

Chomsky, Noam   *World Orders Old and New* (London, Pluto, 1994)

Chomsky, Noam   *American Power and the New Mandarins* (New York, New Press, 2002)

Chomsky, Noam   *Hegemony or Survival: America's Quest for Global Dominance* (London, Hamish Hamilton, 2003)

Choo, Christine   *Mission Girls: Australian Aboriginal Women on Catholic Missions in the Kimberley 1900–1950* (Crawley, Western Australia, 2001)

Chrisman, Laura   *Rereading the Imperial Romance: British Imperialism and South African Resistance in Haggard, Schreiner and Plaatje* (Oxford, Oxford University Press, 2000)

Chua, Amy   *The World on Fire: How exporting free market democracy breeds ethnic hatred and global instability* (London, Heinemann, 2003)

Clancy-Smith, Julia and Gouda, Frances (eds)   *Domesticating the Empire: Race, Gender and Family Life in French and Dutch Colonialism* (Charlottesville, Va., University of Virginia Press, 1998)

Clancy-Smith, Julia (ed.)   *North Africa, Islam and the Mediterranean World: From the Almoravids to the Algerian War* (London, Frank Cass, 2001)

Clayton, Anthony   *The Wars of French Decolonization* (Harlow, Longman, 1994)

Cleary, Joe   'Misplaced Ideas: Location and Dislocation in Irish Studies' in Clare Carroll and Patricia King (eds), *Ireland and Postcolonial Theory* (Cork, Cork University Press, 2003)

Coates, Ken S.   *Global History of Indigenous Peoples* (London, Palgrave Macmillan, 2004)

Codell, Julie F., and Macleod, Dianne Sachko   *Orientalism Transposed: the Impact of the Colonies on British Culture* (Aldershot, Ashgate, 1998)

Cohen, Paul A.   *History in Three Keys: The Boxers as Event, Experience and Myth* (New York, Columbia University Press, 1997)

Cohn, Bernard   *Colonialism and its Forms of Knowledge: The British in India* (New Jersey, Princeton University Press, 1996; preface by Nicholas Dirks)

Coleman, Vernon   *Rogue Nation: Why America is the Most Dangerous State on Earth* (Barnstaple, Blue Books, 2003)

Colley, Linda   'Britishness and Otherness: An Argument', *Journal of British Studies*, 31, 1992a

Colley, Linda   *Britons: Forging the Nation, 1707–1837* (New Haven, CT, 1992b)

Colley, Linda   'What is Imperial History Now?' in David Cannadine (ed.) *What is History Now?* (London, Palgrave Macmillan, 2002a)

Colley, Linda   *Captives: Britain and the World, 1600–1850* (London, Cape, 2002b)

Colley, Linda   'What Britannia Taught Bush,' *The Guardian*, London, G2, 20 September , 2002c

Collingham, Elizabeth M.   *Imperial Bodies: The Physical Experience of the Raj c.1800–1947* (Oxford, Oxford University Press, 2001)

Comaroff, Jean and Comaroff, John   *Of Revelation and Revolution* (Chicago/ London, University of Chicago Press, 2 vols, 1991/97)

Conniff, Michael L. and Davis, Thomas J.   *Africans in the Americas: A History of the Black Diaspora* (New York, St Martin's Press, 1994)

Conrad, Joseph   *Heart of Darkness* (London, Penguin, 1981, c. 1902)

Constantine, Stephen   *Buy and Build: The Advertising Posters of the Empire Marketing Board* (London, HMSO, 1986)

Cook, Noble David   *Born to Die: Disease and New World Conquest, 1492–1650* (Cambridge, Cambridge University Press, 1998)

Cook, S. B.   *Imperial Affinities: Nineteenth Century Analogies and Exchange between India and Ireland* (New Delhi, Sage Publications, 1993)

Coombes, Anne E.   *Reinventing Africa: Museums, Material Culture and Popular Imagination in Late Victorian and Edwardian England* (New Haven and London, Yale University Press, 1994)

Cooper, Frederick   'Colonizing Time: Work Rhythms and Labour Conflict in Colonial Mombasa' in Stoler and Cooper (eds), *Tensions of Empire* (1997)

Cooper, Frederick   *Africa Since 1940* (Cambridge, Cambridge University Press, 2002)

Cooper, Frederick and Stoler, Ann Laura   'Conflict and Connection: Rethinking Colonial African History', *American Historical Review*, 99, 1994

Coquery-Vidrovitch, Catherine   *African Women: A Modern History* (Boulder, Colo., Westview Press, 1997)

Cox, Michael   'Western Capitalism and the Cold War System' in Michael Shaw (ed.), *War, State and Society* (London, Macmillan Press, 1984)

Crais, Clifton, C.   *White Supremacy and Black Resistance in Pre-industrial South Africa: the Making of the Colonial Order in the Eastern Cape, 1770–1865* (Cambridge, Cambridge University Press, 1992)

Crinson, M.   *Empire Building: Orientalism and Victorian Architecture* (London, Routledge, 1996)

Crone, Patricia   *Meccan Trade and the Rise of Islam* (New Jersey, Princeton University Press, 1987)

Crone, Patricia   *Pre-Industrial Societies: Anatomy of the Pre-modern World* (Oxford, Blackwell, 1989)

Crosby, Alfred   *Ecological Imperialism: The Biological Expansion of Europe, 900–1900* (Cambridge, Cambridge University Press, 1986)

Crossman, Virginia   'The Resident Magistrate as Colonial Officer: Addison, Somerville and Ross', *Irish Studies Review*, vol. 8, no. 1, 2000

Crow, Ben and Thomas, Alan (eds) (with Robin Jenkins and Judy Kimble)   'Maps, Projections and Ethnocentricity' in *Third World Atlas* (Open University Press, 1990; first published 1983)

Crowley, Tony   'Forging the nation: language and cultural nationalism in nineteenth century Ireland' in Crowley, *Language and History: Theories and Texts* (London, Routledge, 1996)

Cunningham, Hugh   'The Language of Patriotism, 1750–1914', *History Workshop Journal*, 12, 1981, pp. 8–33

Curtin, Philip D.   *The World and the West: the European Challenge and the Overseas Response in the Age of Empire* (Cambridge, Cambridge University Press, 2000)

Curtin, Phillip D. (ed.)   *Imperialism: Documentary History of Western Civilization, Nationalism, Liberalism and Socialism* (London, Macmillan, 1971)

Curtis, Liz   *Nothing but the Same Old Story: The Roots of Anti-Irish Racism* (London, Information on Ireland, 1984)

Curtis, Liz   *The Cause of Ireland: From the United Irishmen to Partition* (Belfast, Beyond the Pale Publications, 1996)

Curtis, Mark   *Unpeople: Britain's Secret Human Rights Abuses* (London, Vintage, 2004)

Dalrymple, William   *White Mughals: Love and Betrayal in Eighteenth-Century India* (London, HarperCollins, 2002)

Darby, Phillip   'Taking Fieldhouse Further: Post-Colonializing Imperial History' in Burroughs and Stockwell (eds), *Managing the Business of Empire* (1998)

Darbyshire, Neil   'Darkness over Empire', *Daily Telegraph*, London, 26 August 1997, p. 16

Darwin, John   *The End of the British Empire* (Oxford, Blackwell, 1991)

Dash, Michael J.   *The Other America: Caribbean Literature in a New World Context* (Charlotteville, VA and London, University Press of Virginia, 1998)

Daunton, Martin and Halpern, Rick (eds)   *Empire and Others: British Encounters with Indigenous Peoples, 1600–1850* (London, UCL Press, 1999)

Davidson, Basil   *Africa in Modern History: The Search for a New Society* (Harmondsworth, Penguin, 1978)

Davies, Meryll Wynn, Nandy, Ashis and Sardar, Ziauddin   *Barbaric Others: a Manifesto on Western Racism* (London, Pluto Press, 1993)

Davin, Anna   'Imperialism and motherhood', *History Workshop*, Issue 5 (Spring 1978)

Davis, David Brion   *Slavery and Human Progress* (New York, Oxford University Press, 1986)

Davis, David Brion   'Into the Darkness', *The Times Higher Education Supplement*, June 25 1999

Davis, Lance E. and Huttenback, Robert A.   *Mammon and the Pursuit of Empire: The Political Economy of British Imperialism, 1860–1912* (Cambridge, Cambridge University Press, 1986)

Davis, Mike   *Late Victorian Holocausts: El Nino Famines and the Making of the Third World* (London, Verso, 2001)

Davis, Robert   *Christian Slaves, Muslim Masters: White Slavery in the Mediterranean, the Barbary Coast and Italy, 1500–1800* (New York, Palgrave Macmillan, 2003)

Dawson, Geoffrey   *Soldier Heroes: British Adventure, Empire and the Imagining of Masculinities* (London, Routledge, 1994)

Deagan, Kathleen   'Dynamics of imperial adjustment in Spanish America: ideology and social integration' in Alcock *et al.* (eds), *Empires* (2002)

Dean, Bartholomew and Levi, Jerome (eds)   *At the Risk of Being Heard: Identity, Indigenous Rights and Postcolonial States* (Ann Arbour, University of Michigan Press, 2003)

Deane, Seamus   *Civilians and Barbarians in Ireland's Field Day: The Field Day Theatre Company* (London, Hutchinson, 1986)

De la Campa, Román, Kaplan, Ann E. and Sprinkler, Michael (eds)   *Late Imperial Culture* (London, Verso, 1995)

Derrick, Jonathon   'The Dissenters: Anti-Colonialism in France, c. 1900–40' in Chafer and Sackur (eds), *Promoting the Colonial Idea* (2002)

Diamond, Jared   *Guns, Germs and Steel: The Fates of Human Societies* (London, W. W. Norton, 1997)

Dimier, Veronique   'Direct or Indirect Rule: Propaganda around a Scientific Controversy' in Chafer and Sackur (eds), *Promoting the Colonial Idea* (2002)

Dirks, Nicholas (ed.)   *Colonialism and Culture* (Ann Arbor, University of Michigan Press, 1992)

Dirlik, Arif   'The Post-Colonial Aura: Third World Criticism in the Age of Global Capitalism', *Critical Inquiry*, 20, 1994

Dodge, Tony   *Inventing Iraq: the Failure of Nation Building and a History Denied* (New York, Columbia University Press, 2003)

Dos Santos, Theotonio   'The Structure of Dependence', *American Economic Review*, 60, May 1970

Dower, John W.   *Japan in War and Peace: Essays on History, Culture and Race* (London, Fontana, 1996)

Dower, John W.   *Embracing Defeat: Japan in the Aftermath of World War Two* (New York, Norton, 1999)

Doyle, Michael   *Empires* (Ithaka, New York, Cornell University Press, 1986)

Drayton, Richard   *Nature's Government: Science, Imperial Britain and the 'Improvement' of the World* (New Haven, Yale University Press, 2000)

Duara, Prasenjit (ed.)   *Decolonization: Perspectives from Now and Then* (London, Routledge, 2004)

Dube, Saurabh (ed.)   *Postcolonial Passages: Handbook of Contemporary Writing on India* (New Delhi, OUP India, 2004)

Du Bois, W. E. B.   *The Souls of Black Folk: Essays and Sketches* (New York, 1973; first published, Chicago, 1902; new Intro. Herbert Aptheker)

Dubow, Saul   *Scientific Racism in Modern South Africa* (Cambridge, Cambridge University Press, 1995)

Dummet, Ray E. (ed.)   *Gentlemanly Capitalism* (London, Longman, 1999)

Duus, Peter, Myers, Ramon H. and Peattie, Mark R. (eds)   *The Japanese Colonial Empire, 1895–1937* (New Jersey, Princeton University Press, 1989)

Dyer, Richard   *White* (London, Routledge, 1997)

Eagleton, Terry   *The Idea of Culture* (Oxford, Blackwell, 2000)

Edwards, Elizabeth (ed.)   *Anthropology and Photography 1860–1920* (New Haven, Yale University Press, 1994)

Edwards, Penny   ' "Propergender": Marianne, Joan of Arc and the Export of French Gender Ideology to Colonial Cambodia, 1863–1954' in Chafer and Sackur (eds), *Promoting the Colonial Idea* (2002)

Eisenstein, Zillah   *Against Empire: Feminisms, Racism and the West* (London, Zed Books, 2004)

Empire and Commonwealth Museum, Bristol, 'Empire at Home' Gallery, *www.empiremuseum.co.uk*

Engels, Dagmar and Marks, Shula (eds)   *Contesting Colonial Hegemony: State and Society in Africa and India* (London and New York, British Academic Press, 1994)

Escobar, Arturo   *Encountering Development: The Making and Unmaking of the Third World* (New Jersey, Princeton University Press, 1993)

Etherington, Norman   *Theories of Imperialism: War, Conquest and Capital* (London, Croom Helm, 1984)

Evans, Julie, Grimshaw, Patricia, Phillips, Davis and Swain, Shurlee   *Equal Subjects, Unequal Rights: Indigenous People in British Settler Colonies, 1830–1910* (Manchester, Manchester University Press, 2003)

Evans, Martin   'Projecting a Greater France', *History Today*, February 2000

Fairbank, John King   *China: A New History* (Cambridge, Mass., Harvard University Press, 1998)

Falk, Richard   *Predatory Globalization: A Critique* (Cambridge, Polity Press, 1999)

Fanon, Frantz   *Black Skin, White Masks* (London, Pluto, 1993, 3rd impression, first published, 1952; trans. Charles Lam Markham)

Feierman, Steven   'Africa in History: the End of Universal Narratives' in Prakash (ed.), *After Colonialism* (1995)

Ferguson, Niall   *Empire: How Britain Made the Modern World* (London, Allen Lane/Penguin, 2003)

Ferguson, Niall   *Colossus: the Price of America's Empire* (New York, Penguin Press, 2004)

Ferro, Marc   *Colonization* (London, Routledge, 1997)

Fieldhouse, David K.   'Imperialism: A Historiographic Revision', *Economic History Review*, XIV, 2, 1961

Fieldhouse, David K.   *Colonialism, 1870–1945: An Introduction* (London, Wiedenfeld and Nicholson, 1981)

Fieldhouse, David K.   *The Colonial Empires: A Comparative Survey since the Eighteenth Century* (London, Macmillan, 1982)

Fieldhouse, David K.   *The West and the Third World* (Oxford, Blackwell, 1999)

Fitzpatrick, David   *Oceans of Consolation: Personal Accounts of Irish Migration to Australia* (Cork, Cork University Press, 1994)

Fitzpatrick, David   'Ireland and the Empire', in Porter (ed.), *OHBE*: vol. III (1999)

Fletcher, Richard   *The Cross and the Crescent: Christianity and Islam from Muhammed to the Reformation* (London, Allen Lane, 2003)

Flood, Christopher and Frey, Hugo   'Defending the Empire in Retrospect: The Discourse of the Extreme Right' in Chafer and Sackur (eds), *Promoting the Colonial Idea* (2002)

Foley, Conor   *Legion of the Rearguard: The IRA and the Modern Irish State* (London, Pluto Press, 1992)

Forrest, Denys   *The Oriental: Life Story of a West End Club* (London, B. T. Batsford Ltd, 1968)

Forster, Robert (ed.)   *European and Non European Societies, 1450–1800* (Aldershot, Ashgate/Varorium, 1997)

Foster, Roy   *Modern Ireland, 1600–1972* (London, Allen Lane, 1988)

Foster, Roy   *Paddy and Mr. Punch: Connections in Irish and English History* (London, Allen Lane/Penguin, 1993)

Foucault, Michel   *The History of Sexuality, vol. 1, An Introduction* (London, Allen Lane, 1979)

Foucault, Michel   *Power/Knowledge* (New York, Pantheon Books, 1980)

Fowden, Giles   *Empire to Commonwealth: The Consequences of Monotheism in Late Antiquity* (New Jersey, Princeton University Press, 1993)

Frank, Andre Gunder   *Capitalism and Underdevelopment in Latin America; Historical Studies of Chile and Brazil* (New York, Monthly Review Press, 1969)

Frank, Andre Gunder   *ReOrient: The Silver Age in Asia and the World Economy* (Berkeley, UCLA Press, 1998)

Frank, Andre Gunder and Gills, Barry K. (eds)   *The World System: Five Hundred Years or Five Thousand?* (London, Routledge, 1993)

Frank, Andre Gunder and Gills, Barry K.   'World System Cycles, Crises and hegemonic Shifts, 1700 BC to 1700 AD' in Frank and Gills (eds), *The World System* (1993)

Frankenberg, Ruth   *White Women: Race Matters: the Social Construction of Whiteness* (London, Routledge, 1993)

Frederickson, George   *Racism: A Short History* (New Jersey, Princeton University Press, 2002)

Freund, Bill   *The Making of Contemporary Africa: The Development of African Society since 1800* (Basingstoke, Macmillan 1998: first published 1984)

Friedman, Thomas   *The Lexus and the Olive Tree* (Anchor Books, 2000)

Friedman, Thomas   'Global is Good', *The Guardian*, G2, London, 21 April 2005

Fryer, Peter   *Staying Power: Black People in Britain since 1504* (London, Pluto, 1986)

Fukuyama, Francis   *The End of History and the Last Man* (London, Penguin, 1992)

Furedi, Frank   *The New Ideology of Imperialism; Renewing the Moral Imperative* (London, Pluto Press, 1995)

Furedi, Frank   *Colonial Wars and the Politics of Third World Nationalism* (London, I. B. Taurus, 1997)

Furedi, Frank   *The Silent War: Racism, Imperialism and Ideology in the Twentieth Century* (London, Pluto, 1998)

Fyfe, Christopher   'Race, Empire and the Historians', *Race and Class*, 33, 4, 1992

Galbraith, J. K.   *The Economics of Innocent Fraud: Truth for Our Time* (London, Allen Lane, 2004)

Galtung, Johan   'Global Citizenship, Globalized Human Rights and Global Democracy', *http://www.valt.fi/vol/cosmopolis/papers/galtung.html*, 2005

Galtung, Johan   *Sociological Theory and Social Development* (Kampala, Transition Books, 1968)

Gamble, Andrew   'Hegemony and Decline: Britain and the United States' in O'Brien and Clesse (eds), *Two Hegemonies* (2002)

Gandhi, Leela   *Postcolonial Theory: a Critical Introduction* (Edinburgh University Press, 1998)

Garnsey, Peter and Saller, Richard   *The Roman Empire: Economy, Society and Culture* (London, Duckworth, 1987)

Gelber, Harry   *Nations Out of Empires: European Nationalism and the Transformation of Asia* (London, Palgrave Macmillan, 2001)

Gelber, Harry   *Opium, Soldiers and Evangelicals: England's 1840–42 War with China and its Aftermath* (London, Palgrave Macmillan, 2004)

Gerth, Karl   *China Made Me: Consumer Culture and the Creation of the Nation* (Cambridge, Mass., Harvard University Press, 2003)

Gewertz, Deborah and Errington, Frederick   'We Think, therefore They Are? On Occidentalising the World' in Kaplan and Pease (eds), *Cultures of United States Imperialism* (1993)

Gibbons, Luke   'Race Against Time: Racial Discourse and Irish History' in Gregory Castle (ed.), *Postcolonial Discourses: An Anthology* (Oxford, Blackwell, 2001)

Gigantes, Philippe   *Power and Greed: A Short History of the World* (London, Constable, 2002)

Gills, Barry K. (ed.)   *Globalization and the Politics of Resistance* (London, Taylor and Francis, 1997)

Gilroy, Paul   *The Black Atlantic: Modernity and Double Consciousness* (London, Verso, 1993)

Gilroy, Paul   *'There ain't no Black in the Union Jack': the cultural politics of race and nation* (London, Hutchinson, 1987)

Glissant, Édouard   *Le discours antillais* (Paris: Seuil, 1981)

Goerg, Odile   'The French Provinces and "Greater France" ' in Chafer and Sackur (eds), *Promoting the Colonial Idea* (2002)

Goldberg, David Theo   *Racist Culture: Philosophy and the Politics of Meaning* (Oxford, Blackwell, 1993)

Goldberg, David Theo   'Multicultural Conditions' in Goldberg (ed.), *Multiculturalism: A Critical Reader* (Oxford, Blackwell, 1994)

Goldberg, David Theo and Quayson, Ato (eds)   *Relocating Postcolonialism* (Oxford, Blackwell, 2002)

Goldstone, Jack   'Gender, Work and Culture: Why the Industrial Revolution came early to England but late to China', *Sociological Perspectives*, 99, 1, 1996

Gonne McBride, Maude   *The Servant of the Queen: Reminiscences by Maude Gonne McBride* (London, Gollancz, 1938)

Goody, Jack   *The Expansive Moment: Anthropology in Britain and Africa, 1918–1970* (Cambridge, Cambridge University Press, 1995)

Gorer, Geoffrey   *Africa Dances* (London, 1935)

Gott, Richard   'A Seismic Upheaval among Latin America's Indians', *The Guardian*, London, 11 June 2005

Grant, Michael   *The Fall of the Roman Empire* (London, Wiedenfeld and Nicholson, 1990)

Gray, Jack   *Rebellions and Revolutions; China from the 1880s to 2000* (Oxford, Oxford University Press, 2002; 2nd edn; first published, 1990)

Gray, John   *Al Qaeda and What it Means to be Modern* (London, Faber, 2003)

Greene, Graham   *Journey Without Maps* (London, 1962; first published, 1936)

Greenhalgh, Paul   *Ephemeral Vistas: A History of the Expositions Universelles, Great Exhibitions and World Fairs, 1851–1938* (Manchester, Manchester University Press, 1988)

Gregory, Derek   *The Colonial Present* (Oxford, Blackwell, 2004)

Grewel, Inderpal   *Home and Harem: Nation, Gender, Empire and the Cultures of Travel* (Leicester, Leicester University Press, 1996)

Grimal, Henri   *Decolonization: the British, French, Dutch and Belgian Empires, 1919–1963* (London, Routledge, 1978)

Grove, Richard   *Green Imperialism: Colonial Expansion, Tropical Island Edens and the Origins of Environmentalism, 1600–1800* (Cambridge, Cambridge University Press, 1995)

Guha, Ranajit   *Subaltern Studies: Writings on South Asian History and Society* (Delhi, Oxford University Press, 1982–5, 4 vols)

Guttierrez, Ramon A.   *When Jesus Came, the Corn Mothers Went Away: Marriage, Sexuality, and Power in New Mexico, 1500–1846* (Stanford University Press, 1991)

Haggis, Jane   'White Women and Colonialism: Towards a Non-Recuperative History in Midgley (ed.), *Gender and Imperialism* (1998)

Hailey, Sir Malcolm   *An African Survey; A Study of Problems Arising in Africa South of the Sahara: Revised, 1956* (Oxford, Oxford University Press, 1957)

Haldon, John   *Byzantium: A History* (Stroud, Tempus, 2000)

Hall, Catherine (ed.)   *Culture and Imperialism: A Reader* (Manchester, Manchester University Press, 2000)

Hall, Catherine   *Civilising Subjects: Metropole and Colony in the English Imagination, 1830–1867* (Cambridge, Polity Press, 2002)

Hall, Richard   *Black Armband Days: Truth from the Dark Side of Australia's Past* (Sydney, Vintage, 1998)

Hall, Stuart   'The West and the Rest: Discourse and Power' in S. Hall *et al.* (eds), *Formations of Modernity* (Cambridge, Polity Press/Open University, 1992)

Hamelink, Cees   *The Politics of World Communication* (Sage Publications, 1994)

Hamilton, Patrick   *The Empire on Stamps* (London, Peter Davies, 1941)

Han Su Yin   *The Crippled Tree* (London, Panther Books, 1972; first published, 1965)

Hancock, W. Keith   *Argument of Empire* (Harmondsworth, Penguin, 1943)

Hardt, Michael and Negri, Antonio   *Empire* (Cambridge, Mass., Harvard University Press, 2000)

Harraway, Donna   'Teddy Bear Patriarchy' in Kaplan and Pease (eds), *Cultures of United States Imperialism* (1993)

Harrison, Henrietta   'Justice on Behalf of Heaven', *History Today*, vol. 50, 9, 2000

Harvey, David   *The Condition of Postmodernity: An Enquiry into the Origins of Change* (Oxford, Blackwell, 1990)

Harvey, David   *The New Imperialism* (Oxford, Oxford University Press, 2003)

Haynes, Keith   'Capitalism and the Periodisation of International Relations: Colonialism, Imperialism, Ultraimperialism and Postimperialism', *Radical History Review*, 57, 1993, reproduced in Cain and Hamson (2001), vol. 2

Headrick, Daniel R.   *The Tools of Empire: Technology and European Imperialism in the Nineteenth century* (Oxford, Oxford University Press, 1981)

Hechter, Michael   *Internal Colonialism: the Celtic Fringe in British National Development, 1536–1966* (London, Routledge, 1975)

Hegel, George W. F.   *The Philosophy of History* (New York, Dover Publications Ltd., 1956; Intro. C. J. Friedrich, trans. J. Sibree)

Held, David   *Models of Democracy* (Cambridge, Polity Press, 1987)

Held, David, Goldblatt, David and Perraton, Jonathan   *Global Transformations: Politics, Economics and Culture* (Cambridge, Polity Press, 1999)

Held, David and McGrew, Anthony G. (eds)   *The Global Transformations Reader: An Introduction to the Globalization Debate* (Cambridge, Polity Press, 2003)

Hemming, John   *The Conquest of the Incas* (London, Macmillan, 1997; first published, 1970)

Hill, Christopher C.   'Ideology and Public Works: "Managing" the Mahandi River in Colonial North India', *Capitalism, Nature and Socialism: The Journal of Socialist Ecology*, vol. 1, no. 6/4, Issue 24, December 1995

Hill, Christopher C.   *River of Sorrow: Environment and Social Control in Riparian North India, 1770–1994* (Association for Asian Studies, University of Michigan Press, 1997)

Hirst, Paul and Thompson, Graeme   *Globalization in Question: The International Economy and the Possibilities of Governance* (London, Longman, 1996)

Hoare, Q. and Newell Smith, G. (ed. and trans.)   *Selection from the Prison Notebook of Antonio Gramsci* (London, Lawrence and Wishart, 1971)

Hobsbawm, Eric   'Mass Producing Traditions: Europe, 1870–1914' in Hobsbawm and Ranger (eds), *The Invention of Tradition* (1996)

Hobsbawm, Eric   *The Age of Empire, 1875–1914* (London, Sphere, 1989)

Hobsbawm, Eric   *The Age of Extremes: The Short Twentieth Century, 1914–1991* (London, Michael Joseph, 1994)

Hobsbawm, Eric and Ranger, Terence O. (eds)   *The Invention of Tradition* (Cambridge, Cambridge University Press, 1996; first published, 1983)

Hobson, J. A.   *Imperialism, A Study* (London, Unwin Hyman, 1988. 3rd edn; first published, 1902; ed. and Intro. J. Townshend)

Hobson, John M.   'Two Hegemonies or One? A Historical-Sociological Critique of Hegemonic Stability Theory' in O'Brien and Clesse (eds), *Two Hegemonies* (2002)

Hobson, John M.   *The Eastern Origins of Western Civilization* (Cambridge, Cambridge University Press, 2004)

Hochschild, Adam   *King Leopold's Ghost: A Short Story of Greed, Terror and Heroism in Colonial Africa* (London, Macmillan, 1999)

Hoffenberg, Peter   *An Empire on Display: English, Indian and Australian Exhibitions from the Crystal Palace to the Great War* (Berkeley, UCLA Press, 2001)

Hogan, Patrick Colm   *Colonialism and Cultural Identity* (Albany, State University of New York Press, 2000)

Holmes, Michael and Holmes, Denis (eds)   *Ireland and India: Connections, Comparisons, Contrasts* (Dublin, Folens, 1997)

Holmes, Michael   'The Irish in India: Imperialism, Nationalism and Internationalism' in Andy Bielenberg (ed.), *The Irish Diaspora* (Harlow, Pearson Longman, 2000)

Honey, Maureen and Cole, Jean Lee (eds)   *Madame Butterfly/John Luther Long and a Japanese Nightingale: Onato Watanna (Winifred Eaton): two Orientalist texts* (New Brunswick, N.J, Rutgers University Press, c. 2002)

Hooper, John and Baldock, Hannah   'Benetton agrees to hand over land to Indians', *The Guardian*, London, 10 November 2004, p. 22

Hopkins, Anthony G.   'Back to the Future: From National History to Imperial History', *Past and Present*, no. 164, 1999

Hopkins, Anthony G. (ed.)   *Globalization in World History* (London, Pimlico, 2002)

Horne, Gerald   *Race War: White Supremacy and the Japanese Attack on the British Empire* (New York, New York University Press, 2004)

Horsman, Reginald   *Race and Manifest Destiny: The Origins of Anglosaxonism* (Cambridge, Mass., Harvard University Press, 1981)

Howe, Stephen   *Anti-colonialism in British Politics: The Left and the End of Empire, 1918–1964* (Oxford, Clarendon Press, 1993)

Howe, Stephen   'David Fieldhouse and "Imperialism": Some Historiographical Revisions' in Burroughs and Stockwell (eds), *Managing the Business of Empire* (1998)

Howe, Stephen   *Ireland and Empire: Colonial Legacies in Irish History and Culture* (Oxford, Oxford University Press, 2000)

Howe, Stephen   'Review Article: The Slow Death and Strange Rebirths of Imperial History', *The Journal of Imperial and Commonwealth History*, vol. 29, no. 2, May 2001

Howe, Stephen   *Empire: A Very Short Introduction* (Oxford, 2002)

Howe, Stephen   'Review Article: When – If Ever – Did Empire End? Recent Studies of Imperialism and Decolonization' *Journal of Contemporary History*, vol. 40, no. 3, 2005, pp. 585–99

Hoyningen-Huene, G.   *African Mirage: The Record of a Journey* (London, Batsford, 1938)

Huggan, Graham   'Decolonizing the Map: Post-colonialism, Post-structuralism, and the Cartographic Connection' in Adam and Tiffin (eds), *Past the last Post* (1991)

Hulme, Peter and Whitehead, Neil L. (eds)   *Wild Majesty: Encounters with Caribs from Columbus to the Present Day: An Anthology* (Oxford, Oxford University Press, 1992)

Hunt, Nancy Rose *et al.* (eds)   *Gendered Colonialisms in African History* (Oxford, Blackwell, 1996)

Huntington, Samuel P.   *The Clash of Civilizations and the Remaking of the World Order* (London, Touchstone Books, 1997)

Hurd, Percy　*The Empire: A Family Affair (being a Popular Survey of the Self Governing Dominions, Crown Colonies and Protectorates and Mandated Territories Under the British Crown and Recital of Empire Policy* (London, Philip Allen and Co., 1924)

Hutchinson, John　*The Dynamics of Cultural Nationalism: The Gaelic Revival and the Creation of the Irish Nation State* (London, Allen and Unwin, 1987)

Huttenback, Robert A.　*Racism and the Empire: White settlers and coloured immigrants in the British self-governing colonies, 1830–1910* (Ithaca, New York, Cornell University Press, 1976)

Huxley, Elspeth　*East Africa* (London, published for the Penns in the Rock Press by William Collins, 1941)

Huxley, Elspeth　*Four Guineas; A Journey Through West Africa* (London, The Reprint Society, 1955; first published, 1954)

Hyam, Ronald　*Empire and Sexuality* (Manchester, Manchester University Press, 1990)

Ibeji, Mike　'The Darien Venture' *http://www.bbc.co.uk/history/state/nations/ scotland_darien_pri . . .* accessed 28.10. 2003

Inalcik, Halil and Quateart, Donald　*An Economic and Social History of the Ottoman Empire, 1300–1914* (Cambridge, Cambridge University Press, 1994)

Inden, Ronald B.　'Orientalist Constructions of India' (1986) reproduced in Cain and Harrison (eds), *Imperialism:* (2001), vol. 3

Inden, Ronald B.　*Imagining India* (London, Hurst and Company, 1990)

Iriye, Akira　*The Origins of the Second World War in Asia and the Pacific* (London, Longman, 1987)

Ishiguro, Kazuo　*Artist of the Floating World* (London, Faber, 1986)

Ishiguro, Kazuo　*When We Were Orphans* (London, Faber, 2000)

Isichei, Elizabeth Allo　*A History of Christianity in Africa: From Antiquity to the Present* (New York, Barnes and Noble, 1994)

Jacobs, Jane M.　*Edge of Empire: Postcolonialism and the City* (London, Routledge, 1996)

Jameson, Frederick　'Postmodernism or the Cultural Logic of Late Capitalism', *New left Review*, 146, 1984

Jansen, Marius　*The Making of Modern Japan* (Cambridge, Mass, Harvard University Press, 2000)

Jayawardena, K.　*The White Woman's Other Burden: Western Women and South Asia During British Rule* (London, Routledge, 1995)

Jeffery, Keith (ed.)　*'An Irish Empire': Aspects of Ireland and the British Empire*, (Manchester, Manchester University Press, 1996)

Jenks, Leland Hamilton　*Our Cuban Colony: A Study in Sugar* (New York, Vanguard Press, 1928)

Johnson, Chalmers　*The Sorrows of Empire: Militarism, Secrecy, and the End of the Republic* (London, Verso, 2003)

Johnson, Robert　*British Imperialism* (London, Palgrave Macmillan, 2003)

Judd, Denis   *Empire: The British Imperial Experience from 1765 to the Present* (London, Harper Collins, 1996)

Judd, Denis   *The Lion and the Tiger: The Rise and Fall of the British Raj, 1600–1947* (Oxford, Oxford University Press, 2004)

Kamen, Henry   *Spain's Road to Empire: the Making of a World Power, 1492–1763* (London, Penguin, 2002)

Kaplan, Amy   ' "Left Alone with America": the Absence of Empire in United States Culture' in Kaplan and Pease (eds), *Cultures of United States Imperialism* (1993)

Kaplan, Amy and Pease, Donald (eds)   *Cultures of United States Imperialism* (Durham, N.C., Duke University Press, 1993)

Kautsky, Karl   'Ultra-imperialism (Der Imperialismus)'; (first published, 1914 and reproduced in *New Left Review*, 59, January–February, 1970)

Keegan, Thomas   *Colonial South Africa and the Origins of the Racial Order* (Leicester, Leicester University Press, 1996)

Kennedy, Dane   'Imperial History and Post-Colonial Theory', *Journal of Imperial and Commonwealth History*, vol, 24, no. 3, 1996

Kennedy, Dane   *Islands of White: Settler Society and Culture in Kenya and Southern Rhodesia, 1890–1939* (Durham, N. C., Duke University Press, 1987)

Kennedy, Dane   'The Boundaries of Oxford's Empire', *International History Review*, vol. 23, 2001

Kennedy, Liam   *Modern Ireland: Postcolonial Society or Postcolonial Pretensions? Colonialism, Religion and Nationalism in Ireland* (Belfast, Belfast Institute of Irish Studies, 1996)

Kennedy, Paul   *The Rise and Fall of the Great Powers* (London, Unwin Hyman, 1988)

Kenny, Kevin (ed.)   *Ireland and the British Empire*, Oxford History of the British Empire Companion Series (Oxford, Oxford University Press, 2004)

Kenyatta, Jomo   *Facing Mount Kenya: the traditional life of the Kikuyu* (London: Heinemann, 1979; first published, 1938; Intro. B. Malinowski)

Keylor, William R.   *The Twentieth Century World* (Oxford, Oxford University Press, 1992, 2nd edn)

Khalidi, Rashid   *Resurrecting Empire: Western Footprints and America's Perilous Path in the Middle East* (London, I. B. Taurus, 2004)

Kibata, Yoichi and Adamthwaite, Antony   *Anglo-Japanese Relations in the 1930s and 1940s* (London, Suntory-Toyota International Centre for Economics and Related Disciplines, 1986; ed. Ian Nish)

Kibberd, Declan   *Inventing Ireland: The Literature of the Modern Nation* (London, Vintage, 1996)

Kiernan, Victor G.   *The Lords of Human Kind: European Attitudes to Other Cultures in the Imperial Age* (London, Serif, 1995; first published, 1969)

Kiernan, Victor G.   *European Empires from Conquest to Collapse 1815–1960* (London, Fontana, 1982)

Killingray, David and Omissi, David (eds)   *Guardians of Empire: The Armed Forces of the Colonial Powers, c. 1700–1964* (Manchester, Manchester University Press, 1999)

Kimball, Roger   'The Perils of Designer Tribalism', *The New Criterion* on Line, *www. Newcrtierion.com/archive/* 19.04.01, accessed 07.04.04

Kinealy, Christine   *This Great Calamity: the Irish Famine 1845–52* (Dublin, Gill and Macmillan, 1994)

Kinealy, Christine   *The Great Irish Famine: Impact, Ideology and Rebellion* (London, Palgrave Macmillan, 2002)

King, Anthony   'Fame of a Once Proud Empire is fading fast', *The Daily Telegraph*, London, August 26, 1997, p. 4.

King, Jonathan   'Putting on a Brave Face', *The Times Higher Education Supplement*, 25 June, 1999

King, Michael   *Being Pakeha: An Encounter with New Zealand and the Maori Renaissance* (London, Hodder and Stoughton, 1985)

Kirkby, Diane and Coleborne, Catherine (eds)   *Empire's Reach: Law, History and Colonialism* (Manchester, Manchester University Press, 2001)

Kirschenblatt-Gimblett, Barbara   'Objects of Ethnography' in Ivan Karp and Stephen D. Lavine (eds), *Exhibiting Cultures: The Poetics and Politics of Museum Display* (Washington D. C., Smithsonian Institute Press, 1991), p. 398

Klein, Naomi   'Allure of the Blank Slate', *The Guardian*, London, 18 April 2005, p. 17.

Klein, Naomi   *No Logo* (London, Flamingo, 1999)

Kleveman, Lutz   *The New Great Game: Blood and Oil in Central Asia* (London, Atlantic, 2003)

Klitgaard, Robert   *Tropical Gangsters* (New York, Basic Books, 1990)

Klor de Alva, Jorge J.   'The Postcolonialization of the Latin American Experience' in Prakash (ed.), *After Colonialism* (1995)

Knowles, C.   'The Symbolic Empire and the History of Racial Inequality', *Ethnic and Racial Studies*, vol. 19, no. 4, 1996

Kogbara, Donu   'The Chains of History', *The Sunday Times*, London, 30 October 1994

Kuhrt, Amélie   'The Achaemenid Persian Empire (c. 550–c. 330 BCE); continuities, adaptations, transformations' in Alcock *et al.*, (eds), *Empires* (2002)

Kuklich, Henrietta   *The Savage Within: The Social History of British Anthropology, 1885–1945* (Cambridge, Cambridge University Press, 1991)

LaCapra, Dominick (ed.)   *The Bounds of Race: Perspectives on Hegemony and Resistance* (Ithaca, Cornell University Press, 1991)

Laclau, Ernest   *Politics and Ideology in Marxist Theory* (London, NLB, 1977)

Lahiri, Shompi   *Indians in Britain: Anglo Indian Encounters, Race and Identity, 1880–1930* (London, Frank Cass, 2001)

Lake, Marilyn   'Frontier Feminism and the Marauding White Man: Australia, 1990s to 1940s' in Pierson and Chaudhuri, *Nation, Empire Colony* (1998)

Lake, Marylin 'Colonized and Colonizing: The White Australian Feminist Subject', *Women's History Review*, vol. 2, no. 3, 1993

Landes, David S.   *The Unbound Prometheus: Technological Change and Industrial Development in Western Europe from 1750 to the Present* (Cambridge, Cambridge University Press, 1969)

Latouche, Serge   *The Westernisation of the World: The Significance, Scope and Limits of the Drive towards Global Uniformity* (Cambridge, Polity Press, 1996)

Lauren, Paul Gordon   *Power and Prejudice: the Politics and Diplomacy of Racial Discrimination* (New York, Westview Press, 1996, 2nd edn)

Le Sueur, James D. (ed.)   *The Decolonization Reader* (London, Routledge, 2004)

Lenin, Vladimir Ilich   *Imperialism: The Highest Stage of Capitalism* (1916, Reprint, London, Pluto, 1996; Intro. Norman Lewis and James Malone)

Levathes, Louise   *When China Ruled the Seas* (Oxford University Press, 1996)

Levine, Phillippa   *Prostitution, Race and Politics: Policing Venereal Disease in the British Empire* (London, Routledge, 2003)

Levine, Philippa (ed.)   *Gender and Empire*, Oxford History of the British Empire: Companion Series (Oxford, Oxford University Press, 2004)

Lewis, Bernard   *Islam and the West* (Oxford, Oxford University Press, 1993)

Lewis, Bernard   *The Crisis of Islam: Holy War and Unholy Terror* (London, Allen and Unwin, 2003)

Lewis, Reina   *Gendering Orientalism: Race, Femininity and Representation* (London, Routledge, 1996)

Lieven, Anatol   *America, Right or Wrong: An Anatomy of American Nationalism* (London, HarperCollins, 2004)

Lieven, Dominic   *Empire: The Russian Empire and Its Rivals* (London, John Murray, 2000)

Light, Alison   *Forever England: Femininity, Literature and Conservatism between the Wars* (London, Routledge, 1991)

Lindfors, Bernth (ed.)   *Africans on Stage: Studies in Ethnological Showbusiness* (Bloomington, Ind., Indiana University Press, 1999)

Lindquist, Sven   *'Exterminate All the Brutes'* (London, Granta, 1998)

Linebaugh, Peter and Rediker, Marcus   *The Many Headed Hydra: Sailors, Slaves, Commoners and the Hidden History of the Revolutionary Atlantic* (London, Verso, 2000)

Lintott, Andrew   *Imperium Romanum. Politics and Administration* (London, Routledge, 1993)

Lipset, Seymour, M.   *American Exceptionalism: A Double-Edged Sword* (London, Norton, 1997)

Lively, Adam   *Masks: Blackness, Race and Imagination* (London, Chatto and Windus, 1998)

Lloyd, David   *Ireland after History* (Cork, Cork University Press, 1999)

Lockart, James and Schwartz, Stuart B.   *Early Latin America: A Short History of Colonial Spanish America and Brazil* (Cambridge, 1983)

Long, John Luther   *Madame Butterfly: Purple Eyes: A Gentleman of Japan and a Lady* (New York, Century Co., 1898)

Loomba, Ania   *Colonialism/Postcolonialism* (London, Routledge, 1998)

Louis, Wm. Roger   *Imperialism at Bay: The United States and Decolonisation of the British Empire, 1941–1945* (Oxford, Clarendon Press, 1977)

Low, Gail Chiang-Liang   *White Skins, Black Masks: Representation and Colonialism* (London, Routledge, 1996)

Lowe, Lisa   *Critical Terrains: French and British Orientalism* (Ithaca, New York, Cornell University Press, 1991)

Ludden, David   'India's Development Regime' in Dirks (ed.), *Colonialism and Culture* (1992)

Lugard, Lord Frederick, D.   *Political Memoranda; Revision of Instructions to Political Officers on Subjects Chiefly Political and Administrative, 1913–1918* (London, Frank Cass, 1970; first published, 1922; ed. and Intro. A. H. M. Kirk Greene)

Lugard, Lord Frederick, D.   *The Dual Mandate in British Tropical Africa* (Edinburgh and London, William Blackwood and Sons, 1922)

Lyons, F. S. L.   *Culture and Anarchy in Ireland, 1890–1939* (Oxford, Clarendon Press, 1979)

MacDonald, Robert H.   *The Language of Empire: Myths and Metaphors of Popular Imperialism, 1880–1918* (Manchester, Manchester University Press, 1994)

MacFie, A. L. (ed.)   *Orientalism: A Reader* (London, Longman, 2002)

Mackenzie, John M.   *Propaganda and Empire* (Manchester, Manchester University Press, 1984)

Mackenzie, John M.   'In Touch with the Infinite: the BBC and the Empire, 1923–53' in Mackenzie (ed.), *Imperialism and Popular Culture* (1986a)

Mackenzie, John M. (ed.)   *Imperialism and Popular Culture* (Manchester, Manchester University Press, 1986b)

Mackenzie, John M.   *The Empire of Nature: Hunting, Conservation and British Imperialism* (Manchester, Manchester University Press 1997, first published 1988)

Mackenzie, John M.   *Orientalism. History, Theory and the Arts* (Manchester, Manchester University Press, 1995)

MacNeil, Rod   'Time after time: temporal frontiers and boundaries in colonial images of the Australian landscape' in Russell (ed.), *Colonial Frontiers* (2001)

Magdoff, Harry   *Imperialism from the Colonial Age to the Present* (New York and London, Monthly Review Press, 1978)

Majeed, Javed   *Ungoverned Imaginings: James Mill's 'The History of British India' and Orientalism* (London, Oxford University Press, 1992)

Malan, Rian   'The white tribes of Ulster', *The Guardian* (London) Guardian Weekend, 3 April 1993

Man, John   *Ghengis Khan: Life, Death and Resurrection* (London, Bantam, 2004)

Mangan, J.   *The Games Ethic and Imperialism* (Manchester, Manchester University Press, 1986)

Mangan, J. (ed.)   *Benefits Bestowed? Education and British Imperialism* (Manchester, Manchester University Press, 1988)

Mann, Michael   *The Sources of Social Power, vol. 1: A History of Power to AD 1760* (Cambridge, Cambridge University Press, 1986)

Mannoni, Octave   *Propero and Caliban: The Psychology of Colonization* (London, Methuen, 1956)

Marchant, Leslie   'The Wars of the Poppies', *History Today*, vol. 52 (5), May 2002

Marishane, Jeffrey   'Prayer, Profit and Power: The US Religious Right and Foreign Policy', *Review of African Political Economy*, no. 52, 1991

Marks, Shula   'History, the Nation and Empire: Sniping from the Periphery', *History Workshop*, no. 29, Spring 1990

Marshall, Peter J.   'Imperial Britain', *The Journal of Imperial and Commonwealth History*, vol. 23, no. 3, 1995

Marshall, Peter J. (ed.)   *The Oxford History of the British Empire*: vol. II *The Eighteenth Century* (Oxford, Oxford University Press, 1998)

Marshall, Peter J. (ed.)   *The Cambridge Illustrated History of the British Empire* (Cambridge, Cambridge University Press, 1996)

Martin, Bernd   'The Politics of Expansion of the Japanese Empire: Imperialism or Pan-Asiatic Mission?' in Mommsen and Osterhammel (eds), *Imperialism and After* (1986)

Marx, Karl and Engels, Friedrich   *The German Ideology* (London, Lawrence and Wishart, 1940); ed. R. Pascal

Marx, Karl and Engels, Friedrich   'The Manifesto of the Communist Party' 1852 in *Selected Works in One Volume* (Moscow, Progress Publishers, 1968)

Mason, J. (ed.)   *Changing China: Readings in the History of China from the Opium War to the Present* (New York, Praeger, 1977)

Matar, Nabil   *Turks, Moors and Englishmen in the Age of Discovery* (New York, Columbia University Press, 1999)

Maxwell, Ann   *Colonial Photography and Exhibitions: Representations of the 'Native' and the Making of European Identities* (Leicester, Leicester University Press/Continuum, 2000)

Maxwell, David and Lawrie, Ingrid (eds)   *Christianity and the African Imagination: Essays in Honour of Adrian Hastings* (Leiden and Boston, Brill, 2001)

Mayo, Katherine   *Islands of Fear: the Truth about the Philippines* (London, Faber and Gwyer, 1925)

McBride, Ian (ed.)   *History and Memory in Modern Ireland* (Cambridge, Cambridge University Press, 2001)

McCarthy, Justin   *The Ottoman Peoples and the End of Empire* (London, Arnold, 2001)

McCaskie, T. C.   'Cultural Encounters: Britain and Africa in the Nineteenth Century' in Porter (ed.), *OHBE*, vol. III (1999)

McClintock, Anne   'The Angel of Progress: Pitfalls of the term "Post-Colonialism" ' in Williams and Chrisman (eds), *Colonial Discourse* (1993)

McClintock, Anne   *Imperial Leather: Race, Gender and Sexuality in the Colonial Contest* (London, Routledge, 1995)

McCracken, Donal P.   *Gardens of Empire: Botanical Institutions of the Victorian British Empire* (London, Leicester University Press, 1997)

McCrone, I. D.   *Race Attitudes in South Africa: Historical, Experimental and Psychological Studies* (London and New York, Oxford University Press, 1937)

McDevitt, Patrick F.   *May the Best Man Win: Sport, Masculinity, and Nationalism in Great Britain and the Empire, 1880–1935* (London, Palgrave Macmillan, 2004)

McGreal, Chris   'Coming Home', *The Guardian*, London, 21 February 2002

McGrew, Anthony   'The Third World in the New Global Order' in Allen and Thomas, *Poverty and Development in the 1990s* (Oxford, Oxford University Press, 1992)

McLeod, John   *Beginning Postcolonialism* (Manchester, Manchester University Press, 2000)

McNeill, William H.   *The Rise of the West* (Chicago, University of Chicago Press, 1962)

Meade, T and Walker, M. (eds)   *Science, Medicine and Cultural Imperialism* (London, Macmillan, 1991)

Meldrum, Andrew   'San fight to keep Kalahari hunting grounds', *The Guardian*, London, 5 March 2004, p. 19

Melman, Billie   *Women and the Popular Imagination in the Twenties: Flappers and Nymphs* (Basingstoke, Macmillan, 1986)

Melman, Billie   *Women's Orients: English Women and the Middle East, 1718–1818: Sexuality, Religion and Work* (London, Macmillan, 1995; 2nd edn)

Memmi, Albert   *The Colonizer and the Colonized* (London, Earthscan Publications, 1990; first published, 1957; Intro. Jean Paul Sartre; new intro Liam O'Dowd)

Meyer, Karl and Brysac, Shareen   *Tournament of Shadows: The Great Game and the Race for Empire in Asia* (Boston, Little, Brown, 2001)

Middleton, Richard   'The Politics of Cultural Expression: African Music and the World Market' in Allen and Thomas (eds), *Poverty and Development in the 1990s* (1992)

Midgley, Clare (ed.)   *Gender and Imperialism* (Manchester, Manchester University Press, 1998)

Miles, Gary B.   'Roman and Modern Imperialism', *Comparative Studies in Society and History*, vol. 32, 1990

Mill, John Stuart   *John Stuart Mill on Ireland with an essay by Richard Ned Lebow* (Philadelphia, Institute for the Study of Human Issues, 1979)

Mills, Lady D. R. M.   *The Golden Land: A Record of Travel in West Africa* (London, Duckworth, 1929)

Mills, Sarah   *Discourses of Difference: An Analysis of Women's Travel Writing and Colonialism* (London, Routledge, 1991)

Minichiello, Saron A. (ed.)   *Japan's Competing Modernities: Issues in Culture and Democracy, 1900–1930* (University of Hawai'i Press, 1998)

Mishra, Vijay and Hodge, Bob   'What is Post(-)colonialism?' in Williams and Chrisman (eds), *Colonial Discourse* (1993)

Misra, Maria   *Business, Race and Politics in British India, c. 1850–1960* (Oxford, Oxford University Press, 1999)

Mitchell, Angus   *Casement* (London, Haus, 2003)

Mitchell, Timothy   *Colonizing Egypt* (Cambridge, Cambridge University Press, 1988)

Mitchell, Timothy   'Orientalism and the Exhibitionary Order' in Dirks (ed.), *Colonialism and Culture* (1992)

Mitter, Rana   'The Last Warlord', *History Today*, vol. 50, 8, August 2000a

Mitter, Rana   *The Manchurian Myth: Nationalism, Resistance, and Collaboration in Modern China* (Berkeley, UCLA Press, 2000b)

Mitter, Rana   *A Bitter Revolution: China's Struggle with the Modern World* (Oxford, Oxford University Press, 2004)

Mittleman, J. H.   *The Globalization Syndrome* (Princeton, NJ, Princeton University Press, 2000)

Modelski, G. and Thompson, W. R.   *Seapower in Global Politics, 1493–1993* (London, Macmillan, 1988)

Mommsen, Wolfgang J.   *Theories of Imperialism* (London, Weidenfeld, 1980)

Mommsen, Wolfgang J.   'The End of Empire and the Continuity of Imperialism' in Mommsen and Osterhammel, *Imperialism and After* (1986)

Mommsen, Wolfgang J.   *Imperial Germany 1867–1918: Politics, Culture and Society in an Authoritarian State* (London, Arnold, 1995; trans. Richard Deveson)

Mommsen, Wolfgang J. and Osterhammel, Jürgen (eds)   *Imperialism and After, Continuities and Discontinuities* (London, German Historical Institute, 1986)

Monbiot, George   'Driven out of Eden', *The Guardian*, London, 5 August 2003, p. 11

Monbiot, George   *The Age of Consent: A Manifesto for a New World Order* (London, Harper Perennial, 2004)

Morgan, Philip D. and Hawkins, Sean (eds)   *Black Experience and the Empire* (Oxford History of the British Empire Companion Series, Oxford, Oxford University Press, 2004)

Mostert, Noël   *Frontiers, the Epic of South Africa's Creation and the Tragedy of the Xhosa People* (London, Jonathon Cape, 1992)

Motley, Mary   *Morning Glory* (London, Longman, 1961)

Munslow, Alun   *The New History* (London, Pearson Longman, 2003)

Munslow, Alun   *Deconstructing History* (London, Routledge, 1997)

Myers, Ramon H. and Peattie, Mark R. (eds)   *The Japanese Informal Empire in China, 1895–1945* (Princeton, NJ, Princeton University Press, 1984)

Nandy, Ashis   *The Intimate Enemy: Loss and Recovery of Self under Colonialism* (Oxford, Oxford University Press, 1983)

Newman, Andrew J.   *Safavid Iran* (London, I. B. Taurus, 2005)

Ngugi, wa Thiong'o   'Wedding at the Cross' in *Secret Lives and Other Stories* (London, Heinemann Educational, 1975)

Ngugi, wa Thiong'o   *Decolonizing the Mind: the Politics of Language in African Literature* (Oxford, James Currey, 1991)

Ngugi, wa Thiong'o   *Moving the Centre: The Struggle for Cultural Freedoms* (Oxford, James Currey, 1993)

Ninkovich, Frank   *The United States and Imperialism* (Oxford, Blackwell, 2001)

Nora, Pierre   *Les Lieux de Mémoire* (Quarto Edition, Gallimard, 1998, 1984–6)

Nugent, Paul   *Africa since Independence* (London, Palgrave Macmillan, 2004)

O'Brien, Patrick Karl   'The Pax Britannica and American Hegemony: Precedent, Antecedent or Just Another History?' in O'Brien and Clesse, eds, *Two Hegemonies* (2002)

O'Brien, Patrick Karl and Clesse, Armand (eds)   *Two Hegemonies: Britain 1846–1914 and the United States, 1941–2001* (Aldershot, Ashgate, 2002)

Ó'Gráda, Cormac   *Black '47 and Beyond: The Great Irish Famine in History, Economy and Memory* (Princeton, NJ, Princeton University Press, 1999)

O'Hanlon, Rosalind   'Recovering the Subject: Subaltern Studies and Histories of Resistance in Colonial South Asia', *Modern Asian Studies*, 22 (1988)

Ohlmeyer, Jane H.   'Civilizinge of those rude partes: Colonization within Britain and Ireland, 1580s–1640s' in Canny (ed.), *OHBE*, vol. I (1998)

O'Mahoney, Patrick J. and Delanty, Gerard   *Rethinking Irish History: Nationalism, Identity and Ideology* (Basingstoke, Macmillan, 1998)

Omissi, David (ed.)   *Indian Voices of the Great War: Soldiers' Letters, 1914–1918* (London, Macmillan, 1999)

Orde, Anne   *The Eclipse of Great Britain, the United States and British Imperial Decline, 1895–1956* (London, Macmillan, 1996)

Osterhammel, Jürgen   'Semi-Colonialism and Informal Empire in Twentieth Century China. Towards a Framework of Analysis' in Mommsen and Osterhammel (eds), *Imperialism and After* (1986)

Osterhammel, Jürgen   *Colonialism* (Princeton and Kingston, Marcus Wiener/Ian Randle, 1997)

Osterhammel, Jürgen   'Britain and China, 1842–1914' in Porter (ed.), *OHBE*, vol. III (1999)

Overell, Stephen   'Why Myth and Reality must meet', *Financial Times*, London, 3 December 1999, p. 3

Owen, Roger and Sutcliffe, Bob (eds)   *Studies in the Theory of Imperialism* (Harlow, Longman, 1972)

Pagden, Anthony   *European Encounters with the New World* (New Haven, Yale University Press, 1993)

Pagden, Anthony   *Lords of All the Worlds: Ideologies of Empire in Spain, Britain and France c. 1500–1850* (New Haven, 1995)

Paisely, Fiona   'Citizens of the World: Australian Feminism and Indigenous Rights in the International Context, 1920s and 1930s', *Feminist Review*, vol. 58, 1998

Parry, Benita   'Problems in Current Theories of Colonial Discourse', *Oxford Literary Review*, 9, 1987

Parry, Benita   'Directions and Dead Ends in Postcolonial Studies' in Goldberg and Quayson (eds), *Relocating Postcolonialism* (2002)

Parry, J. H.   *The Establishment of European Hegemony 1415–1715* (New York, Harper Torchbook, 1961)

Parsons, Neil   *King Khama, Emperor Joe and the Great White Queen: Victorian Britain through African Eyes* (Chicago, University of Chicago Press, 1998)

Penn, Nigel   'The North African Cape Frontier Zone in South African Frontier Historiography' in Russell (ed.), *Colonial Frontiers* (2001)

Perham, Margery   'African Facts and American Criticisms', *Foreign Affairs*, vol. 22, no. 3, April 1944

Perham, Margery   'France in the Cameroons' *The Times*, May 1933 reproduced in Margery Perham, *Colonial Sequence, 1930–1949: A Chronological Commentary upon British Colonial Policy, Especially in Africa* (London, Methuen and Co. Ltd., 1967)

Petersson, Neils P.   'Gentlemanly and not so Gentlemanly Capitalism in China before the First World War' in Shigeru Akita, ed. *Gentlemanly Capitalism Imperialism and Global History* (London, Palgrave Macmillan, 2002)

Petras, John and Rhodes, Robert   'The Reconsolidation of US Hegemony', *New Left Review*, no. 97, 1976

Phillips, Caryl   'Out of Africa', *The Guardian*, London, *The Guardian Review*, Saturday, 22 February 2003

Phillips, Richard   *Mapping Men and Empire: A Geography of Adventure* (London, Routledge, 1997)

Phillips, Ruth B.   'Why not Tourist Art? Significant Silences in Native America in America Museum Representations' in Prakash (ed.), *After Colonialism* (1995)

Pierson, Ruth and Chaudhuri, Nupur (eds)   *Nation, Empire, Colony: Historicizing Race and Gender* (Bloomington, Ind., Indiana University Press, 1998)

Pieterse, Jan Nederveen   *Empire and Emancipation; Power and Liberation on a World Scale* (London, Pluto Press, 1990)

Pieterse, Jan Nederveen   *White on Black: Images of Africa and Blacks in Western Popular Culture* (New Haven and London, Yale University Press, 1992)

Pieterse, Jan Nederveen   *Globalization and Culture* (Rowan and Littlefield, 2004)

Pilger, John   'Nam Now', *The Guardian*, London, *Guardian Weekend*, April 22 1995

Pollock, Griselda   *Avant-Garde Gambits: Gender and the Colour of Art History 1888–1893* (London, Thames and Hudson, 1993)

Poma, Huamán   *Letter to a King: A Picture-History of the Inca Civilization by Huamán Poma (Don Felipe Huamán Poma de Ayala) c. 1567–1615* (London, George Allen and Unwin, 1978). Arr., ed. and Intro. Christopher Dilke, trans. from *Nueva Corónica y Buen Gobierno*

Pomeranz, Kenneth   *The Great Divergence. Europe, China and the Making of the Modern World Economy* (New Jersey, Princeton University Press, 2000)

Porter, Andrew   *European Imperialism 1860–1914* (Basingstoke, Macmillan, 1994)

Porter, Andrew   ' "Cultural Imperialism" and Protestant Missionary Enterprise, 1780–1914' *Journal of Imperial and Commonwealth History,* vol. 25, no. 3, September 1997

Porter, Andrew (ed.)   *The Oxford History of the British Empire: vol. III: The Nineteenth Century* (Oxford, Oxford University Press, 1999)

Porter, Andrew   'Religion, Missionary Enthusiasm and Empire' in Porter (ed.), *OHBE,* vol. III, (1999)

Porter, Andrew   *Religion Versus Empire: British Protestant Missionaries and Overseas Expansion, 1700–1914* (Manchester, Manchester University Press, 2004)

Porter, Bernard   *Critics of Empire: British Radical Attitudes to Colonialism in Africa, 1895–1914* (London, Macmillan, 1968)

Porter, Bernard   *The Lion's Share: A Short History of British Imperialism, 1850–1995* (Harlow, Pearson Longman, 2004b, 4th edn, 1976)

Porter, Bernard   *The Absent Minded Imperialists: Empire, Society and Culture in Britain* (Oxford, Oxford University Press, 2004a)

Porter, Bernard   'We Don't Do Empire', *History Today,* vol. 55, Issue 3, March 2005

Porter, Dennis   'Orientalism and its Problems' (1983) reproduced in Cain and Harrison (eds), *Imperialism* (2001) 3 vols, vol. 3

Porter, Roy   *Enlightenment: Britain and the Creation of the Modern World* (London, Allen Lane, 2000)

Potter, David   'Colonial Rule' in Allen and Thomas (eds), *Poverty and Development in the 1990s* (1992)

Prakash, Gyan   'Writing Post-Orientalist Histories of the Third World: Perspectives from Indian Historiography' (1990), reproduced in Prakesh (ed.), *After Colonialism* (1995)

Prakash, Gyan (ed.)   *After Colonialism: Imperial Histories and Postcolonial Displacements* (New Jersey, Princeton University Press, 1995)

Prashad, Vijay   *Everyone was Kung Fu Fighting* (New York, Beacon Press, 2001)

Pratt, Mary Louise   *Imperial Eyes: Travel Writing and Transculturation* (London, Routledge, 1992)

Princess Marie Louise   *Letters From the Gold Coast* (London, Methuen and Co. Ltd., 1926)

Procida, Mary A.   *Married to the Empire: Gender, Politics and Imperialism, 1883–1947* (Manchester, Manchester University Press, 2002)

Raban, Jonathan   'Emasculating Arabia', *The Guardian,* London, G2, 13 May 2004

Rafael, Vincente L.   'Surveillance and Nationalist Resistance in the US Colonisation of the Philippines' in Kaplan and Pease (eds), *Cultures of United States Imperialism* (1993)

Rafael, Vincente L.   'Confession, Conversion, and Reciprocity in Early Tagalog Colonial Society' in Dirks (ed.), *Colonialism and Culture* (1992)

Ramamurthy, Anandi   *Imperial Persuaders; Images of Africa and Asia in British Advertising* (Manchester, Manchester University Press, 2003)

Ramussen, Paul   'This World: The Boy from the Block', *British Broadcasting Corporation*, BBC2, 8 July 2004

Ranger, Terence O.   'The Invention of Tradition in Africa' in Hobsbawm and Ranger (eds), *The Invention of Tradition* (1996)

Rattansi, Ali   'Postcolonialism and its discontents', *Economy and Society*, 26, 4, 1997

Raudzens, George   *Empires, Europe and Globalization, 1492–1788* (Stroud, Sutton Publishing, 1999); Foreword Jeremy Black

Restall, Matthew   *Seven Myths of the Spanish Conquest* (Oxford, Oxford University Press, 2003)

Reynolds, Henry   *The Other Side of the Frontier: Aboriginal Resistance to the European Invasion of Australia* (London, Penguin, 1987; first published, 1981)

Richards, Jeffery   'Empire and Cinema in the 1920s and 1930s' in Richards (ed.), *The Age of the Dream Palace* (London, Routledge, Kegan and Paul, 1984)

Richards, Jeffery   *Imperialism and Music: Britain, 1876–1953* (Manchester, Manchester University Press, 2001)

Richards, John F.   *The New Cambridge History of India: The Mughal Empire* (Cambridge, Cambridge University Press, 1993)

Richards, Thomas   *The Imperial Archive: Knowledge and the Fantasy of Empire* (London, Verso, 1993)

Ritzer, George   *The McDonaldization of Society: An Investigation into the Character of Contemporary Social Life* (Thousand Oaks, California, Pine Forge Press, 1993)

Ritzer, George   *The Globalization of Nothing* (Thousand Oaks, California, Pine Forge Press, 2003)

Roberts, A. D. (ed.)   *The Colonial Moment in Africa: Essays on the Movement of Minds and Materials, 1900–1940* (Cambridge, Cambridge University Press, 1986)

Robertson, George *et al.* (eds)   *Travellers' Tales, Narratives of Home and Displacement* (London, Routledge, 1994)

Robertson, Roland   *Globalization: Social Theory and Global Culture* (London, Sage, 1992)

Robertson, Roland   'Glocalization: Time–Space and Homogeneity–Heterogeneity' in M. Featherstone, S. Lash and R. Robertson (eds), *Global Modernities* (London, Sage, 1995)

Robeson, Eslanda Goode   *African Journey* (London, Victor Gollancz Ltd, 1946)

Robinson, R. T.   *Missionary Congregation of the Holy Ghost Fathers*, Publicity Pamphlet, Catholic Truth Society, 1952

Robinson, Ronald and Gallagher, Jack   *Africa and the Victorians: the Official Mind of Imperialism* (London, Macmillan, 1961)

Robinson, Ronald and Louis, Wm. Roger   'The Imperialism of Decolonisation', *Journal of Imperial and Commonwealth History*, vol. 22, no. 3, 1994

Robinson, Ronald   'The Extra-territorial Foundations of European Imperialism' (1961) reproduced in Owen and Sutcliffe (eds), *Theories of Imperialism* (1972)

Rogaski, Ruth   *Hygienic Modernity: Meanings of Health and Disease in Treaty Port China* (Berkeley, UCLA Press, 2004)

Rogin, Michael   ' "Make My Day": Spectacle as Amnesia in Imperial Politics' in Kaplan and Pease (eds), *Cultures of United States Imperialism* (1993)

Rosaldo, Renato   'Imperialist Nostalgia', *Representations*, 26, 1989, p.108

Rose Hunt, Nancy   *A colonial lexicon of birth ritual, medicalization, and mobility in the Congo* (Durham, N.C., Duke University Press, 1999)

Rostow, Walt W.   *The Stages of Economic Growth: A Non-Communist Manifesto* (Cambridge, Cambridge University Press, 1960)

Rotberg, Robert I. and Mazrui, Ali (eds)   *Protest and Power in Black Africa* (Oxford, Oxford University Press, 1970)

Runciman, Stephen   *A History of the Crusades: Volume II: The Kingdom of Jerusalem and the Frankish East, 1100–1187* (Cambridge University Press, 1965; first published 1952)

Russell, Lynette (ed.)   *Colonial Frontiers: Indigenous European Encounters in Settler Societies* (Manchester, Manchester University Press, 2001)

Russell-Wood, A.   *A World on the Move: The Portuguese in Africa, Asia and the Americas 1415–1808* (New York, St. Martin's Press, 1992)

Ryan, James   *Picturing Empire: Photography and the Visualisation of the British Empire* (London, Reaktion Books, 1997)

Rydell, Robert W.   *All the World's a Fair: Visions of Empire at American International Expositions, 1876–1916* (Chicago, University of Chicago Press, 1984)

Sachs, Wulf   *Black Hamlet* (Baltimore, John Hopkins University Press, 1996; first published, 1937). Ed. and new Intro. Saul Dubow and Jaqueline Rose

Said, Edward   *Orientalism: Western Conceptions of the Orient* (Harmondsworth, Penguin, 1985, 1978/9)

Said, Edward   'Yeats and Decolonisation' in Terry Eagelton, Frederick Jameson and Edward Said, *Nationalism, Colonialism and Literature* (Minneapolis, University of Minneapolis Press, 1990)

Said, Edward   *Culture and Imperialism* (London, Vintage, 1994, 1993)

Said, Edward   'In conversation with Neeladri Bhattacharya, Suvir Kaul and Ania Loomba' in Goldberg and Quayson (eds), *Relocating Postcolonialism* (2002)

Said, Edward and Hitchens, Christopher *et al.*   *Blaming the Victims: Spurious Scholarship and the Palestinian Question* (London, Verso, 1987)

Sale, Kirkpatrick   *The Conquest of Paradise: Christopher Columbus and the Columbian Legacy* (London, Macmillan Papermac, 1992; first published, 1990)

Sampson, Anthony   *The Seven Sisters: the Great Oil Companies and the World they Made* (London, Hodder and Stoughton, 1975)

Sampson, Jane   *Race and Empire* (Harlow, Pearson Education, 2005)

Sandall, Roger   *The Culture Cult: Designer Tribalism and Other Essays* (Boulder Co., Westview Press, 2000)

Sanders of the River, London Film Productions, 1935, producer, Alexander Korda, directed by Zoltan Korda

Sartre, Jean Paul   *Colonialism and Neo-Colonialism* (London, Routledge, 2001, first published 1964). Trans. and Intro. Azzedine Haddour, Steve Brewer and Terry McWilliams

Sauer, Elizabeth and Rajan, Balachandra   *Imperialisms: Historical and Literary Investigations, 1500–1900* (London, Palgrave Macmillan, 2004)

Scammel, G. V.   *The World Encompassed: the First European Maritime Empires, c. 800–1650* (Berkeley, University of California Press, 1981)

Scammel, G. V.   *The First Imperial Age: European Overseas Expansion c. 1400–1715* (New York, Harper Collins, 1989)

Schaffer, Kay   'Handkerchief Diplomacy: E. J. Eyre and Sexual Politics on the South Australian Frontier' in Russell (ed.), *Colonial Frontiers* (2001)

Schneer, Jonathan   *London, 1900 – the Imperial Metropolis* (New Haven, Yale University Press, 1999)

Schneider, William H.   *An Empire for the Masses: The French Popular Image of Africa, 1870–1900* (Westport, Conn. and London, Greenwood, 1982)

Schumpeter, Joseph   *Imperialism and Social Classes* (Oxford, Blackwell, 1951, 1919). Ed. and Intro. Paul M. Sweezey; trans. Heinz Norden

Schwabe, Klaus   'The Global role of the United States and its Imperial Consequences, 1898–1973' in Mommsen and Osterhammel (eds), *Imperialism and After* (1986)

Schwartz, Bill   'Conquerors of Truth: Reflections on Post-Colonial Theory' in Schwartz (ed.), *The Expansion of England* (1996)

Schwartz, Bill (ed.)   *The Expansion of England: Race, Ethnicity and Cultural History* (London, Routledge, 1996)

Schweinitz, Karl de   *The Rise and Fall of British India: Imperialism as Inequality* (New York, Methuen, 1983)

Scott, David   *Refashioning Futures: Criticism after Postcoloniality* (Princeton, NJ, Princeton University Press, 1999)

Scott-Stokes, Henry   *The Life and Death of Yukio Mishima* (London, Owen, 1975)

Sharpe, Jenny   'Figures of Colonial Resistance' in *Modern Fiction Studies*, vol. 35, no. 1, 1989

Shaw, Martin   'War, Imperialism and the State System' in Shaw (ed.), *War, State and Society* (London, Macmillan Press, 1984)

Shohat, Ella and Stam, Robert   *Unthinking Eurocentrism: Multiculturalism and the Media* (London, Routledge, 1994)

Shohat, Ella and Stam, Robert   'Contested Histories: Eurocentrism, Mullticulturalism and the Media' in Goldberg (ed.), *Multiculturalism: A Critical Reader* (Oxford, Blackwell, 1994)

Sibeud, Emanuelle   ' "Negrophilia", "Negrology" or "Africanism"? Colonial Ethnography and Racism in France around 1900' in Chafer and Sackur (eds), *Promoting the Colonial Idea* (2002)

Singer, Aubrey *The Lion and the Dragon: the Story of the First British Embassy to the Court of the Emperor Qianlong in Peking, 1792–1794* (London, Barrie and Jenkins, 1992)

Sinha, Mrinalini *Colonial Masculinity: The 'manly Englishman' and the 'effeminate Bengali' in the late nineteenth century* (Manchester, Manchester University Press, 1995)

Sklar, Richard 'Postimperialism: A Class Analysis of Multinational Corporate Expansion' (1976) reproduced in Cain and Harrison, *Imperialism*, vol. 2 (2001)

Sluglett, Peter *Britain in Iraq: Contriving King and Country* (London, I. B. Taurus, 2006, forthcoming)

Smith, Anthony *State and Nation in the Third World: The Western State and African Nationalism* (Brighton, Wheatsheaf, 1983)

Smith, G. A. *When Jim Crow met John Bull: Black American Soldiers in World War 11* (London, I. B. Taurus, 1986)

Smith, Simon *British Imperialism, 1750–1970* (Cambridge, Cambridge University Press, 1998)

Smith, Tony 'American Imperialism is Anti-Communism' in Mommsen and Osterhammel (eds), *Imperialism and After* (1986)

Smyth, R. 'Movies and Mandarins: the Official Film and British Colonial Africa' in J. Curran and V. Porter (eds), *British Cinema History* (London, Wiedenfeld and Nicholson, 1983)

Snooks, Graeme D. *Economics without Time: A Science Blind to the Forces of Historical Change* (Ann Arbor, University of Michigan Press, 1993)

Snooks, Graeme D. *The Dynamic Society: Exploring the Forces of Global Change* (London, Routledge, 1996)

Snowden, Frank M. *Before Colour Prejudice: An Ancient View of Blacks* (Cambridge Mass., Harvard University Press, 1983)

Snyder, Louis L. (ed.) *The Imperialism Reader: Documents and Readings on Modern Expansionism* (New Jersey, Princeton University Press, 1962)

Spivak, Gayatri Chakravorty 'Can the Subaltern Speak? Speculations on Widow Sacrifice', *Wedge* 7/8, 1985.

Springhall, John *Decolonisation since 1945: The Collapse of European Overseas Empires* (London, Palgrave Macmillan, 2000)

Spurr, David *The Rhetoric of Empire: Colonial Discourse in Journalism, Travel Writing and Imperial Administration* (Durham, N.C., Duke University Press, 1995)

Stasiulis, Daiva and Yuval-Davis, Nira (eds) *Unsettling Settler Societies; Articulations of Gender, Race, Ethnicity and Class* (London, Sage, 1995)

Stedman-Jones, Gareth *Languages of Class: Studies in English Working Class History* (Cambridge, Cambridge University Press, 1983)

Steggles, Mary Ann 'Set in Stone: Victoria's Monuments in India', *History Today*, vol. 51, 2, February, 2001

Stepan, Nancy   *The Idea of Race in Science: Great Britain, 1800–1960* (London, Macmillan, 1982)

Stevens, Mary Anne (ed.)   *The Orientalists: Delacroix to Matisse: the Lure of North Africa and the Middle East* (London, Weidenfeld and Nicholson, 1984)

Stiglitz, Joseph E.   *Globalization and its Discontents* (London, Allen Lane/ Penguin, 2002)

Stoler, Ann Laura   'Making Empire Respectable: The Politics of Race and Sexual Morality in Twentieth-Century Colonial Cultures' in Jan Bremen (ed.), *Imperial Monkey Business: Racial Supremacy in Social Darwinist Theory and Colonial Practice* (Amsterdam, 1990)

Stoler, Ann Laura   *Race and the Education of Desire: Foucault's 'History of Sexuality' and the Colonial Order of Things* (Durham, N. Ca., Duke University Press, 1996)

Stoler, Ann Laura   'Sexual Affronts and Racial Frontiers: European Identities and the Cultural Politics of Exclusion in Colonial Southeast Asia' in Stoler and Cooper, *Tensions of Empire* (1997)

Stoler, Ann Laura   *Carnal Knowledge and Imperial Power: Race and the Intimate in Colonial Rule* (Berkeley, UCLA Press, 2002)

Stoler, Ann Laura and Cooper, Frederick (eds)   *Tensions of Empire: Colonial Cultures in a Bourgeois World* (Berkeley, Ca., UCLA Press, 1997)

Stott, Philip   'Jungles of the Mind: The Invention of the Tropical Rain Forest', *History Today*, vol. 51, (5), May 2001

Subrahmanyam, Sanjay   *The Portuguese Empire in Asia, 1500–1700* (Cambridge, Cambridge University Press, 1993)

Sugihara, Kaoru (ed.)   *Japan, China, and the Growth of the Asian International Economy, 1850–1949* (London, Oxford University Press, 2005)

Swingina, Jonathon S.   'The Crisis of Hegemonic Decline: US disinterest in Africa', *Review of African Political Economy*, 38, April, 1989

Taylor, Peter J.   'The "American Century" as Hegemonic Cycle' in O'Brien and Clesse (eds), *Two Hegemonies* (2002)

Thall, Nelson   'Fringeware', *The Guardian*, London, 5 May, 1995

The Empire Exhibition,   Museum of London *http://www.museumoflondon.org.uk* Accessed 09.07.2004

The Glasgow Website,   *http://clydevalley.com/glasgow/empire.htm* Accessed 09.07.2004.

Thomas, Hugh   *Rivers of Gold: the Rise of the Spanish Empire* (London, Wiedenfeld and Nicholson, 2004)

Thomas, Nicholas   *Colonialism's Culture: Anthropology, Travel and Government* (Cambridge, Polity Press, 1994)

Thompson, Andrew S.   *Imperial Britain: The Empire in British Politics c. 1880–1932* (Harlow, Longman, 2000)

Thompson, Andrew S.   *The Empire Strikes Back? The Impact of Imperialism on Britain from the Mid Nineteenth Century* (London, Pearson Education, 2005)

Thompson, William R.   *The Emergence of the Global Political Economy* (London, Routledge, 2000)

Thornton, A. P.   *The Imperial Idea and its Enemies: A Study of British Power* (London, Macmillan, 1959)

Tidrick, Kathryn   *Empire and the English Character* (London, I. B. Taurus, 1990)

Tilzey, Paul   'Roger Casement: Secrets of the Black Diaries' BBC1 History, 1st January, 2002, *www.bbc.co.uk/history/society_culture/protest_reform/casement*

Todd, Emmanuel   *After the Empire: The Breakdown of the American Order* (London, Constable, 2004); trans. C. Jon Delogu

Tomlinson, John   *Cultural Imperialism: A Critical Introduction* (London, Pinter Publishers, 1991)

Tomlinson, John   'Globalization and Cultural Identity' in Held and McGrew (eds), *The Global Transformations Reader* (2003)

Torgovnick, Marianna   *Gone Primitive: Savage Intellects, Modern Lives* (Chicago, University of Chicago Press, 1990)

Tracy, James D. (ed.)   *The Political Economy of Merchant Empires: State Power and World Trade* (Cambridge, Cambridge University Press, 1991)

Tranberg-Hansen, Karen (ed.)   *African Encounters with Domesticity* (New Brunswick, NJ, Rutgers University Press, 1992)

Tremlett, Giles   'Spanish Fury at Slur on the Conquistadores', *The Guardian*, London, 17 March 2003, p. 17

Turner, Frederick   *The Frontier in American History* (New York, Henry Holt and Company, 1921)

Turner, Mary   *Slaves and Missionaries: The Disintegration of Jamaican Slave Society, 1784–1843* (Urbana, University of Illinois Press, 1982)

Ugarte, Manuel   'The US as the "New Rome"' in T. Paterson (ed.), *Major Problems in American Foreign Policy*, vol. 2. (New York, D. C. Heath and Co., 1995, 4th edn.)

UNDP Report   'Patterns of Global Inequality' in Held and McGrew, *The Global Transformations Reader* (2003)

Vail, Leroy (ed.)   *The Creation of Tribalism in Southern Africa* (Oxford, James Currey, 1989)

Van den Anker, Christien   *The Political Economy of New Slavery* (Basingstoke and New York, Palgrave Macmillan, 2003)

Van de Veer, Peter   *Imperial Encounters: Religion and Modernity in India and Britain* (Princeton, NJ, Princeton University Press, 2004)

Vaughan, Megan   *Curing their Ills: Colonial Power and African Illness* (Cambridge, Polity Press, 1991)

Vaughan, Megan   'Health and hegemony: representations of disease and the creation of the colonial subject in Nyasaland' in Engels and Marks (eds), *Contesting Colonial Hegemony* (1994)

Venn, Couze   'History Lessons: Formation of Subject, Post Colonialism and an Other Protest', in Schwartz (ed.), *The Expansion of England* (1996)

Vidal, Gore   *Empire* (London, Abacus, 1994; first published, 1987)

Vidal, Gore   *Imperial America* (Clairview, 2004)

Vlastos, Stephen (ed.)   *Mirror of Modernity: Invented traditions of Modern Japan* (Berkeley, UCLA Press, 1998)

Von Albertini, Rudolf   *Decolonisation: the Administration and Future of the Colonies, 1919–1962* (New York, Africana Publishing Co. 1982, 1971)

Von Albertini, Rudolf with Wirz, Albert   *European Colonial Rule, 1880–1940: the Impact of the West on India, Southeast Asia and Africa* (Oxford, Clio Press, 1982; trans. John G. Williamson)

Von Laue, Theodore H.   *The World Revolution of Westernisation: The Twentieth Century in Global Perspective* (London, Oxford University Press, 1989)

Wallace, Edgar   *Sanders of the River* (London and Melbourne, Ward, Lock and Co., n. d.)

Wallerstein, Immanuel M.   *The Modern World-System: vol. 1: Capitalist agriculture and the origins of the European world-economy in the sixteenth century* (New York and London, Academic Press, 1974)

Wallerstein, Immanuel M.   *The Modern World-System: vol. 2: Mercantilism and the consolidation of the European world-economy, 1600–1750* (New York and London, Academic Press, 1980)

Wallerstein, Immanuel M.   *The Modern World-System: vol. 3: The second era of great expansion of the capitalist world-economy, 1730–1840s* (San Diego and London, Academic Press, 1989)

Wallerstein, Immanuel M.   *Historical Capitalism with Capitalist Civilization* (London, Verso, 1996)

Wallerstein, Immanuel M.   *Utopistics: Or, Historical Choices for the Twenty-First Century* (New York, The New Press, 1998)

Wallerstein, Immanuel M.   'The Rise and Demise of the World Capitalist System' (1974a) reprinted in Cain and Harrison (eds), *Imperialism: Critical Concepts in Historical Studies* (2001) vol. 2

Wallerstein, Immanuel M.   'New Revolts Against the System', *New Left Review*, 18, Nov–Dec, 2002

Wallerstein, Immanuel M.   'Three Hegemonies' in O'Brien and Clesse (eds), *Two Hegemonies* (2002)

Walvin, James   *Fruits of Empire: Exotic Produce and British taste, 1660–1800* (London, Macmillan, 1997)

Walvin, James   *Britain's Slave Empire* (Stroud, Tempus, 2000)

Walvin, James   *The Making the Black Atlantic* (London, Cassell, 2000)

Walvin, James   *Atlas of Slavery* (Harlow, England; New York, Pearson Longman, 2005)

Ward, Stuart (ed.)   *British Culture and the End of Empire* (Manchester, Manchester University Press, 2001)

Ware, Vron   *Beyond the Pale: White Women, Racism and History* (London, Verso, 1992)

Warren, Allen   'Citizens of Empire: Baden Powell, Scouts and Guides and an Imperial Ideal, 1900–40', in Mackenzie (ed.), *Imperialism and Popular Culture* (1986)

Warren, Bill   *Imperialism: Pioneer of Capitalism* (London, Verso, 1980, ed. John Sender)

Washbrook, David   'India 1818–1860: the Two Faces of Colonialism' in Porter (ed.), *OHBE*, vol. III (2001)

Washbrook, David   'Orients and Occidents: Colonial Discourse Theory and the Historiography of the British Empire' in Winks (ed.) *OHBE*, vol. V (1999)

Waugh, Evelyn   *When the Going Was Good* (London, Duckworth, 1946)

Weber, Max   *The Protestant Ethic and the Spirit of Capitalism* (London, Routledge, 1992, first published 1904/5. Trans. by Talcott Parsons)

Webster, Wendy   *Englishness and Empire, 1939–1965* (Oxford University Press, 2005)

Wesserling, H. L.   'Imperialism and Empire: An Introduction' in Mommsen and Osterhammel (eds), *Imperialism and After* (1986)

Wesserling, H. L.   *Imperialism and Colonialism: Essays on the History of European Expansion* (Greenwood Press, 1997)

Wheatcroft, Geoffrey   'No Regrets, No surrender: Profile of Connor Cruise O'Brien', *The Guardian*, London, Saturday Review, 12 July 2003

White, Donald W.   *The American Century: the Rise and Decline of the US as a World Power* (New Haven, Yale University Press, 1996)

White, Owen   *Children of the French Empire: Miscegenation and Colonial Society in French West Africa, 1895–1960* (Oxford, Oxford University Press, 1999)

Wildenthal, Lora   *German Women for Empire, 1884–1945* (Durham, N.C., Duke University Press, 2001)

Wilkinson, James A.   *Great Britain and the Empire: A Discursive History* (London, 1944)

Williams, Patrick and Chrisman, Laura (eds)   *Colonial Discourse and Postcolonial Theory: A Reader* (New York; London, Harvester Wheatsheaf, 1993)

Wilson, Kathleen   *The Sense of the People: Politics, Culture and Imperialism in England, 1715–1785* (Cambridge, Cambridge University Press, 1998)

Wilson, Kathleen   *The Island Race: Englishness, Empire and Gender in the Eighteenth Century* (London, Routledge, 2002)

Windshuttle, Keith   'Edward Said's "Orientalism" revisited' in *The New Criterion*, vol. 17, no. 5, January 1999

Winks, Robin W.   *The Imperial Revolution: Yesterday and Tomorrow*, Inaugural lecture delivered before the University of Oxford, 10 May 1993 (Oxford, Oxford University Press, 1994)

Winks, Robin W. (ed.)   *The Oxford History of the British Empire, vol. V Historiography* (Oxford, Oxford University Press, 1999)

Wolfe, Patrick   'History and Imperialism: A Century of Theory, from Marx to Postcolonialism', *American Historical Review*, 102, 2, April 1997

Wolfe, Patrick   *Settler Colonialism and the Transformation of Anthropology: The Politics and Poetics of an Ethnographical Event* (London and New York, Cassell, 1999)

Wolski, Nathan   'All's not quiet on the western front – rethinking resistance and frontiers in Aboriginal historiography' in Russell (ed.), *Colonial Frontiers* (2001)

Wong, Roy Bin   *China Transformed: Historical Change and the Limits of European Experience* (Ithaca, New York, Cornell University Press, 1997)

Wood, Michael   *In the Footsteps of Alexander the Great: A Journey from Greece to India* (London, BBC Books, 2004, 1997)

Wood, Michael   *Conquistadors* (London, BBC, 2003; first published 2000)

Woolf, Greg   'Inventing empire in ancient Rome' in Alcock *et al.* (eds), *Empires* (2002)

Woolf, Leonard   *Imperialism and Civilization* (London, Hogarth Press, 1928)

Woollacott, Angela   'Inventing Commonwealth and Pan Pacific Feminisms: Australian Women's International Activism in the 1920s and 1930s', *Gender and History*, vol. 10, no. 3 1998

Worsley, Peter   *The Third World* (London, Wiedenfeld and Nicholson, 1964)

Wright, Patrick   *Living in an Old Country: the National Past in Contemporary Britain* (London, Verso, 1985)

Yates, Robin D. S.   'Cosmos, central authority, and communities in the early Chinese Empire' in Alcock *et al.* (eds), *Empires* (2002)

Yee, Chiang   *A Silent Traveller in Lakeland* (London, Country Life Ltd, 1946, 1937)

Yee, Chiang   *The Silent Traveller in the Yorkshire Dales* (London, Methuen and Co., 1951, 1941)

Young, Emma   'Koalas fight, shepherd's delight', *The Guardian*, London, 23 November 2003

Young, Louise   *Japan's Total Empire: Manchuria and the Culture of Wartime Imperialism* (Berkeley, UCLA Press, 1998)

Young, Robert J. C.   *White Mythologies: Writing History and the West* (London, Routledge, 1990)

Young, Robert J. C.   *Colonial Desire: Hybridity in Theory, Culture and Race* (London, Routledge, 1992)

Young, Robert J. C.   *Postcolonialism: An Historical Introduction* (Oxford, Blackwell, 2001)

Younge, Gary   'Distant Voices, Still Lives', *The Guardian*, London, 2 November 2002

Youngs, Tim   *Travellers in Africa: British Travelogues, 1850–1900* (Manchester, Manchester University Press, 1994)

Index